22.513

The E

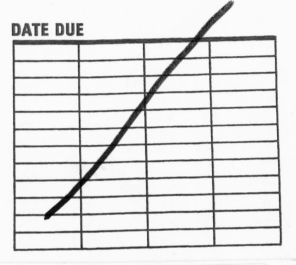

DATE DUE

HARRY K. GIRVETZ

The Evolution of Liberalism

Introduction by Arthur Schlesinger, Jr.

Collier Books / Collier-Macmillan Ltd., London

Library of Congress Catalog Card Number: 63–7205

First Collier Books Reissue 1966.

Second Printing 1969

The Evolution of Liberalism *originally appeared*
under the title From Wealth to Welfare.

This edition, revised for Collier Books,
is published by arrangement with the author.

The Macmillan Company
Collier-Macmillan Canada Ltd., Toronto, Ontario
Printed in the United States of America

To My Sons

Contents

Preface   13

Introduction   17

Part One/Classical Liberalism

Introduction   23

1 The Psychological Creed   27

    Egoism
    Intellectualism
    Quietism
    Atomism
    Qualifications

2 Initiative and Incentives: The Problem of Motivation   49

    Protection of Property
    Protection Against Involuntary Servitude
    Deprivation as an Incentive to Effort

3 The Political Creed:
  Political Quietism in Theory and Practice   65

    The Rejection of the State
    From Adam Smith to Herbert Spencer
    The American Version
    The Sequel in England
    The Sequel in America

4 The Political Creed: The Functions of the State   91

    Preservation of Order
    Enforcement of Contract
    Promotion of Exchange
    Protection of Freedom of Competition
    The Meliorative Function

5   The Political Creed: Checks and Restraints   103
        Constitutionalism
        Jusnaturalism
        The Division of Power
        Suffrage
        Revolution

6   The Economic Creed:
    The Natural Harmony of Interests   137
        The Division of Labor and Exchange
        The Role of the Market
        The Role of Competition
        Harmony and Dissonance

Part Two/Contemporary Liberalism

Introduction   153

7   Of Human Nature   157
        The Fallacy of Egoism
        The Spirit of Workmanship
        The Misuses of Reason
        Critical Conclusions

8   "Frictions" and "Exceptions"   181
        The Consumer: Sovereign or Subject?
        Competition, Free and Fettered
        Trade Cycles

9   The Wealth of Nations   203
        Production and Productivity
        The Postwar Record
        Growth and Unemployment
        Concealed Unemployment
        Economic Lag and Waste
        The Great Ambivalence

10 The Welfare of Nations   225
        The Distribution of Income
        The Standard of Living
        The Problem of Priorities

11 The Positive State   249
      In Historical Perspective
      Institutional Changes and Interventionism
      The Commissional Revolution

12 The Road to Freedom   263
      The Anatomy of Power
      Economic Power
      Totalitarianism: A Faulty Diagnosis
      A New Separation of Powers

13 The Welfare State: First Phase   297
      From the Cradle to the Grave
      Economic Recovery and Compensatory Spending
      The Limitation of Power

14 The New Challenge   333
      Challenge of the Soviet Union
      The Emerging Nations
      The Impact of Automation
      The Urban Crisis

15 Liberalism Today   353
      Optimum Growth
      The "Public Sector"
      Liberals and American Conservatism

Conclusion   385

Notes   389

Index   441

THE DOGMAS of the quiet past are inadequate for the stormy present. The occasion is piled high with difficulty and we must rise with the occasion. As our case is new, so must we think anew and act anew. We must disenthrall ourselves and then we shall save our country.

—LINCOLN, Message to Congress,
December 1, *1862*

Preface

THIS VOLUME began as a revision of my earlier *From Wealth to Welfare*, but the changes were so extensive in Part Two that a new title became appropriate. This is not to suggest that anything said in the earlier volume has had to be withdrawn. However, in the perspective of another decade, it becomes possible to discern new emphases in the liberal philosophy and to cite fresh evidence for the old emphases.

In its classical form liberalism appeared in England in the seventeenth century, spread to France in the eighteenth century, and dominated the thought of Western civilization by the late nineteenth century. In the course of this remarkable development, liberalism, both as precept and as practice, has undergone changes so great that the term as currently used has come to have contradictory meanings. Liberalism is differently understood by Americans and Europeans, and even among Americans, rivals are divided into camps over the issues raised by liberalism, with only the haziest knowledge of the ground on which they have pitched their tents. One is bound to be perplexed when men so diverse in their views as Herbert Hoover, Franklin Roosevelt, Walter Lippmann, John Dewey, Ludwig von Mises, John Maynard Keynes and Friedrich Hayek refer to themselves, or are characterized by others, as liberals. If the result has been confusion, this is surely no asset in the great competition which history has thrust upon us.

This is not a treatise on world politics and I have resisted a temptation to deal with the international crisis. Nevertheless, it would be a grave error to suppose that a study of liberalism has no implications for the contest between the democratic and totalitarian worlds. Whether or not the struggle deteriorates into a collision between the armed forces of America and one or all of the Communist states, a decisive phase of it is and will be a competition for the hearts and minds of the other peoples of the world. We can hardly succeed in that competition until we achieve a greater measure of clarity concerning our own social arrangements and needs. And we shall very probably fail in the competition—as we so far largely have with the peoples of Asia—until we become more sensitive to the popular aspirations of economically backward countries and discover that in our social tradition which attracts and that which repels the less favored peoples of the world. To say this is to ask for a better understanding of liberalism, its shifting content and enduring form.

Contemporary liberalism differs markedly from the classical liberalism of the eighteenth and nineteenth centuries. To define this difference is to treat of the central social problem of our day: the degree to which we shall have collective control over individual behavior—the degree, that is, to which individual interests shall be subordinated to social purposes. Thus a discussion of liberalism may not only aspire to clarity where confusion now prevails; it may throw light upon the most vital social issue of our time.

An analysis of liberalism may serve another purpose. Albert V. Dicey in his *Law and Public Opinion in England* suggested this purpose when, referring to the variant of liberalism that prevailed in England between 1825 and 1870, he wrote,

Benthamism was a coherent system; its ethics, its constitutional theories, its jurisprudence, and its political economy were indissolubly linked together, and were indeed different aspects of one and the same theory of life and human nature.

An analysis of liberalism affords an opportunity to view capitalism not as a mere set of economic relationships but as a part, perhaps the most important part, of a way of life. The neglect of this approach, however unavoidable, is a shortcoming of most technical economic discussions. To concentrate upon the economic trunk of capitalism and ignore the roots and leaves and branches is to see it as so much dead lumber and not as a living thing modifying and modified by a surrounding world. Harold Laski wrote in *The Rise of Liberalism*,

The inner idea of capitalism is inherently a philosophy of life. Those who accept it do not need extra-capitalist sources to validate their activities. Their search for wealth as individuals colours and shapes their attitude to every department of behaviour. Unless this had been the case, capitalism could not have achieved the revolution it effected.

Whatever one may think of the economic determinism suggested in Professor Laski's statement, the point he makes is profoundly important.

Let the economists have the term "capitalism." Happily, usage allows the term "classical liberalism" for the philosophy of life inseparably identified with capitalism. The glossary of no single one of the social sciences is adequate for an explanation of liberalism. The liberal movement in its various historical manifestations has rudely defied the boundaries by which social scientists have defined, often too neatly, their separate spheres of interest. An adequate discussion of liberalism will take freely from political science, economics, the sociology of religion, the sociology of welfare, social anthropology and social psychology.

Some readers may find the neglect of liberals and liberalism outside of France, Britain, and the United States a glaring omission. The experience of other nations has already been described, however, by Ruggiero. Moreover, liberal ideas have not been markedly transformed when they have crossed national boundaries. The cradle of liberalism is in England and France, and there is no reason for doubting the wisdom of the poet who taught us that the child is father of the man.

The best extended studies of classical liberalism are Elie Halévy's *The Growth of Philosophical Radicalism*, Guido de Ruggiero's *The History of European Liberalism*, Sir Leslie Stephen's *The English Utilitarians*, Harold Laski's *The Rise of Liberalism*, and Albert V. Dicey's *Law and Public Opinion in England During the 19th Century*. The more persevering reader may wish to consult them.

A teacher of philosophy who has served some years of apprenticeship in the field of the social sciences will be forgiven,

I hope, by professional economists and political scientists for trespassing on their fields of competence. For the most part, as the documentation will indicate, I have relied heavily on their advice. For the rest, the student of philosophy enjoys certain advantages in addressing himself to questions of public policy: he wears the mantle of the generalist more easily than most; and there is precedent in his discipline for pleading the cause of justice more ardently than is permitted the "detached" practitioners of a science—even a social science. Ours is not a world in which one can avoid passing judgment. Accordingly, as the reader will discover, I have taken sides—I hope with a proper appreciation of the difference between conviction and preconviction. The former is a moral imperative; the latter is the nemesis of progress.

For this revised edition I have had the help of a wife patient enough to read a manuscript much of which she had read before, of Sharon McKenna, a peerless secretary, and of Professor Walter Mead of the Economics Department at the University of California, Santa Barbara, who generously consented to warn me against statements in the text which would affront economists.

HARRY GIRVETZ

University of California, Santa Barbara
January 28, 1962

Introduction

Liberalism is not only a word: it is a battlefield across which contending forces have marched in different directions for nearly two centuries. Professor Girvetz's book is a thoughtful account of the ebb and flow of the battle, written from the viewpoint of one who tempers his ardent commitment to modern liberalism by a respect for facts and by a belief in historical perspective.

The battle of liberalism goes on to this day. The word is claimed by opponents as well as advocates of government intervention in economic affairs and is thereby invoked to cover a variety of incompatible ideas. Professor Girvetz suggests that the confusion is rooted in historical circumstance—that, while the ends of liberalism have remained constant, the means have varied according to the stages of economic and technical growth. His basic distinction is between "classical liberalism" and "contemporary liberalism," and his main contribution is to show wherein they are alike and wherein different.

He begins with an admirably lucid reconstruction of the intellectual world of classical liberalism. He then suggests that the basic principles of the classical creed failed to stand up to the harsh demands of industrial society. As a consequence, he argues, liberals abandoned their old belief that that government was best which governed least and turned instead to the idea of the affirmative state. He concludes with a provocative survey of the present problems and hopes of contemporary liberalism.

Whatever liberalism is, it is not a rigid ideology nor a dogmatic system; and it would be futile to expect any version of the evolution of liberalism to command universal assent. Historians might say, for example, that Professor Girvetz's ac-

17

count of American development assumes too tidy a division between a laissez-faire and an interventionist phase. In fact, intervention was an accepted means of economic policy in the early years of the American republic, and laissez-faire became a sacred faith only in the years after the Civil War. As one American economic historian (Thomas C. Cochran) has written in the *American Historical Review,* recent scholarship demonstrates, not a consistent belief in the sanctity of private enterprise, but a shift of American opinion "from the early nineteenth-century view that government was the most efficient agency for large-scale development . . . to the late nineteenth-century conviction that government enterprise was generally corrupt and inefficient."

Similarly some liberals will doubtless differ with some of Professor Girvetz's views of contemporary liberalism. Many will follow Galbraith and Berle in regarding economic bigness as an opportunity rather than as a menace; and these will certainly object to the suggestion that Galbraith's countervailing power thesis, "to the extent that it assumes the *spontaneous* emergence of countervailing power, has been rather thoroughly discredited," since Galbraith's argument is precisely that government intervention is an organic and indispensable part of the countervailing system. Some, too, will wish that Professor Girvetz had directed more attention to the distinction, as developed by W. Arthur Lewis and J. E. Meade, between direct and indirect economic planning—a distinction which might perhaps have clarified his somewhat obscure argument for a structure of national economic planning. (This distinction, if pursued, would also have made it harder for Professor Girvetz to mistake Walter Lippmann's *The Good Society,* with its advocacy of compensatory state action, for Hayek's *The Road to Serfdom.*) I imagine also that there are many who believe that Reinhold Niebuhr has plumbed the philosophical and psychological foundations of modern liberalism much more profoundly than John Dewey. And many will wish that Professor Girvetz had given more space to the mounting concern of many modern liberals with the qualitative aspects of American life and culture.

But, since debate is the essence of liberalism, such disagreements will only increase the effectiveness of *The Evolution of Liberalism* as a spur to a further evolution of the liberal outlook. Professor Girvetz's valuable book documents the historical permutations of the liberal idea and offers a trenchant, if personal, view of liberalism's contemporary agenda.

ARTHUR SCHLESINGER, JR.

August 1962

PART ONE/CLASSICAL LIBERALISM

Thus God and Nature planned the general frame
And bade self-love and social be the same.

—ALEXANDER POPE

Introduction

THE EPIC transition of the Western world from an agrarian, handicraft society to the urban mechanized civilization of the present century was marked by the appearance of a new social philosophy, which has come to be known as liberalism. To distinguish it from the quite disparate liberal creed of today, it had better be called classical liberalism.

Classical liberalism, which took on its characteristic form in the eighteenth and nineteenth centuries, has with modifications become the conservatism of our time. But it was not always a "remembrance of things past." The same doctrine which now feeds the defensive backfire of reaction once kindled the spreading flame of revolution. The same arguments which now bolster an established order once reduced the castles of feudalism. There are thus two contexts within which the classical liberal creed may be examined: as a weapon designed to help in the destruction of an obsolete order and as a set of generalizations about man and society for which universal validity is claimed— for our day as for the time of Charles II and Louis XVI.

Whatever conclusions are reached as to its absolute validity, classical liberalism cannot be understood unless one is aware of two factors which profoundly influenced its formulation: the impact of the physical sciences on the thinking of the seventeenth and eighteenth centuries, and the aspirations of the new capitalist class.

On its theoretical side the classical liberal philosophy was shaped as to method by the physical sciences, which enjoyed enormous prestige after the publication of Newton's *Principia*. The social science of the eighteenth century consciously patterned itself after the physical sciences, in particular, the science of mechanics with its reliance upon universal and invariant, mathematically formulable laws. Whatever may have been the result of this approach in the physical sciences, where Galileo cautioned that experience is the "true mistress of astronomy" and Newton emphasized experimental confirmation, in the social sciences the result, with few exceptions, was an emphasis upon deductive procedures. The logic of the social sciences, upon which classical liberalism founded itself, aped the rationalism and generally neglected the experimentalism of the physical sciences. The prestige of the physical sciences led also to an insistence upon extending mechanical principles to the science of man and of society and, with this, to the facile assumption that wholes are completely understood by analyzing them into their simplest elements. It led finally to an identification of the natural and the reasonable and an appeal to Nature as the ostensive model of order and regularity. Thus, the Age of Reason could aptly ask that the "natural order" be substituted for the arbitrary and irrational social arrangements contrived by men.

It was no mere coincidence that these "arbitrary" social arrangements were precisely those which were objectionable to the emerging and eventually ascendant middle classes. On its practical side, classical liberalism was largely determined as to content by the needs and aspirations of the merchants and manufacturers, great and small, who came into their own with the commercial and industrial revolutions. Classical liberalism was born of protest and most particularly of the dissatisfaction which led the new and energetic middle classes to reject their inheritance.

What, in general, did the commercial and industrial middle classes need and want as they emerged from the wings of the medieval stage and appeared for the first time in the glare of the footlights? They were not unique in wanting relief from strife and disorder, but they differed from their feudal predecessors in requiring peace and order over areas large enough to embrace an expanding trade. This was their first requirement. Second, they wanted to free production and trade from what they regarded as unnecessary restraints, sacred and secular—the Church's doctrine of the "just price" and its restrictions on usury, as well as the *règlements* of Colbert and the

English Navigation Laws. Regulation shortly came to be construed as restraint, so that Richard Cobden could one day protest humanitarian factory legislation with the same fervor which he directed against the Corn Laws. Third, merchants and manufacturers wanted to protect the profits of trade and industry from arbitrary confiscation, from the expense of costly social services, indeed, from all taxes save those necessary to maintain services regarded as essential. They wanted a voice in determining what these services should be and how much should be paid for them—a voice commensurate with their growing power.

Finally, they sought a world in which their characteristic activities would be regarded as normal and necessary, not as marginal and even disreputable. It is difficult for us to comprehend the hostility with which the Middle Ages regarded the pursuit of gain. The nobility viewed trade with polite scorn. The Church regarded moneylending—to which today we erect our tallest temples—as amoral if not, in many of its phases, downright immoral.[1]* For that matter even the Protestant Luther condemned those who, like the Fuggers, made a religion of business, as vigorously as he condemned the churchmen who made a business of religion. This suggests that business motives were present in the so-called precapitalist Middle Ages, as, of course, they were. But the comments of R. H. Tawney on this subject are illuminating. "If it is proper to insist on the prevalence of avarice and greed in high places," he writes of the Middle Ages, "it is not less important to observe that men called these vices by their right names, and had not learned to persuade themselves that greed was enterprise and avarice economy."[2] Merchants and manufacturers of the new era wanted mores which honored thrift, industry, and enterprise, just as they wanted social institutions that dispensed with obsolete hierarchical arrangements in which the honored places were reserved for functionless aristocrats. An exaggeration of the economic motive often leads one to oversimplify the purposes of the entrepreneurial class. Entrepreneurs were not animated exclusively by a desire for gain. As much as anything, they needed a philosophy which would

* Notes, numbered consecutively for each chapter, will be found on pages 389-439.

demonstrate that the welfare of the community was dependent on their efforts; their pecuniary zeal notwithstanding, they wanted to feel that they were making an indispensable contribution to society.

Such were the influences, theoretical and practical, which dictated the classical liberal creed. They impose a twofold task: to trace the internal logic of the classical liberal creed with a view to showing how its conclusions are derived deductively from a set of universal generalizations about human nature; to indicate how these conclusions coincide with the interests of the middle class.

Before proceeding to this task, however, one must guard against possible misunderstanding. It must not be thought that the intellectuals who formulated the philosophy of classical liberalism were subservient spokesmen for special interests. The greatest of them were independent and critical thinkers. They were often men of compassion, usually with a strong sense of social responsibility. Adam Smith spoke of the "sneaking arts of underling tradesmen"; Bentham squandered his fortune on a "panopticon," designed to revolutionize penal institutions; Voltaire and Diderot grew caustic about the greed of their contemporaries. If most of them feared the masses, it must be remembered that men can hardly grow larger than the crevices in which they live. If the regard of the classical liberal philosophers for property verged on reverence, property is a protean word, and masters and latter-day disciples often use it with quite different meanings.

A final caution is in order. Classical liberalism is a broad stream fed by many tributaries. If I linger where the waters mingle I am not unaware of their varied sources. Great distances separate the eighteenth-century Whigs from the nineteenth-century Benthamite radicals, the planting artistocracy of the Founding Fathers from the Jacksonian "rabble," the traditionalism of Burke from the iconoclasm of the French Revolution. But there is a point of confluence at which men have erected what the late Carl Becker (recalling St. Augustine) named the Heavenly City of the Philosophers. It is here that I shall for the most part dwell.

Chapter 1

The Psychological Creed

ANYONE who has taken part in extended discussions of social problems knows that, invariably, some reference is made to human nature. Moreover, the conception of human nature involved is usually fundamental to the whole argument. We are admonished against stifling initiative—presumably man's most perishable virtue. We are warned against coddling people and destroying the incentive to work. We are reminded of man's natural greed and cupidity. Man is a creature with his eye constantly on the main chance. His ruling ambition is to get something for nothing, and the creative life of a community flourishes only if it has evolved rules, arrangements, and institutions, which somehow foil this ambition. Issues of the gravest public import have been and still are resolved by reference to such a conception of human behavior.

The use of human nature as a final court of appeal and an ultimate ground of proof is a favorite recourse of the conservative. But if human nature is the fixed star by which conservatives would guide public policy, this is an inheritance, received undiminished from the classical liberals of the seventeenth and eighteenth centuries. Liberals of our time have found the "facts of human nature" factitious. But the classical liberals of yesteryear regarded them as manifest and immutable and used them as the foundation upon which to build a whole system. Classical liberalism owed its popular acceptance primarily to the operation of powerful social and economic forces. But as a reasoned and logically coherent social philosophy, classical liberalism takes its start from certain basic psychological assumptions. One cannot clearly understand the social, political, and economic expressions of classical liberalism—any more than the conservatism which is nourished by them in our time—unless one first formulates and later critically examines the psychological assumptions upon which this liberalism is based. These assumptions compose a creed which can be broken down into four articles.

Egoism

The first of these four articles, if considered in terms of the formulation given it by Thomas Hobbes (1588–1679), may be called psychological egoism; if considered in terms of the approach employed by Jeremy Bentham (1748–1832), psychological hedonism. Although distinguishable, the two views are closely related, particularly in their bearing upon the immediate problem.

Although Hobbes, who wrote during the English civil wars, intended his work to serve as a defense of absolute monarchy, it was in fact an important influence in the development of eighteenth-century liberalism. Starting from the assumption that all reality is essentially matter in motion, Hobbes described human nature as a special instance of this same principle. All conduct, he held, is motivated by desire for that which aids the "vital motion" of the organism and by aversion to that which retards this "vital motion." Human organisms conform to this law as ineluctably as all material bodies to Newton's laws of motion. Consequently, every organism seeks its own preservation. Whatever makes for such preservation is regarded as good, whatever endangers it, as bad.

Upon this foundation Hobbes constructs his famous "selfish system." Man is by nature self-seeking. He may employ elaborate subterfuges to conceal the self-interest which permeates his conduct, but for him to be other than self-interested would be for him to be other than he actually is. Men associate in political groups from no motives other than a consideration of the destructiveness to themselves of the "state of nature." They obey a king from selfish motives. They conform to law for the same reason. Even compassion —Hobbes refused to halt before the most extreme consequences of his logic—is a species of self-interest. He wrote in the *Leviathan*, "Grief for the calamity of another is *pity*, and ariseth from the imagination that the like calamity may befall himself; and therefore is called . . . *compassion*, and

. . . *fellow-feeling* . . ." The difference between man in a state of nature and civilized man is not the difference between brute selfishness and altruistic consideration for the welfare of others; it is the difference between the reckless egoist who yields to his immediate impulses and the cool, calculating egoist who perceives that he must reckon with the welfare of others if his own well-being is to be secured.

The "selfish system" was not originated by Hobbes. It enjoyed a considerable vogue in ancient Greece, as the arguments of Glaucon and Thrasymachus in Plato's *Republic* attest. But, unlike Glaucon, Hobbes is unwilling to rest his case on the slender point made in the myth of Gyges' ring. Hobbes's psychological egoism is distinguished by the fact that he sought scientific vindication for it through an appeal to the laws of nature.

The doctrine of psychological hedonism is best formulated in the writings of Jeremy Bentham, who belongs to a later generation. His hedonism has much the same social implications as the views expounded by Hobbes. Psychological hedonism differs from psychological egoism primarily in its insistence that all conduct is motivated by the desire for pleasure. Hobbes had asserted that pleasure accompanies the promotion of self-interest, but he had not supposed that pleasure was the object of interest. Bentham writes in a famous passage:

Nature has placed mankind under the governance of two sovereign masters, *pain* and *pleasure*. It is for them alone to point out what we ought to do, as well as to determine what we shall do. On the one hand the standard of right and wrong, on the other, the chain of causes and effects, are fastened to their throne. They govern us in all we do, in all we say, in all we think . . .[1]

Bentham was an indefatigable reformer—one of the greatest in English history. He and James Mill (1773–1836) were primarily responsible for formulating the moral gospel of the nineteenth century—the utilitarian principle of the greatest happiness to the greatest number. But Bentham's theory of motivation, like Hobbes's, contains no moral prescription.

Indeed, moral prescriptions are gratuitous, and all moral comparisons and evaluations become pointless once one assumes that men are governed solely by their desire for pleasure and their aversion to pain. If the intensity of the yield in pleasure or pain is the sole measure which the individual can employ in guiding his conduct, invidious comparisons between saints and sinners become reflections of our personal bias. Passion is no less noble than compassion. And, more significantly in the rough youth of capitalism, the callousness and venality of the most aggressive businessman are morally indistinguishable from the humanity and generosity of the dedicated idealist: each has exercised his preference and, while anyone may err in what best satisfies his preference, here error halts.

Pleasures differ, then, in intensity but not in kind, and men are bound to prefer the greater pleasure over the less, no matter what the object of that pleasure may be. Unlike some hedonists, Bentham accepted the logical consequences of this position. "Quantity of pleasure being equal, pushpin is as good as poetry," he said quite consistently.

Contained in these words is the suggestion that pleasure is measurable, and that is, indeed, a basic and significant assumption of hedonistic doctrine. It led Bentham and his followers to suppose that they had devised an exact science of conduct. The method of the physical sciences in reducing qualitative to quantitative differences could now be applied to the direction of conduct. Pleasure, it was assumed, can be broken down into units that can be compared with each other quantitatively.

Accordingly, Bentham devised the famous "hedonistic calculus." A pleasure or pain varies in (1) intensity, (2) duration, (3) certainty, (4) propinquity; when we take into account the other pleasures or pains that might result from the act or event which produced it, it varies in (5) fecundity and (6) purity; and, when we take other persons into account, it varies in (7) extent. In directing our conduct, we seek that pleasure which is most intense, of longest duration, most certain, nearest, and so forth. These "dimensions of value," as Bentham calls them, are significant only because they indicate Bentham's conviction that we are able to fix these dimensions quantitatively, add up the quantities, balance the totals against each other with more or less mathematical precision, and select the greater. "Sum up all the values of all the *pleasures* on the one side," Bentham advised, "and those of all the pains on the other. The balance, if it be on the side of pleasure, will give the *good* tendency of the act upon the whole, with respect to the interests of that *individual* person; if on the side of pain, the *bad* tendency of it upon the whole."

Psychological egoism and its hedonistic variant have seldom received the frank, clear, and consistent formulation which is found in the writings of Hobbes and Bentham. The view has often been obscured by its association with supplementary hypotheses designed to explain the possibility of conduct prompted by regard for others. Psychological egoism has been amended in various ways to avoid criticisms which have been leveled against it. But, in one form or another, it has been the accepted theory of motivation for an overwhelming majority of spokesmen for the classical liberal tradition.

John Locke (1632–1704), by whom so much of the classical liberal creed was formulated, was a hedonist. "Good or evil," he writes, "are nothing but pleasure and pain, or that which occasions pleasure or pain to us." The French Physiocrats, who knew Locke's work well, leaned heavily on the selfish theory of motivation in laying the foundations of modern political economy. Bernard de Mandeville (1670–1733) in his *Fable of the Bees or Private Vices Made Public Benefits* argues in an ironical vein that moral distinctions are fictitious, and that it is only through the vices of men, i.e., their self-interest, that progress is possible. David Hartley (1705–57), that curious combination of crude materialist and devout Christian believer, derives all the sentiments from the feelings of pleasure and pain, while the Frenchman, Helvetius (1715–71), in the same decade which marked the publication of Hartley's *Observations on Man*, gave hedonism the formulation which influenced Bentham so greatly. The same view was taken by other adherents of the French school of sensationalist psychology, notably by La Mettrie (1709–51), Voltaire (1694–1778), Condillac (1715–80), and Diderot (1713–84).

Among the men who exercised a considerable influence upon Adam Smith (1723–90) was Abraham Tucker (1705–74), moralist and well-to-do country gentleman, who spent twenty years writing *The Light of Nature Pursued*. In a chapter entitled "Doing All for the Glory of God," Tucker declares that a man must have a "thorough conviction . . . that acting for the divine glory is acting most for his benefit." Self lies at the bottom of everything we do, and the purest affections grow from these roots. Even the Ten Commandments are given a hedonistic rendering by the painstaking Tucker. Tucker's immediate disciple was William Paley (1743–1805), one of the most influential and most widely read theologians of the time, who continued in much the same vein. Such a conclusion as Tucker's might easily find lawyers in accord with theologians. The great Blackstone (1723–80) wrote that "the Creator . . . has been pleased to contrive the constitution and frame of humanity that we should want no other prompter to enquire after . . . but only our self-love, that universal principle of action."[2]

Adam Smith's emphasis on sympathy in *The Theory of Moral Sentiments* might seem to suggest a departure from the egoistic tradition. However, in *The Wealth of Nations*, his later and more influential work, he takes the selfish system for granted. So, too, do Adam Smith's immediate followers. Thomas Robert Malthus (1766–1834), for example, in his famous *Essay on Population*, refers to the "apparently narrow principle of self-interest" to which we are indebted —along with the laws of property and marriage—"for all the noblest exertions of human genius, for everything that distinguishes the civilized from the savage state." James Mill, David Ricardo (1772–1823), and John Ramsay McCulloch (1789–1864) were directly under the influence of Bentham, Malthus, and Smith. Indeed, the egoistic theory of motivation has been accepted as axiomatic by the overwhelming majority of orthodox economists, from Adam Smith's time until our own day. Its eventual rejection by psychologists and philosophers did not deter great economists like Alfred Marshall (1842–1924) and members of the marginal utility school, like William Stanley Jevons (1835–82) in England and John Bates Clark (1847–1938) in America, from employing explicitly or implicitly a hedonistic theory of motivation.

Among those mentioned above, James Mill occupies a pivotal position, because in his work the primarily economic emphasis of Smith and Ricardo converges with the primarily psychological emphasis of Bentham. His son, John Stuart Mill (1806–73), was Bentham's most renowned disciple. The younger Mill labored vainly to effect Bentham's attempted reconciliation of hedonism and utilitarianism. Finally, lest the multiplication of instances become tedious, one may mention Alexander Bain (1818–1903), a close follower of Mill, and Herbert Spencer (1820–1903), who wedded the theories of hedonism and evolutionism.

In all of these examples two characteristic features require special emphasis: first, the assumption that the various terms of the egoistic vocabulary are unambiguous and meaningful as they are commonly employed; second, the attempt to ground egoism in human nature. Adherents of the egoistic point of view find it simpler to appeal for an explanation of the direction of our interests and the course of our conduct to immutable laws which govern human nature than to the changing institutional setting which constitutes our social environment. This, in the end, is the most significant feature of the doctrine of egoism.

The foregoing account may provoke mixed reactions. Some will wonder why such pains have been taken to document a perfectly simple and self-evident proposition. In this they will testify to the degree in which egoism has come to be taken for granted. The fact that so many distinguished thinkers have taken pains to defend the proposition should lead one to suspect that it is perhaps not as pellucidly clear as originally supposed.

Others will argue that the selfish system libels human nature. Egoism, it may be contended, is a historical aberration, natural perhaps to a society in which the forms of capitalism were still young and crude, but a theory which few people would entertain today. It would, indeed, appear that egoism, like other aspects of the wider social philosophy with which it is associated, has fallen into disrepute with a considerable majority of the intellectual spokesmen of our time. But it is equally apparent that egoism continues to survive as the accepted theory of motivation among people in general and practical men of affairs in particular. We are likely to be told that everyone asks the question, "What's in it for me?" except a few "starry-eyed idealists," and even they, the "realist" sagely assures us, have their ax to grind if we only knew.

Intellectualism

The second article in the psychological creed of classical liberalism is the view that men are basically rational. Such a conclusion is already suggested in Bentham's attempt to find a mathematically exact formula for the guidance of conduct, a "felicific calculus" as he called it.

At first glance the teachings of the hedonists might seem to argue the contrary: men are given over to a brute desire for pleasure. Pleasure or selfishness, not reason, is the motive power of conduct. But what distinguishes man from the brute is that the behavior of brutes is entirely instinctive, whereas the behavior of men is deliberate and calculated. Graham Wallas reminds us that a century ago professors and schoolmasters distinguished between men and animals by characterizing the former as completely "rational" and the latter as completely "instinctive." The word "instinct," he observes, is conspicuously absent from the enormous index to Bentham's collected works, interested as Bentham was in the human sciences. That Professor Henry Sidgwick, writing in the 1890's, should actually have undertaken to prove that "unreasonable action" is possible, and that instances of such action can be found, is evidence of the degree in which the contrary assumption had come to be taken for granted.

Men are moved to action, not by reason, but by the nonrational force of egoism. But if

> Self-love, the spring of motion, acts the soul;
> Reason's comparing balance rules the whole.

If self-interest or the desire for pleasure supply the compelling motive power, the *degree* of pleasure or satisfaction
which an individual shall enjoy is not determined by blind,
irrational forces. Self-love is cool; self-interest is enlightened;
reason is at the controls. With Olympian detachment it dis-
passionately surveys the field of assorted and competing
enticements, blandishments, and temptations, and determines
which will yield the greater pleasure. This decision is not
governed by the blind caprice of instinct, habit, custom, or
convention. It is determined by the inherent power of reason
to discern the intrinsic capacity of various experiences to
satisfy. Reason looks to the consequences, carefully balances
one promised pleasure or pain against another, and then,
solely by reference to the quantity of pleasure or pain involved, delivers the verdict. The verdict having been rendered,
conduct follows automatically. If the verdict should prove to
be wrong, this will be because of imperfect education or inadequate information. However, "the evil of ignorance admits
of cure." And, as a matter of fact, Bentham and his followers
addressed themselves to such a cure, becoming, to their eter-
nal credit, ardent advocates of universal education. At the
same time, their tendency to regard education as the panacea
for all social ills is striking evidence of a supreme confidence
in the rationality of men.

It might be objected, Bentham noted, "that passion does
not calculate," but "this, like most of these very general and
oracular propositions [*sic*], is not true." On the contrary,
"when matters of such importance as pain and pleasure are
at stake . . . who is there that does not calculate?"

If Paley's *Evidences of Christianity* (1794), reigning theological textbook of its time, is to be believed, even Christ was
not a man of "impassioned" devotion. "There was no heat in
his piety." On the contrary, his discourses were models of
"calmness," "sobriety," and "good sense."

There are, to be sure, evidences among the classical liberals
of a recognition of the influence of nonrational factors in
conduct. This is true of Adam Smith in *The Theory of Moral
Sentiments,* and particularly true of Malthus, whose melancholy conclusions concerning human passion helped to give
economics its reputation as the dismal science. There were

times when even Bentham doubted the felicity of the felicific calculus. But, on the whole, it was "rational man" who prevailed.

Bentham's fame rests in large part upon his remarkable activities in behalf of legal reform. Interest here is not in his concrete proposals, excellent as many of these were, but in the characteristic logic by which he arrived at them. Criminals, Bentham argued in his well-known discussion of penology, must be treated with a view to discouraging further crime and reforming the criminal. He rejects the idea that the criminal must make retribution through suffering, since this of itself merely adds to the quantity of pain in the world. Pain must be inflicted upon the criminal but only in sufficient measure to barely exceed the pleasure which he derived from his crime. More pain than this would embitter him and turn him against society; less would encourage him to further crime.

Here in application are all the assumptions of the hedonistic calculus: that pleasures and pains can be measured and nicely balanced against each other; that felons, not to mention honest men, will engage in the kind of calculation which Bentham describes.

In whatever measure men are rational, Bentham was preeminently so. He and his close friend, James Mill,[3] lived a cerebral life as nearly as men can approach such a life. God made man in his own image. So did Bentham, one may add.

Quietism

The third article of the psychological creed of classical liberals, like the second, is closely associated with their assumptions about egoism. It may be called psychological quietism. The proposition that all purposive activity must be explained in terms of self-interest or the desire for pleasure suggests that action must be induced, that in the absence of the enticement provided by pleasure or advantage the organism would remain apathetic, inert, quiescent. This is implicit in the psychological hedonist's view that when we engage in various activities—playing tennis, painting landscapes, making love—we do so not because we find these activities intrinsically interesting but because they are means to an end beyond themselves, namely, pleasure. Pleasure, the psychological hedonist asserts, is not merely the accompaniment of a fulfilled desire or a desire in prospect of being fulfilled. Pleasure is the *cause* of desire. In this way of thinking, activities do not generate desires; desires generate activities. The original datum is not an organism already engaged in a variety of activities, with the question remaining open as to how these activities will be directed. The direction which behavior will take is a closed question for the egoist; that direction must be self-advancement or the pursuit of pleasure. The question which concerns him is the provision of the requisite conditions for inducing action.[4]

The assumption that activity is episodic and that the organism is normally in a state of rest is not, indeed, confined to egoistic theories of motivation. As John Dewey has pointed out, it is often tacitly suggested in descriptions of the stimulus-response situation or of motivation in general, even when the point of view is avowedly nonhedonistic. When motives are viewed as causes of conduct rather than as factors *in* conduct whereby conduct is redirected, or, one might say, whereby behavior becomes conduct, the implication is clear that there are periods prior to the operation of the motive during which the agent is inactive. Any psychology of motivation which detaches motives from behavior as something external and apart—as when we say that men are "moved" by hunger—commits us to the view of human nature that is here imputed to psychological egoism.

One may view the office of motives as that of imparting meaning to activity already ongoing, activity which would otherwise be blind and mechanical. Or one may regard motives as instigating activity.[5] The alternatives were hardly envisaged in precisely these terms by the psychological egoists. Their views on this score are clear: it is only by dint of effort that the organism engages in activity, and that effort will not be made without the promise of a reward. Effort is painful. Since men are averse to pain and seek pleasure, they will avoid the pain of effort, work, labor, unless compensated by the prospect of a correspondingly greater amount of pleasure. Bentham writes, "*Aversion*—not *desire*—is the emotion —the only emotion—which *labour,* taken by itself, is qualified to produce: of any such emotion as *love* or *desire, ease,* which is the *negative* or *absence* of *labour*—*ease,* not *labour*—is the object."[6]

In the judgment of Malthus not even the desire for the means of his own subsistence suffices to overcome "the acknowledged indolence of man." It is only because we desire marriage and are forced after marriage to provide subsistence for our families that we arouse ourselves. So great is the force of human inertia that the melancholy herald of the dire consequences of overpopulation refuses to condone birth control. "I should always particularly reprobate any artificial and unnatural modes of checking population," he writes, "both on account of their immorality and their tendency to *remove a necessary stimulus to industry.*"[7]

Whatever the practical considerations which inspired psychological egoism, its theoretical source is to be found in the associational psychology which, beginning with Hobbes, almost completely dominated English and French thought for two centuries. Because a satisfied desire is *associated* with or accompanied by pleasure, it was assumed that pleasure is the object or motive of all desire. However, the view that human nature is passive is implied by the associationist theory of knowledge as well as by its theory of motivation. Here, as in so many cases, the great Englishman, Locke, is one of the most influential and articulate spokesmen.

In addressing himself to the question that was the chief theoretical preoccupation of the Enlightenment—the question of the origin and nature of knowledge—Locke finds that the mind is to begin with a *tabula rasa,* a blank sheet, passively registering the "ideas" or sense impressions which come to it through experience. These simple ideas combine to form complex ideas, and, although Locke is equivocal in indicating the part which reflection plays with respect to these combinations, they appear on the whole to take place quite mechanically, according to the laws of association, while mind participates only as a passive onlooker. Mind appears to be a wax which accepts the seal of sensations, without imparting any character of its own.

If Locke was somewhat ambiguous concerning the role of reflection in modifying the content of experience, followers like Hartley in England and Condillac in France were not. To them the process whereby simple impressions or ideas associate to form the complex content of the mental life becomes a completely mechanical one—governed by the law of contiguity, according to Hartley, and operating without any principle of association, according to Condillac. Here the dependence on sensory factors is almost complete; not even the attenuated functions which Locke assigned to mental life were permitted to complicate the mechanical process. No activity on the part of the agent by way of selecting or transforming the content of experience is allowed. Thus, in their epistemology, as in their theory of motivation, the thinkers of that day came to the conclusion that man, to use Thorstein Veblen's words, is an absorbent rather than an agent.

Psychological quietism must not be dismissed as a discarded or uninfluential dogma. Whatever its fate among recent psychologists, the proposition that effort is painful has been a cardinal, if not indispensable, premise of orthodox economics. And Middletown, as the Lynds have shown, still stands by Bentham. "Men won't work if they don't have to." Work isn't fun. None of us would do a lick of work if he didn't have to."

Indeed, we have been so much under the influence of this doctrine that we are jolted when we learn from an eminent anthropologist, Melville J. Herskovits, that the primitive inhabitants of the South Sea Islands "work and work hard, despite the fact that here, almost uniquely in the world, man is furnished by nature with practically all he needs." Some of us had been taught to believe that the South Sea Islands are a place where contented natives luxuriate in a life that is idyllic because it is idle. Professor Herskovits calls this the "coconut tree" position concerning labor in primitive societies, the view, namely, "which envisages the 'savage' as a man who, commonly living in a climate where his needs are bountifully provided by nature, neither is required to exert himself, nor is willing to do so when he can obtain even the necessary minimum to support life by abstaining from effort." Lest this view be dismissed as the afternoon aberration of weary escapists, Herskovits reminds us that Alfred Marshall, most influential English economist of modern times, wrote of the savage that "Laborious and tedious tasks are avoided as far as possible; those which are inevitable are done by the compulsory labor of women."[8]

Man's natural indolence is often tacitly assumed without giving the view explicit formulation. Writing in the *Scientific Monthly,* an authority on public health chides us for our disparagement of the microbes which cause disease. There is something to be said for pestilence, he claims, as there is for glaciation, floods, and famine. Like these other disasters, "disease makes man active, versatile, and inventive by shattering his complacency, rendering him supremely uncomfortable, developing his foresight, and forcing him to assume some responsibility for his destiny."[9] The author appears, to be sure, to have forgotten notable exceptions—if they are not indeed the rule—such as China and India. At best, such unqualified generalizations are precarious, but the accuracy of this statement is not so relevant here as is the view of human nature of which it affords a typical illustration: man is disposed to be complacent; he is bovinely incapable of activity, versatility, and inventiveness unless threatened with disaster. In the absence of powerful external incentives, he will remain as in Pope's *Essay on Man*:

> Fix'd like a plant on his peculiar spot,
> To draw nutrition, propagate and rot.

The assumption that men are normally indolent is by no means limited to the public health authority quoted, the nineteenth-century liberals, and the creator of the bearded hillbillies who people the pages of *Esquire*. The uncritical acceptance of the apothegm that necessity is the mother of invention indicates that a great many of us are committed to the same point of view. To be sure, Veblen once suggested that invention is the mother of necessity—but even in academic circles Veblen was regarded as an eccentric genius with a weakness for paradox which clouded his judgment.

Atomism

One further article in the psychological creed under discussion remains to be considered. This psychology is essentially atomistic. Atomism treats the character of any complex entity as entirely derivative from the character of its parts, viewed as independent, homogeneous, unitary existences. Every complex whole can be broken down or analyzed into its parts without remainder, the whole being no more than the sum of its parts. The behavior of any complex entity is thus the sum total of the behavior of its parts. Priority is assigned to the ultimate components out of which an aggregate or whole is composed; they constitute the fundamental reality. Moreover, they possess their essential character quite independently of their relations to each other and to the whole which they compose. These relations are entirely external and do not, therefore, alter the character of the component parts.

The atomistic point of view is frequently contrasted to the organic. The two views are often defined by comparing a heap of billiard balls to a multicellular organism. The cell loses its identity when separated from the whole. The behavior of an organism is, moreover, something more than the sum total of the behavior of the component cells taken as individuals. On the other hand, a billiard ball retains its essential characteristics when separated from the heap, and the whole of which the billiard ball is one part is no more than the sum of the parts. One could describe the behavior of a group of billiard balls from one's knowledge of one of them; no amount of knowledge about an individual cell would enable one to say anything about the organism of which it is a part. The strict atomist thinks of every whole as analogous to a heap of billiard balls.

The atomistic basis of eighteenth- and nineteenth-century psychology expressed itself in the first place in the sensationalism whose premises have already been examined in a slightly different context. From this point of view the complex content of the conative and cognitive life is regarded as having been built up from simple ideas, impressions, or sensations, which are treated not as the products of abstraction but as discrete unitary existences possessing a reality of their own. All knowledge is viewed as having originated in separate sense impressions, and David Hume (1711–76) characterizes the mind itself as no more than a "bundle of perceptions." Even when mind is not completely identified with its sensory content and is viewed as more than an aggregate of atomic sensations, its status is extremely vague, as in the shadowy substantiality accorded it by Locke, or flagrantly inconsistent with his premises, as in the writings of Bishop George Berkeley (1685–1753). It is characteristic of the great majority of English and French thinkers of this time that, in all their numerous inquiries into human nature, they went back to simple atomic sense impressions, out of which they sought to reconstruct the entire content of mental and emotional life. For the most part they shared with Hartley the judgment that "it is of the utmost consequence . . . that the affections and passions should be analyzed into their simple compounding parts, by reversing the steps of the associations which concur to form them."[10]

All this is suggestive as indicating a frame of mind and as illustrating a postulate of method. More important is the way in which the atomistic point of view expressed itself in the eighteenth-century view of the relation between human nature and its social environment. "Most people," Charles H. Cooley wrote at the turn of our century, "not only think of individuals and society as more or less separate and antithetical, but they look upon the former as antecedent to the latter. That persons make society would be generally admitted as a matter of course; but that society makes persons would strike many as a startling notion . . ."[11] That Professor Cooley's well-known defense of the latter thesis should generally be regarded as a turning point in the history of social psychology is evidence of the accuracy of his observation. The recency of scientific social psychology, assuming, as it does, that human nature is in large measure a product of the social environment, is further testimony to the aptness of Professor Cooley's observations. In a marked degree they apply to the view of human nature which prevailed in the eighteenth and nineteenth centuries.

The classical liberals, in accord with their atomistic outlook, regarded social institutions as the handiwork of pre-existing individuals whose characteristic mental and emotional endowments antedate the social arrangements into which these individuals enter. Even rights are often regarded as natural, that is to say, as antedating the state. Social arrangements affect individual human nature only superficially. They are additive and artificial, and their importance is largely negative, an importance which consists mostly of removing obstacles which might prevent individuals from achieving complete self-expression. The relationship between individuals and society is an external one; the individual with his various propensities and faculties is given, and society is an arrangement of convenience, whereby faculties operate more effectively and propensities are more likely to find fruition. To repeat, social institutions are created by the fiat of self-contained individuals; they are instruments, even expedients, which the individual can employ or discard without fundamentally altering his own nature.

Thus, although John Stuart Mill declared that "circumstances" altered individuals, he could write in a discussion of the logic of the social sciences as follows, "Men . . . in a state of society, are still men; their actions and passions are obedient to the laws of individual human nature. Men are not, when brought together, converted into another kind of substance with different properties, as hydrogen and oxygen are different from water . . . Human beings in society have no properties but those which are derived from, and may be resolved into, the laws of individual men."[12]

An earlier variant of the same atomistic outlook is to be found in Locke. The following passage from his *Second Treatise of Civil Government* may be regarded as fairly typical. Here one finds Locke quoting with approval the "judicious" Hooker to the effect that inasmuch ". . . as we are not by ourselves sufficient to furnish ourselves with a competent store of things needful for such a life as our nature doth desire—a life fit for the dignity of man—therefore to supply these defects and imperfections which are in us, as living single and solely by ourselves, we are naturally induced to seek communion and fellowship with others; this was the cause of men's uniting themselves at first in politic societies." Locke adds, "I moreover affirm that all men are naturally in that state and remain so, till by their own consents they make themselves members of some politic society . . ."[13]

The suggestion is clear that prior to the social arangements into which they enter, individuals in all their singleness and solitude are still sufficiently civilized, sophisticated, and reflective to consider the unhappiness of their isolated state and the improvements which life in society might bring. These attributes are not conferred by membership in society. Individuals already possess them. Society is merely an instrument whereby individuals may more fully satisfy otherwise imperfectly satisfied needs.

The same atomistic outlook is also exemplified in a characteristic tendency to regard individuals as basically homogeneous. They are all driven by the same self-interest and the same desire for pleasure. In short, like Democritean atoms, individuals may differ in the human equivalents to "fineness," "smoothness," and "mobility," but the same fundamental stuff is more or less equally distributed through all of them. Consequently, according to Bentham, each is to count as one and no one as more than one. Bentham, to be sure, could become quite caustic about the egalitarian "jargon" of the American and French Declarations. Nevertheless, he was himself so far under its spell that he could offer his services as lawmaker, after scant concessions to the "influence of time and place," to such disparate peoples as the English, the Russians, and the Latin Americans. Underneath the differences wrought by ancient custom and rooted habit there apparently resides a natural man whose fundamental sameness renders him equally amenable to the legislative wisdom of a Benthamite whether he resides in Cambridge or the Cameroons.[14]

The primacy of the atomic individual—uniform, discrete, ultimate, is thus affirmed. This is, indeed, the logical consequence of the egoistic premise with which the classical liberals start. The animus which Bentham and his contemporaries bore against traditionalism may have been limited, but the egoistic theory in which this animus received theoretical formulation is not. Egoism in any of its varieties is, after all, a revolt against the authority of custom and law and the claims of duty. Repudiate these and the individual stands forward and apart, self-contained, atomic, bound only by the ties of interest to the society in which he lives.

It is thus understandable why, ever since the advent of classical liberalism, it has been possible to think in terms of the "opposition" between society and the individual, an opposition which clearly assumes that individuals have separate existences, apart from the society in which they live. One can account also for the plausibility of the "social contract" theory in the eighteenth century. Whatever its implications for political and social philosophy, the view that the state is the product of a contractual agreement among individuals involves certain psychological assumptions: that men are rational enough to pause in the heat of the "warre of every man against every man," which characterizes their natural state, and consider the advantages of an ordered social relationship; that human nature as we know it antedates society and is not, therefore, dependent on society in any, save a secondary, sense.

With this apotheosis of the individual, the social nature of man became a doctrine to be left to classical scholars who study Platonism and deal in other ancient superstitions. It has remained for a comparatively recent era to revive the ancient Platonic teaching, without retaining the metaphysical and class bias which rendered the great master's insights so unpalatable to the liberal preference of the eighteenth and nineteenth centuries.

Qualifications

The psychological assumptions of the classical liberals have encountered varying fortunes in the course of time. Some retain their original popularity, although they have been modified in minor respects and the character of their adherents has changed. Others have lost favor. On the whole, they remain the psychological creed of most of those who still profess adherence to the tradition of classical liberalism.

This account is obviously incomplete from the standpoint of the history of psychology. But one need be concerned here with eighteenth- and nineteenth-century psychology only as it bears on the major purpose—an understanding of classical liberalism as a self-consistent social philosophy. This is not out of harmony with the actual procedure of the eighteenth- and nineteenth-century thinkers for whom psychology had not yet become a separate and specialized science. Their own approach to the study of human nature was always from the point of view of a more or less fully developed social philosophy.

Finally, and perhaps most importantly, one must not be deceived by the appearance of complete consistency and agreement, which the foregoing account may convey. This is equally true of the forthcoming stages of the discussion. No man, let alone a movement, is completely self-consistent. If we get approximate consistency that is a great deal. Rousseau and others attacked the "selfish system." In their heyday the associationists were challenged by the philosophers of the Scottish School. Both Bentham and Mill inadvertently departed from the standpoint of psychological hedonism when they defended utilitarianism; the moral obligation to seek the greatest happiness for the greatest number is clearly contradicted by the assumption that there is a natural compulsion to seek one's own pleasure. John Stuart Mill's distinction between higher and lower kinds of pleasure, after he adopted Bentham's and the elder Mill's view that pleasure is the *only* criterion of value, may do credit to his sense of realities, but not to his sense of consistency.[15] Rousseau refused to regard the mind as a passive recipient of external sense impressions. Unlike Bentham, he emphasized the social nature of man. Bentham, on the other hand, rejected the social contract theory so dear to Rousseau, as a fiction, although it accorded nicely with his own atomistic approach to human nature. Adam Smith appeared to forget his *Theory of Moral Senti-*

ments when he became occupied with *The Wealth of Nations*. Locke's equivocations occasioned endless differences among his followers.

Nevertheless, after all this is said, the degree of consistency which one finds is impressive. It was extensive enough throughout the work of a long succession of influential leaders and acute thinkers to warrant our designating them as forming the classical liberal school. If from the contributions of many men one must inevitably select and reject, the procedure is not abstract or forced. One emerges with a pattern of ideas which, even though no man or no generation has entertained it in its entirety, has influenced the intellectual climate of the "Great Society" for some two hundred years.

Chapter 2

Initiative and Incentives: The Problem of Motivation

THE KIND OF QUESTION the classical liberals posed to themselves was determined by their generalizations about human nature. If human nature is as it has just been described, the problem which at once suggests itself is twofold: (a) How may men indolent by nature be stimulated into productive activity? (b) Once this result is secured, how, if men are inherently selfish, can this productive activity be made to serve the general welfare? An answer to these questions embodies no less than the substance of classical liberalism as a social philosophy.

Protection of Property

What is the most effective way of overcoming what Malthus calls "the natural inactivity of man" and of stimulating his inventiveness, ingenuity, and effort? Since man is selfish, the arousal must be by way of his self-interest, an appeal which consists in the first place of *making him secure in the possession, enjoyment, and disposition of the fruits of his labors.* That is why men quit the state of nature and bind themselves together into societies, according to Locke. "The great and chief end . . . of men's uniting into commonwealths . . . is the preservation of their property . . ." And by property Locke explicitly understands whatever "he [man] hath mixed his labor with." If Locke justifies a title to the fruits of one's labor primarily by an appeal to the "law of reason," and in so far to a logical principle of self-evidence, in Bentham the appeal to psychological principles of motivation is clear. "If I despair of enjoying the fruits of my labour," writes Bentham, "I shall only think of living from day to day: I shall not undertake labours which will only benefit my enemies." Shocked that Beccaria, for whom he had a great admiration, had called the property right into question, Bentham responded that "It is this right which has overcome the natural aversion to labour." The younger Mill declared that "Insecurity of person and property is as much as to say uncertainty of the connexion between all human exertion or sacrifice and the attainment of the ends for the sake of which they are undergone. It means uncertainty whether they who sow shall reap, whether they who produce shall consume . . ."

Now the apparently simple proposition under discussion has had a remarkably checkered career. Beginning as an argument for guaranteeing to the worker the fruits of his toil, it has become one of the chief apologies for the institution of private property in general. "The property which every man has in his own labour . . . is the original foundation of all property . . . ," writes Adam Smith. In our own time Tawney reminds us that, "Whatever may have been the historical process by which they [proprietary rights] have been established and recognized, the rationale of private property traditional in England is that which sees in it the security that each man will reap where he has sown."[1]

If the logic of this rationale is to be understood, one must in the first place note the historical circumstances in which it was conceived. For a long time the overwhelming majority of Englishmen were anything but secure in the possession of the fruits of their toil, and Frenchmen suffered from a similar insecurity until the revolution ended the ancient regime. They were compelled to support an extravagant monarch and an aristocracy which, in France particularly, was entirely functionless. They had little real voice in determining the amount or the disposition of the frequently confiscatory taxes which were levied against them. They were often the victims of monopolists who were in a position to impose charges without rendering corresponding service. Under such circumstances it was to be expected that those who were not fed by these taxes, or sustained by feudal rights and titles, would plead that effort was being penalized and idleness rewarded.

Even when, as in England after the revolution, property was no longer in danger of outright expropriation, its disposition was hedged about by so many restrictions that owners could well plead for the substance of possession as well as the form.

Of those who were in this predicament only the middle class was articulate. The classical liberals, both early and late, although they expressed varying degrees of concern for the plight of "the laboring poor," were primarily spokesmen for the middle class and for its proprietary interests. Peasants and artisans of the seventeenth century might find a few spokesmen like Gerrard Winstanley, the leader of the Diggers, but theirs were voices in the wilderness, audible only because of the general silence. Consequently, it was to be expected that "effort" should be construed to include the initiative and ambition of the entrepreneur.

In the second place, given the doctrine of psychological quietism, it was natural that the energy displayed by the entrepreneur should become the chief object of concern. It is not, after all, a matter of prime importance whether the average artisan or the factory worker or the tiller of the soil is assured the full fruits of his toil. He must work under any circumstances in order to eat. Should his "take-home pay" fall short of his desert, he is in no position to question why. The curse of Adam is on him or a niggardly nature is about him; at any rate, whether the necessity be theological or ecological, he must submit.

The crucial question is to incite effort over and above that which is needed to provide subsistence. The case is different, in other words, with a Manchester textile manufacturer, a Shropshire ironmaster, a Texas oil operator, or a Detroit motor magnate. They may choose to continue at the head of their enterprise or they may not. And, given the irksomeness of labor, they will not so choose unless the reward is sufficiently high and sufficiently certain. In the case of the entrepreneur, therefore, the incentive must not be jeopardized. Nothing must be done to diminish his assurance that he will receive the "wages of superintendence."[2] If the difference is not usually formulated so explicitly, it is nonetheless clearly implicit.[3]

Thus far such terms as effort and energy, on the one hand, and fruits and reward, on the other, have not been given a precise meaning. This omission has been deliberate. The looseness with which these terms are habitually employed is notorious. Effort might have been the labor of a grimy-faced collier, picking away at a coal seam for most of the daylight hours of his life, or the "assiduity and skill" of the ironmaster whose hearth the coal would heat. It might be the labor of a switchboard operator or the "trouble" to which Mr. Wrigley went in making her chewing-gum conscious. It might be the toil of an assembly-line worker at the River Rouge plant or the energy of Mr. Ford in providing America with a cheap motor car. As for reward, one need not explore the endless difficulties of finding the pecuniary equivalent to the goods which any one of these may by his effort have created. In short, the very elasticity of the terms employed makes it possible to justify a wide variety of titles over a considerable array of property when one argues that men will not labor unless they are assured of the fruits of their toil.

Finally, and from a social point of view most importantly, the protection of property in general could easily be justified by the classical liberals on the score that this assurance was indispensable to the exercise of productive activity, because in the eighteenth century property actually was to a considerable extent functional, and the property owner was actually and directly associated with the production of the wealth to which he claimed ownership. This was an era of small-scale enterprise in which the entrepreneur worked side by side with his employees, and in which the property to which he claimed title were tools and personal possessions rather than stocks, bonds, and debentures. So, too, with the landowner during a period in which property in land was widely distributed. At first no more than a master craftsman, the entrepreneur shortly became a small-scale industrialist, but even so, he frequently drove himself more ruthlessly than he drove his men and had in addition countless problems whose urgency did not end with the eighteenth-century equivalent to our punch on the time clock.

Here in meager outline are some of the considerations which have often tended to blur the distinction between wages and profits and to justify the property right in general by an appeal to psychological principles, which, whether spurious or valid, ostensibly apply at the outset to actual instances of effort—the acorns picked under an oak, the apples gathered from trees in the wood, the deer killed by an Indian. The illustrations are provided by Locke, who, ever since the second of the famous *Two Treatises* appeared in 1690, has been regarded as the classic spokesman for the institution of private property.

Protection Against Involuntary Servitude

If we are not likely to exert effort when we cannot claim possession to the fruits of our toil, neither are we likely to exert ourselves when, in the second place, *we are not free to choose the task at which we shall labor*. This freedom is clearly denied the slave and the serf. It is also denied when the law of indenture permits one to bind himself over to another for an indefinite period. Finally, it is denied when guilds which enjoy monopolies in the performance of special tasks become exclusive societies from which newcomers are barred by excessive fees or extended apprenticeship. Slave and serf must perform what their master directs. Those whom the guilds exclude can work only at tasks which the guilds have not pre-empted. Similar arguments came to be used, not only against trade-union abuses, but against every effort of workers to bargain collectively with their employers.

Freedom of occupational choice is from any point of view profoundly important to all workers. Clearly, the contributions of many of our most resourceful business and industrial leaders could not have been made had they not enjoyed such freedom. However, *it is characteristic of the classical liberal point of view that it abhors compulsions which have their origin in law and custom and tends to overlook the economic compulsion which may keep the head of a family at an assembly line as inescapably as any black slave was held to a Southern plantation.* To suggest that the abstract right to reject employment is often meaningless when balanced against practical compulsions to accept employment in almost any circumstance still strikes many employers as splitting hairs. The fact is, however, that when the supply of labor exceeds the demand—*as it generally has in peacetime*—such compulsions prevail, and they are no less strong for being economic rather than legal.

Deprivation as an Incentive to Effort

If, in the first place, men must be assured of the fruits of their toil, and if, in the second place, they must labor voluntarily, in the third place, *they must not have access to the fruits of toil without toiling*, provided, of course, that they are able. Since labor is onerous, men will avoid it if they can acquire its fruits in some other way.

The proposition that reward must be contingent upon labor would appear to be susceptible of a variety of applications. It would appear, for example, to apply to legatees as well as to the "able poor" in connection with whom it has received special emphasis. However, we are told that, if property implies the right of each to what he can produce by his faculties, it implies also the right "to give this to any other person if he chooses, and the right of that other to receive and enjoy it."[4] To deny the right of bequest on the basis of the present proposition would, therefore, controvert the property right implied by the first proposition. In such an event the latter is promptly accorded priority.

Nonetheless it is evident that the proposition that no one shall reap where he has not sown, despite this recourse to an order of priority among incentives, presents a sword which cuts both ways. It may, indeed, be an incentive to production that one's children shall reap what one has sown, but it is often argued that where the harvest is large there is a net loss of incentive if children receive all of it or even so considerable a portion as that enjoyed by the legatees of, say, the Woolworth, Duke, or Manville fortunes.

John Stuart Mill, perhaps the most critical of the thinkers who formulated the creed of classical liberalism, finally accepted the fuller implications of the proposition that reward should be contingent on performance. In his *Autobiography* he writes of looking forward to a time "when the rule that they who do not work shall not eat will be applied not to paupers only, but impartially to all . . ."[5] Mill was over sixty when he wrote his *Autobiography* and hardly in a position, if question should arise, to plead the time-honored prerogative of youth in such a display of "socialistic" tendencies. However, there is nothing socialistic in this statement. It is simply a logical deduction from the premises of classical liberalism.

Despite these embarrassments, the general proposition that rewards should be earned continued to be affirmed with vigor. The decadence, particularly in eighteenth-century France, of a titled elite who reaped without sowing was in part responsible for this insistence. But there was another cause—one which overshadowed all the others. This was the dissatisfaction due to the English poor laws.

This is not the place to trace the history of legislation for care of the indigent. However, it may be noted that the English problem was a peculiar one. On the continent the clergy were primarily responsible for supplying aid to the needy. In England the dispossession of the monasteries compelled the state to assume responsibility. A law of 1572 provided for collectors and overseers to compel heretofore voluntary payments for poor relief. The Elizabethan Poor Relief Act of 1601 definitely accepted the principle of state responsibility for care of the needy, and set up, among other things, a forerunner of our depression-born WPA, by providing that the able-bodied poor be put to work. However, the administration of the Elizabethan law was lax and, not unlike the WPA, it was vigorously criticized because the conditions under which aid was granted were being construed too loosely. Here, then, was occasion to invoke the principle that payment must not be made to the able-bodied in lieu of labor. It is not known whether or not the dinner talk of prosperous Elizabethans often turned to poor-law workers seen leaning on their shovels in reposeful attitudes, but it may be surmised that controversies precipitated by the WPA were not new ones.

Criticism of the system of outdoor relief and concern over the increasing number of indigents led to the adoption of the Knatchbull Act of 1722, which put the able-bodied poor to work building workhouses (later nicknamed Bastilles) and farmed them out to contractors.[6] But even this effort to keep the able-bodied poor at work was gradually relaxed, largely, we are told, because the justices of the peace feared the spread of revolutionary ideas from France to England. Outdoor relief was restored, and, in 1795, the remarkable Speenhamland system was adopted. This system embodied a provision for minimum subsistence by supplying an allowance from the public treasury for workers whose wage fell below a specified level. It did not require them to perform additional labor in return. This amounted to support of the employed as well as the able unemployed, where the wages of the former fell below the subsistence level. An additional grant was allowed for each child, thereby outraging Malthus.

Presumably, the same result could have been secured by fixing a minimum wage instead of virtually subsidizing employers to pay low wages. But the era of the free market was dawning and the free market abhorred price-fixing, whether of labor or other commodities, as nature was said to abhor a vacuum. However, if the classical liberals opposed direct price-fixing, they also opposed indirect tampering of the kind made possible by the Speenhamland system. The cost of poor relief was mounting, aggravated, paradoxically enough, by the emergence of modern industry. The administration of poor relief was usually unenlightened, inefficient, and corrupt. This was the situation which presented itself when, with liberal sponsorship, the Poor Law of 1834 was passed, a statute whose object, says Dicey, "was in reality to save the property of hard-working men from destruction by putting an end to the monstrous system under which *laggards who would not toil for their own support* lived at the expense of their industrious neighbors . . ."[7] It is against this background that one must understand the emphasis which was placed on the proposition that to permit consumption in the absence of production is to encourage or perpetuate indolence. In many quarters the emphasis is much the same today as it was a hundred or a hundred fifty years ago.

In our country the most popular exemplars of congenital shiftlessness have been the poor whites and Negroes of the South. In eighteenth-century Britain the Irish cottier, better known as shanty Irish, enjoyed a similar notoriety. As a matter of sentiment or of public health and morals, it will be conceded that even the "undeserving poor" may become the object of private efforts at rehabilitation and charity, but to give them public aid is to encourage them in their idleness and to invite others to seek the same way out. Why should men toil in mills and mines when they can live on the WPA or enjoy the largess of a seventeenth- or eighteenth-century poor law? In the rather austere judgment of Herbert Spencer even private philanthropy is hazardous. Thus, in commenting on philanthropists, he writes, "That rigorous necessity which, when allowed to act on them, becomes so sharp a spur to the lazy . . . these paupers' friends would repeal, because of the wailings it here and there produces."[8]

On the other hand, it is often recognized that there is a class of "deserving poor," who, even though able-bodied, are impoverished through no fault of their own. That this is unjust is freely granted, but the psychological principles involved are not thereby modified and should have undiminished application. Partial and short-term aid may be given as a matter of common decency, but should the aid become certain, should it extend over a considerable period of time, should it be ample, should the social stigma be removed from the state of dependency,[9] should the insistence on work in return be relaxed—and these are the characteristics which public in contrast to private aid takes on, we are often told —dire consequences will ensue. Not only will the admitted former industriousness of the recipient lapse into parasitic indolence, but others, presumably always on the alert for relief from the pains of labor, will seek the same way out.

A word of caution is necessary. One must not suppose that the classical liberals were insensitive to the claims of the able-bodied needy.[10] The fact that these claims were met, however crudely and imperfectly, suggests that their co-operation was forthcoming in some measure at least. Moreover, it would be unfair to say that this co-operation was based entirely upon considerations of expediency. It should be added that many of the critics of poor relief deserve a great share of credit for rectifying some of the more flagrant abuses in the administration of public aid. All this may be said of present-day conservatives in connection with the relief problems arising out of the last economic crisis.

But the fact remains that the considerations cited above argue against public aid to the needy save in a rigidly qualified way. And these considerations were formulated for the most part by adherents, past and present, of the classical liberal creed. Classical liberals could accept such arguments all the more readily because they assumed that all human values are rooted in the property right. Hence, they were able with easy conscience to subordinate the problem of public aid for the needy to considerations of the effect of such aid on property owners. The impetus to social legislation, including more generous aid to the needy, has not come from the classical liberals, but primarily from the nineteenth-century antiliberal humanitarians, like Southey, Oastler, Sadler, and above all, Lord Shaftesbury,[11] and, more recently, from the British and American labor movements, the American New Deal, and kindred groups in other countries. Whether this is to the credit of the latter and the discredit of the former will depend, among other things, upon what one thinks about the psychological assumption under discussion. Judgment may be reserved until a view contesting the congenital indolence of human nature is presented in the following section. That there are wide differences of opinion concerning the point at which public aid can and should meet the basic needs of the indigent will not be disputed. That the conservative heirs of the classical tradition are prone to estimate this point rather modestly will perhaps be suggested by the following passage in which Mr. Herbert Hoover, referring to the world-wide depression of the early 'thirties, writes, "It is one of the greatest testimonies to the staunchness of the structure of American Liberty that immediately upon this disaster the country was organized and giving unfailing food and shelter to those in distress . . ."[12]

In 1905 a now famous minority report of the royal commission appointed to investigate English poor-law administration found that all prior poor-law legislation had been designed merely to relieve destitution. It urged that measures be taken for the prevention as well as the relief of poverty.[13] The opinion of the minority has gradually become the opinion of the majority and, under the leadership of David Lloyd George, England embarked upon a program of social insurance, matched only by the program which Bismarck had inaugurated in Germany. As a result, the British people have provided for workmen's compensation, old-age pensions, insurance against sickness and unemployment, and public housing; and the program is now more or less taken for granted in Britain by almost all parties.

But the full development of this program was relatively recent. Vigorous opposition had to be overcome. Were it not for the growing strength of the heretofore inarticulate laboring classes, it is safe to say that the program would never have gotten under way. France lagged far behind Britain, and, in America, at least until the depression, the idea of an extensive program of social security was as remote as the Kremlin and often attributed to that source. Meanwhile the same arguments have been raised against a program of social security in general and social insurance in particular that were brought to bear against poor relief. Among these are arguments which presuppose the psychological generalization under discussion.

Social security in the form of social insurance against unemployment, sickness, and old-age dependency or in the form of provisions for a minimum standard of subsistence is regarded as "getting something for nothing" and, therefore, as discouraging effort and initiative. The assumption is that the income received by any wage earner, as represented by the price his services command on the market, is on the whole a fair measure of his productivity. To provide him with more goods and services than his wage can purchase on the open market is, therefore, to supply him with what he has not earned, and, in so far, to destroy the incentive to earn more. On the other hand, if he is already putting forth a maximum effort, a program of social insurance will lead him to relax his effort, since he is assured of security even if he fails to do his best. So great is the aversion to labor, that a guaranty of the meager "necessities" of life removes the only incentive powerful enough to goad men, or, at any rate, the "average man" into action. Assure him and his family of barely adequate or even slightly less than adequate food, clothes, shelter, and medical care, and more will be regarded as hardly worth the effort it will cost. If the desire for more than the admittedly meager provisions of most social insurance programs is not enough to stimulate initiative and effort, it follows that only when prodded by the threat of deprivation, only, that is, when haunted by the sense of insecurity, will the average man arouse himself to effort.[14]

All of these considerations are part of the implicit if not the explicit logic behind most of the opposition to social legislation. "Everyone but an idiot," wrote the widely read Arthur Young in 1771, "knows that the lower classes must be kept poor or they will never be industrious."[15] Patrick Colquhoun echoed the same sentiment in 1806.

Without a large proportion of poverty, there could be no riches, since riches are the offspring of labour, while labour can result only from a state of poverty. Poverty is that state and condition in society where the individual has no surplus labour in store, or, in other words, no property or means of subsistence but what is derived from the constant exercise of industry in the various occupations of life. Poverty, therefore, is the most necessary and indispensable ingredient in society, without which nations and communities could not exist in a state of civilization.[16]

These statements are more forthright than the average. But that they are not quite a caricature of influential opinion current in our country is suggested by Abraham Epstein in his well-known study of social legislation. Behind the "opposition to every form of social insurance among the business and industrial leaders in the United States," writes Mr. Epstein, is a philosophy which "presupposes that only the constant threat of unemployment, sickness, old-age dependency, widowhood, and orphanage maintain the character and aspiration of the poor. Should these terrors be removed and security established, there will be neither striving nor desire for work among the masses."[17]

Mr. Epstein's generalizations are well illustrated by the

remarks of Mr. J. E. Edgerton, speaking as president of the National Association of Manufacturers, before the Permanent Preventives of Unemployment Conference. His comments may be regarded as typical of the attitude prevalent among the dominant economic group in this country in the 1930's. Mr. Edgerton objected to unemployment insurance for many reasons: it did not originate in America and was not in harmony with the Constitution, it was impractical, would encourage graft, would dry up the springs of private charity, and would lead to a repudiation of God and the church; he also found a serious objection to unemployment insurance and proof that "it is unmoral in its nature, however beautiful in its motive," in the fact that "its natural effect would be to subsidize idleness and encourage thriftlessness by removing those *necessities* which stimulate effort."

Mr. Edgerton was able to document his judgment with the words of Calvin Coolidge:

It has always been supposed that *strong motives* were necessary to insure continuous effort . . . If when unemployed he [the workman] is to receive something he did not pay for, no one can say how that would affect the will of the wage earner to hold his place by doing his best . . . The duty to relieve unemployment is plain, but not even the unemployed have a right to what they do not earn.

Mr. Edgerton commented,

Never was a sounder doctrine from a clearer thinker than that suggested by these words of the sage of Northampton. I cannot conceive anything that would more quickly sap the virility of the nation and be a more serious blow to the vital sense of individual responsibility than for the government to set up a protectorship over any particular class and make public wards of any except those reduced to helplessness by physical misfortune.[18]

Here again is an example of a double-edged sword which, although wielded in one direction, can be used to cut both ways. Some will comment on Mr. Edgerton's failure to perceive that the very arguments which he uses against unemployment insurance can be used against the institution of private property. They may argue that the security for which unemployment insurance tries to provide is considerably less than the security enjoyed by virtue of the possession of wealth, and that, if the former dulls the initiative of the worker, the latter should completely destroy the initiative of the owner. These considerations do not prove that the possession of wealth does in fact destroy initiative. The question raised is one of consistency rather than fact. If human nature is such that the enjoyment of security destroys initiative, this would apply to all classes and not to just one. Human nature is the great leveler: for good or for ill, all classes have it.[19]

The attitude of the dominant economic group in America is reflected in a *Fortune* magazine poll of more than ordinary significance. Asked their opinion concerning a "cradle to grave" program of minimum [*sic*] security, executives of business and industry answered in the following proportions:

	Percent
Impossible and undesirable	44.0
Economically possible but undesirable	15.2
Desirable but impossible	21.0
Economically possible and desirable	19.8

As late as 1943, some 59.2 percent of the dominant control group in America were opposed to an inclusive program of minimum security.

Obviously shocked by this overwhelming preponderance of adverse opinion, the editors of *Fortune* seek an explanation in the semantic difficulties occasioned by the phrase "cradle-to-the-grave security."

If he [the executive] rejects a social program tagged "cradle-to-the-grave security," it is more likely because the term has unfavorable semantic values connoting socialization than because he turns his back firmly upon all measures of social security that will surely be among the laws of our land. For in times past this poll has shown that the U.S. business man possesses a much more social view than he is generally credited with by his detractors.

But even the editors of *Fortune* find this explanation rather lame. "Yet with full allowance for the semantic difficulties," they go on, "it would seem that a lamentably large section of the business community is still unaware of—or still refuses to face up to—the political and economic forces at work in the fifth decade of the twentieth century."[20] Clearly, the nineteenth-century view of social security as giving something for nothing and therefore as weakening the motive to work still prevails.

The several conditions which must be given if men who are normally indolent are to be stimulated to productive activity have been enumerated. Men must, in the first place, be secure in the possession of the fruits of their toil. By a series of permutations this comes to mean that the property right in all its forms must be held inviolate. Men must, in the second place, enjoy freedom of occupational choice, with freedom defined exclusively as absence of legal restraint rather than as emancipation from economic compulsion. Finally, men must be barred from access to goods for which they have not labored. This is interpreted to mean that aid to the needy must be kept at such an intolerable minimum and dispensed under such odious circumstances that the beneficiary may be expected to exercise every effort to help himself. If, owing to circumstances over which he has no control, he is unable to help himself, his misery must not occasion faintheartedness. We must bravely steel ourselves against his suffering and think of the far greater misery of a society in which men could relapse into sloth and extravagance in the comfortable assurance that aid would be forthcoming from the industrious and thrifty; in such a society all men would soon become drones and misery would be universal.

Chapter 3

The Political Creed:
Political Quietism in Theory and Practice

To EXAMINE the conditions that must prevail if men are to be made industrious and enterprising is to be led at once to a consideration of the formidable obstacles which may lie in the way. Clearly, no one can enjoy the rewards of his labor if these are at the mercy of individuals prepared and able to use force to appropriate them or to do actual violence, for whatever reason, to one's person. Neither can one enjoy the fruits of his toil if he can easily be cheated of them through guile, fraud, deception. The possibility of foreign aggression is still another threat to one's person and the products of one's effort. Likewise praetorianism—a situation in which the military uses its armed might to exercise independent political control and to exact tribute as it wishes from the civilian population—has in times past endlessly plagued the productive groups in the community.

To deal with these threats to enterprise requires the agency of government. But government itself threatens the individual in both his person and property. The classical liberals denounce criminals, they fear foreign aggressors, they distrust their own military establishments—but the real burden of their contumely is reserved for the state. For, if it is the state, acting through government, upon which they must rely to apprehend criminals, to oppose foreign aggressors, and to control armies, it is the state also which, as the supreme coercive authority, can corrupt the innocent, plunder the thrifty and industrious, enslave the free. Thus, the liberals are torn between their need for the state and their fear of it. They define the authority of the state and the liberty of the individual as opposites, only to find that they cannot dispense with either of them. It is upon the task of extricating them-

65

selves from this dilemma that most of the political virtuosity of the liberal has been exercised, from the time when Gournay first proclaimed the doctrine of laissez faire to the day when Walter Lippmann confessed his animadversions concerning the "providential state." It is, therefore, to the classical liberal solution of this problem that one must now turn.

The Rejection of the State

In the judgment of the classical liberal the state is always suspect, for it possesses power, and power corrupts. Consequently, that state is best which governs least. Government, as the instrument of the state, rarely intervenes; it "interferes." Government functionaries rarely act; they "meddle." They rarely err; they "blunder." Whether it is the Radicals who gather about Bentham or the political economists who stem from Smith and Ricardo, the landed middle class of the Continent or the industrial *bourgeoisie* of England, they all share this same fear and distrust. It expresses itself now in the Physiocrats' "*laissez faire, laissez passer*"; again in Jeremy Bentham's admonition to the state to "be quiet"; now in the comment of Burke that "it is in the power of government to prevent much evil; it can do very little positive good"; again in the judgment of Herbert Spencer that "government is essentially immoral."

One of the most celebrated expressions of the sentiment may be found in the opening passages of Tom Paine's *Common Sense*. There Paine wrote,

Some writers have so confounded Society with government, as to leave little or no distinction between them; whereas they are not only different, but have different origins. Society is produced by our wants, and government by our wickedness; the former promotes our happiness *positively* by uniting our affections, the latter negatively by restraining our vices. The one encourages intercourse, the other creates distinctions. The first is a patron, the last is a punisher.

Society in every state is a blessing, but government, even in its best state, is but a necessary evil; in its worst state an intolerable one . . . Government, like dress, is the badge of lost innocence; the palaces of kings are built upon the ruins of the bowers of paradise.

In seeking the reasons for the animus to which Paine gave such eloquent expression, one must remember some of the more urgent practical considerations which prompted the flight of early liberals from what has been called *étatisme*. Whatever the merits of the universal proposition that the state is inherently oppressive, corrupt, and inefficient, these titles did aptly fit most government in the eighteenth and much of the nineteenth century, even after the more tyrannical regimes had been ousted. England's parliamentary government was notoriously unrepresentative when it was not downright despotic. The middle classes, not to mention the masses, were virtually excluded from participation or control until 1832. *La belle France* bore revolutionaries and suckled Bonapartists in 1848 as in 1789. In short, government intervention in economic life *was* arbitrary and repressive, and such intervention was rarely in the interest of the classes excluded from participation in government.

Indisputably, interference served to restrict enterprise and to retard production. The complaint of the classical liberals against government was the grievance of those who sought to liberate the forces of production from governments which held these forces in restraint. It is no accident that the decade made notable by James Watt's use of steam power to drive machinery (1769) and Arkwright's establishment of the first cotton factory run by water power (1771) was also featured by the appearance of Adam Smith's *Wealth of Nations* and Bentham's *Fragment on Government,* both arguments in behalf of restricting government activity.[1] While Adam Smith was writing his masterpiece, the Physiocrats were striving, quite independently, to liberate French agriculture from destructive state interference. The year 1776, which marked the publication of Bentham's *Fragment* and *The Wealth of Nations,* is also the year when the American Declaration of Independence, the most historic of all protests against political oppression, appeared.

Men live and act in a world of particulars, but think in a world of universals. The particular political abuses with which the classical liberals were all too familiar became the basis of a number of generalizations which condition their every attempt to define the functions of the state. The state is the supreme coercive authority in society. It differs from all other social institutions in that it enjoys a monopoly in the use of force—sheer, brute, physical force. But this force must be wielded and the activities of the state conducted by persons. Even if human nature is not inherently corrupt, many men are corruptible. This is particularly true of men in politics, confronted, as they are, by greater than average temptation. Indeed, the opportunities for plunder are so great that at the very outset political office attracts men with few scruples. Government, therefore, is bound to be featured by an extraordinary amount of corruption.

If politicians are not all corrupt, certainly they are all fallible. In ordinary situations individual errors of judgment, at worst, affect only a limited number of people; errors of judgment by men in political office affect the whole social order. There is, moreover, a greater tendency toward error by men in political office. We are told that they are almost invariably men who are long on the social graces and short on "practical experience." The ingratiating arts of the politician do not ordinarily appeal to competent men of affairs, nor for that matter do they appeal to scholars. Consequently, such men shun political office. Even when specialists adequate to some particular task are found, they tend to become remote, immersed in their own routine, arbitrary, inflexible—in short, bureaucrats. Or worse (in our time), they are "starry-eyed" professors with an ideological ax to grind. In any event, the very nature of government service is such that men are removed from the actualities of everyday experience. Also, they are often spared the deterring punishments attendant on bungling and error in everyday life. Unlike businessmen, they need not fear bankruptcy.

This error and inefficiency, say the classical liberals, is multiplied beyond measure when government endeavors to escape its own proper and narrow sphere. Modern society is far too complex to lend itself to government by distant bureaucrats acting, necessarily, according to general rule. This is particularly true of economic relationships at the present time. Only those directly involved in the countless relationships which prevail in the modern business and industrial world know what these are all about, and even their knowledge is limited to the small area in which they move. This situation is aggravated by the dynamic, fluid character of these relationships which renders law archaic as soon as it leaves the legislature.[2]

Also, so long as they are spending other people's money, bureaucrats, however honest, are bound to be extravagant. In their case there is a special temptation, for their power and authority usually depend on the number of their subordinates and the scope of their operations.

Lurking in the background of these indictments is a haunting fear that men, thus beset by temptation and liable to vice, may defy attempts to prescribe and limit their functions and use their seductive political wiles[3] to capture the formidable apparatus of state power for themselves. How real this fear is—how genuine, for example, was the fear that President Roosevelt aspired to be a dictator—one cannot easily say. Certainly, this is a factor which is responsible for some of the allergy to government.

The items enumerated are not particular criticisms directed at stubborn Stuarts and blind Bourbons, although it was the situation precipitated by the Stuarts and Bourbons which clearly inspired them. They are universal indictments directed at all governments, however well-intentioned. They suggest why, in the judgment of the classical liberals and those who still adhere to their point of view, government action, even in the province in which it may be said properly to fall, is always a near and often an immediate threat to individual enterprise and productivity. It burdens the individual with unnecessary taxes, thereby depriving him of at least part of the fruit of his labors; it limits his freedom of action, weighing him down with countless "forms," and enmeshing him in red tape; and, finally, it multiplies the hazards of doing business and creates uncertainty and insecurity by tampering with the laws of economics. At its worst, it becomes Caesarism which, from the point of view of enterprise, is as stultifying as anarchy, for both designate a condition of lawlessness, the one organized, the other fortuitous.

From Adam Smith to Herbert Spencer

The classical liberal's concern with defining and limiting the functions of government can be understood only in the light of this general fear and distrust of state power. The limits of government action have been marked off differently by different spokesmen for the classical liberal tradition. Judgments concerning where the boundaries between government activity and individual initiative should be drawn vary all the way from holding government rigidly and undeviatingly to the exercise of its police function—the negative role of protecting persons and property from violence and fraud —to allowing the exercise of certain positive functions in carefully defined areas. But there is enough community of doctrine among spokesmen, past and present, for the classical liberal tradition to warrant a clear distinction between them and the advocates of collective control of individual action.

It is useful to begin with the well-known enumeration of government functions which appears in *The Wealth of Nations*. The sovereign has only three duties, according to Adam Smith. The first of these is the protection of the social group from outside violence. The second is the protection of the individual members of society from the injustices or oppression of their fellow citizens. The third is "the duty of creating and maintaining certain public works and certain public institutions which it can never be for the interest of any individual, or small group of individuals, to erect and maintain; because the profit could never repay the expense to any individual or small number of individuals, though it may frequently do much more than repay it to a great society . . ."[4]

In connection with the third responsibility, Adam Smith would allow public support of schools for children where they might be taught to "read, write, and account." Even so, the master must not be paid wholly by the public, "because, if he was wholly, or even principally paid by it, he would soon learn to neglect his business."[5] Such support for education he justifies, not only because of the advantages accruing to the beneficiaries of such education, but because "the more they are instructed, the less liable they are to the delusions of enthusiasm and superstition, which, among ignorant nations, frequently occasion the most dreadful disorders." They are, moreover, more disposed to respect their lawful superiors and "less apt to be misled into any wanton or unnecessary opposition to the measures of government."

In connection with the discharge of this third function he also provides for public works and institutions which facilitate commerce in general, such as roads, bridges, canals, harbors, coinage, the post, and the like. Also, particular branches of commerce may be facilitated by maintaining forts, garrisons, and commercial representatives in foreign lands.

Jeremy Bentham was in almost complete agreement with Adam Smith concerning the functions of the state and in at least two instances applied the doctrine of "quietism," as he called it, more rigorously than his master. Adam Smith contents himself with a mere revision of the laws through which the state intervened against usury. Bentham declares that "no man of ripe years and of sound mind, acting freely, and with his eyes open, ought to be hindered, with a view to his advantage, from making such a bargain in the way of obtaining money, as he thinks fit; nor (what is a necessary consequence) anybody hindered from supplying him, upon any terms he thinks proper to accede to."[6]

So, too, Bentham is perhaps clearer than his master in condemning colonialism. While criticizing colonialism, Adam Smith concedes that colonization of the new world had served a useful purpose. Bentham denies that colonies have any economic utility. To the French revolutionists, for example, he addressed the categorical advice, "Emancipate your Colonies!"[7]

When John Stuart Mill wrote his *Principles of Political Economy* in 1848 he had already come under the influence of Coleridge and Comte, both of whom implanted in him a dislike for the pure doctrine of laissez faire as it had been expounded by the political economists, e.g., John Ramsay McCulloch and Nassau W. Senior. The influence of Coleridge and Comte also led him to break in certain important respects with the Benthamite school in which he had been raised, quite literally, from infancy. After noting that Coleridge was "at issue with the *let alone* doctrine, or the theory that governments can do no better than do nothing," Mill adds that laissez faire was "a doctrine generated by the manifest selfishness and incompetence of modern European governments, but . . . as a general theory, we may now be permitted to say that one-half of it is true and the other half false."[8]

It is in this mood that Mill later distinguished between the "necessary" and the "optional" functions of government.[9] The former are universally accepted as inseparable from the idea of government; the latter, while important, are not indispensable and are the subject of some disagreement. The necessary functions of government, Mill reminds his readers, are not as simple and definite as many would like to believe. They include more than the mere protection against force and fraud to which many of Mill's contemporaries believed that government action should be confined. If government must act against the evil of violence and fraud, why not against other evils? "If nothing but what people cannot possibly do for themselves, can be fit to be done by government, people might be required to protect themselves by their skill and courage even against force, or to beg or buy protection against it . . ."[10]

Among the functions of government which elicit general consent, although they do not come under the head of protection against force and fraud, are those which have to do with the regulation of inheritance, the use of natural resources, the performance of contracts, the prevention and conciliation of disputes, the care of the incompetent, the coinage of money, the provision of standards for weights and measures, the maintenance of communications, and the sanitation and lighting of cities.

Besides these, Mill favored certain more controversial forms of intervention. He believed that governments should support elementary schools, so as "to render them accessible to all the children of the poor, either freely, or for a payment too inconsiderable to be sensibly felt," provided the government did not insist upon an educational monopoly. He believed that "the certainty of subsistence should be held out by law to the destitute able-bodied," provided that "the condition of those who are supported by legal charity can be kept considerably less desirable than the condition of those who find support for themselves . . ."[11]

Mill, like Adam Smith, regarded colonization as a long-range solution to the population problem and, accordingly, favored government intervention of this nature. He believed also that government might act to aid geographic and scientific exploration as well as to assist in the cultivation of speculative knowledge in general.

By far the most venturesome of Mill's concessions to government is the idea, contemplated rather than proposed, that government might regulate the hours of work. The great majority might desire a reduction of the workday from twelve to ten hours but be unable to accomplish this without the aid of government, Mill observes.

Assuming . . . that it really would be the interest of each to work only ten hours if he could be assured that all others would do the same, there might be no means of their attaining this object but by converting their supposed mutual agreement into an engagement under penalty, by consenting to have it enforced by law.

He cautiously goes on,

I am not expressing any opinion in favour of such an enactment, which has never in this country been demanded, and which I certainly should not, in present circumstances, recommend: but it serves to exemplify the manner in which classes of persons may need the assistance of law, to give effect to their deliberate collective opinion of their own interest, by affording to every individual a guarantee that his competitors will pursue the same course, without which he cannot safely adopt it himself.[12]

Mill's general position has sometimes been regarded as a perfect example of individualism and laissez faire. He writes in his great essay, *On Liberty*, that "the sole end for which mankind are warranted, individually or collectively, in interfering with the liberty of action of any of their number, is self-protection." To justify "the subjection of individual spontaneity to external control," the conduct from which it is desired to restrain an individual "must be calculated to produce evil to someone else." Compulsion is justifiable, he says, only for the security of others, only, that is, "in respect to those actions of each which concern the interest of other people."[13]

Clearly, the test of Mill's position will depend upon where he actually draws the line between those of an individual's actions that concern himself and those that concern others. The passages cited above do imply, among other things, liberty of thought and discussion, as Mill shows in a magnificent chapter whose brilliance has not been tarnished by time. But there is nothing in these passages which excludes the regulation of hours and conditions of work, the quality of merchandise offered for sale, of wages, prices, etc. We are told of trade that it is "a social act." In selling goods to the public, Mill declares, we are doing what affects society and therefore comes within its jurisdiction. If restraints in the form of restrictions on trade and production are wrong, this is solely because they fail to achieve the results desired of them, not because they encroach on individual liberty.

It may be concluded that, while limiting the agenda of government, Mill is by no means among the most extreme partisans of this point of view. Mill was one of the few classical liberals who, while accepting the institution of private property and the system of free private enterprise for the visible future, was willing to re-examine both and even to contemplate the possibility, at least in the remote future, of such a radical program of government intervention as socialism. He was willing to allow numerous exceptions to the proposition, universally entertained by the classical liberals, that men are the best judges of their own interests. But basically he favored "restricting to the narrowest compass the intervention of a public authority in the business of the community." "Laissez faire," he wrote, "should be the general practice: every departure from it, unless required by some great good, is a certain evil."[14]

The views of Mill, the younger, have been dealt with at such length because of the great prestige he enjoyed in the middle of the nineteenth century and because he achieved a peculiar intellectual balance and eminence which enabled him to see both backward and forward. For a more extreme partisan of the view under discussion one may turn briefly to the work of Herbert Spencer.

Perhaps the greatest speculative tragedy from which the position of antistatism has suffered is the desuetude into which Spencer's works have fallen. To be sure, as late as 1905 Justice Holmes felt constrained to remind his colleagues on the United States Supreme Court that "the Fourteenth Amendment does not enact Mr. Herbert Spencer's *Social Statics*." Nevertheless, by 1915, Elihu Root was noting with evident regret that "under the law to which books are subject," the writings of Herbert Spencer had entered upon a period of comparative neglect.

In the works of Herbert Spencer the idea of limiting state power is carried to a doctrinaire extreme. "Granting," he says, "the proposition that men are selfish, we cannot avoid the corollary, that those who possess authority will, if permitted, use it for selfish purposes."[15] The essential function of the state is the protection of the citizen against internal and external aggression. The moment that the state tries to do more than protect, it becomes itself an aggressor. Accordingly, Spencer opposed all regulation of commerce. "In truth," he wrote, "it is a sad sight . . . to see these political schemers, with their clumsy mechanisms, trying to supersede the great laws of nature." We are called upon to witness some "flippant red-tapist get upon his legs and tell the world how he is going to patch up nature!" These meddlers, these self-appointed nurses, these creation-menders—the epithets are Spencer's—tamper with the "inherent sufficingness of things," and they ignore the beautiful simplicity of those principles by which every defect is remedied:

> . . . principles that show themselves alike in the self-adjustment of planetary perturbations, and in the healing of a scratched finger —in the balancing of social systems, and in the increased sensitiveness of a blind man's ear—in the adaptation of prices to produce and in the acclimatization of a plant.[16]

His objections to law-enforced plans for relief to the needy are so many and so various that they need not be set forth here, although they have a certain historical interest as an example of the length to which doctrine can be carried. Many of these objections would now be repudiated even by admirers of Herbert Spencer. Public education, government colonization, even sanitary and health superintendence are condemned. The state may not interpose between quacks and their patrons, nor may it forbid unlicensed persons from prescribing. We are told that "to do so is directly to violate the moral law." Let the invalid buy from whom he pleases and let the unlicensed practitioner sell to whomever will buy. "On no pretext can a barrier be set up without the law of equal freedom being broken . . ." So, too, sanitary administration by public authorities, state or municipal, is evil, implying, as it does, a tax upon the citizen's property "greater than is needful for maintaining his rights," and, by the same token, "the levying of compulsory rates for drainage, and for paving and lighting is inadmissible . . ." Such legislation is called "aggression."

By this time it is abundantly evident that the distance between Spencer's version of liberalism and what Carlyle called "anarchy plus the constable" is not a long one. Herbert Spencer is, on the whole, an extremist among the more thoughtful spokesmen for classical liberalism, but few men have had the immense vogue he once enjoyed among the laity.[17] However, even among the social philosophers, it is arguable that Spencer was exceptional only because he refused to join them in subordinating cold logic and doctrine to warm sympathy and emotion. He started from the same premises. His peculiarity, it can be contended, consists of carrying these premises to their bitter conclusion. That this conclusion does not strike everyone as preposterous is evident not only from the lament of Elihu Root and the caustic comment of Justice Holmes. As recently as 1935, Albert Jay Nock wrote in *Our Enemy, the State* that "With our public affairs in the shape they are, it is rather remarkable that no American publicist has improved the chance to reproduce these essays [Spencer's *The Man Versus the State*] verbatim . . . If this were properly done, it would make one of the most pertinent and useful works that could be produced at this time."[18]

The American Version

When attention is turned to America, it is found that the prevalent ideas concerning the role of government were, of course, received from abroad and recast to suit our needs.

Cultural laissez faire, that is, the freedom of individuals from government interference with religious worship, speech, publication, and assembly, was the creed of American liberals, as it was of their English cousins. America had its Sedition Act of 1798 and English Tories exploited the Massacre of Peterloo to pass the repressive Six Acts of 1819, but such legislation was in opposition to the prevailing trend. Serious infractions of civil rights might occur in the course of time and go unchallenged, but in our country, after the expiration of the Sedition Act of 1801, the principle of cultural laissez faire was never itself in question, with the one great exception, of course, of the slaves. With economic laissez faire the case is more complicated.

If by laissez faire one means government cast in the role to which Spencer later assigned it, the term does not apply to the thought of the Founding Fathers, however apt it may be to the Supreme Court's late nineteenth-century interpretation of their thought. The Founding Fathers were familiar with mercantilist practices in their own states where trade was controlled through tariffs and, in the case of eight of the states, by actually fixing the price of many retail commodities. Those who hailed from states which chartered commercial corporations and granted bounties and subsidies could scarcely be called strangers to the idea of state intervention.[19]

Consulting the Constitution one is confronted by the vexing question of interpretation. The powers of the states are residual and unenumerated; that is, the states may exercise those powers not forbidden them under the Constitution and not delegated by the Constitution to the federal government. Legislation for public health, morals, safety, and welfare has always been regarded as falling within the compass of state powers. Nevertheless, the powers of the states are nowhere clearly and specifically defined. Consequently, their boundaries, particularly in the case of social legislation, have varied with the social and political philosophy of the Supreme Court.

An examination of the powers granted in the Constitution to the federal government makes it clear that the Founding Fathers intended to give the federal government powers commensurate with the problems that faced it. Although alert to the need for securing ratification by the states, they were anxious to avoid the weakness of the governing instrument created by the Articles of Confederation. Accordingly, the Constitutional Convention was called to "render the federal constitution adequate to the exigencies of government and the preservation of the Union." The Committee of Detail was instructed by the convention to formulate a constitution according to which the legislature could act "for the general interest of the Union."

On the basis of such evidence, one may agree with Charles Beard when he says, "Certainly the convention did not confine the Constitution to a mere enumeration of specific powers";[20] or one may insist that the limitation of federal authority to the enumerated powers is a basic feature of the Constitution. In any event, a glance at the clauses which designate these powers discloses that, given the will, they suffice for a wide exercise of authority.

In practice the chief constitutional grants of power to the federal government have been found in its authority to regulate interstate and foreign commerce, to levy taxes, and to spend revenues for the general welfare. The interstate com-

merce clause, under judicial interpretation, has been notoriously elastic and adaptable. In all sorts of ways, from taxing
imports to taxing incomes, the power to tax has served as a
device for social control. There remains the general welfare
clause which, although the most sweeping grant of power,
did not come into its own until quite recently. It deserves a
word of special comment.

The Constitution contains two important references to the
general welfare. The preamble declares that the purpose of
the Constitution is "to form a more perfect Union, establish
Justice, insure domestic Tranquility, provide for the common
defence, promote the *general Welfare*, and secure the Blessings of Liberty to ourselves and our Posterity . . ." A similar
reference to the general welfare will be found in the paragraph which gives Congress the power to tax in order "to
pay the Debts and provide for the common Defence and
general Welfare of the United States . . ."[21] It was on the
basis of the "necessary and proper" and "general welfare"
clauses that Alexander Hamilton defended the constitutionality of the first United States Bank. While Jefferson took a
contrary view, his party re-established the bank in the difficult years which followed the War of 1812, employing Hamilton's own arguments.

There is nothing in the constitutional provisions protecting
property which prevents government from regulating property
for the promotion of the general welfare. These provisions,
Charles Beard reminds us, "do not declare any absolute rights
in property. They merely protect property against arbitrary,
high-handed, and discriminatory actions of government and
its officials. They mean a certain equality of treatment for the
various classes of property owners in the enactment of laws
which tax, regulate, and take property for public use."[22] It
was not until the Supreme Court reversed itself and tardily
interpreted the "due process" clause of the Fourteenth Amendment as forbidding a state to regulate the prices charged by
grain elevators or to limit the length of a baker's work week
to sixty hours that action in behalf of the general welfare
was explicitly limited by the property right.

Clearly, then, no Founding Father turned in his grave

when Justice Holmes refused to conform the Constitution to Spencer's *Social Statics*. However, if one means by laissez faire not the rigid doctrine expounded by Spencer and the Manchester school but the standpoint taken by men like Adam Smith and John Stuart Mill—a standpoint which still defines the functions of government in negative terms—the authors of our basic law were in complete accord. Constitutional exegesis aside, the fact remains that the Founding Fathers believed in restricting government action to the minimum implied by an essentially negative conception of government. The separation of powers and the system of checks and balances are ample proof of that. So, too, is the record of legislation after the adoption of the Constitution.

The Founding Fathers were by no means unanimous in their judgment concerning the role of government, as the classic controversy between the strict and loose constructionists shows. But the area of agreement is invariably greater than partisans in the heat of controversy are prone to realize. Historians who accept the version of the participants concerning these controversies are likely to neglect the fundamental agreements which often underlie them.

The outstanding exponent among the Founding Fathers of quietism in government, in theory if not always in practice, was Thomas Jefferson.[23] Although Adam Smith's influence in this country was felt only tardily, Jefferson knew and praised *The Wealth of Nations*. He also approved of the *Political Economy* of the Frenchman, Jean Baptiste Say, another defense of laissez faire. In his first inaugural address Jefferson declared, "A wise and frugal Government, which shall restrain men from injuring one another, shall leave them otherwise free to regulate their own pursuits of industry and improvement and shall not take from the mouth of labor the bread it has earned. This is the sum of good government, and this is necessary to close the circle of our felicities."

Now Beard contends that there is no way of knowing whether Jefferson would have uttered these words had he lived in the city of Manchester—had he been thinking, that is, in the context of an industrialized urban society instead of the handicraft, rural society of early nineteenth-century

America. This raises a familiar issue which involves men like Adam Smith and Bentham and Mill, as well as Jefferson. When Adam Smith wrote *The Wealth of Nations*, he had in mind the commercial society of England which, in the last quarter of the eighteenth century, had not yet been Manchesterized. As for the others, what would their attitude have been in the twentieth century? Their objections to government are couched in general terms. Inevitably one must ask how they would have defined the functions of government in an era of corporate ownership and after two world wars separated by a decade of feverish speculation and another decade of unremedied depression. The record discloses that, if the men referred to were not pre-Spencerians, they were also, both in theory and in practice, far from embracing collectivism.

The Sequel in England

In England the original doctrine of laissez faire eventually passed, for the most part, from the care of intellectuals like Adam Smith, Jeremy Bentham and the Mills—and Albert V. Dicey (1835–1922), Walter Bagehot (1826–77), and William E. H. Lecky (1838–1903)—into the custodianship of businessmen and industrialists and their hired spokesmen. A similar transition took place in America at a considerably later date. Meanwhile, at a time placed by Dicey between the years 1865 and 1870, the interpretation and application of the doctrine of laissez faire underwent a number of changes which have led some to assert that laissez faire strayed from the course its earlier spokesmen had charted.

Between 1800 and 1830, as Dicey points out, the foundations of Benthamism and radicalism, the intellectual expressions of laissez faire, and Manchesterism, its commercial expression, were being laid. After 1830 the doctrine of laissez faire was unmistakably in the ascendant. In the years 1833–54 laws were passed which abolished the crime of usury. In the year 1844 the statutes that made forestalling and regrating[24] crimes were repealed. The Corn Laws were repealed in 1846 and the Navigation Laws in 1846 and 1849. By 1867 the last protective duties had been removed. The Combination Act was repealed in 1824, although it was re-enacted in revised form a year later. During the same period, a long list of legislative acts sought to clear away the jungle of restrictions impeding trade in property, especially property in land. Civil and religious liberties were extended by the Toleration Act (to Unitarians, 1813), the Corporation and Test Acts (1828), and the Roman Catholic Relief Act (1829), which—with a long list of Oath Acts—had the effect of giving religious minorities access to Parliament and the courts of law. Even the Poor Law of 1834 was a direct reflection of the ascendancy of laissez faire. The period was also marked by an impressive body of humanitarian legislation, having to do with matters as various as abolishing the pillory, ending slavery, reducing the number of crimes punishable by death, protecting the insane, and preventing cruelty to dumb animals.

Now all this legislation possesses characteristics which distinguish it from the outstanding legislation of the period which follows. The laws dealing with the abatement of suffering were confined almost entirely to the type of cases that did not involve the individual's freedom of action, as in the prohibition of flogging, hanging in chains, and cock-fighting. Where limitations upon individual freedom of action were involved, as in the law prohibiting the hiring of children as chimney sweeps, the beneficiaries were minors and others similarly incapable of guarding their own interests. The other legislation (the Navigation Act, Oath Acts, etc.), not strictly humanitarian and on the whole far more characteristic of the period, deals almost entirely with the removal rather than the imposition of restrictions upon individual conduct.

From 1870 on there occurred, according to Dicey, "a revolution of social or political belief." The "revolution" was, indeed, foreshadowed by the Ten Hours Bill, which was passed in 1847 over the fierce opposition of the liberals. Much significance has been attached to this measure. The Ten Hours Bill limited the labor of women and children to ten hours a day or fifty-eight hours a week. In his private diary, Shaftesbury, who put the measure through, wrote, "I had to break every political connection, to encounter a most formidable array of capitalists, mill-owners, doctrinaires, and men who, by natural impulse, hate all 'humanity-mongers' . . . In very few instances did any mill-owner appear on the platform with me; in still fewer the ministers of any religious denomination . . . Bright was ever my most malignant opponent. Cobden, though bitterly hostile, was better than Bright . . . Gladstone is on a level with the rest . . . Lord Brougham was among my most heated opponents . . . Miss Martineau also gave her voice . . . in resistance to the measure." These were all Benthamites or adherents of some variant of Benthamism. A successful rear-guard action finally secured an amendment of the measure in 1850 which extended the workday to ten and one-half hours!

The controversy over the Ten Hours Bill raged so fiercely, because it appeared to involve a new principle of government action. Writing in 1905, Dicey declared, "The Ten Hours Act has not ruined British industry, and has put an end to much suffering. . . . But the Ten Hours Act has tended towards socialism, and contains within it the germs of an unlimited revolution, of which no man can as yet weigh with confidence the benefits against the evils. . . ."[25]

It is one thing, the liberal argued, for the state to protect the individual, as when the weak are protected from the violence of the strong or when incompetent individuals (infants, madmen) are given care and protection. In such an event government action merely serves to protect the freedom of the individual. It is quite another matter when government intervenes to do for the individual what he is able to do for himself, and even constrains the individual when he should be left free to decide for himself. This leads to helpless dependency and the loss of freedom. The Ten Hours Bill represented such intervention and compulsion, in the judgment of the classical liberal. If women or children of fourteen wish to work more than ten or ten and a half hours a day, the state in effect tells them that they are not the best judge of their interests and limits their freedom of choice.[26]

From 1870 on, legislative action was largely of this latter type. Legislation like the Adulteration of Food Act of 1860 and the Sale of Food and Drugs Act of 1899 safeguards individuals from mistakes "which often may be avoided by a man's own care and sagacity," which, in other words, "might be warded off, though at the cost of a great deal of trouble, by individual energy and circumspection . . ." Accordingly, "these enactments rest upon the idea . . . that the State is a better judge than a man himself of his own interest . . ." These words do not appear in the "handout" of a food and drug lobby; they express the judgment of A. V. Dicey, eminent scholar and writer.

The Workmen's Compensation Acts of 1897 and 1900 deprive a worker of the freedom to give up the benefit or "contract himself out" of compensation in the event of injury. In 1880 legislation was passed, depriving parents of the freedom to keep their children from school; while a law of 1891 compelled childless citizens to share the cost of schooling other people's children. One could go on and on.[27]

It is legislation of this type which Dicey, writing in the classical liberal tradition, describes as "collectivist" and "socialistic." The difference between the legislation of the two periods (approximately before and after 1870) is, he says, "essential and fundamental." The "interventionist" type of legislation was for the most part opposed by the dominant economic control group, now completely under the spell of Adam Smith and Ricardo. Were the intellectual and political guardians of liberalism, needled by the slowly awakening masses, turning renegade? Had they abandoned laissez faire?

It is clear that the scope of state action was appreciably widened after 1870. But whether this represents so radical a departure from the principles of laissez faire as to be called a "revolution of social and political belief" is another question. What name would Dicey have reserved for the Beveridge plan? Can Dicey and Lippmann and the others who write wistfully of the classical era have mistaken a modification in the philosophy of laissez faire for its repudiation? Are they not confusing tactics with strategy, a change in means with a change in end? If an army of mere soldiers can find more than one route to Berlin and Seoul, an army of theorists and politicians should be able to find more than one route to Manchester.

The issue is in part a verbal one, depending upon what is meant by laissez faire, and in part the more basic one of understanding when a change in degree becomes a change in kind. In historical perspective, British reform legislation, at least until the regime of Lloyd George, is hardly the departure from traditional laissez faire which purists would have us suppose. This is equally true of legislation in America, as late as the advent of the New Deal. There was indeed a break with the tradition of individualism in certain collectivistic tendencies and centripetal forces at work *inside the business and industrial world*. But these forces had not yet formally affected to any great extent the legal, governmental, and other institutional arrangements of the time. As for the so-called "paternalistic" legislation of this period, which is usually cited as evidence of the lapse of laissez faire, it is neither socialism nor "*le socialisme sans doctrines.*"

It requires no more than a casual glance to discover that the legislation was essentially a patchwork, a series of improvisations, both in its conception and in its administration. The career of employers' liability and workmen's compensation legislation is a case in point. The first laws were easily evaded, limited to only a few workers, and cumbersome in their administration. Some twenty-six years had to elapse between the passage of the first act and the passage in 1906 of effective compensation legislation. Some might call this sort of thing a departure from basic principles; the British Joint Industrial Conference of 1919 was closer to the truth when it referred to "tinkering with particular grievances." Even the trade unions, until the turn of the century, were preoccupied with their own sick and accident funds, not interested in the great mass of unskilled workers, and often as averse to government intervention as the liberals whose leadership they accepted.

Reform legislation amounted, then, to a yielding to pressure here in order to resist it more firmly there. Its object was not to abandon the idea of a negative state, but to strengthen the idea where it really counted. A concession to the idea of a welfare state is not a consecration. What Laski says of the social legislation that followed 1914 applies *a fortiori* to the legislation of the period following 1870, namely, that "it seemed far more impressive to those who bestowed it than it did to those upon whom it was bestowed."[28]

Histories are notoriously deceptive, particularly if we take from them only what we seek. As we read of reform following reform, we receive the impression that state intervention took on the dimensions of a tidal wave. Actually, relatively few people were touched by the reform movement until quite recently. We also receive an exaggerated impression of the part—considerable as it was—played by reformers, cabinet ministers, and the like, forgetting that the leaders and lawmakers yielded, in many cases reluctantly, to anonymous mass pressures in the conviction that they were wise to pay hush money. This is not to say that a great many of them were not genuinely moved by a desire to ameliorate mass suffering and that some of the conservatives like Shaftesbury, Carlyle, and Ruskin, did not despise laissez faire. However, there is no question also but that many of them regarded reform as a sedative. Others might talk of precedents; they were thinking in terms of preventives.

It may be argued that the particular character of the source from which social legislation issued is unimportant; the forces demanding such legislation, however humble and obscure, finally won out. But the point of the stress upon the expedient attitude of many, if not most, of the reformers and lawmakers is this: in the end they wrote the laws and they administered them. Their attitude might well warn us, therefore, against committing laissez faire to premature burial.

The Sequel in America

The fortunes of laissez faire in England are significant because, as usual, the English experience is a fairly accurate clue to what later happened elsewhere. Developments in this country lagged behind developments in England, and the result is a rather curious historical anomaly. During the very period when the English were expanding the functions of government, these functions were being narrowed in the United States. This development is reflected in the changing interpretations of constitutional law, that is to say, in the shifting positions of the Supreme Court, which, thanks to our doctrine of judicial review, have a crucial bearing on the subject.

There is a general consensus that, for a long period starting in the 1880's, laissez faire was given a doctrinaire interpretation by the Supreme Court which ignored the spirit and tortured the letter of the Constitution. The shifts which led to this consequence fall into four periods.

Under the leadership of Chief Justice Marshall the Supreme Court sought to expand the scope of federal power. His interpretation of the interstate commerce clause of the Constitution laid the foundations for later federal regulation. On the other hand, the constitutional provision that no state shall make or enforce laws impairing the obligations of contracts and the Fifth Amendment, forbidding Congress to deprive any person of life, liberty, or property without due process of law, were used freely to prevent state legislatures from regulating private interests. Marshall presided from 1801 to 1835.

During the second period, from 1836 to 1864, Chief Justice Taney followed Marshall in relying upon the clause granting Congress control over interstate commerce as a support for enlarged federal authority. However, under the influence of Jacksonian democracy, the court was disposed to allow freer rein to the state legislatures.

During the third period, from the Civil War to 1885, the mood of the court in these matters was expressed in the Granger decisions of 1877. In these decisions the court refused to invoke the Fourteenth Amendment to outlaw legislation regulating grain elevators and railroads. In this period, which marked the dawn of the new industrial era, the court showed little disposition to curb the expanding activities of government, and the "police power" was loosely interpreted to give the states freer action in promoting the public welfare.

The fourth period began in the middle 'eighties. It was in this period that the quadrumvirate of Field, McKenna, Brewer, and Sutherland crowned Spencer philosopher laureate and made America the true abode of laissez faire in one of its most doctrinaire forms. The state withered and "free" private enterprise came into its own.

The legal device which court interpretation converted into a club with which to beat the bloody head of government was that same "due process" clause which it had earlier refused to invoke in the Granger decisions.

From a procedural limitation, originally designed to prevent federal encroachment upon individual rights and extended into the states to protect the Negroes of the South, the clause was transformed into a substantive limitation upon any social or economic legislation which, in the eyes of the Court, appeared unreasonable, arbitrary, or capricious. Its protection of 'persons' was extended to corporations. Its prohibition upon deprivations of liberty and property was construed to enact into the Constitution the classical economic doctrines of laissez faire and of liberty of contract.[29]

"The aristocracy of the robe," as John W. Burgess admiringly called the judiciary, was to protect America from the blandishments of "collectivists" until the constitutional crisis precipitated by Franklin Roosevelt's attempt to reform the court in 1937. To be sure, there were dissenters like Holmes, Brandeis, and Cardozo, but for the most part they had to content themselves with writing brilliant minority opinions. Also a number of important laws were passed which marked a withdrawal from the extreme position of the 'eighties and 'nineties. Typical of these were the Mann-Elkins Act of 1910, which empowered Congress to place a ceiling on the rates charged by interstate carriers, the Farm Loan Act of 1916, the Industrial Rehabilitation Act of 1920, the Adamson Law establishing an eight-hour day for trainmen engaged in interstate commerce, and a host of state laws. Such legislation did not, however, represent a defeat for laissez faire: it was merely a strategic retreat. It was even farther from representing a concession to social planning than the late nineteenth-century English legislation of the same type.

Herbert Hoover might write in 1933 that laissez faire "has been dead in America for generations,"[30] but his supreme confidence in the system of free competition and his identification of planning with regimentation suggest that the obituary of laissez faire could not be written until his own administration had passed into history.[31] Even if a display of new wrinkles in its old age rendered laissez faire unrecognizable to Mr. Hoover, the Supreme Court continued to believe in its vitality as evidenced by a series of decisions in which the court in effect informed the federal government that under the Constitution it lacked the power to deal with the problems of the depression in a direct and comprehensive way. Laissez faire sickened in 1933 but it did not really die until the great constitutional crisis of 1937. Its ghost still haunts the annual meetings of the National Association of Manufacturers, the American Bankers Association, the United States Chamber of Commerce, innumerable occupational and professional associations, such as the American Medical Association, and varyingly large segments of the United States Congress. It prefers in our time, however, to be known by the name of "freedom of enterprise." Its despised antithesis is the "welfare state."

Chapter 4

The Political Creed:
The Functions of the State

THE MAJOR FUNCTIONS of the classical liberal state, as they emerge from this background of theory and practice, may now be fixed. It is now possible to define the area of agreement concerning the functions of the negative state, as this agreement has prevailed among the great majority of classical liberals and their living descendants.

In enumerating these functions, one must bear in mind the fundamental principle which determines their exercise: When government controls the action of individuals, this may be in behalf of the individuals controlled or in behalf of others. In principle, classical liberalism rejects all attempts by government to do for the welfare of individuals who are sane and adult what they would not do for themselves. It reserves the name "paternalism" for government intervention of this kind. It rejects paternalism, not only because of misgivings about government, but—to recur to the psychological preconceptions cited at the outset—because paternalism is said to sap initiative and self-reliance and because, in general, rational adults are said to know their own interests better than any government could know them.

The activities of the individual are to be controlled, then, not as they affect him, but as they affect others. However, an individual's relationships to others may be governed in two ways: he may be constrained to help others; he may be restrained from doing them harm. In principle, only the latter is permitted by the classical liberal creed. Exceptions may be allowed, but they are carefully labeled as such. So, too, concessions may be made in the interest of expediency, but the basic principle is retained.

Preservation of Order

First and foremost among the functions of the classical liberal state is the protection of persons and property against the mischief of others. The term "mischief" is used advisedly. What is mischief?

Individuals must be protected both in their person and property from foreign aggression. They must be protected from the domestic turmoil provoked by factional strife. They must be protected from murderers and thieves.

But mischief embraces much more than mere violence. It embraces fraud, which cheats men of their property, and slander, which cheats them of their reputations. The contents of fraud and libel vary with a thousand shifting eddies, but whatever the muddy waters at the top may contain, time and custom have left a solid deposit at the bottom into which judges have sunk the pilings on which they build decisions.

Mischief also embraces hazards to health, so that persons are forbidden to contaminate drinking water, to sell putrefied meat (at least after the publication of Upton Sinclair's *The Jungle*), to engage in the more obvious forms of medical quackery,[1] and so on. It embraces reckless conduct which threatens the safety of others even though it may be perpetrated without malice, as when a motorist drives at excessive speed. It embraces affronts to the moral sense of the community, as when lottery, polygamy, nudity, traffic in narcotics, and white-slave trade are forbidden. To be sure, once the state acts in behalf of the moral sensibilities of the community, it enters upon *terra incognita,* where the classical liberal must tread warily if not deviously. It is difficult, for example, to see how the classical liberal state can justify its interference in certain sumptuary matters (e.g., the use of alcohol, narcotics, etc.), or in defining the conditions under which childless couples may be divorced; but in these matters conscience defies and custom usurps the role of logic, particularly when the practices involved have become the special concern of churchmen.[2]

Where injury to person and damage to property have been caused, the state must fix responsibility, apprehend the culprit, exact damages, impose punishment. This requires the elaborate apparatus of police, courts, and institutions of correction.

All this (with the exception of defense against foreign aggression) is implied by the idea of the police power, which is loosely defined as the protection of the "health, safety, and morals" of the community and which, in this country, is generally exercised by the state governments. Presumably "general welfare" is broader than "health, safety, and morals," so that the protection of the latter must fall short of what is required for the preservation of the former, if only in its emphasis on negative rather than positive action. Thus, in its exercise of the police power the classical liberal state may remain quite indifferent to wide areas of the general welfare.

The exercise of the police power justifies preventive measures of a narrowly restricted sort. An army of inspectors may be retained to test scales, inspect meats, report fire hazards and so on. Examinations may be devised to test skills, and licenses may be issued to persons and businesses. The owner of a substandard house may be required to remove it without compensation, as a protection to the health of the community.[3] To be sure, if the health of the community requires as much as this, it would appear to require also, at the very least, that slum dwellers be assured adequate housing elsewhere. But from such positive measures the negative state is bound to recoil. Its task is over when it has forbidden the operation of a nuisance. The gap thereby left must be filled through individual ingenuity and co-operation, not through political "coercion."

Enforcement of Contract

The classical liberal state in general refuses to coerce individuals in respect to their acknowledged positive obligations. Its emphasis is on what the individual *shall not* do rather than on what he *shall* do. Now, the only alternative to social control in the sphere of positive action is voluntary agreement. But voluntary agreement is grossly inadequate as a basis on which to conduct the business of a complex society, unless there is some assurance that agreements will be kept. Thus, if the state refrains from imposing positive obligations upon individuals, it must nonetheless require that individuals fulfill the positive obligations which they have themselves undertaken. Accordingly, the state has a prime responsibility to require performance of the engagements which individuals freely and honestly contract. If the protection of the health, safety, and morals of the community may be taken as the first major function of the negative state, the enforcement of contract may be taken as its second major function.

Henry Sidgwick writes, "once their respective relations to the surrounding material world have been determined so as to prevent mutual encroachment and secure to each the fruits of his industry, the remainder of their positive rights and mutual obligations ought to depend entirely on that coincidence of their free choices, which we call contract."[4] Both in the scope he assigns to contract and the definition he gives it as a "coincidence of free choices," Sidgwick is merely pronouncing the judgment reached by the generations of classical liberals who preceded him. Whatever its role in primitive or precommercial societies, contract evidently took on a new significance with the advent of the commercial and industrial era.

In the preliberal era social relationships in general and economic relationships in particular had been more or less carefully defined and rigidly fixed by established custom and law. Prices, interest rates, the condition of work, the quality of merchandise, the relationships of vassal to lord or journeyman to master, all these were determined, not by a contract or agreement representing the upshot of a bargain or negotiation among the parties to the transaction or relationship, but by pre-established rule and practice.

But it was precisely these rules and practices which stifled the initiative and enterprise of rising generations of merchants, traders, and industrialists. Feudal custom and royal decree were, therefore, discarded as a basis on which to determine individual rights and responsibilities in large areas of human intercourse. They were discarded for very practical and very particular reasons, which in the course of time were buttressed by theoretical and universal reasons derived primarily from the accepted interpretation of human nature. Thus, if each man is indeed the best judge of his own interest, he should be allowed as far as possible to decide for himself the commitments he will make and the circumstances under which he will make them. If every agreement or bargain is, as Sidgwick says and most liberals have believed, a consensus of two or more free wills and if, moreover, these are the wills of enlightened egoists—each engaged in the pursuit of his own happiness—it is evident that the less interference with such agreements the more general happiness is promoted.

Quite apart from the practical ambitions of entrepreneurs and such theoretical rationalizations of them, there were factors inherent in the actual historical situation itself which imparted a new importance to contracts. The rapidly expanding economic system multiplied endlessly the occasions on which individuals had to rely on each other's promises. The old system of rights and obligations was not and could not have been developed with reference to a situation in which hundreds of workmen labored under a single roof, or hundreds of owners pooled their capital in a single corporation, or laborers transformed materials brought from two corners of the earth to make it salable at the other two corners. The very tempo of change made reliance on precedent difficult and recourse to agreement necessary. Finally, the sheer complexity of the modern business and industrial system has been said to defy the regulation of law and to require reliance on promises.

If for these reasons contract or agreement was in part, at least, to supplant law and usage as the basis on which to define rights and responsibilities, it can be understood why the classical liberals attached so much importance to making promises legally binding. Sidgwick writes,

Withdraw contract, suppose that no one can count upon anyone else fulfilling an engagement—and the members of a human community are atoms that cannot effectively combine; the complex co-operation and division of employments that are the essential characteristics of modern industry cannot be introduced among such beings. Suppose contracts freely made and effectively sanctioned, and the most elaborate social organization becomes possible, at least in a society of such human beings as the individualistic theory contemplates—gifted with mature reason, and governed by enlightened self-interest.[5]

The kinds of contract which the coercive power of the state might be invoked to enforce,[6] the nature of the indemnity in the event of nonperformance, all this need not concern us. The main object is to see why the classical liberal places the enforcement of contract on the state's agenda next to the protection of person and property from violence and fraud. If he encounters the reproach that the use of the coercive power of the state to enforce contracts represents a departure from the doctrine of noninterference, the classical liberal might respond that certain departures are necessary in the interest of protecting initiative and enterprise and that, after all, the exercise of the police power to protect person and property is such a departure. Or he might deny that the use of the state's power to enforce contracts is a form of interference, by reverting to the definition of contracts cited at the outset. According to that definition, in enforcing contracts the state does not regulate, direct, or interfere with the conduct of individuals; it merely gives effect to their expressed will.

Promotion of Exchange

It is yet to be shown how, through the free market, an aggregate of enlightened egoists become accessories to the happiness of the community as a whole. Somehow this is brought about by the phenomenon of exchange when buyers and sellers, producers and consumers, employers and workers are free to contract on the open market. It is imperative, therefore, that they have the freest possible access to the market and that all possible measures be taken to facilitate those acts of exchange for the totality of which the term "market" is in fact the inclusive designation. Hence, the promotion of exchange may be cited as the third function of the classical liberal state.

Facilitation of exchange requires first of all the standardization of the essential elements that acts of exchange involve.

These elements are a medium of exchange and a commodity possessed of determinable quantity and quality. By providing a stable and uniform currency, the state immeasurably simplifies the act of exchange at the same time that it protects the individual from fraud. By providing standard weights and measures and requiring that all claims regarding size conform to these standards, the same end is accomplished.

The same logic would appear to extend to the quality of a commodity as well as to its quantity. But here the classical liberal state has proven remiss. Legislation requiring that commodities carry a correct description of their parts, contents, and ingredients is relatively recent and hard-won. Although legal remedies have been available against some of the more flagrant forms of misrepresentation, there has been little administrative enforcement until quite recently.

In this country, a federal Pure Food and Drug Act was not passed until 1906. The still weak Food, Drug, and Cosmetic Act of 1938, designed to overcome the glaring weaknesses of the old act, would very probably have failed of passage had it not been for the fortuitous death in 1936 of some one hundred persons from the new proprietary drug, Elixir Sulfanilamide. More recently "grade-labeling" has been fought as though it were an attack on capitalism itself.

The National Bureau of Standards, established in 1901, has supplied invaluable information to large-scale purchasers, but its information is virtually unavailable to the average consumer. While government orders to "cease and desist" are directed in a steady stream against the more extravagant claims concerning quality of performance and content, advertising presents a hard shale of mendacity, distortion, and exaggeration which has so far defied erosion. Some standardization of quality has indeed been achieved, but this has not been the work of those following the classical liberal school.

Facilitating exchange is only in one part a matter of setting and enforcing standards. It consists in its other part of providing the physical means through which to transact the business of exchange: roads, canals, harbors, railways, the telegraph and telephone, the mail, and so on. Much of this was and still is left to private enterprise. In strictest logic there is no more reason for the maintenance of roads by government than for the maintenance of automobile factories. There is, moreover, no logic in assigning highways to the province of public and railways to the province of private enterprise. Practice in these matters varies, of course, from country to country.

The reasons given for public ownership or regulation of the mail, railways, highways, and the like differ. In some cases the inherently monopolistic character of the enterprise is cited, in others the needs of defense. But governments, however averse to public ownership and regulation in principle, have usually recognized that the dependence of the economic life of the community on transportation and communication facilities is too great to be left to the uncertainties of private enterprise.

Members of the community are now protected in their person and property against violence and fraud, free to contract in the secure knowledge that bona fide contracts will be performed, and provided with easy and reliable access to a market in which transactions are simplified because all parties can rely upon official standards. Two major functions remain.

Protection of Freedom of Competition

According to the classical economists, competition is central and crucial in the process whereby a multitude of unrestrained egoists create something called the general welfare. If this is so, competition must be preserved at all cost—even the cost of government intervention. Since men often prefer the calms of combination to the tempests of competition, action by government is necessary to prevent combinations which are destructive of competition or "in restraint of trade."

This is not the place to examine the long history of government attempts in our country and elsewhere to curb monopoly. For a long time, followers of the classical liberal tradition have been involved in a conflict between an impulse to trustification and a conviction that trusts are wrong. By whatever procedure that conflict has been in fact resolved—

possibly by giving way to the impulse and then, as Thurman Arnold points out, inventing elaborate ceremonials (such as antitrust laws) to conceal the surrender—the point is that government in the classical liberal state has always been charged with the duty of destroying or regulating monopolies. In the case of so-called "natural" monopolies, like telephone communication or railway transportation, where competition is clearly wasteful and destructive, the government either owns or operates the enterprise or is given a measure of control over rates, service, and financing, from which competitive enterprise is strictly exempt. The prevention and control of monopoly is, then, the fourth function of the classical liberal state.

The Meliorative Function

The vaguest and least well-defined of the functions has been left to the last in this enumeration. It may be called the meliorative function. This designation is employed as a kind of catchall for a multitude of activities, some of them logically compatible with the premises of classical liberals, others decreed by the practical needs of a civilized society.

To begin with, the rejection of paternalism does not exclude aid for those who, by reason of youth or congenital disability, are unable to care for themselves. The negative state acknowledges a positive obligation in the case of young children. The age at which child dependency ends, the extent to which the state may interfere in abuses of the relationship between parent and child, and the kind of aid to be made available to dependent children have been matters of considerable dispute. But ultimate responsibility of some kind or other is reposed in the state, and interventions in family affairs are usually justified on this basis. So, too, is public education.

Some responsibility is also accepted for the victims of acquired disabilities—the insane, the sick, the blind—although aid has not been distinguished for its munificence. Purists have argued that it is the individual's own responsibility to prepare for illness and old age. The extent to which they have made concessions to humanitarian and other considerations has already been discussed in another context. These concessions have been least to the so-called able-bodied poor, but even here the force of circumstance has thrust obligations upon the hesitant negative state. In noting this gesture in behalf of the helpless and needy, one must not forget that it is strictly meliorative—serving merely to diminish the more revolting aspects of suffering. More generous action is considered to be the province of private charity, and the state's scant provision is justified by alleging the basic irresponsibility of the needy or by invoking the doctrine of "social Darwinism."

The meliorative function of the negative state has in our time appeared in quite a different role. The waste of irreplaceable natural resources, of forests and top soil, for example, has required state intervention. Nature has its own way of prompting the dangerously laggard and negligent, and disastrous floods have been a persistent reminder of lack of prudence. Although the principles of classical liberalism generally permit intervention by government to protect natural resources, the conservation movement did not become a powerful political force in this country until the turn of the century. The energies of a business society were absorbed in exploiting rather than conserving and, in America, nature has been so generous that it seemed waste could go on with impunity. When the need was finally recognized, action was only meliorative, receiving its greatest impetus from the need during the depression of the 'thirties to provide employment through noncompetitive public works.

For lack of a better place, one may also list under the meliorative function a host of activities, ranging from major to minor, which are difficult to classify: those "certain public works and certain public institutions which it can never be for the interest of any individual, or small group of individuals, to erect and maintain; because the profit could never repay the expense to any individual . . . though it may frequently do much more than repay it to a great society . . ." One thinks at once of institutions of higher learning, museums, public monuments, public parks. Whatever other motives may have inspired them, they too serve a meliorative function in a society which regards it as the responsibility of the individual to secure the basic amenities of civilized life.

In the preceding discussion the term melioration has been deliberately used instead of "general welfare" to designate the function described. Our constitution does, indeed, assign the "general welfare" as a responsibility of government, but it was not until recently, with the advent of a new philosophy of liberalism, that the clause came to have a comprehensive and really significant meaning. It is one thing to soften the rigors of adversity; it is quite another to plan systematically so that all people may live fuller lives. The difference is the difference between a handout or a dole and acceptance of responsibility for the basic security of everyone. The former is meliorative; the latter is "general welfare" in an authentic sense.

Chapter 5

The Political Creed: Checks and Restraints

IT IS ONE thing to enumerate the functions of the state and to define the limits of state action; it is quite another to prevent the state from exceeding these limits. How is the state to be restrained from encroaching upon the areas from which the foregoing enumeration of functions denies it entry? To discuss what the state should or should not do is, after all, idle unless there are effective devices for restraining the state's power. How does the classical liberal implement the limitation of power? The individuals entrusted with the powers of government will, in James Mill's words, "infallibly have the strongest motives to make a bad use of them," but "it is possible that checks may be found sufficient to prevent them." "It is," he says, "sufficiently conformable to the established and fashionable opinions to say that upon the right constitution of checks all goodness of government depends."[1]

Constitutionalism

The first and most basic check upon the power of the state is to be found in the conscious and explicit employment of the *principle* of constitutional government. In the parlance of the liberal, constitutionalism is the idea that sovereignty must be limited, no matter where sovereignty resides, whether in a monarch, a class, or a people.[2] As so defined, constitutionalism antedates liberalism, for the idea of limiting power is no new one. Indeed, in an important and often neglected sense power always has been limited, for power must be wielded by men, and men always move in a climate of opinion and live by customs and traditions which effectively shape their ideas and restrain their will even if they are as little conscious

103

of the restraint as of the air they breathe. Nevertheless, constitutionalism takes on a new and special significance with the advent of liberalism, in association with which it becomes universalized, popularized, and formalized, and through which it achieves a central importance in theory and in practice.

One may leave to students of law and political science a discussion of the varieties of constitutions and of the desiderata of a good constitution. The problem here is to define more carefully the distinguishing feature of constitutionalism per se, as understood by the liberals, and to develop briefly its implications. That feature, to repeat, is the idea that legal limitations must be imposed upon the exercise of power, that is to say upon the sovereign power and the agencies through which this power is wielded. Since limitations on the sovereign power always include unwritten usage and tradition, most notably in the case of the British constitution, one cannot accurately distinguish constitutional limitations as those that are expressed in codes, written upon parchments, or embodied in formal and solemn resolutions. Indeed, many such resolutions are inoperative and meaningless. A limitation upon power is constitutional and in so far distinguished from other limitations, because it expresses the clear *sense of the community*—or of the dominant control group in the community—that power *ought* to be limited in that particular way. When this sense is strong enough, it acquires the force of law.

Law is inherently restrictive and limiting, decreeing what may or may not be done. Accordingly, government by law means a government with limited rather than plenary powers, a government which is not based upon the arbitrary will, the whim or caprice, or the "intuition" of the person or group of persons in charge. The Duke of Wellington saw the point when, after defining military law as the "will of the general who commands the army," he added, "in fact . . . no law at all."

The law may, indeed, be generous to those in power and permit them a wide range of authority. It may permit the exercise of almost despotic powers, concerning itself primarily with holding the ruler to the requirement of constancy or regularity. All this is compatible with constitutionalism. On the other hand, the law may employ devices for strictly limiting the power of government—a bill of rights, a system of checks and balances, federalism—all the contrivances, so dear to liberals, for guarding against the possibility that governments might govern. But all this is by the way. Constitutionalism means simply that those who govern are subject to some law or other within the confines of which they must operate.

To say this is to say that those who govern are *subject*. Constitutionalism suggests, therefore, not only the idea of a limit upon the power of government but a power beyond government. For if those who govern are subject only to laws of their own making, they are limited not at all. But the law must issue from some source. If those who govern cannot in the nature of the case make the law which limits their authority, whence then does the law come?

The law may have divine origin, but historically this claim has been made by sovereigns intent on concealing the fact that they were making their own laws. In that it has been used only as a cloak to disguise the very opposite of constitutional government. If, by definition, constitutional law cannot be created by those who govern and if the theory of divine origin (if not of divine inspiration) is rejected, constitutional law must have its origin in those, or in a part of those, who are governed. Thus, constitutional government implies in the first place a limitation on the power of government and, in the second place, the sovereignty of those or some of those who are governed. Historically speaking, the rise of constitutional government coincides with the spread of the idea of popular sovereignty. "The Constitution of the United States," according to John Quincy Adams, "was a return to the principles of the Declaration of Independence and the exclusive constituent power of the people." Just who, in the judgment of the classical liberals, the people are and how they exercise their constituent powers are often far from clear, and an examination of the famous constitutional assemblies of history renders it less so. However, the idea of popular sovereignty eventually emerges—more or less closely associated with the idea of constitutional government.

But constitutionalism implies the limitation of *all* exercises of power, and although it implies the right of the governed to restrain those who govern, by definition, this right cannot be unlimited. Constitutionalism must also imply limitations upon the sovereignty of the governed, or where all the governed are included, upon popular sovereignty. This is usually managed by setting up a distinction between the action of a constitutional assembly in mapping the boundaries of power and any subsequent action to redraw these boundaries; or, to use other terms, by distinguishing between the original decisions according to which a constitution is drawn up and any subsequent decisions to alter it. A special and quite distinctive character is accorded the former, and original constitutional law comes to be invested with clear priority over subsequent legislation, save under carefully defined circumstances.

The distinction is made possible in the first place by the more or less inclusive and systematic nature of the decisions usually arrived at by a constituent assembly. This factor may be referred to as structural. Inclusiveness often carries the suggestion of conclusiveness. It is argued that the work of an assembly, convened for the specific purpose of planning the structure of the state, deliberating with a view to the outlines as a whole, and sensible of its special mission, should not be lightly disregarded for some later piecemeal proposal blown in upon a gust of popular passion.

The distinction is based, in the second place, on the emergence of a tradition which, in the case of successful constitutions, grows stronger year by year. This tradition attaches unique importance to the original decisions which gave birth to the constitution, no matter what the circumstances surrounding them, an importance so great that all sorts of obstacles in the way of repeating a similar process on later occasions are acceptable. Those who arrived at the original decision are invested with a halo. They are said to have been divinely inspired. Their anniversaries are occasions for impassioned encomia. Subsequent generations are taught that they could never hope to equal them in wisdom and purity of motive. The day the decisions were reached becomes a holiday, the spot at which the decisions were made, a shrine, and the parchment upon which they were inscribed, holy writ. All this is bound up with national pride and prestige. Obviously, this and more has happened in connection with the Founding Fathers and their work at the Philadelphia Convention, even if an impudent historian like Charles Beard has sometimes been accused of impugning the purity of their motives. We rarely recall that its authors viewed the Constitution as an imperfect instrument.

This second factor may be referred to as traditional. Here, the basis for the distinction between the original constituent judgments and later judgments intended to modify the original is supplied by a grateful posterity happy with the first allotment. But the authors of the original judgment are at least as zealous as a contented posterity that their work be kept relatively intact. Consequently they themselves make provision, on the occasion of arriving at their original judgment, for placing obstacles in the way of alterations. This third factor may be called procedural.

In our country, and this is true of most, with the notable exception of England, procedural differences between the enactment of constituent and statutory law are established, making it much more difficult to secure enactment of the former. Thus, an amendment to the Constitution of the United States (i.e., a constituent law) must be proposed by two-thirds of both houses or by a convention called by two-thirds of the state legislatures, and it must be ratified by the legislatures of three-fourths of the states or three-fourths of the state conventions assembled for this purpose.[3] The presence of these procedural obstacles may be indicated in another way by saying that Congress is subordinate to the Constitution. Whereas an act of the English Parliament is forthwith a part of the English constitution, an act of our lawmaking body is not part of our Constitution. On the contrary, all acts of Congress must conform to the provisions of a constitution, in the making of which Congress played no part. These acts are subject to judicial review, and if they fail to meet the test of constitutionality, they are rejected by the Supreme Court. Thus statutory law is made subordinate to constituent law.[4] It is in this manner that a constitution becomes a kind of monarch, ruling by accident of birth—a regency of the past over the present and future, or of the dead over the living and the not yet born. Our legal structure is, perhaps, the most extreme example of this regency.

England has no equivalent to our system of judicial review. Parliament is supreme, combining in itself both the constituent and lawmaking powers. Legally there is no procedural difference between the enactment of an ordinary statute by Parliament and the enactment of a fundamental law, like the Reform Act of 1832 or the Act of Union or the Statute of Westminster. Neither is the English constitution—composed, as it is, of assorted charters, petitions, and statutes, of established precedents, of the common law, and so on—the work of a constitutional assembly. In this respect it differs from most of the constitutions of the world.[5] No "Founding Fathers" assembled in London or anywhere else to plan a comprehensive constitutional framework for the English government. Consequently, it might seem to lack the prestige attaching to a document which, like our own, was the handiwork of many able men solemnly assembled to plan their basic law. But the appearance is misleading. Any proposal to narrow the suffrage or to give the Lords coordinate legislative power with the Commons would probably be condemned by the English as unconstitutional, with as much vigor as Americans would display in denouncing a proposal to abolish the Supreme Court.

Thus, the British constitution is nothing to be tampered with either. It commands the respect and obedience of posterity because tradition, as with our Constitution, has invested it with special significance. Moreover, the procedural factor comes into play even with the British constitution. Although it is true that there is no formal difference between ordinary and constituent law, as a matter of practice, Parliament before acting on any highly controversial issue of great concern to the country seeks a mandate from the people. This is accomplished by the simple device of dissolving Parliament and ordering new elections, a decision which is not likely to be made lightly. Great constitutional changes, like the Reform

Acts of 1832 and 1867 and the Parliament Act of 1911, were not enacted until the electorate had expressed itself in this indirect way at least once.

In the end, however, the British constitution, like the American Constitution and like all constitutions which have withstood the test of time, survives most efforts to change it drastically, because *it commands the respect of the living community and inspires among most of the members of the community a sense of its general rightness and fairness.* This is the rock upon which every enduring constitution ultimately rests. Without it, structure, tradition, procedure are so much sand.

It is now clear that the constitutionalist effects a division of power not only between ruler and ruled but between the past and the present. The several factors—structural, traditional, procedural—enable the constitutionalist to achieve the latter division. Through them the past acquires a hold upon the present. But, in the final analysis, a constitution must survive the test of contemporary scrutiny; it must embody the prevailing will on matters that are deemed fundamental. If the hand of the past is indeed a dead hand and if it weighs too heavily, the present will assert itself.

Such an assertion may take the form of a recourse to amendments. Almost all modern constitutions make some provision for amendment. Where the process of amendment is too cumbersome, impatient critics will insist upon a broader interpretation of the original law, as in the case of the pressure placed upon the Supreme Court during the first term of the Roosevelt administration. If this too proves unavailable, the result may be revolution, which, in at least one of its manifestations, is the appropriation by a living majority or ascendant minority of a constituent power otherwise denied it.

At this point an inherent ambivalence in the liberal position discloses itself. For on the one hand, an analysis of constitutionalism, as understood by the liberal, indicates that it not only implies a limitation upon the power of rulers, but also a restraint upon the direct action of the ruled, and revolution is, of course, the most extreme form of direct action. On the other hand, tyrants sometimes defy constitutions and all other efforts to restrain them, as the early liberals well knew. In such an event liberals must hold that revolution, the ultimate effort to curb tyranny, is justified. This is inherent in the constitutional concept itself. If a constitutional limitation of power has been correctly defined as one which expresses the clear sense of the community that power *ought* to be limited in a given way, this implies a release from all obligation to acquiesce in any exercise of power which is not so limited. Why should not the same provocation which justified an exercise of the constituent power in the past justify its exercise in the present? Constitutionalism thus both denies and implies the right of revolution.

The nature of this ambivalence as it affects the liberal's theory of revolution will be examined at a later stage of this inquiry. The less drastic devices which liberals have written into their constitutions for limiting the power of government must be first enumerated. This necessitates shifting from a discussion of the general to a discussion of the particular.

Jusnaturalism

The principle of constitutionalism does not, as such, imply the specific limitation of power in which liberals were primarily interested, a limitation which secures the individual *as* individual from the encroachment of the state. A constitution might scrupulously protect classes of individuals and leave the individual, as such, completely limited by the nature of his class relationship. A constitution might curb the tyranny of the state only to substitute the restraint of status.

Accordingly, liberals wrote into their constitutions guaranties specifically designed to protect the rights and liberties of individuals. For example, our own Constitution establishes the writ of habeas corpus, it forbids ex post facto laws and bills of attainder, it guarantees trial by jury, and so on. Such guaranties were enough for men like Alexander Hamilton,[6] but the majority of his contemporaries insisted upon a separate and detailed enumeration of rights. All liberal countries

were able to boast a "bill of rights"—in England the Bill
of Rights of 1689, in our country the first ten amendments
to the Constitution as well as the bills of rights included in
most of the state constitutions, in France the famous Declaration of the Rights of Man and of the Citizen.

All of these great documents bear a close relationship to
each other. Our own Bill of Rights shows the influence of
the English Bill of Rights as well as of the state constitutional
guaranties after which it was patterned. The French were
influenced by us in formulating the Declaration of 1789. With
the exception of our Declaration of Independence, which
refers to "life, liberty, and the pursuit of happiness" but
omits reference to the ownership of property, these documents
show a common emphasis on the property right. Besides this,
they enumerate the right of free speech, of free press, of free
assembly, and of free worship. Our Bill of Rights, like the
English one, forbids excessive bails and fines as well as cruel
and unusual punishments, it provides for jury trial, and so
on. Most of this will also be found in the French Declaration.[7]

Now all this would appear to leave the protection of individual rights on the constitutional level, a special application
of the constitutional limitation of power. But to leave it so
would be to neglect the characteristic treatment which the
doctrine of individual rights received from the champions of
liberalism—at any rate from a majority of them. For the
authors of the liberal manifestoes of the seventeenth and
eighteenth centuries were not content with flimsy legalistic
guaranties. They sought stronger confirmation—and they
found it in the doctrine of natural rights, sometimes called
"guarantism," sometimes "jusnaturalism."[8] No doctrine is
more typical of the period.

In effect, the doctrine of natural rights shifts the whole
question of limiting power from the level of constitutional
law to the level of metaphysics or, better, since the implications of the shift are political, to the level of what may be
called metapolitics. The age of Newton and Descartes had
already substituted nature for God. Consequently, it was
easy for liberals to pit the natural rights of man against the

divine right of kings; they were not merely engaging in a political maneuver against royal absolutists; they were effecting the logical completion of a system—the system of nature.

Natural rights are to be distinguished in the first place from customary rights. Natural rights are not conferred; men are born with them. Natural rights are possessed indifferently by all men, simply by virtue of their being men. Accordingly, natural rights are unaffected by birth and station, time and circumstance. Individual rights are not the product of a historic process; they issue from the universal nature of man. Our Declaration refers not to British subjects, nor to "citizens," but to "all men," and the French National Assembly declared "the following rights *of the man* and the citizen." Moreover, to discover natural rights requires no precarious empirical search; like the immutable laws of nature they are self-evident. "We hold these truths to be *self-evident*," Jefferson wrote in the Declaration of Independence, and some might find poetic justice in the fact that in thus defending our separation from England, he was using the thought and language of Locke, who may be called the father of English jusnaturalism.

There are natural rights, then; and they are absolute, indefeasible, inalienable. "The end of every political association is the conservation of the *natural and imprescriptible* rights of man."[9] An individual may not surrender them any more than a state may encroach upon them. This is the essence of the jusnaturalism through which men sought to limit the claims of the state.

But the doctrine of natural rights fell substantially short of producing unanimity among the classical liberals. The English fogs dampened the ardor with which the doctrine of natural rights had been asserted on the French side of the channel. If the reasons for this are historical rather than meteorological, they are to be found in the limited character of the English revolution as contrasted with the French Revolution. R. H. Tawney defines the contrast with his usual brilliance:

In England the idea of right had been negative and defensive, a barrier to the encroachment of Governments. The French leapt to the attack from trenches which the English had been content to defend, and in France the idea became affirmative and militant, not a weapon of defense, but a principle of social organization.

He continues,

English practical men, whose thoughts were pitched in a lower key, were a little shocked by the pomp and brilliance of that tremendous creed [of the French revolutionists]. They had scanty sympathy with the absolute affirmations of France. What captured their imaginations was not the right to liberty, which made no appeal to their commercial instincts, but the expediency of liberty, which did; and when the Revolution had revealed the explosive power of the idea of natural right, they sought some less menacing formula.[10]

To be sure it was the very English Locke who gave the doctrine of natural rights the formulation which was to influence the Americans and the French so greatly. The natural rights to which Locke had reference were "life, liberty, and estate," but it was the estate or property right upon which he lavished his attention and, indeed, he sometimes used the property right as synonymous with all three.[11]

But, while proclaiming the sanctity of the property right, the doctrine of natural rights contains an implied threat to precisely the distribution of property which the middle classes of the eighteenth and nineteenth centuries were interested in defending. For, if property is a universal and natural right, then, clearly, all men should have property, and any dispensation in which they do not abridges this right. As Guido de Ruggiero points out,

. . . from the conception of property as natural right follow certain unexpected consequences, which undermine the foundations of that conception. If property is essential to the development of man's natural liberty, it ought not to be enjoyed exclusively by a few, as an odious privilege; all ought to be owners of property. Thus the same theory of natural rights which consecrated individual property, and for its sake demolished the castle of feudalism, issued in the opposite conception, namely, communism.[12]

Locke himself had derived "unexpected consequences" when he wrote in the *Second Treatise* that "the same law of nature that does by this means give us property, does also bound that property too." It binds it by as much "as anyone can make use of to any advantage of life before it spoils . . ." He added, "whatever is beyond this, is more than his share, and belongs to others."[13]

Thus, too, Thomas Jefferson might write to Madison: "Whenever there is, in any country, uncultivated land and unemployed poor, it is clear that the laws of property have been so far extended that they violate natural right." Clearly, the extension in recent times of this logic to idle factories would have devastating consequences. No wonder many Englishmen sought a less menacing formula.

Most influential spokesmen for the opposition were Burke, Hume, and Bentham—a truly formidable trio. Brilliant apologist for the conservatism of his day, darling of complacent Whigs, class-conscious defender of the "faith," which is to say, the traditions and institutions of England, Edmund Burke (1729–97) must be regarded in longer historical perspective as one of the great advocates of liberalism. Few defenses of quietism in government have been more explicit than his; he exalted the constitutional principle as reflected in English practice; in a limited sense he was an ardent exponent of individual rights, even the rights of the American colonists.

But Burke feared the French Revolution as men in recent times have feared the revolution of the Bolsheviks. He loathed its egalitarianism and absolutism. In particular, he recoiled from the assertion of the right of revolution. The Declaration of the Rights of Man he called "a sort of institute and digest of anarchy." The rights upon which the jusnaturalists had conferred the absolute and timeless authority of nature became in Burke's treatment derivative and conditional; they issue from law and custom, and they are dependent on the acceptance of duties and the recognition of obligations.

Meanwhile, in the realm of speculative philosophy Hume had already demolished the foundations upon which the whole superstructure of natural rights had rested. In his famous *Treatise of Human Nature*, the penetrating Scotsman had undermined the self-evidence of natural law in general. When he was finished, nature was no longer an abode in which men might find the certainty which eluded them elsewhere. The doctrine of natural rights fell casualty to the same corrosive analysis. With Hume, expediency and convention replaced self-evidence and reason as the bulwark of individual rights, and, if his influence was for the time being limited, this was because most of his contemporaries recoiled from the iconoclastic consequences of a positivism which swept away the foundations of religion and metaphysics as well as the fictions and abstractions of politics.

With Hume's work before him it was easy for Bentham, a less acute thinker with greater immediate influence, to reject jusnaturalism. The doctrine of natural rights not only affronted Bentham's practical instincts, it ran counter to the principle of utilitarianism which is associated primarily with his name. "Natural rights is simple nonsense . . . rhetorical nonsense,—nonsense upon stilts," he wrote. The French Revolution left Bentham cold, and he referred to our own Declaration of Independence as so much "jargon." To the Frenchman, Brissot, he wrote, "I am sorry that you have undertaken to publish a Declaration of Rights. It is a metaphysical work—the *ne plus ultra* of metaphysics. It may have been a necessary evil—but is nevertheless an evil. Political science is not far enough advanced for such a declaration. Let the articles be what they may, I will engage they must come under three heads [said the inveterate classifier]—(1) Unintelligible; (2) False; (3) A mixture of both . . . You can never make a law against which it may not be averred, that by it you have abrogated the Declaration of Rights; and the argument will be unanswerable."[14]

Bentham and his followers most assuredly believed in individual rights. But they treated rights as qualified and derivative. Rights exist only in and through law, and they can be voided by law; not in a law anchored, as by Burke, to tradition, but in a law which has socially useful consequences. Thus, the supreme test to which all rights should be submitted is the test of utility. If the exercise of a right results in anti-social consequences, if it subtracts from the total happiness, the right should be waived. Locke had grounded rights in nature and Burke in history; it remained for Bentham to ground them in social expediency.

Thus, on the issue of jusnaturalism liberalism became a

house divided against itself. Sometimes the differences amounted to no more than a lovers' quarrel, sometimes they threatened to produce a serious schism. The fortunes of controversy went something like this: a revolutionary crisis would place the doctrine of natural rights in the ascendant. However, victorious revolutionaries would shortly discover that in the doctrine of natural rights they had forged a weapon which could be used to threaten the tangible rewards of victory. Appropriate revision would ensue. Here, as elsewhere, are evidences of a deep inner conflict in the liberal ideology, which is never successfully reconciled: it is forever torn between degenerating into middle-class apologetics and developing into a creed of emancipation for all mankind.[15]

The Division of Power

"Any society in which rights are not securely guaranteed, and *the separation of powers* is not determined, has no constitution." This is one of the most seminal articles of the French Declaration. Metapolitics is to have the aid of political mechanics in curbing the power of the state, for in the separation of powers the liberals were concerning themselves with the actual arrangement and relation of the working parts of the machinery of government. But the separation of powers, as conventionally understood, is a special application of the broader division of power which may take a variety of forms: politico-economic, politico-social, politico-ecclesiastical, and political.

The first of these, and the most fundamental by far, is associated with the favorite political (as distinguished from psychological and economic) argument against socialism. Private ownership of the means of production provides an economic power to balance the state's political power, it is contended. The socialization of production, by concentrating economic as well as political power in the state, abandons this division of power, thereby rendering the state omnipotent. If, in other words, the two chief sources of power in modern society are economic and political, these had better be kept in separate hands or the state will have an exclusive monopoly.

Much more venerable is the argument that a desirable division of powers is achieved by creating co-ordinate branches of government, corresponding to the class composition of the social group: monarchic, aristocratic, democratic. Under such an arrangement the representatives of one class cannot act without the concurrence of the representatives of the others. This is what is meant by a "mixed" government or constitution. It would be realized, for example, if the House of Commons could not act without the concurrence of the House of Lords and the King and vice versa. Such a division of powers has been hailed as the glory of the Roman constitution. In his famous *Commentaries,* "the judicious" Blackstone, misled perhaps by Montesquieu, celebrated its embodiment in the English constitution. A similar division of powers was in the minds of some of the Founding Fathers and, at the outset—when United States Senators were elected by the members of the state legislatures and the President was elected in a manner which removed him farther from the people—mixed government was by no means a remote possibility, even in this country.

A third division of power may be achieved by distributing power between the church and the state, God and Caesar. The political theory of the Middle Ages defended such a division, although in practice it proved itself unstable.

When attention is transferred to the narrower sphere of government per se the distinctive separation of powers is achieved by differentiating the functions of government and distributing power in greater or less measure among the agencies or branches responsible for the discharge of these functions. The most celebrated formulation of this doctrine is to be found in Montesquieu's *Spirit of the Laws.* Montesquieu classified all political functions as legislative, executive, and judicial. By creating separate branches of government for the discharge of these functions, Montesquieu believed that the naturally despotic propensities of the state could be curbed. He received the idea from Locke, who had suggested a similar view without developing it fully.

Montesquieu found his model in the English government, although, as a matter of fact, the English system did not in his time, and does not now, embody a separation of powers. The Glorious Revolution settled once for all the supremacy of Parliament. Moreover, Montesquieu's ideas had their greatest influence, not in England, but in revolutionary France[16] and on this side of the Atlantic. It was in America that the doctrine of a separation of powers and the related system of checks and balances was first embodied in many of the revolutionary state constitutions. It was then given classic formulation in our Constitution and in that brilliant apology for the Constitution, *The Federalist,* by Hamilton, Madison, and Jay. "The accumulation of all powers," wrote Madison in *The Federalist,* "legislative, executive, and judiciary, in the same hands, whether of one, a few, or many, and whether hereditary, self-appointed or elective, may justly be pronounced the very definition of tyranny."[17] On this score even Jefferson was in agreement with the Federalists.

Liberals were by no means unanimous, however, in accepting the principle of a division of powers along the lines laid down by Montesquieu. Bentham, although he later changed his mind, condemned the idea vigorously as an undesirable limitation upon the legislative power and, ultimately, upon the people. Although the formal status of the doctrine is still taken for granted in the United States, two wars and a great depression, as well as the increasing complexity of modern society, have concentrated more and more power in the hands of the executive, thereby compelling a general re-examination of the trifurcation of power as it has been traditionally understood. The best evidence of this is the debate now raging over "bureaucracy," a debate in which, unfortunately, the issues are so obscured by ulterior political motives that a truer understanding of the nature of "government by commission" is rendered discouragingly difficult.

The division of power among co-ordinate branches of the government achieves its purpose by pitting the state against itself. The same result can be achieved by the simple device of duplicating as well as differentiating the functions of government. This is accomplished in the bicameral legislature in which two equal and co-ordinate chambers perform approximately the same duties, the one duplicating the work of the other.

"Of all the forms of government that are possible among mankind," wrote the historian William E. H. Lecky, "I do not know any which is likely to be worse than the government of a single, omnipotent democratic Chamber."[18] And Madison, defending an upper chamber, wrote in *The Federalist* the now familiar argument that "It doubles the security to the people, by requiring the concurrence of two distinct bodies in schemes of usurpation or perfidy, where the ambition or corruption of one would otherwise be sufficient."[19] Obviously, the same result could be achieved by creating a plural executive (e.g., the dual kingship of Sparta) or several courts with identical jurisdiction (so that an act of Congress could be tested in two or more supreme courts) as well as by multiplying the number of legislatures.

Still another device for achieving a division of powers is federalism, of which the United States is again the chief exemplar. By the Tenth Amendment to the Constitution "all powers not delegated to the United States by the Constitution, nor prohibited by it to the states, are reserved to the states respectively or to the people." The fifty states, it is clear, are not mere administrative subdivisions. Although federalism, like bicameralism, is without doubt a result of the special circumstances attendant on the founding of the republic, the fact remains that states' rights have been used deliberately as a device for curbing the power of government. The relationship between liberalism and federalism is, however, an inherently contradictory one, for the rise of liberalism is associated with the centralizing tendencies involved in nationalism; on the other hand, fear of a strongly centralized government has often inspired, as in our country, a professed affection for localism in the form of states' rights. Here as elsewhere the logic of events rather than the arrangements of men has determined the actual distribution of power.

Suffrage

The several political devices for restraining the state by dividing and distributing its power have this in common: they are directed against the despotism of the mob as well as the despotism of the state. The tripartite division of the government into co-ordinate branches, the bicameral partition of the legislative branch, and the doctrine of states' rights, all serve to delay and obstruct expression of the popular will, a consequence which often weighed more with the sponsors of these devices than any limitation on the power of the state. But the power of government may also be limited by making it more sensitive to the group will. If an exercise of power can meet with rebuke from those who are affected by it, this power is bound to be exercised sparingly and discreetly.

Suffrage is the first and most obvious device for securing this result. Suffrage, may, of course, be limited or popular, and a brief canvass of liberal opinion and action on this subject affords an invaluable insight into the liberal point of view. Between the Whig aristocrats satisfied with the revolutionary settlement of 1688 and the utilitarians and radicals of the nineteenth century, between the fear of the mob which haunted the Founding Fathers and the democratism of Jackson, between Voltaire's contempt for the common man and Rousseau's respect for the people, a considerable gap intervenes. Although, historically speaking, the attitude of liberals toward extension of the franchise constitutes a continuous development, on no subject is there less unanimity among them.

All liberals agreed that suffrage is a necessary check on the tyranny of government. But some of them wanted class suffrage and others wanted mass suffrage. Some feared the tyranny of the mob much more than they feared the tyranny of the state; others feared the tyranny of a class, particularly a business class *sans noblesse oblige*, at least as much as they feared the mob. Many liberals favored an economic qualification for suffrage; others, in increasing number as time went on, recognized that this encouraged class conflict and that the working class, like the middle class when it was disfranchised, would try to win by violence what it was excluded from seeking by vote. It is worth while indicating in some detail how these mixed motives are reflected in typical utterances and in the course of events, not merely to explain the role of suffrage as a means of limiting the power of government, but for a fuller understanding of historical liberalism.

In America some of the colonial constitutions accepted universal male suffrage. Together, the Fifteenth and Nineteenth Amendments to the federal Constitution forbid states from denying citizens the right to vote on account of race, color, sex, or previous condition of servitude; otherwise the Constitution leaves the regulation of suffrage to the discretion of the states. For a long time the states limited voting to male property owners almost exclusively, and it was not until 1860 that most states provided for universal white male suffrage.

According to John Adams, leader of the Federalist party, "the majority has eternally and without one exception usurped over the rights of the minority," and Benjamin Franklin believed, "as to those who have not landed property [that] the allowing them to vote is an impropriety." These views express the consensus that prevailed among the Founding Fathers. On the other hand, Tom Paine's great paean to democracy in the *Rights of Man* presaged the day when the Whig liberalism of the Founding Fathers would give way under the influence of men like Jefferson and Jackson to a liberalism accepting the idea of popular government.

In England the beliefs of men like Thomas B. Macaulay, the great Whig spokesman, contrasted sharply with views of the kind expressed by Cartwright. According to Macaulay, universal suffrage is "incompatible, not with this or that form of government, but with all forms of government," as well as with property and civilization. On the other hand, much earlier, in 1776, Major John Cartwright, English parliamentary reformer, had already published his remarkable pamphlet, entitled *Take Your Choice! Representation and Respect: Imposition and Contempt* . . . , in which he declared that "*personality* is the sole foundation of the *right* of being represented: and that property has, in reality, nothing to do with the case." This was the view which eventually prevailed with that wing of liberal opinion known as the philosophical radicals whose leaders were Bentham and the two Mills.

However, the fight over the great Reform Act of 1832 was

waged over extending the franchise to the middle class; the possibility of extending it to the working class was not even seriously considered. That is why Macaulay, who detested universal suffrage, could plead for the Reform Bill of 1832, urging in its behalf that "at present we oppose the schemes of revolutionists with only one half, with only one quarter of our proper force . . . we exclude from all share in the government great masses of property and intelligence, great numbers of those who are most interested in preserving tranquility, and who know best how to preserve it."[20]

Even the Reform Bill of 1867, in which the Conservative party "shot Niagara,"[21] did not completely abolish property qualifications; only the more highly paid urban workers (as well as tenant farmers) were admitted to suffrage, although by this time the trend was unmistakable.

The French Revolution proclaimed the ideal of popular sovereignty and universal manhood suffrage, but democracy in France underwent many vicissitudes in the years which followed. The Revolution of 1830, in which workingmen seeking a democratic republic triumphed over the last Bourbon to hold a French throne, ended under the control of the *bourgeoisie* who placed Louis Philippe, the Orleanist "citizen king," on the throne. His advent marked the ascendancy of the middle class which established parliamentary government, but refused to lower the property qualifications for voting to the point where workingmen would have a voice. France's electorate at this time numbered some two hundred thousand in a population of about thirty millions. The ideal of universal manhood suffrage proclaimed by the Revolution of 1789, though briefly revived, was not effectively realized until 1875.

In France, as in England and America, liberals were divided on the issue of suffrage. Some, like Alexis de Tocqueville, feared that bourgeois liberalism might become a class despotism without class responsibility. De Tocqueville, accordingly, favored universal suffrage, which he regarded as "inevitable" and "providential." But until the birth of the Third Republic, the judgment of men like Guizot and Thiers prevailed, and they feared popular rule.

Enough has been said to indicate that, until quite recently, the great weight of liberal opinion was on the side of class suffrage rather than popular suffrage, and it is in this light primarily that liberal recourse to suffrage as a device for curbing the state must be viewed. In the end it was not so much the decisions of the more democratic liberals, like Jefferson, de Tocqueville, or Mill, which universalized the franchise, but the logic of history: as Western society became urbanized and industrialized, the heretofore inarticulate masses acquired the power to demand the voice in government which apprehensive property owners had denied them.

However, popular suffrage does not of itself mean that the state will be subject to democratic control, nor does limited suffrage mean that the state will be subject to the group enjoying suffrage. One need merely be reminded of Hitler's and Stalin's plebiscites and the plebiscites of Napoleon III. Most liberals would agree that at least six basic conditions must first be satisfied. If suffrage is to be more than a ruse designed to create the illusion of control over government (a) there must be free appeal to the electorate through the written and spoken word, (b) there must be elections at regular and reasonably frequent intervals, (c) voters must be free of coercion, (d) all electors must be eligible at some period of their lives to public office, (e) all policy-making officials must be subject to election or, if appointed, subject to dismissal by elected officials, and (f) the electorate must be presented with a choice between real alternatives.

The effectiveness of suffrage in limiting the state power is often lost by virtue of the very separation of powers. The group will finds itself baffled in a Minoan maze of checks and balances—not to mention other obstacles—and before it finds embodiment in actual law, it is all too likely to have been diverted and dissipated. Needless to say, public officials whom suffrage is designed to control are familiar with these obstacles and their responsiveness to the popular will is correspondingly weakened.

To compensate for this limitation, direct legislative action in the form of recall, initiative, or referendum may be instituted. Although these deserve discussion in an exhaustive enumeration, far more significant is the classical liberals' view respecting the ultimate form of direct action, for in the event that governments defy all other efforts to control them, there remains the final recourse—revolution: the action of "the massed, angered forces of common humanity."

Revolution

Liberalism, it is well to remember, is the child of revolution, and the ideas of liberals concerning the right of revolution were bound to be shaped by the circumstance of this parentage. Each of the three men primarily responsible for formulating the classical liberal position on the subject of revolution is inseparably linked with major revolutionary upheavals: Locke, whose *Treatise of Civil Government* appeared in 1690, with the Glorious Revolution; Rousseau, whose *Social Contract* was published in 1762, with the French Revolution; Jefferson, author of the Declaration of Independence, with the American Revolution.

Now, whatever may have been the abuses which provoked them, neither these men nor their contemporaries were content to cite a mere list of grievances in justifying their recourse to revolution. They sought a framework of universal principles into which to fit their bill of particulars. Thus the Declaration of Independence contains a long list of specific grievances against the king of Great Britain:[22] "quartering large bodies of armed troops among us," "cutting off our Trade with all parts of the world," "imposing Taxes on us without our Consent," and so on and on. But it also invokes with all the majesty of Jefferson's impeccable prose a set of universal principles which might justify all men in any time in rebelling against tyrannical authority. What are these principles?

Actually, liberal doctrine concerning revolution stems from two sets of principles: one set associated with the names of Locke and Rousseau and having to do with an analysis of sovereignty and of the contract by which the relationship between the governors and the governed is established; the other associated with Hume and Bentham and based upon the more prosaic principle of utility.

A caution is in order. Liberalism is the child of revolution. But the child of a revolution may become the parent of a regime. In such an event, reference to its revolutionary ancestry may produce the same embarrassment which social climbers experience upon meeting their *arriviste* parents. Consequently, one may expect the emphasis to shift among those later generations of liberals who are concerned, not with undermining a regime, but with preserving one.

Indeed, not only do liberals separated from one another by several generations differ in their conclusions and inferences; any particular liberal spokesman may vary his verdict with the purpose he has in mind. When Alexander Hamilton undertook in *The Federalist* to persuade the representatives of a majority of the people of his state, New York, that they ought to repudiate the constitution of 1781, called the Articles of Confederation, as well as important provisions of the constitution of the State of New York and substitute the work of the Philadelphia Convention, he referred circumspectly to "that fundamental principle of republican government, which admits the right of the people to alter or abolish the established Constitution, whenever they find it inconsistent with their happiness . . ."[23] These are strong words for the man who, at the Philadelphia Convention, when discussing the general proposals for the new constitution, declared, "The people are turbulent and changing; they seldom judge or determine right . . . Nothing but a permanent body can check the imprudence of democracy. Their [the people's] turbulent and uncontrollable disposition requires checks."[24]

With this caution in mind, the way in which contractualism has served as a doctrinal basis for revolution may now be examined. Such an examination must go back beyond Rousseau and beyond Locke to that remarkable Englishman, Thomas Hobbes, who feared revolution like the plague and tried to banish it from the affairs of men. For it was Thomas Hobbes who shaped, even if he did not create, the universe of ideas within which Locke and Rousseau were later to move.

In search of the basis of sovereignty Hobbes goes back to a hypothetical state of nature, described in the *Leviathan* in terms which are among the most famous in the literature of political philosophy. The state of nature is one in which individuals, driven by their appetites and aversions, are engaged in an endless quest for power. The result is a condition of warfare of indefinite duration, because the participants are so nearly equal in ability that one is unable to prevail permanently over the other. In this state of *bellum omnium contra omnes,* as Hobbes calls it, every man has a right to everything, but no man is secure; every man is free, but no man is happy. There is "no culture of the earth, no navigation . . . no commodious building . . . no knowledge of the face of the earth . . . no arts; no letters; no society . . ." Life is, in Hobbes's famous phrase, "solitary, poor, nasty, brutish, and short."[25]

In these circumstances men, searching for peace and protection, enter into a covenant to give up the freedom which they have by natural right, the freedom, that is, to use their power for self-preservation. In this covenant or contract each agrees to surrender his natural right to govern himself to any man or group of men whom the majority selects. All are bound by the decision of this majority. Thus, for many sovereign wills, one will vested with absolute power and authority is substituted. Lest the contract prove to be no more than a truce in the war of all against all, it is made forever binding, or, at any rate, binding for so long as the sovereign is able to enforce his authority. Nothing which the sovereign may do can abrogate the agreement, since the contract is among the individual members of society and not between them and him. Having surrendered their rights to the sovereign by agreement with each other, they are left without any right to challenge his authority.

All this is part of the original contract to which the parties consented, be it understood, not because they underestimated their natural rights, but because they found the surrender of these rights less hateful than the anarchy produced by retaining them. Thus the social contract becomes under Hobbes's manipulation a device whereby absolute dictatorship is founded on the free consent of enlightened egoists. Majoritarianism is made to yield authoritarianism.[26] Their use of the plebiscite to secure an irrevocable delegation of power places Bonapartism and the *Führerprinzip* quite in the tradition of Hobbes.

Both Locke and Rousseau follow Hobbes in returning to an original state of nature. Also both agree with Hobbes, albeit with quite different emphases, that the state of nature becomes intolerable. Finally, both follow Hobbes in resorting to the social contract as a device through which men substitute civil society for the state of nature.

However, their debt to Hobbes is somewhat greater than these resemblances indicate. After all, Hobbes was by no means the first political philosopher to use the idea of a social contract. The idea goes back to the Romans and even to the Greeks, and it played a prominent part in the thinking of the medievalists, not to mention Hobbes's immediate predecessors on the Continent. But in the social contract as expounded by Hobbes several features appear that are especially significant: the compact is an arrangement among free and equal men, and the delegation of powers to the sovereign[27] is a democratic decision of the majority, which is binding on the minority; the whole question of sovereign power is settled, not by invoking divine right, but by appeal to the law of reason. The process whereby the materialistic Hobbes derives the authority of the sovereign is part of a rational deductive system: in it there is no place for appeals to faith or to divine sanction. Locke and Rousseau seized upon these features of Hobbes's contract theory. More significantly, they used them to develop a point of view in diametric opposition to his.

That which men give they may retract. Once one accepts the fiction that government rests upon a contract among free individuals, in which they agree to delegate all or part of the rights they enjoy in a prepolitical or "natural" state to a political authority selected by the majority, Hobbes's contention that their decision is irrevocable is bound to seem arbitrary. The need which drove men to substitute civil society for the state of nature, namely, the need for protection —in Locke's phrase—of "life, liberty, and estate," may again drive them to alter the society so created. Why must they heed the first need and ignore the second? If the authority of government rests upon an original act of consent—and Hobbes had postulated precisely such an act—then why should it not require a renewal of consent? If a majority of free and equal men has the power to select the form of government under which all shall live, a subsequent majority may choose not to abide by the decision of its predecessor.

Moreover, the authority vested in government has no divine origin, Hobbes had declared. It is a reasonable delegation of authority, but it is not sacrosanct. It was conferred by anonymous men in a mundane contract. Succeeding generations of anonymous men, in choosing not to be bound by that decision, do not even have to defy the will of God. Such was the generation of men, anonymous and otherwise, who fought and won the Glorious Revolution. And Locke was their professed apologist. It is not surprising, therefore, that he should have used the social contract not as a device through which the people forever surrender their sovereignty but as a reason for arguing that sovereignty can never reside anywhere else. He did not use the term sovereignty—Hobbes and others had made the term savor of irresponsible power—but his insistence on the right of revolution can mean nothing else.

Locke declares, "The end of government is the good of mankind," and he asks, "which is best for mankind, that the people should be always exposed to the boundless will of tyranny, or that the rulers should be sometimes liable to be opposed when they grow exorbitant in the use of their power, and employ it for the destruction and not the preservation of the properties of their people?"[28] Accordingly, he enumerates the circumstances which may justify a people in taking revolutionary action against government, domestic or foreign, which is not of their choosing: when an executive or prince substitutes his arbitrary will for the laws which reflect the will of society; when he tries to prevent the assembling of the legislature; when he uses his arbitrary power to control the electors, alter the ways of election, and hand-pick the candidates; when he uses force, money, and patronage to corrupt the legislature; when he so neglects and abandons his charge that the laws cannot be put into execution; when he or the legislature act so contrary to their trust that they "invade the property of the subject . . . and make themselves or any part of the community masters . . . of the lives, liberties, or fortunes of the people." When such circumstances are present, the "community" may retract the power which it has delegated to government and set up a new government.

Jean Jacques Rousseau (1712–78) also knew his Hobbes and, like Locke, recoiled from Hobbes's conclusions. But, unlike Locke, Rousseau is difficult to classify. He is closer in many ways to the romantic idealism of nineteenth-century Germany than to the French Enlightenment. His pages are replete with inconsistencies. Burke could damn him for his individualism and later damn him doubly for his collectivism. At least Moses knew whither he led his people if he did not live to enter the promised land. This "insane Socrates," as Burke called him, neither lived to witness the revolution which made him its patron saint, nor did he suspect that he was building the barricades from behind which revolutionaries would one day leap. He had in mind only the abuses of the aristocratic regime of his native Geneva when he wrote the *Social Contract*. But, as Ferrero points out, "The Revolution, seeking justification for its doctrine after the collapse of the monarchy, made Rousseau, who had wanted to be the physician for an aristocratic disease, the obstetrician for modern democracy."[29]

However, on one score Rousseau is quite clear, and it is in this respect that his work has particular significance for the growth of liberalism. He takes his stand with Locke in contending that the sovereignty of the people is inalienable. He has no fear of this Hobbesian term, and he explicitly locates sovereignty in the general or group will. This will he identifies with the common interest. In the welter of conflicting interests there must be a common interest, else a civil society could never come into being. This common interest is ascertained, he tells us, by consulting the majority. All law has its source in this sovereign general will, and government, whatever its form, is merely the agent or executive of this will.

Although it is possible for the sovereign to function as executive or government, this is not practical, declares Rousseau, except in a small community. Thus the sovereign, or state, as he also calls it, and the government are almost always two separate entities. Consequently, even though all laws originate with the sovereign, government may fail to execute the laws and in that to serve the interests of the sovereign. In fact, government tends to become more and more an inner clique with interests counter to the general interest.

Spontaneous assemblies of the people, convening in complete independence of the government, are the sole corrective of this tendency. That these are constituent assemblies engaged in formulating basic law is indicated by the two questions they consider: "First, is it the pleasure of the sovereign to preserve the existing form of government; second, is it the pleasure of the people to leave the administration to those who at present have it in charge." They are revolutionary assemblies, even if these questions are not answered in the negative, in that the functions of government are suspended during their deliberations. Clearly, the French National Assembly in requiring that the first statue commissioned by the republic be in the image of Rousseau was merely returning a compliment; it regarded itself as the image of the assembly depicted in the *Social Contract*.

It was natural that Locke should be better known to the Americans than Rousseau, although both were familiar. The difference between the reception of the *Second Treatise* in England and in America is the difference between exculpation and exhortation. In England Locke's work defended an accomplished fact; in America it was a summons to action. The Declaration of Independence rings out in Jefferson's unforgettable words:

> We hold these truths to be self-evident, That all men are created equal, that they are endowed by their Creator with certain unalienable Rights, that among these are Life, Liberty, and the pur-

suit of Happiness.—That to secure these rights, Governments are instituted among Men, deriving their just powers from the consent of the governed,—That whenever any Form of Government becomes destructive of these ends, it is the Right of the People to alter or abolish it, and to institute new Government, laying its foundations on such principles and organizing its powers in such form, as to them shall seem most likely to effect their Safety and Happiness.

No more forthright assertion of the right of revolution was ever framed. Even before the Declaration, James Madison and others had incorporated similar affirmations in the constitution of the state of Virginia.

In 1778 and in 1787 the American people availed themselves of this right. But the very Constitution which was the fruit of their revolutionary action raised a profoundly important question to which liberals have failed to give a consistent answer, a question which suggests again the internal conflict between mass and class consciousness, which haunts the soul of the liberal. The Constitution describes the procedure whereby changes in the basic framework of the government are to be made. The procedure is cumbersome, and it is arguable that it is designed to obstruct, if not to prevent, majority action on any matter concerning our fundamental law. How is this to be reconciled with the idea of popular sovereignty, in particular with the brave words of the Declaration? How, indeed, is constitutionalism as such to be reconciled with the plenary powers assumed by the majority when it engages in revolutionary action, if by constitutionalism one is to understand the limitation of power, no matter who exercises it?

Daniel Webster, in pleading before the Supreme Court, took the position that it could not be reconciled. He declared, while the court listened sympathetically, that

the constitution goes on the idea, that, within and under the Constitution, no new form of government can be established without the authority of the existing government. Unless [there] be some authentic way of ascertaining the will of the people . . . all is anarchy . . . and all constitutions and all legislative rights are prostrated and disregarded.

He was echoed by the Supreme Court under Taney, when it declared in Dodge *v*. Woolsey, "that the Constitution is supreme . . . it is supreme over the people of the United States, aggregately and in their separate sovereignties, because they have excluded themselves from any direct or immediate agency in making amendments, and have directed that amendments should be made representatively for them."

The Founding Fathers in their day fully understood the motives which prompted Webster and the members of the Supreme Court to arrive at this conclusion. They were haunted by the same fears, particularly when someone like Daniel Shays was starting a rebellion in Massachusetts. Few of them would have gone as far as Jefferson, that "atheist and leveler from Virginia," when he said (unlike an atheist, but possibly like a leveler), "God forbid that we should ever be for twenty years without a rebellion." Still, they were themselves revolutionaries as well as the authors of our basic law. Thus Madison, "Father of the Constitution," declared that the people have "the transcendent and precious right" to "alter and abolish their governments as to them shall seem most likely to effect their safety and happiness." So, too, Justice Wilson, one of the most learned men among them, commented that

A revolution principle certainly is, and certainly should be taught as a principle of the Constitution of the United States, and of every State in the Union. This revolution principle that the sovereign power residing in the people, they may change their constitution and government whenever they please, is not a principle of discord, rancor or war; it is a principle of melioration, contentment, and peace.[30]

Even Lincoln, removed in time as he was from the Revolution, was nevertheless close enough to it in spirit to say in his famous first inaugural address,

This country, with its institutions, belongs to the people who inhabit it. Whenever they shall grow weary of the existing government, they can exercise their constitutional right of amending it, or their revolutionary right to dismember or overthrow it.

Were Lincoln and Madison and Jefferson and Sam Adams and John Quincy Adams and Justice Wilson and all the others oblivious to the danger seen by Webster? Webster and the justices of Taney's court and the many others who have shared their point of view were, after all, only echoing Hobbes in denying the right of revolution, and Hobbes had denied it because he feared its acceptance would lead to endless strife. The Founding Fathers, while sharing his fear and stressing the unruliness and turbulence of the "mob," nevertheless affirmed the right of revolution. Sometimes they ignored the problem and, like Hamilton, stressed the right of revolution when they were the revolutionists, only to stress the turbulence of the mob when they were the regime.[31] Others found the solution in the amending process. The reasoning of the latter went something like this:

The sense of outrage and the energy necessary to start and carry through a revolution would easily suffice to quicken the cumbrous process of amendment set up in the Constitution. Long before it acquires explosive violence, resentment will have found satisfaction through the amending process. It is easier to amend the Constitution than to start and win a revolution. So long as the amending process is available, the energies which would otherwise become explosive act upon the Constitution to change it through the prescribed machinery, even if that machinery is ponderous and slow. Thus, so long as the Constitution is respected by those in power, the changes sought through revolutionary action not only could be but in the normal course of events would be effected within the framework of the Constitution. The authors of our basic law wisely provided a method of amending the Constitution, which would not require the cooperation of the government. However, if those in power should use their power to keep the Constitution from being changed, they would be guilty of usurpation; and revolution, however hazardous, would be justified.

For the rest, the Founding Fathers were able to turn to Locke, who had addressed himself to the issue frequently and with more than usual eloquence. Locke quotes the familiar objection to the right of revolution, before demolishing it:

May the commands, then, of a prince be opposed? May he be resisted, as often as anyone shall find himself aggrieved, and but imagine he has not right done him? This will unhinge and overturn all politics, and instead of government and order, leave nothing but anarchy and confusion.[32]

Locke's answer is worth citing in some detail. People, he declares, are not easily aroused. They are slow to become provoked over acknowledged faults, let alone imagined ones. He points to the continuity in the English system of government despite "the many revolutions which have been seen in this kingdom . . ." On the other hand, if they are sufficiently provoked they will act against their rulers, whether the right to rebel is acknowledged or denied. But,

such revolutions happen not upon every little mismanagement in public affairs. Great mistakes in the ruling part, many wrong and inconvenient laws, and all the slips of human frailty will be borne by the people without mutiny or murmur. But if a long train of abuses, prevarications and artifices, all tending the same way, make the design visible to the people—and they cannot but feel what they lie under, and see whither they are going—it is not to be wondered that they should then rouse themselves and endeavor to put the rule into such hands which may secure to them the ends for which government was at first erected, and without which ancient names and specious forms are so far from being better that they are much worse than the state of nature or pure anarchy . . .[33]

The weight of Locke's response is even more evident in the following paragraph, which is worth citing in nearly full length. It is one of the most significant passages in the literature of political philosophy.

Nor let anyone say that mischief can arise from hence as often as it shall please a busy head or turbulent spirit to desire the alteration of the government. It is true such men may stir whenever they please, but it will be only to their own just ruin and perdition. For till the mischief be grown general, and the ill designs of the rulers become visible, or their attempts sensible to the greater part, the people, who are more disposed to suffer than right themselves by resistance, are not apt to stir. The examples of particular injustice or oppression of here and there an unfortunate man moves them not. But if they universally have a persuasion grounded upon manifest evidence that designs are carrying on against their liberties, and the general course and tendency of things cannot but give them strong suspicions of the evil intention of their governors, who is to be blamed for it? Who can help it if they, who might avoid it, bring themselves into this suspicion? Are the people to be blamed if they have the sense of rational creatures . . . ? And is it not rather their fault who put things in such a posture . . . ?[34]

Times change. The Whig aristocrats of the next century and the conservative beneficiaries of the American Revolution preferred to open their Locke to other passages; their living descendants often denounce revolution as the mad dream of men under the influence of Marx or Moscow; but Locke wrote the right of revolution into the liberal tradition, Tom Paine trumpeted it to the whole world, and there it is in the precious Declaration of Independence for every schoolboy to read and recite and, conceivably, to reaffirm.

These men for the most part tried to justify revolution by using the idea of contract and the doctrine of natural rights. Another school of liberal opinion preferred a consideration of consequences to an analysis of hypothetical social contracts, and the principle of utilitarianism to the idea of jusnaturalism. On the whole, the eighteenth-century English preferred to discuss revolution in terms of interests, the French in terms of rights.

Hume, Adam Smith, Priestley, Paley, and Bentham, all exemplify this eighteenth-century English refusal to employ fictions, however vital. Thus Hume argues that, since promises and the obligation to keep them are "founded on the necessities and interests of society,"[35] the duty to obey government derives not from a promise, i.e., a contract, but from the public interest. Since the reason for keeping the social contract is the public interest, nothing is lost and clarity is gained if revolution is discussed in terms of social interest, omitting references to contract altogether. The only principle which can justify obedience or disobedience is the principle of utility. To this Bentham gave a vigorous second. Although Bentham wrote the *Fragment on Government* while he was still a Conservative—he began as a Tory but ended as a "Radical"—and Hume always remained a Conservative in politics, the principle of utility was hardly likely to render the head that wears the crown less uneasy than the Lockian or Rousseauan version of the social contract.

This completes the discussion of the checks and restraints whereby the liberal creed proposes to keep government within allotted bounds, and concludes the discussion of the political philosophy of classical liberalism.

The individual is now surrounded by all possible safeguards against the forces, within or without himself, which might deter him from becoming productive. He is protected from himself by the threat of economic insecurity; he is protected from the violence and vices of others by government; and from government by the several devices enumerated. The elaborate logic according to which slothful man becomes the "hustler," the "go-getter," the enterprising, aggressive, tireless man personifying the spirit of modern capitalism has been traced.

But such a transformation will have been of no avail unless this energy serves a social purpose and promotes the general welfare. It is by no means immediately evident that, in rendering men more energetic in pursuing their own interests, the good of society is served. Indeed, on the surface, if not beneath it, the contrary would seem to be the case. The second of the two problems raised at the outset must therefore be faced: how do the efforts of selfish individuals benefit the whole? The liberal believes that there is an automatic harmony between the self-interest of the individual and the welfare of the whole. If such a conviction were not an essential part of his creed, he could hardly preach the release of the individual from positive social controls with that missionary zeal which has come to be associated with liberals. "Law and government can do little or nothing toward eliminating self-interest, even if it were desirable to do so, which it is not," declares a twentieth-century exponent of the classical liberal tradition, "but it is possible to harness it to the good of the nation." It remains to be seen how the straining steed of self-interest is harnessed to the social good.

Chapter 6

The Economic Creed:
The Natural Harmony of Interests

THE FORMULA BY which the interest of the individual is identified with the interest of the community is the culmination of the classical liberal creed, its very summit. Here at last one confronts classical liberalism in its economic aspect and comes face to face with "economic man." How men may remain, nay, must remain calculating egoists while they serve the public good, this is the formidable question to which the classical political economy addressed itself. It found the answer in the "natural harmony of interests." If a hundred fifty years of affirmation have made the answer seem commonplace, at the time it was framed it had all the charm of boldness and originality.

The Division of Labor and Exchange

The classical economists lived at a time when the division of labor with its consequent reliance upon exchange had become the most striking feature of man's effort to make a living. It is not surprising, therefore, to find the opening passages of *The Wealth of Nations* embarking upon this theme.

The greatest improvement in the productive powers of labour, and the greater part of the skill, dexterity, and judgment with which it is anywhere directed, or applied, seem to have been the effects of the division of labour.

The proposition hardly admits of doubt, even without the profusion of logic and illustration by which Adam Smith demonstrates it. Neither does the proposition that a division of labor would be impossible in the absence of exchange. Thus, in a famous passage, Adam Smith turns his attention secondly to the phenomenon of exchange.

This division of labour, from which so many advantages are derived, is not originally the effect of any human wisdom, which foresees and intends that general opulence to which it gives occasion. It is the necessary, though very slow and gradual, consequence of a certain propensity in human nature which has in view no such extensive utility; the propensity to truck, barter, and exchange one thing for another.

He goes on,

. . . the certainty of being able to exchange all that surplus part of the produce of his own labour, which is over and above his own consumption, for such parts of the produce of other men's labour as he may have occasion for, encourages every man to apply himself to a particular occupation, and to cultivate and to bring to perfection whatever talent or genius he may possess for that particular species of business.[1]

Once the division of labor is established, all of us live by exchanging. The scope and frequency of such exchange will depend upon the extent of the market, as determined, for example, by the availability and efficiency of transportation facilities, by population, and so on.

Exchange is at least a two-way process. It throws the acquisitive individual at once into a relation of dependence upon others. That dependence consists specifically in his being compelled to satisfy the needs of others in order to satisfy his own. In serving others it is his own interest that the individual has in view. As far as economic activity, at least, is concerned, the individual is an egoist from first to last. Thanks, however, to the requirements of an exchange economy, where *all* little pigs go to market, "the study of his own advantage naturally, or rather necessarily, leads him to prefer that employment which is most advantageous to the society."[2] Again in one of the most widely quoted passages of *The Wealth of Nations,*

He generally, indeed, neither intends to promote the public interest, nor knows how much he is promoting it . . . by directing . . . industry in such a manner as its produce may be of the greatest value, he intends only his own gain, and he is in this, as in many other cases led by an invisible hand to promote an end which was no part of his intention. Nor is it always the worse for the society that it was no part of it. By pursuing his own interest he frequently promotes that of the society more effectually than when he really intends to promote it. I have never known much good done by those who affected to trade for the public good. It is an affectation, indeed, not very common among merchants, and very few words need be employed in dissuading them from it.[3]

The same note is struck by others with remarkable regularity. "Private vices, public benefits" was the somewhat disconcerting way in which Bernard de Mandeville stated the same formula before Adam Smith. The "friendly qualities" and "kind affections" are not the foundations of society, Mandeville declared. On the contrary, "what we call evil [i.e., egoism] in this world . . . is the grand principle that makes us sociable creatures."[4] The point of view still has its ardent advocates.

The Role of the Market

Before an act of exchange can take place, those who buy and those who sell must come together, not merely in the physical sense which makes possible a transfer of the commodities involved, but in the sense that they must somehow come to an agreement concerning the value of these commodities. This is accomplished in the "market" through the mechanism of "price."

At the market everything—capital, labor, land, the endless variety of things which men prize for whatever reason—takes on the character of a commodity and has a price placed upon it. That this is a "money" price is important. More important is the fact that the price arrived at through the higgling of the market reflects the value at which the buyer is willing to acquire and the seller to relinquish the commodity, in short, its "power in exchange." This price will be something which the individual regards as "worth while." In the normal case, what is "worth while" will be something in excess of what the commodity has cost him, where the cost may be so many hours of labor (as in the case of workers),[5] so much "abstinence" (as in the case of one who is saving capital), and so much risk (as in the case of one who is investing capital). Labor is onerous, and so too, presumably, are the feelings associated with abstinence and risk. Accordingly, each individual weighs these "pain costs" against the "pleasure gains" represented by wages, profits, and interest, and selects the alternative which will yield him the maximum amount of pleasure.

This hedonistic or "felicific" calculus became more explicit in the theory of orthodox economics as early classicism passed into late classicism and this in turn into marginalism (e.g., Léon Walras in France, William Stanley Jevons in England, Herman H. Gossen in Germany, and the Austrian School), and as economists, focusing on theory of value, shifted their emphasis from production to distribution.[6] In the psychologically more sophisticated language of neoclassicists, like Alfred Marshall and his disciples, the vocabulary of literal hedonism is altered. Each individual exercises a preference, "the outward manifestations of which appear as incentives to action in such a form that the force or quantity of the incentive can be estimated or measured with some approach to accuracy." This measurement is accomplished "by the sum of money which [the individual] will give up in order to secure a desired satisfaction; or again by the sum which is just required to induce him to undergo a certain fatigue."[7]

The prevalence of hedonism, either implicitly (as with Marshall) or explicitly (as with Jevons and F. Y. Edgeworth), in the thinking of the orthodox economists may be traced in great part, as far as the lineage of ideas is concerned, to the influence of the Benthamite dogma that pleasure is measurable. Economics thereby acquired the status of an exact science in the minds of its practitioners, at the same time that the pecuniary aspect of the highly institutionalized behavior of men in the market was first abstracted and then saved from the profane hands of economic heretics by calling it "human nature."

Economic man is assertedly rational. Accordingly, his "pecuniary sagacity" prompts him to buy in the cheapest market and sell in the dearest. More specifically this means that of two products of equal quantity and quality he will always prefer the cheaper. If, on the other hand, the price is the same and the quantity and quality vary, he will prefer the greater quantity or superior quality. For his part, the owner of a commodity will try to sell the least amount and the poorest quality at the highest price. Workers in selling their labor power will always seek the least laborious work and the highest wage. Employers will try to exact a maximum amount of work at a minimum wage. Similar considerations will apply to the lending of capital, the renting of property, in brief, to any transaction which takes place on the market.

The market price of any commodity is governed by the law of supply and demand. When the quantity of a commodity exceeds the demand, the price declines until it falls below the cost of production or below the point at which the producer is willing to continue making more of the commodity. When the quantity of a commodity falls short of the demand, its price will rise until supply and demand are in equilibrium. This is as true in a free market for the wages paid a coal miner as for the price of a ton of coal. If the number of miners exceeds the demand for them, the wages of miners will decline until they seek work in more remunerative employments. If the demand for miners exceeds the supply, the wages of miners will rise until so many workers are attracted from other less remunerative occupations that the supply approximates the demand. If the amount of coal exceeds the demand, the price will go down until operators find it more profitable to invest their capital elsewhere. If the demand exceeds the supply, the reverse takes place.

The market thus determines how society shall invest its resources, human and material. It decrees when, where, and how men shall labor. It determines the disposition of capital. The market becomes the regulator of what shall be produced, its quality, quantity, and price. The market is truly called sovereign.

No AAA, no Gosplan, no production board or planning commission of any kind—not even the planning of a private association of producers—determines how many acres of wheat shall be sown and how many hogs raised, or how wheat and hogs shall exchange for other commodities. No sovereign state decrees how many motor cars shall be manufactured, what gadgets they shall contain, or what the length of their wheel base shall be. No department, commission, or bureau and, in pure theory, no labor union tells men where to labor, in what number, at what wages, nor how the wealth of society shall be distributed among the several factors involved in production. Quite apart from other considerations, no agency, public or private, can have the knowledge to make such decisions.[8] Instead of one or several decisions, there are countless decisions, each party to a transaction making his own.

In his memorable description of a locust invasion, Donald Culross Peattie writes, "No communal swarm are they, with mutual helpful purposes, like bees and men, but an anarchic mob, each ravening appetite out for itself." Unlike Mr. Peattie, the classical economists denied that men are a "communal swarm" with "mutual helpful purposes." Why, then, are they not an "anarchic mob"? If the result is something other than the frenzied throng comprised by Mr. Peattie's locusts, this, presumably, is because the countless decisions made by individuals obey an inner law of their own, which is no more than human nature responding to the motives of the market under the conditions prevailing in an exchange economy.

The Role of Competition

No orthodox economist ever claimed that any of the results so far described are realizable, save in a *free* market, a market to which everyone has equal access and in which, therefore, everyone is in competition with everyone else. When individuals are in a competitive relationship, they are pitted against each other in seeking an object which not all of them can possess. Economic rewards are such an object. With respect to these rewards competition functions both as a spur and a bridle: loiterers, blunderers, and wastrels will soon find themselves outdistanced by the energetic and skillful and abstemious; the venal will encounter limitations upon their greed.

Competition functions as a spur because each producer

must produce with relative efficiency, else he will lose the market to someone who can produce a superior commodity at a reduced price. The mere quest for profits is of itself static as far as its implications for the improvement of productive techniques are concerned. A producer with a "good thing" might actually be deterred from seeking innovations if he had no competition to fear. But competition imparts a dynamic quality to the productive system, compelling producers to eliminate waste and to search out the most efficient methods of production, including the latest technological improvements. It accomplishes this by confronting them with the threat that their profits will be pre-empted by rivals with greater ingenuity—all to the endless benefit of consumers. The same considerations govern wages as well as profits.

So, too, competition functions as a bridle by preventing producers from charging "what the traffic will bear." There is nothing in the relationship of exchange, taken by itself, to prevent one of the parties to the exchange from fleecing the other, if the offender controls the quantity of the commodity and the victim wants it badly enough. But where free competition prevails, the recipient of exorbitant profits is likely to find himself undersold by someone willing to accept less. The logic of classical economics is transparently clear on this score, that human nature being what it is, i.e., inordinately acquisitive, profit degenerates into plunder unless controlled by competition.

Thus, free competition seems to proportion reward to merit among producers—wage earners as well as entrepreneurs—and to afford indispensable protection to the consumer. The consumer is protected doubly: by receiving the benefit of the best effort of the producers and by being shielded from the otherwise unrestrained greed of producers. On the other hand, producers are protected because consumers are themselves in competition for the scarce goods supplied by producers.

In the absence of the protection provided by competition, it is recognized that the public has no recourse but to fall back on official price-fixing. Price-fixing is ordinarily anathema to the classical economist, but not even he would deny that, if prices are to be fixed, this had better be the work of a public than a private agency. Thus, in the several areas where competition is universally acknowledged to be impractical, as in the case of certain utilities, the regulation of rates is conceded to government agencies. In the absence of free competition, the idea of laissez faire becomes untenable by the logic of its own exponents.

Toward the end of the nineteenth century the competitive system, as so described, found itself buttressed by a theory which came subsequently to be known as social Darwinism, although Darwin was only indirectly and quite unintentionally responsible for it. Darwin himself had been guided by the suggestion contained in Malthus' famous *Essay on Population*, which called attention to the mathematical inevitability of overpopulation in a world where resources increased in arithmetic ratio (1, 2, 3, 4, 5 . . .) while population increased in geometric ratio (2, 4, 8, 16, 32 . . .). This suggested to Darwin the idea of a competition for survival, which he extended to all living species, a competition in the course of which only the fittest survive.

Darwin did not attempt to apply this idea to the sphere of social relations,[9] but men like Walter Bagehot and Herbert Spencer in England and William Graham Sumner in America were quick to make its implications a foundation for the belief that the system of free competition was simply another instance of the struggle for survival, and that here as in the order of nature the fittest remained and prospered. If those who received only crumbs, or were cast by the way entirely, complained, or found others to protest in their behalf, they were simply railing against nature. The survivors in this process of natural selection could blandly assure their defeated rivals that a competitive order which distributed individuals according to merit and eliminated the unfit was good not only for the select but for society as a whole. The "poverty of the incapable, the distresses that come upon the imprudent, the starvation of the idle, and those shoulderings aside of the weak by the strong, which leave so many 'in shallows and in miseries,' are the decrees of a large, far-seeing benevolence."[10]

Social Darwinism is no longer proclaimed as official doctrine and, in any event, the logic of the system of free competition was formulated without the aid of Darwinism and does not require it. But in the nineteenth and early twentieth centuries the notion exercised a powerful sway over the minds of businessmen,[11] professors, college presidents, and even ministers of the Gospel, and it continues to flourish in some business quarters.

This, then, is the "consummately conceived and self-balanced mechanism" from which issues the natural harmony of interests. As described by the orthodox economists the mechanism is nothing if not a model of efficiency. No wonder it moved Sir Arthur Salter to exclaim that it was "more like one of the marvelously intricate structures built by the instincts of beavers or ants than the deliberately designed and rational works of man."[12] But the orthodox economists have described only the bones, the merest skeleton upon which practice has grafted the flesh and blood of "exceptions," "frictions," "disturbing influences," "artificial interferences"; and these in turn have been clothed with an attire of extenuating circumstances, supplementary hypotheses, saving qualifications, revisions, and all the other paraphernalia, which have made orthodox economics a much more complex science than it set out to be. Whether the skeleton must creak and ultimately collapse under the burden is a question which the critics of orthodoxy shall be called on to answer in the sequel. Meanwhile the popularity among laymen of works by such stalwart friends of the free market as Ludwig von Mises, Friedrich A. Hayek, John Chamberlain, Henry Simons, John Jewkes, and Lionel Robbins suggests that, if a skeleton, it is by no means in a closet.[13]

Harmony and Dissonance

It is a commonplace among logicians that an impeccably consistent system of ideas may have no reference to the real world. Logic, no matter how flawless, cannot coerce the sometimes stubbornly refractory world of events. Not even the heirs of the orthodox tradition will deny that at first the doctrine of a natural harmony of interests suffered this unhappy fate.

The convincing demonstrations of the economists failed

to rain the blessings of the free market upon the great populations huddled together in the sordid cities of the English Midlands where the industrial revolution first came into its own. Women and children were cruelly exploited under circumstances which beggar description. The English cities which became the workshops of the world were ugly, filthy, and utterly without provisions for a decent community life. Men labored endless hours in mine and mill for niggardly wages and returned to squalid slums to sleep briefly so that they might labor more. These were the years when Ricardo's "brazen law of wages" sounded a discordant note in the natural harmony of interests. Malthus' dismal prophecies concerning the uneven race between the arithmetic and geometric ratios hardly lightened the gloom. Nature contributed to the somber scene with several years of bad crops.[14] Here was a cacophony rather than a harmony of interests, and, if the heralds of the new day had not been able to confute it with something more than syllogisms, their case would shortly have been demolished with that same "large brutal effectiveness" which Mr. Lippmann's *Good Society* imputes to the free market.

But tangible evidence was soon at hand, which lent some point to the classicists' praise of the free market and seemed to give the economists' demonstrations needed empirical verification. The story has been told often.

In a short period of some seventy-five years goods were produced in quantities beyond the wildest imaginings of the most incorrigible optimist. Men built great factories. They penetrated the bowels of the earth and roamed its remotest recesses to feed their ravenous industries with an endless stream of raw materials. They spanned continents with railroads and highways, reduced space with the wireless and telephone and radio. Steam power replaced water power and was in turn replaced by electricity. Machines, endlessly versatile, promised to banish hard and tedious labor. Great cities of steel and concrete grew up, brilliantly lighted, ingeniously supplied with fresh foods and pure water, and filled with goods in sufficient variety to tickle the most jaded taste. Automobiles, radios, bathrooms, electric refrigerators, and a thousand conveniences became available in enormous quantity, not indeed to all, but to a rapidly increasing number of the population.

All this transpired during the relatively brief span of time when Capitalism came into its own. In that period men far exceeded the total of their previous physical achievements through all the long centuries of human history. And, so runs the argument, besides all this, wages were increased, the workday was reduced, and child labor and the cruder exploitation of women were virtually abolished. Concomitantly, the ownership of wealth became so diffused that one of our greatest banking institutions was able to accurately represent the number of its stockholders by picturing in its advertisements a great stadium full to the brim with people.

Even if all this is platitude, there have been and are still endless panegyrics upon this theme. Two are worth citing as typical of the remainder. "The triumph of our degree of economy of plenty over an economy of scarcity represents the highest achievement of civilization," former President Hoover has written. "We can say without qualification," he declares, "that the motivation of production based on private initiative had proved the very mother of plenty." There follows an impressive enumeration of America's achievements: ". . . four times as many telephones, five times as many radios, and six times as many automobiles as any great nation of Europe."[15]

Mr. George Sokolsky has dilated upon this theme about as frequently as anyone. Even the American so modestly situated that he has no bank account or insurance premium is the owner of great wealth, according to Mr. Sokolsky.

Take two items, for instance: electricity and running water. The possession of them today would not be regarded by most Americans as a mark of wealth. Yet, as short a time ago as seventy-five years back, nobody in this world possessed either of them. No king, no emperor, no millionaire possessed them.

He goes on,

Science, invention, mass production, the factory system, modern transportation—and many more agencies of modern life have made wealth in its many diverse forms more accessible to an increasingly large number of people. Let me take two or three items to show you how true this is: In 1920, there were 50,000 radios in this country; in 1930, there were 12,000,000; today, there are 27,000,000. In 1920, there were 935,000 washing machines; in 1930, there were 7,000,000; today 13,000,000 are in use. In 1920, only 10,000 electrical refrigerators were in use in this country; by 1930, this number had grown to 2,250,000; today 12,000,000 are in use.

This is an absolute evidence of the wide diffusion of wealth in America under our American economic system. Whereas in 1920 only 10,000 Americans possessed wealth in terms of electric refrigerators, by 1930, 2,250,000 Americans had become wealthy in this respect.

These words were written in the 'forties. The figures are much more impressive today.

So the story goes, varying only with the eloquence of the teller. No wonder that those who thought in the classical liberal tradition became ardent converts to the idea of progress. Wars and depressions have, indeed, interrupted the steady march forward, and the orthodox economists have, of course, been troubled by them. But for such economists, as for all classical liberals, wars and depressions are not a reason for transforming or abandoning the system of free private enterprise so much as a consequence of our failure to adhere to its principles with sufficient fidelity. Thus, the most prolonged depression and the worst war in history—not to mention a series of post-war recessions—leave the faith of many classical liberals unshaken. We are being punished for our economic heresies. We must return to the ways of our fathers. Then the dissonances will die away, and we shall have that "natural harmony" promised us by the classicists and recklessly scorned by intransigent moderns.

Such are the outlines of liberalism in its classical formulation. Time has aged the mansions of the nineteenth century. Events have jarred them, and the fierce winds of doctrine blow. Today men are finding themselves new abodes. The scope of this study prevents a systematic consideration of the challenge of Fascism and Marxism to the liberal ideals of the eighteenth and nineteenth centuries. Instead, the inquiry will be limited to a new variant of liberalism at once continuous with the classical liberal tradition and a vigorous protest against it.

PART TWO/CONTEMPORARY LIBERALISM

Ill fares the land, to hastening ills a prey,
Where wealth accumulates and men decay!

—OLIVER GOLDSMITH

Introduction

THE *New York Times*, in a mood induced by the season, was editorializing about the month of September. "September," the editor wrote, "is a fickle month. It does not exactly belong to either Summer or Autumn, and often has an unpleasant touch of each." The month, the editor observed, "is a period of restlessness." "In more ways than one," he found, "September is a month which seems to have no great character of its own. Its very name shows how little of settled place it has."

Preoccupied with these observations, the reader might turn from a perusal of the *Times* to reflections on liberalism in transition. Contemporary liberalism, he might say, has come into vogue during "a period of restlessness." In more ways than one it has "no great character of its own." It does not "exactly belong to either the Right or Left" and "often has an unpleasant taste of each. Its very name shows how little of settled place it has."

I acknowledge my own indebtedness to the *Times* editor, although I shall be on guard, in what follows, against his petulant overtones.

Contemporary liberalism, at the very outset, bears this dissimilarity both to its classical forerunners and to its revolutionary contemporaries: It is not a fixed or systematically elaborated body of doctrine, nor is it a product of the practical and theoretical labors of one or two or even of several great men. There are no towering figures like John Locke and Adam Smith or Karl Marx and Friedrich Engels associated with the standpoint of contemporary liberalism. There is no monumental treatise like *The Wealth of Nations* or *Capital* to which contemporary liberals may turn for guidance and inspiration. Contemporary liberalism is essentially a fluid and frequently elusive doctrine. It is eclectic in point of view.[1] As such, it is often regarded with suspicion by the Right and with contempt by the doctrinaire Left.

Liberalism—and henceforth the term when not otherwise qualified will designate contemporary liberalism—is, to begin with, a frame of mind. In contrast to the conservative, the liberal is more hospitable to change, more willing to re-examine established institutions and accepted practices in the light of new problems and new needs. He thinks of the conservative as one who constantly appeals to the experience of the past but refuses to learn from it. The liberal is less reverent of the status quo, more venturesome in the realm of ideas, more hopeful of the possibilities of exploration, experiment, and discovery. In this respect he continues in the tradition of the classical liberal, who was, as we have seen, a social frontiersman, albeit one who often gave way to a nostalgic yearning for home.

In contrast to the revolutionary, the liberal is more apprehensive of the consequences of sudden change, more prone to prize and conserve values which have been inherited from the past, more disposed to pause at the brink of action. Violent social action is likely to be rejected as culminating in new forms of tyranny or as ignoring fundamental changes in the strategy of revolution in technologically advanced societies, where the barricades of 1848 and 1917 are as obsolete as the flintlock.

In any case, the liberal is likely to be a good deal more discriminating in his choice of means and to perceive that they can impair and sometimes completely transform the ends they serve. Thus "liquidations" and "purges" are not for the liberal, no matter what end they are expected to realize. For all these reasons the liberal worships at the shrine of legality —sometimes to his own detriment.

Liberals are usually at their best when they play the part of critic. By disposition, even if no longer always by circumstance, they are the "loyal opposition." There is a sense in which liberals may remain the "opposition" even after an electoral victory—opposed, that is, to established economic interests whose hold on power may or may not be weakened by the defeat of their advocates at the polls. Since the liberal is most comfortable, not to say formidable, as critic, it is appropriate, as attention is turned from the general to the particular, to begin with the contemporary liberal in the exercise of his critical function. This criticism takes two forms: (1) a re-examination of the theoretical foundations of classical liberalism, and (2) an evaluation of the practical achievements of the world for which classical liberalism has been the reigning philosophy. The discussion will begin with the former but not without first warning against the mood to which liberals themselves have sometimes yielded during the "cold war" in which we now find ourselves.

The "cold war," so-called, has ended the uneasy alliance between the USSR and the Western democracies. The truculence and aggressiveness of the Soviet Union and its allies have diverted attention from the continuing menace of other forms of totalitarianism and the forces in the capitalist democracies which breed them. In some quarters the menace of domestic communism has been fantastically exaggerated, and the fears thereby generated have been unscrupulously exploited to suppress criticism and silence dissent. In other quarters, the fact that Communists, to serve their own ulterior objectives, have paraded the shortcomings of the capitalist democracies has generated a tendency among non-Communists to overlook our weaknesses, lest emphasis upon them aid the communist cause.[2]

But the shortcomings of the capitalist democracies either exist, or they do not exist. If they do not exist, this must be determined by an appeal to the enduring facts and not by a transient humor induced by an international crisis. If they do exist, systematic criticism, now as always, is an indispensable preliminary to correction and, therefore, to averting the social ills upon which communism and fascism both thrive.

Chapter 7

Of Human Nature

CONTEMPORARY LIBERALISM, borrowing heavily from recent psychological and anthropological studies and from the relatively new science of social psychology, begins by demolishing the theory of human nature from which classical liberalism takes its start. It is this work of demolition which must first be examined.

The Fallacy of Egoism

The psychological tenet which has suffered severest attack is the view that "it's human nature to be selfish." The attack on the doctrine of psychological egoism and its hedonistic variant did not originate with economists but with psychologists and philosophers. Confronted with a powerful barrage of argument against the hedonistic presuppositions of their science, orthodox economists either adopted an altered terminology, as in the case of Marshall,[1] or like Gustav Cassel, renounced psychology as a source of economic postulates altogether. Few economists now accept psychological hedonism. But it is still sometimes retained as a preconception, even when it has been discarded as a postulate.[2] In any case, the fact that egoism in both its variants is still the prevalent conception of human nature among the dominant economic group and that it is taken for granted by many amateur social philosophers, particularly those engaged in practical politics, exempts one from the charge of flogging a dead horse.

What is self-interest? Merely to ask the question is to discover that the term is so vague as to be utterly meaningless. The self is *anything* it happens to be identified with; and self-interest may be interest in amassing a fortune, in helping down-and-outers, in agitating for social reform, in hunting big game in Africa, or in risking one's life to further the revolutionary struggle of some remote people.

But to say this is to divest self-interest of any special meaning. Self-interest acquires meaning, and to speak of conduct as "selfish" acquires significance, only because by such designation certain types of conduct seem to be excluded.[3] If no variety of conduct is excluded, and if a selfish individual may indeed identify himself with and act in behalf of any objective, clearly, to say that all conduct is selfish is to say that all conduct is conduct—an indubitable but hardly significant proposition.

Just as clearly, the classical liberals did not regard themselves as expounding this empty truism. The proposition that conduct is selfish was more than merely tautological as they employed it; it had significance just because they tacitly identified self-interest with the pecuniary interest which dominated their time.

Thus, the otherwise empty concept of egoism (empty just because it is so full) was identified with acquisitiveness, or, more precisely, with the quest for pecuniary gain which passes as the profit motive. As a result, the profit motive could be understood without reference to its institutional origins and historical antecedents; it received its credentials from human nature and, like human nature, it was thought ineluctable, given—and therefore accepted. The identification of self-interest and the profit motive was thus mutually advantageous; self-interest acquired a specific meaning, and the profit motive was lifted out of the flux of history, was fixed, fastened, and made firm.

In this fashion the datum to be explained became a principle of explanation. The contingent and, from any long historical point of view, the novel motives of the assertive, entrepreneurial middle classes were read into human nature. The psychological egoists then appealed to human nature, as so described, to account for the operation of these motives and to argue that they are as indefeasible as human nature itself.

That all conduct is selfish in the truistic sense described above is indisputable. That the profit motive, i.e., the identification of the self with certain pecuniary goals, can be a powerful motive is clearly evident from an inspection of the conduct of acquisitive individuals. That all conduct must be in behalf of *this kind of self* to the exclusion of other kinds of self—the only sense in which the doctrine of psychological egoism can be said to have significance—is palpably false.[4] Thus, psychological egoism must be either trivial or false: in the use in which it has significance it is false; in the use in which it is true it is trivial.

There is another fallacy associated with the doctrine of self-interest, based, as that doctrine is, on a failure to perceive the identity of a self with the ends it pursues. The kind of end pursued, varying as it does with time and place, determines the kind of self. There is, then, no single self, complete and aloof, and therefore no self set up over against other persons or selves in relationship to which it as an entity may be either benevolent or selfish—according to the egoist, only selfish.[5] Thus, the fundamental issue is not between "self-regarding" and "other-regarding" conduct; it concerns rather what *kind* of self one shall become, and this is a matter, not of catering to something antecedently fixed and given, but of guiding conduct in the pursuit of ends whose character changes with time and circumstance.

The comments of William James on this subject are especially illuminating. In his famous *Principles of Psychology*, he delivered the *coup de grâce* to the selfish system with characteristic brilliance and clarity:

But what is this abstract numerical principle of identity, this "Number One" within me, for which, according to proverbial philosophy, I am supposed to keep so constant a "lookout"? Is it the inner nucleus of my spiritual self . . . ? Or is it perhaps the concrete stream of my thought in its entirety, or some one section of the same? . . . Or, finally, can it be the mere pronoun I? Surely it is none of these things that self for which I feel such hot regard . . . To have a self that I can *care* for, nature must first present me with some *object* interesting enough to make me instinctively wish to appropriate it for its *own* sake, and out of it to manufacture one of those material, social, or spiritual selves, which we have already passed in review . . . *The words ME, then, and*

SELF, so far as they arouse feeling and connote emotional worth, are OBJECTIVE designations, meaning ALL THE THINGS which have the power to produce in a stream of consciousness excitement of a certain peculiar sort . . .[6]

To sum up . . . we see no reason to suppose that self-love is primarily, or secondarily, or ever, love for one's mere principle of conscious identity. It is always love for something which, as compared with that principle, is superficial, transient, liable to be taken up or dropped at will.[7]

The hedonistic variant of egoism suffers from the difficulties cited above, plus a number peculiar to itself. To say that individuals seek pleasure makes no more sense than to say that they seek to further the self. The proposition that individuals amass wealth, attend the theater, hunt game, help neighbors in need, listen to music, or collect postage stamps because they regard these as means to an end which is pleasure, is a complete distortion of the experience involved. Nor is the situation helped by substituting the word "satisfaction," to which some hedonists have had recourse. This at any rate is now the nearly unanimous verdict of those engaged in the study of human nature.

The object of interest, that which is sought in any case of endeavor, is not pleasure or satisfaction—any more than it is the self—but some specific experience: listening to music, wielding financial power, enjoying security, or taking a chance. We like, we enjoy *these things* in and for themselves. Our desire for *them* incites our action. Satisfaction will accompany successful action. But the cause of the action is not this satisfaction or pleasure, or whatever we choose to call it. As Walter G. Everett aptly points out, "we find things pleasant because we desire them; we do not in the first instance conceive them to be pleasant and afterwards feel the desire."[8] Satisfaction is not an object of desire and therefore not a stimulus to action.[9] Rather it is a feeling state accompanying a satisfied desire or consummated action. According to Edward Tolman, "pleasantness and unpleasantness are . . . as conscious feelings, probably present in an introspective moment only. As conscious entities, they are undoubtedly artifacts of introspection."[10]

As noted earlier, egoism took a hedonistic form, among other reasons, because it seemed to many hedonists, particularly Bentham, that in the hedonistic calculus they had discovered the foundations for a science of conduct which might be comparable to physics. The spectacular success of physics dates from the time that men learned to relate (or, as some thought, reduce) qualitative differences to the quantitative variations of a single common denominator. Benthamite hedonists supposed that in pleasure they had found such a quantitative variable.

The general run of psychologists are hardly doing more than confirming the simplest introspection when they deny that pleasure and pain are amenable to measurement and computation. Ardent Benthamite that he was, John Stuart Mill nevertheless found it necessary to distinguish pleasures into kinds, and the truth is that pleasures and pains, whatever the role they play in conduct, are so diverse that one can no more add or subtract them than one can add a bushel of wheat and a sack of potatoes or subtract a cord of wood from a bolt of cloth. Even Bentham sometimes conceded this point, although he did not allow the concession to alter his general position. Nevertheless, the idea that feelings of pleasure and pain are commensurate and therefore amenable to mathematical calculation played a decisive part in leading men like W. Stanley Jevons and F. Y. Edgeworth to suppose that in hedonism they had found the basis for an exact science of economics.[11] If the foregoing analysis is sound, the doctrine of hedonism cannot sustain such a science.

The Spirit of Workmanship

Egoism, either in its general or in its specifically hedonistic form, implies a quietistic conception of human nature and a description of conduct as predominantly, if not exclusively, rational—particularly in those aspects that are the proper concern of economics. These assumptions are also rejected in the current understanding of human nature.

The rejection of psychological egoism does much to weaken the notion that human nature is inert and passive. At once attention is shifted from subjective and private feeling states to the objective situations with which we are in dynamic interaction. It then appears that activity is not a means to an end, not something carried on for the sake of something else, but a manifestation of the life-process itself. The description of human organisms as needing to be stimulated into activity and bribed into displaying initiative and inventiveness is, critics now contend, a libel on human nature. And yet it is this conception of human nature that lies at the basis of the system of incentives and rewards as understood by the classical liberals in general and the orthodox economists in particular. Thorstein Veblen put it with his usual irony:

> It is one of the commonplaces of the received economic theory that work is irksome . . . common sense opinion is well in accord with current theory on this head. . . . According to the common sense ideal, the economic beatitude lies in an unrestrained consumption of goods, without work; whereas the perfect economic affliction is unremunerated labor. . . . No one will accept the proposition when stated in this bald fashion, but . . . it is scarcely an overstatement of what is implied in the writings of eminent economists. If such an aversion to useful effort is an integral part of human nature, then the trail of the Edenic serpent should be plain to all men, for this is a unique distinction of the human species.[12]

Typical of the altered approach to human nature are the comments of John Dewey. Because Dewey, with Veblen, was one of the most influential American critics of the theoretical foundations of classical liberalism, his observations are worth pursuing at some length.

Ends or objectives function as foreseen consequences which influence deliberation and guide action, declared Dewey. But ends arise and function as redirecting pivots within action. The utilitarian who sets up pleasure (or, indeed, any end) as a kind of "outside and beyond," an external goal in which action culminates after it has been induced, misses this essential point. We may indeed *say* that every conscious act has an incentive or motive. But this is no more significant than to say that every event has a cause. Neither statement explains anything.

Those who attempt to defend the necessity of existing economic institutions as manifestations of human nature . . . take the saying to mean that nobody would do anything, or at least anything of use to others, without a prospect of some tangible reward. And beneath this false proposition there is another assumption still more monstrous, namely that man exists naturally in a state of rest so that he requires some external forces to set him into action.[13]

Confirmation of the position taken by John Dewey—if the position any longer needs confirmation—comes from an interesting quarter in the work of recent anthropologists. As noted before, natives of certain South Pacific islands, blessed with a generous natural environment, were for a long time described by armchair anthropologists as living in a state of blissful indolence. But, according to Melville Herskovits, "Even those primitive folk who inhabit that most romantic area, the South Sea Islands, work and work hard, despite the fact that, here, almost uniquely in the world, man is furnished by nature with practically all his needs . . ."[14]

The distinguished anthropologist, Edward Sapir, makes the same point concerning the work of the Andamanese.

In the manufacture of their weapons, utensils, and other articles, they . . . spend . . . hour after hour in laboriously striking pieces of iron with a stone hammer, for the purpose of forming spear or arrowheads, or in improving the shape of a bow, etc., even though there be no necessity, immediate or prospective, to stimulate them to such efforts. The incentive is evidently a spirit of emulation, each one priding himself on being able to produce work which will excel, or at least compare not unfavorably with, that of his neighbors.[15]

Recent epistemology has also thrown its weight against the quietism of eighteenth- and nineteenth-century psychology. "The mind," declares William McDougall, "is no longer regarded as a mere *tabula rasa* or magic mirror whose function it is passively to receive impressions from the outer world or to throw imperfect reflections of its objects . . . Nor are we any longer content to supplement this Lockian conception of mind with only two principles of intrinsic activity, that of the association and reproduction of ideas and that of the tendency to seek pleasure and to avoid pain."[16] His comment may be regarded as typical of recent trends.

One of the more salutary results of Darwinism has been a tendency among philosophers, especially among American pragmatists (e.g., Peirce, James, Mead, Dewey) to stress the functional role of mind in the life-process. The description of the knower as a passive spectator of reality is abandoned. Knowing, we are told, is more than a mere noting or beholding. The old psychology of the sensationalists and associationists is abandoned, and with this the description of mind as the passive recipient of external sense impressions and of knowledge as a product of the mechanical combination of these impressions, according to the laws of contiguity and similarity.[17]

"We are only just now commencing to appreciate how completely exploded is the psychology that dominated philosophy throughout the eighteenth and nineteenth centuries," wrote Dewey. The effect of the development of biology has been to reverse the picture of the mind as wholly acquiescent in knowing, he points out. Once knowing is understood as a function of the interaction of the organism and its environment, a new notion of experience and knowledge becomes possible. "Experience becomes an affair primarily of doing. The organism does not stand about, Micawberlike, waiting for something to turn up. It does not wait passive and inert for something to impress itself from without." So, too, knowledge is seen not as "something separate and self-sufficing," but as "involved in the process by which life is sustained and evolved."[18]

Whatever opposition may have been provoked by pragmatism on other scores, this account of the role of the knower in experience has won widespread acceptance.

When he adds all this up, the critic charges that psychological quietism is no more than a convenient rationalization of prevailing economic institutions and their shortcomings. The idea that men must be prodded into activity accords nicely, the critic points out, with the emphasis in a capitalist society on the profit motive. When, during the war, the President of

the United States proposed a twenty-five-thousand-dollar limitation on net earnings, Mr. Arthur Krock of the *New York
Times* echoed conservative opinion throughout the country
when he declared that "personal incentive, necessary to develop new instrumentalities of war as well as of peace, will
be deeply depressed . . ."[19] Similarly every attempt to tax or
otherwise limit profits and income is opposed on the ground
that initiative and enterprise will be discouraged.

There is an important sense, of course, in which this is
true. Most beneficiaries of an "acquisitive society," habituated
as they almost exclusively are to pecuniary institutions and
the pecuniary system of motivation, may indeed lose initiative
if deprived of the incentives which they have been taught to
regard as right and proper. But it is one thing to say that
men do not change long established habits easily; it is quite
another, to say that in the event of the destruction or drastic
modification of the profit motive, human nature would be
incapable in ordinary situations of displaying the energy,
initiative, and enterprise which have made our great industrial
civilization possible. It is the latter proposition which psychological quietism has been invoked to demonstrate.

In our society the hero is the tycoon. Teachers, writers,
artists, research workers, ministers, and the like are supposed
to be sentimental or marginal people who lend interest to the
façade of the social structure but are hardly "pillars of society" (i.e., the people of substance who pay the taxes, support
the churches, build the art museums, and belong to the best
clubs). Nevertheless, the fact is that many, if not most, able
men prefer to be healers, teachers, engineers, artists, scholars,
preachers, legislators, social workers—occupations which, save
in rare instances, are not noted for their pecuniary induce-
ments. And it is arguable that, in the final analysis, these are
the men who make the wheels of society turn.

These men labor for many things—security, power, prestige. Needs, habits, loyalties, ambitions keep them at labor
which is often tedious. But also they labor out of a joy in
workmanship, a sheer desire to engage in productive activity,
an incorrigible urge to be creative. It is this creative impulse
to which psychological quietism does violence.

If this is true today it was no less true yesterday. It is often said that the incentives provided by the profit system made possible the rapid expansion of production in the nineteenth century. No doubt the zeal of profit seekers imparted a dynamic character to the economy of England and America which would otherwise have been lacking. However, we must be on guard against the old *post hoc* fallacy for which the cock is the legendary symbol who believes his crowing ushers in the sunrise. Other significant developments besides the institutionalizing of the profit motive preceded the Industrial Revolution, notably the appearance of parliamentary government, the rise of Protestantism and the revolution in scientific thinking which came into its own in the seventeenth century. Certainly the great scientific revolution, crowned by the work of men like Copernicus, Kepler, Tycho Brahe, Galileo, and Newton is hardly to be imputed to the zeal of egoists striving to maximize gains at the market-place. Neither is the work in a later day of Faraday, Pasteur, Darwin, Maxwell, Lister, Helmholtz, Agassiz, and others, if we may accept the testimony of those who have studied their lives. They were, we are told, quite untouched by the profit motive.[20]

David Rockefeller, president of the nation's second biggest bank and described by *Time* as "one of that little group of men who sit at the hub of the world's wealthiest nation and . . . wield vast powers," recently explained his strenuous way of life thus: "I work because I enjoy work and because it is my duty to use whatever talent I have for a worthwhile purpose." Mr. Rockefeller may not know it, but these words are clearly subversive of the classical liberal creed.

Psychological quietism is more than a covert justification of the profit motive. It is a way of explaining the odiousness of work in terms of a congenital laziness—which is beyond remedy—thereby diverting attention from the disagreeable conditions under which most work is done—which are not beyond remedy. Perhaps the old charwoman was lazy whose epitaph is said to have read:

> Don't mourn for me, friends, don't weep for me never,
> For I'm going to do nothing for ever and ever.[21]

It is much more likely that she was a pathetic victim of inhuman exploitation.

The industrial system took men from the bench and field and chained them to the machine. It subjected them to the discipline of the factory and the time clock. It made automatons of them and sought no recompense for the drabness, monotony, and routine of factory labor. It cut them off from sunlight and fresh air and a chance to toil, quite literally, in their own gardens. It deprived them of a sense of participation in the productive process, even of their self-respect. No wonder that labor was "painful." In the words of Justice Felix Frankfurter, "The crucial fact of modern industry is its failure to use the creative qualities of men, its deadening monotony, and its excessive fatigue."[22]

Perhaps these have been the unavoidable results of industrialization in its early phases. Perhaps they were the price society paid for the rapid pace of industrialization. But surely the machine need not exact this price today. If mechanization means anything, it means that monotony can be reduced by shortening the workday, that heavy drudgery can be lessened, that men can be left with the energy to be creative. They would, moreover, have the will to be creative as well as the energy if they were treated not as robots but as men, not—to use a Kantian phrase—as means but as ends. This, however, is a matter of modifying social institutions and not of defying human nature.

The words of John Dewey are an apt summary:

It is "natural" for activity to be agreeable. It tends to find fulfillment, and finding an outlet is itself satisfactory, for it marks partial accomplishment. If productive activity has become so inherently unsatisfactory that men have to be artificially induced to engage in it, this fact is ample proof that the conditions under which work is carried on balk the complex of activities instead of promoting them, irritate and frustrate natural tendencies instead of carrying them forward to fruition. Work then becomes labor . . . Paradise Regained means the accumulation of investments such that a man can live upon their return without labor. There is, we repeat, too much truth in this picture. But it is not a truth concerning original human nature and activity. It concerns the form human impulses have taken under the influence of a specific social environment. If there are difficulties in the way of social alteration—as there certainly are—they do not lie in an original aversion of human nature to serviceable action, but in the historic conditions which have differentiated the work of the laborer for wage from that of the artist, adventurer, sportsman, soldier, administrator, and speculator.[23]

Dewey made the foregoing criticisms of the "current economic psychology" in 1921. Whatever change this psychology has undergone among orthodox economists, its prevalence among their lay cousins renders Dewey's trenchant criticism as timely today as it was the day he wrote it.

Psychological quietism has been used not only to divert attention from the disagreeable conditions which once made most work and still make much work objectionable; it is also invoked to excuse unemployment. Never was this better illustrated than in the now famous words of President Eisenhower's first Secretary of Defense, Charles Wilson, on the occasion of one of the several "recessions" which plagued the Eisenhower administration. While professing sympathy "for the jobless in surplus labor areas," he always "liked bird dogs better than kennel-fed dogs." "The bird dogs like to go out and hunt around for their food, but the kennel dogs just sit on their haunches and yelp," explained the late head of General Motors. One need not question Mr. Wilson's knowledge of man's best friend to conclude that he betrayed in these words an impressive and perhaps typical ignorance of man— all the more so in that the tempting analogy between kennel dogs and jobless workers left unexplained how millions, employed some months before and therefore presumably to be reckoned as bird dogs, had suddenly become transformed into the kennel variety.

One may venture a final comment: Psychological quietism, besides justifying the profit motive and providing an explanation of unemployment and the aversion to disagreeable employment which exculpates prevailing economic institutions, has served a third purpose. It was once widely used and is still invoked to argue against an adequate program of social security. But if the foregoing analysis has merit, men no more need the prodding of insecurity to display enterprise than they need the promise of great pecuniary reward. On the contrary, "freedom from want" might well provide an atmosphere in which the creative energies of man would find expression on a scale dwarfing everything that has gone before.

The Misuses of Reason

The rejection of psychological egoism undermined the influence of intellectualism, just as it discredited psychological quietism. This is not the place to review the successive retrenchments which men have recently made in their claims for Reason. The scope of these claims was once very wide indeed. Quite apart from the eighteenth- and nineteenth-century theoretical conception of the role of reason, on the practical level of conduct man was described as generally "taking thought," as acting for "sufficient reason," as deliberating carefully over ends and selecting the means consistent with their realization. From this it was easy enough to conclude that men not only follow their own interest but are the best judges of it—a theme which recurs in nearly all the writings of the classical liberals.

The assertion by later generations of liberals that rational man is a myth does not mean that they have embraced the cult of unreason. In disputing the claims of reason they are not defending the vicious relativism of the moral skeptic any more than the worse obscurantism of those who "think with their blood."[24] Neither do they deny that in some ways, if not in others, the earlier belief in the rationality of man made an important contribution to that growing respect for human dignity without which the Great Society would have remained ignominiously small. The contemporary liberal is simply calling attention to the irrational and nonrational in human conduct, concerning which recent psychology has accumulated an overwhelming mass of evidence, and, in particular, he is challenging certain uses to which the concept of rational man has been put.

One does not need to accept economic determinism to affirm with Marx that reason is often the servant of class interest; nor does one need to subscribe to pansexualism to agree with Freud that reason is far from master of the libido; nor does one have to accept his theory of instincts to agree with McDougall that "man is only a little bit reasonable and to a great extent very unintelligently moved in quite unreasonable ways."[25] These men and others have taught us that we fail to deal realistically with conduct unless we reckon with brute compulsions, vital drives, basic urges; unless we understand the role of such nonrational factors as customs and conventions in conduct; unless we recognize the part played by myths, stereotypes, ideologies, and the other tools for manipulating the masses, which have only a very little to do with the intellect and a great deal to do with the will and the emotions.

Why, from the point of view of the liberal, is all this important? In the first place, and from the most general point of view, proper recognition by the liberal of the irrational and nonrational factors in conduct renders them subject to use and control.[26] It has sometimes been said that liberals who insist upon limiting the claims of reason have played into the hands of fascists and their kind, who make a cult of unreason. Quite the contrary is the case. To ignore the factors which restrict the scope of reason is to yield the rabble-rouser a monopoly in their use. Those who fight on the side of the angels are in an uneven contest, indeed, if they proceed on the assumption that man is wholly or predominantly rational and leave to the forces of evil the manipulation of the nonrational instruments of social control.[27]

Quite apart from this general consideration, liberals have concentrated their fire on the uses which have been made of intellectualism in the field of political economy. Egoism and hedonism led easily to a preoccupation with man as a forward-looking and end-seeking creature. The self-satisfaction or pleasure sought lies in the future and, in any case, no egoists or hedonists contended that the nature of man required him to seek his *immediate* gratification. That interest is enlightened and that men weigh and calculate pleasures and pains before embarking upon a course of action is what distinguishes man from the beast, according to the classical liberal.

In economic theory the result was something like that described by P. T. Homan in discussing the work of the distinguished orthodox economist, John Bates Clark. In Homan's words,

Stripped of technical jargon, the man presented to view is one forever taking counsel with himself how he may attain a maximum of pleasure; forever debating whether he will be best served by another bushel of potatoes or another rabbit, whether he shall go fishing or start a new canoe, whether a lean-to to his hut or ten hours' additional leisure will constitute the greater benefit. It is not permitted that these matters resolve themselves into any habitual routine. Every choice of one thing against another, of the present against the future, of work against leisure, must be rationally made in pursuit of the maximum of personal satisfaction. This is in no sense a parody, but expresses the implicit or explicit assumption of the system we are examining.[28]

Likewise, Wesley C. Mitchell, writing in 1910, called attention to the psychological unreality of most discussions of the theory of value in economics. Bargainers are usually described, he pointed out, as coming to the market with clearly formulated ideas of how many units of the good in their possessions they will give to get a successive unit of the other good. "The artificiality of the whole picture is further enhanced by using diagrams to show the varying marginal utilities of goods and the varying disutilities of successive hours of labor."[29]

The classicist's account of economic conduct is undermined not merely because pleasure does not prove amenable to calculation. The most recent generation of orthodox economists has specifically repudiated the hedonistic calculus. Lionel Robbins, for example, believes that economics need concern itself only with acts of choice—of choice, that is, among the "alternative uses" of "scarce means."[30] The economist need not be concerned with addition or subtraction of hedonistic magnitudes but with "the fact that individuals can arrange their preferences in an order and, in fact, do so."[31] Robbins is clearly no hedonist. Even so his account of economic behavior, like that of all neoclassicists, is still engrossed with man as a calculating animal who sets up a schedule of preferences and then governs himself by it. This is not to say that when men buy and sell they do not in a great many instances engage in a careful calculation of profits and losses. It is to say that *economics in its classical and neoclassical expressions has excessively emphasized such transactions, to the neglect and exclusion of activity whose economic bearing is at least as significant and often a great deal more significant than that concerned with the balancing of utilities against costs.* For, while the economic theorist takes rational economic behavior for granted, what happens in the real world?

Is it rational or libidinal men to whom the advertisers appeal when they display a nearly nude bathing beauty smoking the world's "mildest" cigarette? Is it rational or paranoid man who during the war complained bitterly and believed honestly that the government was enslaving him, while he continued to applaud his favorite government detractor, worshiped freely, voted at regular elections—and more than doubled his net profits?[32] Are those rational men, even if they are in one sense calculators, who accumulate dollar symbols far beyond the amount needed to satisfy any other needs which they contemplate, or are they, as one economist suggests, more akin "to the mentally unbalanced who collect bits of paper and hide them in their chamber"?[33]

It was not rational man engaging in a shrewd calculation of profit and loss whom Mr. Sewell Avery incarnated when he defied the government's war directives to Montgomery Ward; as a result of public resentment the sales of his company suffered a precipitate decline while the sales of the rival firm of Sears Roebuck enjoyed a corresponding increase. It was not as *homo economicus* that the elder Henry Ford acted when he declared that he would shut down his plant rather than deal with the union. It is arguable that Mr. Avery and Mr. Ford were refusing upon mature reflection to do something they regarded as inconsistent with some conception of their future advantage which they had first carefully defined and now forthrightly sought. A more likely explanation would reckon with the institutional forces that had produced Mr. Avery and Mr. Ford, with their long established habit patterns and their love of power. We might even find that, in their own way, Messrs. Avery and Ford were crusaders, not calculators.

Neither are they "human calculators"—despite their occupation as bank clerks—who refuse to avail themselves of pay increases which union membership affords because, along with most other white-collar workers, they regard labor unions as *déclassé*. Nor, as Malthus himself reminded us, are they calculators, who, while having the benefit of clergy, beget children without the benefit of cost accountants or even the counsel of a "planned parenthood" clinic. Or is it a calculation of costs and benefits which prompts a weary woman, vacation bound and hence not recognizable by her uniform, to respond to the Pullman porter's urgent call for a nurse to help a suddenly stricken passenger. Even Balzac, so mercenary, we are told, that he calculated the sale price of each line as he wrote his love letters, corrected his works with excruciating care, though they were just as salable in the first draft.

The case against the orthodox economists' "rational man" may be put in two ways. In the first place it may be contended that the assumption of rationality fails to describe man even when he "goes to the market." In the second place it may be contended that the market activities of men are only one of many other significant economic activities in which they engage and that the reduction of economics to "pecuniary logic" ignores important areas of economic interest. This latter is the burden of Rexford Tugwell's assertion that the economists' study of the producer and consumer "cannot be confined to their transient appearances in the spotlight of the market place." This means, Tugwell continues, that economists "are to say what it is the industrial system does to men and to define what it is men have a right to expect from industry."[34]

The point which Tugwell makes is a crucial one. Its preoccupation with the rationality of economic behavior focuses the attention of classical economics on only one aspect of economic life and that a highly specialized one. Social welfare, while it remains the ultimate ground of ethical appeal, plays no part in the deliberations of economists. The utilitarian economists, declares Veblen, "make exchange value the central feature of their theories rather than the conduciveness of industry to the community's material welfare."[35]

There can indeed be no a priori objection to abstracting man's rational behavior at the market from his other activities and confining attention to the former. All sciences proceed by just such abstraction. But in connection with the process of abstraction, by which every science delimits its subject, one must always ask: is the abstraction a useful one—does it, that is to say, yield the increased power to predict and control, which is the aim of all science?

The current critic of classical economics answers this question in the negative. As evidence of the barren abstractness of their science, he points to the way in which the attention of orthodox economists is inadvertently transferred to "frictions" and "exceptions" (i.e., situations not anticipated by and incomprehensible in terms of their postulates) and away from the "normal," which is left more and more to the "long run." "All things being equal," we might not have wild fluctuations in the business cycle, monopolistic price-fixing, etc.; but an economist who expects to be taken seriously will study these even if he neglects the "norm."

Realistic economists will insist, moreover, that economics concern itself with more than de facto schedules of wants or preferences, as these express themselves in buyers' bids and sellers' offers; economics must study why men have such wants and how these wants change.[36] Also, instead of taking the pecuniary phase of the economic interest for granted, they will want to know how it affects the production and distribution of goods—precisely how, for example, production is affected by the fact that in a pecuniary society the making of goods is subordinate to the making of money. They will address themselves to other questions: How does the corporate organization of industry affect the efficiency of production? What are the economic effects of advertising? What are the consequences in terms of efficient production and consumer satisfaction of the presence in a given industry of both public and private enterprise? How is labor efficiency affected by the requirements of the factory system? What are the economic consequences of various methods of public control and administration? To what extent does private enterprise shift part of the costs of production to third persons and to society as a whole?[37]

It would be doing them an obvious injustice to charge that orthodox economists do not concern themselves with these questions. But by their own conception of economics, when they do so they are not acting as economists, and, in any event, such concern is regarded as incidental to the main work of the science which "treats phenomena from the standpoint of price."

Critical Conclusions

It is now possible to conclude this discussion of the influence upon orthodox economics of its psychological preconceptions. In the judgment of the so-called "critical school,"[38] the hedonistic-rationalistic bias of the orthodox economists led them to frame their science in a rigid deductive cast, thereby imparting to it that abstractness and arid scholastic quality that was once the bane of the natural sciences. Instead of attending to man as he behaves in the here and now of concrete circumstance, they described how man would behave *if*, propelled by pleasure and repelled by pain and careful to calculate the units of each so as to procure a favorable balance, he competed freely in an economy based upon private ownership. Thus was born "economic man," a computative creature presumably free of the play of those causal influences which it is ordinarily the business of science to investigate, a constant, always and forever the same, amid the ebb and flow of changing circumstance.[39] By assuming that men *must* act in a given way, namely after the model of a hypothetical businessman exclusively absorbed in balancing profits against costs, they spared themselves the task of explaining why men act sometimes in this way, more often in other ways. Instead of a search for the causal antecedents of conduct found in institutions as they grow and decay, brute compulsions as they are released or restrained, social conventions as they are accepted or rejected, they elaborated the logical consequences of an abstract definition suggested by the observation of human behavior in the very special, relatively novel, and possibly fugitive set of circumstances which a small part of the world presented in the eighteenth and nineteenth centuries.[40] These were, of course, the set of circumstances which included free competition, private ownership of the means of production, and so forth.

Accordingly, orthodox economics was driven by its hedonistic preconceptions into a slavish imitation of the Newtonian science of the seventeenth century, concerned with fixed universal laws and their implications.[41] The result was a science whose approach was static and mechanical rather than genetic and evolutionary, a science more like an internally coherent logical system than a set of generalizations about the real world.

Another closely related and profoundly important consequence must be noted. It is already indicated in what has been said above. To take as explanatory principles traits of human nature, which are themselves products of a specific institutional environment, and to treat these as static instead of evolving phases of conduct is to render the prevailing order immutable.

When the profit motives becomes "selfishness," when the act of exchange becomes a reflection of the light of reason playing upon our preferences, when the aversion to odious conditions of labor becomes "indolence," all these are placed beyond the reach of inquiry and causal explanation; since they are manifestations of original human nature, criticism and evaluation are quite as pointless as an appraisal of the law of gravity. *The result of these psychological preconceptions in classical economics is that the existing system of property rights and pecuniary incentives is taken for granted.* Thus, if the "science of wealth" did not quite become, as Cliffe Leslie charged, a science for wealth, it often served the latter purpose.

Are we to conclude that the psychological creed of classical liberalism is no more than a rationalization of the interests of the middle classes? Such a judgment would be unfair. The creed under examination marked a first attempt to understand the social and economic aspects of conduct in terms of general principles and systematic conceptions instead of rules of thumb and random conjecture. It functioned as an effective solvent of hardened and outworn custom and archaic law. It focused attention upon human experience, however limited, thereby rescuing the study of social institutions from the turgid waters of metaphysics and theology. All this is applauded by current critics.

If the psychological creed under discussion led the orthodox economists to concentrate on wealth to the neglect of welfare,[42] they and particularly their cousins, the utilitarians, often displayed a great zeal for the public good. The utilitarians and their numerous followers were, indeed, mistaken in the assumption that "the greatest good to the greatest number" was a formula that solved social problems or even served as a guide to specific social policy: Bentham used it to defend private property as others have used it to denounce private property. The utilitarians were mistaken also in their attempts to found this formula upon hedonism. But there is no substitute for the "greatest happiness to the greatest number," as the ultimate justification of policy. In the end, what is done must commend itself in terms of human happiness. If hedonism led utilitarians to this conclusion, so much to its credit.

So, too, with the proposition that every individual is the best judge of his own interest. When it takes the form that each man, "gifted with mature reason," *knows* his best interest or knows better than anyone else what he will receive from a given exchange, the proposition is clearly false. The use of this intellectualist fallacy as an apology for the free market and as an argument against social intervention is repudiated by the contemporary critic. At the same time he will grant that the individual should be the final judge of his interest. In the end there is no substitute for the individual in the determination of his preferences. His approval or disapproval is the conclusive test. Here the classical liberal proposes the emancipation of individual tastes from external dictation, a proposal which every contemporary liberal will approve.

In the final summation, however, the science of those who

have preached the classical liberal creed has been, in Carlyle's happy phrase, "the supplement of their practice." This science almost invariably suggested an approach to private owner- ship, taxation, wages, social security, and public control that coincided with middle-class interests. "Benthamism," a warm admirer like Dicey confesses, "was fundamentally a middle- class creed."[43] Such subordination of psychological generali- zation (to still confine ourselves to this branch of the science of man) to class interest is, after all, nothing new. One may suppose that there was some connection between Aristotle's discovery that some men are by nature slaves and the interests of the Greek upper classes. The psychological attributes have changed; new class interests have appeared. But the appeal to nature remains now, as in the day of Aristotle, a favorite device for bulwarking the existing order and opposing social change.

Classical liberalism can no longer claim acceptance by insisting on its derivation from immutable natural law. This does not mean that classical liberalism must be rejected along with the psychological creed upon which it took its stand. It means that the basis of discussion must be shifted from the psychological to the institutional level. The economic and political aspects of classical liberalism must now be judged on their merits. The appeal must now be directed, not to inexorable natural law, but to results, consequences.

Reading some of the orthodox economic tracts of the nine- teenth century, one gets the impression that the unavailability of food, clothing, and shelter to large numbers of the popu- lation is a matter of sentimental and subordinate concern; the main object is not to do violence to human nature by departing from the principles of orthodox economics. Pre- cisely the same impression is left by those who strenuously opposed large-scale relief in the 1930's and the postwar re- cessions; many appeared to believe that a balanced budget is more important than a balanced diet.

The contemporary liberal, on the other hand, insists that institutions be judged in terms of their consequences for human welfare. If they fail by this test, he will not say that human nature forbids their alteration. Having listened to professional psychologists and discovered the tentative and limited character of their conclusions, he does not share the assurance with which conservatives so often generalize about human nature. But this much he has learned and does know: human nature is compatible with considerable variation in our institutional arrangements, and many of these arrangements have yet to be explored; there is, moreover, no unbreakable link between human nature and the institutions which have given the commercial and industrial middle classes their position of hegemony in the Great Society. As Thoreau tells us in *Walden*, ". . . man's capacities have never been measured; nor are we to judge of what he can do by any precedents, so little has been tried."

Chapter 8

"Frictions" and "Exceptions"

THE ECONOMIC WORLD of the classicists is sometimes known as an economy based upon production for profit, sometimes as a price or market economy. Actually both characterizations are essential. The owners of the means of production, or their agents, must first give the signal to proceed before the economic mechanism can move, and they will not give this signal unless they anticipate a profit. Merely to dwell upon the profit motive, however, is to fail to distinguish between the capitalist economy of the classicists and such highly regimented capitalist economies as that of the Third Reich. The difference is emphasized when we refer to the economic systems of Ricardo and Senior and Marshall as a price economy. Before turning to some of the basic criticisms of a price or market economy, it may be well to recapitulate the claims which have been made for it.

In any economy other than a price economy individual decisions concerning what shall be produced and consumed are governed by a plan which, however formulated and for whatever purpose, determines how the factors of production (labor, land, capital) shall be employed and how the goods which are produced shall be distributed. In every society, of course, the central economic question of what to produce and how to distribute what is produced must somehow be decided. But it need not be decided, so the classical liberal contends, by vesting such vast powers in the membership of a single or even of several agencies. On the contrary, it can be decided by distributing these powers among all producers and consumers. The means by which this may be accomplished is the mechanism of price.

In a free market, price, responding to the law of supply and demand, tells producers when to produce more of a commodity and when less. For when the demand is great, the price will rise and producers will find it profitable to produce more. They in turn will offer more for the capital, labor, and other factors necessary for the production of that commodity, thereby guiding the appropriate productive resources to the use for which they are wanted. On the other hand, if supply exceeds demand, if, in other words, producers are making something that is not wanted, they are soon warned. For prices will fall and will continue to fall until supply and demand are in equilibrium.

Thus the price mechanism achieves without duress the solution of one of the fundamental economic problems in a society; how so to allocate productive resources (scarce means) as to realize the closest possible coincidence between what is produced and what is wanted. Most people want more than their limited incomes permit them to buy—this is freely granted—but, given the existing distribution of incomes, a price system is the only method by which those who have these limited incomes can spend them as they please. The universal conviction that incomes should be higher must not blind us to the fact that they have been growing higher and that meanwhile the mechanism of price, operating in a free economy, enables the possessors of these incomes to gear the productive system to their preferences. This is the significance of von Mises' coronation of the consumer in a market or price economy:

Within the market society the working of the price mechanism makes the consumers supreme. They determine through the prices they pay and through the amount of their purchases both the quantity and quality of production. They determine directly the prices of consumers' goods, and thereby indirectly the price of all material factors of production and the wages of all hands employed.

. . . In that endless rotating mechanism [i.e., a market society] the entrepreneurs and capitalists are the servants of the consumers. The consumers are the masters, to whose whims the entrepreneurs and capitalists must adjust their investments and methods of production. The market chooses the entrepreneurs and the capitalists, and removes them as soon as they prove failures. The market is a democracy in which every penny gives a right to vote and where voting is repeated every day.[1]

The Consumer: Sovereign or Subject?

If the consumer fails to recognize himself in the royal raiment in which von Mises has attired him, this is because the real world is as far from the smoothly working mechanism just described as the frog in the Grimm fairy tale is from the prince.

That consumers should be free, with certain exceptions,[2] to spend their incomes as they please is a laudable ideal to which all people who believe in democracy are committed. But it must be noted, to begin with, that great numbers of people are prevented by their limited income from exercising such freedom of choice in a real or significant sense. For those people whose income is exhausted in purchasing the simplest fundamentals of life, freedom of choice has a hollow ring. It must be meager consolation to the millions of families with an annual income of $3,000 or less to learn that they could spend an income of $20,000, if they had such an income, any way they pleased. The man who spends his last eighty dollars making a payment or paying the rent on his house is not likely to bless the freedom which would permit him to buy a suit of clothes instead. Freedom of choice presupposes an income large enough to open up real alternatives. If the free market as we have known it results in a distribution of incomes such that large numbers are limited to purchasing the basic necessities of life or less, then just that many do not enjoy real freedom of choice.

With incomes distributed as unevenly as they are, freedom of choice means that the resources of society are often allocated to the production of the most inane extravagances while basic needs go unsatisfied. Von Mises may describe the market as "a democracy in which every penny gives a right to vote," but others will wonder whether the system of plural voting which results from so many pennies falling to so few can properly be called "democracy."

If freedom of choice presupposes the availability of real alternatives, it also presupposes the possession by a free agent of a substantial measure of knowledge concerning the alternatives among which he is attempting to choose. This knowledge must be of two kinds: a free agent must know something about the nature of the alternatives themselves—brands of food, makes of motor cars, kinds of dentifrice, etc.—as he goes about satisfying his preferences; he must know also (and this kind of knowledge is too often taken for granted) what his preferences really are. Critics of the market economy contend that in the real world, as distinguished from the ideal world defined by orthodox economists, a variety of forces conspire to prevent the consumer from having either kind of knowledge in adequate amount.

In the first place, buying and selling is no longer a simple affair of horse trading. A knowledge of the commodities he buys requires a technical competence which is far beyond the average consumer. Laborious progress has been made in the direction of honest labeling, but labeling is still far from informative. A proposal to require the grade-labeling of canned goods, to cite one example, was successfully defeated by producers. As the Kefauver Committee has shown, not even physicians can penetrate beyond the brand names by which manufacturers of pharmaceuticals keep the public in ignorance of what it is buying. Even interest and insurance rates, once susceptible of easy comparisons, are now described so deviously that the consumer is unable to make intelligent choices among alternatives. In any case, it must not be supposed that informing the consumer is merely a matter of labeling. Each trade has its tricks, and the average buyer has no way of knowing the particular ruse by which he has been victimized. Meanwhile, the ubiquitous art of the advertiser reduces even more the consumer's chance of determining the true nature of the alternatives which are presented to him. It is clear that, confronted by bafflingly complex and artfully misrepresented merchandise, the consumer all too often lacks the knowledge indispensable to genuinely free choice.

Perhaps worse, the consumer is often confused concerning his own true preferences. This is a matter of considerable significance, which necessarily escapes those who, like Professor von Mises, describe the producer as the obedient servant of the consumer. They seem to miss the point that producers are engaged in influencing our preferences as well as satisfying them, and that, moreover, consumers are not the rational men described by the classicists. The fact is that in his effort to alter what economists call our demand schedules in his favor, the producer often has us so confused that we do not know what our demands really are. American consumers were the target of approximately $11 billion worth of advertising in 1959, not to mention the cost of other forms of high-pressure salesmanship. They can hardly avoid being confused and stunned by such a barrage, so much so that they are no longer able to recognize what their preferences really are.

The point will be developed in some detail later;[3] here it need only be recorded that there is a note of fantasy in the statement that the sovereign consumer has willed the prevailing disposition of our resources—the treasure spent on advertising and the trifles on medical research, the production of luxury articles for "conspicuous display" and the failure to build sufficient housing. It must be evident too that deliverance from such absurdities lies not in forcing people to consume what an enlightened person or group of persons believes they ought to want—it involves providing those conditions under which people may find out what they themselves want and recognize clearly the things which satisfy these wants. These conditions, the liberal argues, are far from universally present in the market economy as we know it.

Another, more formidable weapon employed against consumers is the power to regulate prices and output. By common consent, the producer is the obedient servant of the consumer in a market economy only if free competition prevails. If the producer can control prices, it will be he and not merely the buyer who determines what shall be consumed, for what consumers buy is influenced not only by their wants but by the price of getting their wants satisfied. How do producers control prices? "This can be achieved either by fixing standard or minimum prices, which the firms concerned agree not to undercut, or by fixing a standard of minimum output, which they agree not to exceed. The effect is much the same; for whoever fixes output indirectly fixes price and whoever fixes price indirectly fixes output. So much can be sold, at such and such a price; so large an output will fetch such and such prices."[4]

The point is an extremely important one. The chief argument against planned production is that the actual purchases of consumers are the only reliable guide to their preferences. However, before such purchases can be said to be a true reflection of their preferences, consumers must be able to buy at the most economical price. If building materials are selling at artificially inflated values in consequence of price-fixing agreements in the building industry and automobiles are selling at highly competitive prices (just barely enough to pay the cost of attracting and borrowing capital, paying wage and salary costs, etc.), expenditures on houses and automobiles are not a measure of the relative value which consumers place upon these two commodities. Obviously, in such an event, automobiles would be selling in much larger quantity in relation to houses than would be the case if building materials could be bought on a competitive market at the most economical possible price.

For years (until 1958) the so-called Big Three, fearful of jeopardizing the market for costly cars, ridiculed the notion that Americans might prefer a small, inexpensive motor car to the oversized, overstyled, overpowered machines which they had cajoled the public into buying; and, since they controlled the market, there was no way of ascertaining consumer preference in this allegedly competitive field until foreign imports, abetted by a clamorous American "independent," finally forced a change.

"We can, in fact, only draw conclusions about what pattern of production best pleases consumers," writes Barbara Wootton, "when we are sure that all the articles offered for sale are being produced in the most economical possible way and offered at the most economical possible price."[5] But the fact is that the state of perfect or even approximate competition, in which alone the minimum economic price can be determined, does not exist except in textbooks.

Competition, Free and Fettered

The dubious sovereignty of the consumer suggests a broader examination of monopolistic practices, a kind of interference with the "system of natural liberty" to which the classical economists gave scant attention. They did indeed concern themselves with monopoly; but, in the era of relatively small-scale production with which they were familiar their chief concern was with legal monopolies, i.e., monopolies based upon government grants of privilege rather than private monopolies, produced, in the words of the Supreme Court, "by the act of mere individuals." The father of the system of natural liberty, Adam Smith, did indeed observe that "People of the same trade seldom meet together, even for merriment and diversion, but the conversation ends in a conspiracy against the public, or in some contrivance to raise prices." He added, "It is impossible indeed to prevent such meetings, by any law which could either be executed, or would be consistent with liberty and justice."[6] Such behavior was considered irregular and deplorable. All the same, Adam Smith and his followers did not waver in regarding the competitive system as the natural order.

The subject of monopolistic practices has been so thoroughly explored by others that only a summary statement is needed here. In the foregoing discussion monopolistic practices have been considered primarily from the point of view of the claim that purchases are an index to the preferences of consumers. But the prevalence of monopolistic practices has equally damaging consequences for claims concerning the role of producers in a market economy.

The description of a market economy on its production side is of a system into which individuals with ambition and ideas may freely enter, provided they have accumulated or attracted enough capital to launch the enterprise. The enterprise once launched, its future depends upon its relative merits, that is to say, on the approval of the buying public. Since this approval will be given to the best product selling at the cheapest price, it must follow that producers in vying with one another for public favor will seek more and more efficient ways of producing a more and more attractive article. The result should be an endless flow of new products, new techniques, new inventions.

Clearly, enough of this has actually come to pass to make the account plausible. There are many American industries in which competitive relations prevail. This is true of much of agriculture, lumber, coal mining, petroleum production, fishing, the textile and garment industry, and the boot, shoe, and leather industries. Although the rubber industry has been concentrated, it has also been competitive, and this is true likewise of the production of many household appliances and food products. In many other industries the presence of more than one or two or several producers suggests the prevalence of competition. Moreover, the effects of competition are suggested by gradual reductions, the war period and other periods of rapid inflation excepted, in the price of articles like motorcars and in the sustained rate of technological progress. Most striking evidence of the latter is the American record of output in manufacturing per man-hour, which more than doubled between 1919 and 1939. But the evidence may be misleading and generalizations from it deceptive.

It must be clear at the outset that in many industries the cost of financing highly mechanized establishments engaged in mass production is so great that only a very few can support such an undertaking. John Stuart Mill foresaw this long ago. In the *Principles* he wrote that "If a business can only be advantageously carried on by a large capital, this in most countries limits so narrowly the class of persons who can enter into the employment, that they are enabled to keep their rate of profit above the general level." The number of such businesses and the amount of capital required have obviously increased greatly since Mill's day. *Fortune* magazine, hardly biased against big business, finds that "in many industries a man must be a success—i.e., big—before he can even enter the competitive struggle." It adds, "By the same token, the established corporation in such industries has economic advantages that free it from many of the risks of competition and render its profits relatively secure."[7]

To be sure, from the point of view of establishing or preserving a regime of competition, the field of enterprise need not be accessible to everyone who is ambitious and fancies himself able. But there must be enough in the field so that, in the words of economist Clair Wilcox, no "single seller . . .

or number of sellers acting in unison control enough of the supply of a broadly defined commodity to enable them to augment their profit by limiting output and raising price."[8] Also, those who are in the field must not act in such concert that the effect achieved is the same or nearly the same as if there were only one.

A great many important fields of enterprise in America, as elsewhere, do not satisfy these conditions. They may vary from fields in which there are one (monopoly in the literal sense) to two (duopoly) to many (oligopoly) producers. Those who are in the field may vary their practice from rigidly excluding all newcomers to admitting those who "play the game." But the evidence is incontrovertible that most of the major fields of enterprise are either carefully fenced off to keep out intruders or, if there are gates, everything is done to avert rivalries that might benefit consumers at the expense, fancied or real, of producers.

A great government-sponsored study of monopoly and competition in American business and industry was undertaken in the late 'thirties by the Temporary National Economic Committee. It found that, although most of the early trusts (e.g., Standard Oil, American Can, International Harvester, etc.) no longer enjoy exclusive control of their fields, one company in each field controlled all, or nearly all, of the nation's supply of aluminum, nickel, magnesium, shoe machinery, glass-container machinery, and scientific precision glass; and provided nearly all of the domestic telephone service and all of the transoceanic service. Other instances are cited, including "important segments" of the markets for international cable and radio communication, oil pipe line, railway freight transportation, and transoceanic aviation.

There are many markets in which two firms are cited as being in complete control: "Two companies [now one] provide all of the domestic telegraph service; two control all of the submarine cables between the United States and several foreign countries; two offer the only radio-telegraph service to many points abroad. Two companies in each field account for all, or nearly all, of the nation's supply of bananas, of plate glass and safety glass, of bulbs, tubing and rod, and bases for electric lamps, of electric accounting machines, of railroad air brakes . . ."9

Such cases, in which one or two producers control nine-tenths or more of the supply in their fields are not as significant, however, as the industries in which a single or several firms govern the market, even though they produce a much smaller proportion of the total output. "Among 1,807 products, representing nearly half, by number, and more than half, by value, of those included in the Census of Manufacturers for 1937, there were 291, or more than one-sixth of those in the sample, in which the leading producer accounted for 50 to 75 percent of the total supply." The same census reported that twenty-eight commodities were being produced in each case by only three firms, and that "among the 275 categories included in the Census of Manufacturers for 1935, there were 54 in which the 4 largest firms produced more than two-thirds, by value, of the total supply." Finally, among the 1,807 products in the sample for 1937, five to ten firms accounted in each case for the whole supply of 382 products.10 The most recent industrial census discloses a similar pattern.

As Mr. Berle has pointed out in his *20th Century Capitalist Revolution,* while American law forbids monopoly,

. . . it has sanctioned and even encouraged a system, industry by industry, in which a few large corporations dominate the trade. Two or three, or at most, five, corporations will have more than half the business, the remainder being divided among a greater or lesser number of smaller concerns who must necessarily live within the conditions made for them by the 'Big Two' or 'Big Three' or 'Big Five' as the case may be.11

What are the devices by which the multiplication of producers in any given field is avoided? Often mergers are preferred. Often the producer will establish a quasi-monopoly by creating through advertising a false sense of difference in the public mind between his own commodity (e.g., a brand of gasoline or cigarette) and other similar commodities. With the outlawing of some of the cruder practices of the nineteenth century, a favored device has been the patent system which may give to a single or to several firms complete control over basic processes without which an enterprise in that field cannot be successfully operated. Often the entrenched or dominant firm will be in a position to exclude or select newcomers by virtue of its control, through exclusive contract or through ownership, of indispensable equipment or raw-material supplies. Often distributors are required to sign exclusive contracts. Methods vary with time and place, the moods of lawmakers, the machinations of lawyers, and the personnel of the Attorney General's office.

The phenomenon of merger calls for special comment, not only because it is commonly supposed that consolidation is outlawed by the Clayton Act, but because here is an interesting example of how legislation can be reduced, in the words of the Federal Trade Commission, to a "virtual nullity." Although the Clayton Act forbids corporations from purchasing the stock of competing firms, its provisions do not govern firms not engaged in interstate commerce and, more importantly, the act did not forbid one corporation from *purchasing the physical property* of another, until the tardy passage in 1950 of the Kefauver-Celler Anti-merger Act. That is why, in a 1948 report, the Federal Trade Commission declared that "the fundamental objective of the antitrust laws is plainly circumvented."[12] The anti-merger bill, an amendment to the Clayton Act, was blocked in Congress for five years, curiously opposed, it so happens, by some of the most vehement spokesmen for "free" private enterprise. The door is still not completely closed.

Even though there be a multiplicity of producers, competition among them is often subverted by a bewildering variety of collusive practices. Price agreements, although forbidden as conspiracies in restraint of trade, are common, with the result that producers may compete in salesmanship and advertising for customers, but act collectively in all matters concerning the price and quality of their products. The agreement need not be stated. By means of price leadership, basing-point systems, uniform cost-accounting systems, open-price systems, and the like, producers tell each other what they are charging and end up like "little steel" and the United States Steel Corporation, by playing follow-the-leader. This is the basis of that "higher telepathy," as Walton Hamilton calls it, by which General Electric and Westinghouse, to take another typical example, arrive at identical schedules of prices.[13] When Professor Hamilton used this term he could not predict that twenty years later, in 1960, ranking officials of both corporations would ignominiously end up in jail for blatantly conspiring to fix prices.

In some industries competition is avoided by dividing the market, each firm confining itself to its allotted area or limiting itself to an agreed-upon quota. Such pooling arrangements, as they are called, closely resemble the cartel arrangements prevalent in European countries. More recently pools and other cartel arrangements have been effected through trade associations, industrial institutes, and the like, which, while purporting to engage in activities of common interest to their members without interfering with competition, do in fact bring prices and production under common control. Despite the Clayton Act, competition is often averted as a result of common ownership of the stock of ostensibly different firms. Interlocking directorates, the "friendly" relations of directors from two firms in a given field, who sit together as board members of another firm in a different field, "Gary dinners," holding-company arrangements of various kinds, all serve to achieve a harmony that is quite remote from the "natural harmonies" of the orthodox economists. If "independents" refuse to "play ball," price wars, patent controls, special legislation, and financial pressures of assorted kinds can bring them into line. Many state governments have actually co-operated in price-fixing through so-called "fair trade" laws.

The intention here is not to criticize. Some of the enterprises referred to can boast convincing records of efficiency and price reduction. It may be that "what helps business helps you," or to borrow from former Secretary of Defense Wilson again, that "what's good for General Motors is good for the country." Moreover, competition is by no means an unmixed blessing; it often makes for duplication of effort and facilities, it encourages unscrupulous practices, it leads to the destruction of irreplaceable resources. *So far the main concern has been to show that one may not speak of our world of economic Brobdignagians as though it were a world of little men each striving to outdo the other.* It required the imagination of a pre-Roosevelt Supreme Court and the "due process" clause of an innocent constitutional amendment to transform these agglomerates into persons; it requires a folklore buttressed by the vast powers of press, television, and radio, of full-page advertisements and spot announcements, to represent the private enterprise in which they engage as "free." The plain fact is that the productive side of our economy is only in part a world open to all comers and only in part a world in which producers are in actual competition with one another. For the rest it is a closed world, where men lead double lives, talking and perhaps believing in competition, but acting in concert and collusion.

What are the effects upon producers who have achieved this relative immunity from the rivalries of the economic world? Are they still spurred to turn out the best possible product, to seek the most economical methods of production, to explore new frontiers of technology, and to pass on the benefits of their effort to the public? Orthodox economic theory requires a negative answer, to the unrelieved embarrassment of the monopolists who speak in its name. Apart from orthodox theory the issue is a subject of much debate, but professional economists have interpreted the data so variously and shifted their position so often that the issue is in danger of becoming thoroughly confused.[14]

Professor Galbraith (who may be classified as a liberal despite a pose of aloof neutrality) regards oligopolistic arrangements as actually encouraging innovation. Taking his cue from Schumpeter's well-known theory of innovation,[15] he argues that the large corporation, provided it is not the only enterprise in the field, is "an almost perfect instrument for inducing technical change."[16] This is so because (*a*) only the very large corporation can command the great resources necessary in these times for financing research and development and absorbing the cost of failures; and (*b*) only firms commanding a large segment of the market will find the reward of innovation sufficient to justify the cost, especially since most innovations are easily copied by imitators. Actually, so this argument goes, control over prices encourages innovation by insuring "that the resulting gains will not be passed on to the public by imitators . . . before the outlay for the development can be recouped.[17]

Others take a different view. Professor J. M. Clark, while he agrees with much that Galbraith says, cautions that "when he [Galbraith] . . . recommends throwing competition out the window in favor of a substitute, he is surely overplaying his hand."[18] Professor W. R. Maclaurin, an authority on the economics of technological innovation, while conceding that some degree of monopoly is essential to technological progress, declares: "My own conviction is that any industry today which fails to incorporate a research conception will languish and die. *The inclusion of such a conception into an industrial structure seems to me more important, both to the industry itself and to the public, than the degree to which the industry is monopolistic.*"[19]

Professor Walter Adams goes farther, arguing that Maclaurin has overemphasized the significance of monopoly as an incentive for innovation and urging that "the maintenance of competition is imperative if innovations are to serve the public welfare." He cites, as example, an important study of the electric lamp industry indicating that General Electric's control over the manufacture of lamps retarded the introduction of fluorescent lighting and other innovations, and Gilfillan's conclusion that "the incessant ballyhoo of patent lawyers and their friends that the patent system is the fount of all inventive progress, needs a great transformation to attain truth."[20]

An equally vigorous view is taken by Mr. Wendel Berge, former Assistant Attorney General of the United States, whose book *Cartels* fills in the lacunae about free enterprise left by the full-page newspaper advertisements and the symphony-hour sermons. Referring to cartels, which he describes as trusts magnified to an international scale, Mr. Berge writes,

Through the abuse of our patent system, cartel controls have been established over large segments of technology. With this leverage, industrial monopolies of international compass have at times deliberately brought about the deterioration of quality standards. When it might be to their advantage in maintaining or exploiting their monopoly position, they have adulterated their products to an extent and in a manner endangering the health, and even the lives of consumers. Almost incredible as these assertions may be, they are not subject to contradiction—the incontrovertible facts are clearly set forth in Congressional investigations and in the evidence in antitrust cases of the Department of Justice.[21]

Mr. Berge's remarks concerning the influence of monopoly on technological progress are especially illuminating. "In a system based upon freedom of enterprise," he writes, "access to technology is the fundamental condition of rapid advancement toward the goals for which our nation is striving." This is a statement with which everyone would agree. But the fact is, as Mr. Berge points out, that monopolistic interests control vital areas of research through which they perpetuate their grip on the advancement of science and technology and retard the introduction of new goods and services.[22]

This is far indeed from the endless benefits which would ensue to the public as entrepreneurs vied with one another for public favor—as the idyllic theory avers. A now classical illustration is to be found in the interesting details of how the du Pont Company and Rohm and Haas sold the same plastic, methyl methacrylate, to industrial users at 85 cents a pound and to dentists, for the making of dental plates and dentures, at $45 a pound.[23] Again, when du Pont developed a pigment which could be used either in paints or as a textile dye, the director of one of its laboratories—no doubt unaware of the notoriety his words would one day enjoy—wrote: "Further work may be necessary on adding contaminents to 'Monastral' colors to make them unsatisfactory on textiles but satisfactory for paints." It is well known that the Standard Oil–I. G. Farben prewar agreements greatly retarded the development of the synthetic rubber industry in this country. Clearly, at innumerable points—the important drug industry, for example—private enterprise verges dangerously on privateering.

The public record of antitrust proceedings and Congressional hearings is available for the multiplication of instances,[24] but to dispel our last doubts Mr. Berge quotes from the comments of Dr. F. B. Jewett, late vice-president of the American Telephone and Telegraph Company and chief of Bell Laboratories, in which Dr. Jewett discusses an agreement into which his company has entered:

Broadly speaking, the practical effect of the agreement is to limit the field of possible development of each party to the present major activities . . .

Thus, while a casual reading of the agreement by one not thoroughly conversant with all the factors may appear to establish the basis for an enlarged free development in most of the fields, this is not actually the case.

Dr. Jewett testified from experience. As the Bell empire has grown, its rulers have become less and less intrepid. The introduction of improvements has been delayed, and innovations have been suppressed. Professor Walton Hamilton cites the Federal Communications Commission report on nine new Bell devices whose period of gestation has varied from nine to more than thirty years, a long interval indeed between the time when they were conceived and the time of making their appearance in the telephone user's world. The fact is that monopolistic interests, to the extent that they are comfortably in control, have less need of innovation and tend to fear it, so that under their manipulation the patent system— originally designed to "promote the Progress of Science and the useful Arts"—tends to become in effect a method of technological contraception.[25] This, plus the monopolist's interest in maintaining price structure through restricting the supply of his product, adds up to what Thorstein Veblen variously called "industrial sabotage" and the "conscientious withdrawal of efficiency."

Up to this point, monopolistic practices have been examined from the point of view of their related implications for the consumer and the producer in an economy based upon production for profit. A subsequent chapter will deal with the political implications of monopolistic enterprise, that is to say, its role in determining the distribution of power, and its bearing on the stratification of incomes, and the chain of consequences thereby set in motion. Meanwhile enough has been said to show that the consumer is something less than sovereign and the producer something more than servant in the so-called market economies of the real world.

There is, indeed, much more to say about "frictions" on the producers' side even when competition is roughly approximated: of the frequent immobility of capital, of entrepreneurial errors of judgment,[26] of the tendency of true competitors in an unplanned economy to overproduce commodities which they have been selling at a profit, with consequent losses to everyone involved. But a comprehensive critique of this kind belongs more appropriately to an essay in economics. Likewise, there is much that might be said about so-called "frictions" and "exceptions" associated with the compensation and disposition of labor in an unregulated economy. Here, too, details may appropriately be omitted. As regards the compensation of labor, liberal critics of an unplanned economy have long emphasized the glaring weaknesses of the workers' bargaining position, especially after the mechanization of production substituted the unskilled workman for the craftsman whose skill endowed him with a measure of bargaining power. They have noted that, with rare exception, the labor market has been a buyers' market in which supply exceeded demand and that in such circumstances it was to be expected—indeed the advance of democracy made it inevitable—that workers would seek to improve their position through collective action and often through recourse to the restrictive methods practiced by management.

As regards the disposition of labor, liberal critics point out that orthodox economics grossly overestimates the mobility of labor, as it does the mobility of capital, ignoring the manifold circumstances which prevent workers from becoming so many iron filings drawn by the magnet of price: their family and neighborhood ties, their possible financial involvements, their ignorance of the state of the market. As for freedom of occupational choice, that blessing which, according to the classicist, is conferred exclusively by the market in a capitalist economy, contemporary liberals contend that, when the labor market is a buyers' market, freedom of occupational choice is only a hollow promise for the great majority of workers. Much too often it is Hobson's choice. Many liberals contend, moreover, that genuine freedom of choice is not incompatible with a planned, not to mention a regulated economy.[27]

Trade Cycles

If the system of economic harmonies elaborated by the classicists overlooks serious immobilities in the movement of capital and labor, if it neglects the ignorance and helplessness of the average consumer, if it takes no adequate account of the monopolistic proclivities of private enterprise, it also fails to reckon with the evident irregularities in business activity which are such a familiar feature of modern economic life. Crises are an old story, to be sure. But heretofore they have been associated with a shortage of goods (and a rise in prices) brought about through crop failures, political disturbances, and the like. In recent times they have been produced by economic rather than by extraeconomic forces. They are associated with overproduction and a fall in prices. Moreover, after the middle of the nineteenth century they ceased to be mere "crashes," to be attributed to a wave of ill-considered speculation; they came to take the form of "depressions," which reached deeper, lasted longer, and had far more widespread consequences. More recently, they manifest themselves as protocrises and are variously known as "recessions," "downturns," "pauses," "periods of adjustment," etc. Some of the consequences of depressions and recessions will be considered in later chapters. Here, concern is with the incidence of crises and near crises and with the fact that the so-called equilibrium theory of the orthodox economists, dealing as it does with the "normal" case, does not help us to comprehend them.

A depression is more accurately described as the contraction phase of a business cycle which in its expansion phase is known as a boom. Business cycles are recurrent, but it is generally agreed that they are not periodic. Their manifestations are too familiar to require detailed description. Although no two cycles are alike, the peak of every cycle is associated with high prices, an expansion of credit and investment, feverish speculation, a large volume of sales, high profits, relatively high wages, and a relatively high level of employment;[28] the trough of every cycle is marked by a fall in prices and profits,[29] bankruptcies and bank failures, restriction of credit and investment, a low volume of sales, low wages, and a large volume of unemployment. Between 1855 and 1927, years which roughly demarcate the heyday of capitalism, there were nineteen business cycles in the United States. Thirteen of these occurred between 1885 and 1927. The average duration of each cycle has been 46.1 months, of which 25.4 months is the average duration of the period of expansion, 20.7 months, of the period of contraction.[30] These figures do not take into account the boom of 1928 and the long period of depression which, while marked by some revival, was not brought to an end until the advent of the war, nor do they reckon with the numerous recessions which have troubled the economy since World War II.

Now, in terms of the orthodox concept of a self-adjusting mechanism such violent fluctuations of the business cycle are quite incomprehensible. Static equilibrium theory, as economists term it, demonstrates with infallible logic that when any part of the system gets out of balance, forces are released which soon restore the balance. If too much of a commodity is produced, the price will fall, thereby reducing the number of sellers and increasing the number of buyers. If there is an excess of savings, interest rates will fall and borrowers will be attracted. If there is an excess of labor, wages will fall, the cost of production will be less, prices will fall, demand will increase, and workers will be re-employed. In each case, the consequences must follow with inexorable logic. But they have nothing to do with the general and recurrent discrepancy between supply and demand, with the glutted markets and failure of buying power, which is the striking feature of the business cycle, or, indeed, with violent oscillations of any kind.[31]

A hypothesis which assumes the absence of such widely prevalent phenomena as monopolistic restraints of trade and business cycles, not to mention the other data cited, may still lend itself to highly complex elaborations and nice exercises in deductive logic, but its applicability to the real world will be strictly limited. The experts who are initiated in this logic are men of the real world, however. They are aware of trusts and cartels, booms and slumps, and the familiar "rigidities" which afflict the markets of the real world. But for them, these must be frictions, disturbances, aberrations, which do not affect the "normal" case. The most ubiquitous features of economic life become mere "residue," to use Lionel Robbins' word. Thus, the science which deals with the economic laws of a static and unchanging society in a world of flux diverts orthodox economists and their lay admirers and popularizers from dealing with the world as it really is.[32] It condemns them again to that abstractionism of which they were found guilty on the psychological level. More importantly, it leads them to suppose that there is no causal connection between our basic economic institutions and the world of trade restraints, of underconsumption and mass unemployment.

A fitting epitaph for the system of the classical and neoclassical economists could be *ceteris paribus*—"other things being equal." Unfortunately they rarely if ever are. "The trouble is I'm always off my game," one golfer remarked disconsolately to another, after a bad day on the links. The market economy as represented in the classical model and still preserved, even if only in the imagination of large numbers of business and professional leaders, seems always "off its game."

There are three ways of treating the data which have been described. The first way is to deny their existence. Young children sometimes shut their eyes and then assume that others cannot see them. Our monopolists are sometimes like them, especially those who insist that ours is with minor exceptions a competitive economy. For a time we tried winking at the depression of the 'thirties; it could not be an actual state of affairs, many said; it was only a state of mind. Eventually even the blind began to see.

The second way is to acknowledge the data but to treat them as exceptional and accidental. This is the method of the classical and neoclassical economists and it dictates the platform of present-day conservatives. There is nothing inherent in the market economy, that is, in our basic economic institutions, which makes for practices in restraint of trade, for booms and slumps and their evil consequences. These are the result of short-sighted interference by the ignorant, the impatient, and the wicked. At most, all we need do is tighten a few bolts, oil a few gears, and keep "planners" and "bureaucrats" out of the driver's seat, and we shall have smooth driving to the best of all possible worlds.

The third way is to dismiss classicism, or today's conservatism, as unrealistic and to regard the facts as evidence of the need either for reconstruction or for abandonment of our basic economic institutions. Contemporary liberals have called for reconstruction.

But even the call for reconstruction runs into the defense that it would be folly to tamper with an economic system which, depressions and monopolies—or "irregularities" and "abuses"—notwithstanding, has been the most productive in the history of mankind. The argument is fundamental. The proof of this pudding *is* in the eating. It is important that liberals undertake this decisive test.

Chapter 9

The Wealth of Nations

"FRICTIONS" AND "EXCEPTIONS" notwithstanding, American practice has afforded, apart from Victorian England, the closest historical approximation of a free enterprise system, and this is the image of the American economy which most advocates of the system today carry in their minds. The merits of free private enterprise are therefore likely to be judged, whether fairly or unfairly, by reference to the American record.

The extent to which America's economy any longer resembles a system of free private enterprise on the classical model is a question which may be deferred until later. Here it may be agreed that the tests of any economic system, classical or other, are fundamentally four: the amount of goods, services, and leisure it produces; the extent to which it realizes its productive potentialities; the degree to which what is produced in goods, services, and leisure is made available to the members of society; the extent to which what is made available coincides with what is needed and wanted. Surely these are tests to which all parties will assent. They may now be applied to the present case.

Production and Productivity

In the seventh decade of the twentieth century America presents a spectacle of opulence that would defy the descriptive powers of a Toqueville or Bryce. The total annual output of its goods and services exceeds an astronomical $500 billion. Its 180 million people, comprising 7 percent of the world's population, produce almost 50 percent of the world's manufactured goods.

The wealth produced by the American people so far exceeds anything achieved in the three-thousand-year-long history of civilized man as to suggest a mountain peak soaring steeply above low-lying plains. The industrial complexes that cluster about Chicago, Detroit, Pittsburgh, Los Angeles, Cleveland, San Francisco, are awesome in their immensity; their voracious appetite for fuel and raw materials is fed by far-flung power and extracting industries; they are linked by a bewilderingly complex communications and transportation network; they are sustained by elaborate laboratory and re-search facilities; their accounts are reckoned in steel and masonry towers that are emblems of the power of a great industrial colossus. The Golden Gate Bridge, Grand Coulee, Rockefeller Center, the Ford plant at River Rouge, Pitts-burgh's Golden Triangle, the Los Angeles freeway interchange, Dallas' Nieman-Marcus, Mies' towers on the Chicago lake-front, all these and hundreds more, epitomize in different ways America's vast wealth and productive power. While this has been accomplished the workweek has been greatly reduced, the crude exploitation of women workers mitigated, and the use of child labor nearly banished.

If there is one accomplishment upon which our system of free private enterprise has prided itself, that accomplishment has been "production." To suggest any criticism of the system is almost invariably to invite an account of past accomplish-ments such as the foregoing, or a reminder that we are pres-ently due to witness "an upturn of explosive proportions" such that the annual value of our output in goods and services will soon reach $600 billion. Such figures are dis-arming. The system may have scorned beauty, it may have cast truth to the mercies of the advertising man, it may have sacrificed goodness to the requirements of a pecuniary moral-ity, but it has *produced*. This much at least can be said for it, according to its apologists. This is its great strength.

Is such an account of American production and produc-tivity a complete and therefore accurate one, and to what extent may the record of performance in America—and, for that matter, the earlier record of nineteenth century England —be regarded as a vindication of the system of free private enterprise? We shall find at the outset that the impressive arrays of production figures conceal some serious ambiguities. For example, to say that we produced some $500 billion worth of goods in 1960 is hardly as revealing as it seems. The statement becomes more informative when viewed in relation to production figures for the preceding years. But it becomes most revealing when compared with the volume of goods which could have been produced in that year had we fully and efficiently employed our productive resources. We want and need more goods. In a great many cases the need has been desperate. If we have the producing facilities—willing workers and idle tools—and do not employ them, no amount of talk about millions of bathtubs, radios, TV sets, and automobiles can conceal the fact that we are behaving irrationally.

The phenomenon, greatly magnified in the 'thirties, of forced unemployment and idle fields and factories in the midst of acute need convinced many people that they were indeed in the presence of organized and institutionalized irrationality. But until several decades ago the measure of this irrationality had not been taken. We knew how much we produced, but we had no accurate, or even nearly accurate, idea of how much we were able to produce. Accordingly, experts turned their attention to a study of productive capacity.

A relatively early study that approached the problem from the point of view of waste and inefficiency was entitled *Waste in Industry*. This is an authoritative report issued in 1921 by a committee of the Federated American Engineering Societies. The study was initiated by Mr. Herbert Hoover, who wrote the introduction to the report. The committee found that the average waste of the *best* plants in six basic industries was approximately 22 percent out of a possible 100 percent waste. The *average* efficiency for each industry was in most cases less than 50 percent of the efficiency of the best plant. Moreover, the report attributed the overwhelming burden of responsibility for this failure to management. These are impressive findings, accustomed as we are to the idea that government has a monopoly on inefficiency.

At about the same time, the United States government in its Census of Manufacturers asked for information concerning "actual output as percentage of maximum possible output." According to answers received, industrial production in 1921 was 57.1 percent of capacity and in 1923, 72.4 percent. "Maximum possible output" is an ambiguous term, and the replies may have been inaccurate, but the finding is nonetheless suggestive.

The first comprehensive study of productive capacity was published in 1934 by the Brookings Institution, in its now famous report called *America's Capacity to Produce*.[1] The Brookings report does not concern itself with waste, as such, but with unused capacity. The authors of the report based their concededly conservative estimates of capacity on the productive system as they found it, including single-shift and seasonal patterns, wherever these prevailed. They concluded that in the year 1929—until that time, and for some time to come, our year of maximum production—19 percent of our productive capacity went unused. The Brookings Institution authors concluded that this 19 percent would have added $15 billion to the national income.

Before the findings of the Brookings Institution had been made known, the Federal Government, through the Civil Works Administration, had set up the National Survey of Potential Product Capacity, by all odds the most comprehensive survey of this kind ever undertaken. The results of a year of research by sixty technicians were summarized by their director, Mr. Harold Loeb, in *The Chart of Plenty*. These results constituted a startling criticism of the claim that our economic system "worked."

Basing its estimate on the existing plant, and employing methods more exact than those used by Brookings, the National Survey found that in the same year, 1929—until then, let us remember, our most productive year—we failed to produce $42 billion worth of goods that we could have produced.

In 1929, under the open-market system, the consumer *lost* the difference between the goods and services which *might* have been produced and the goods and services *actually* produced. This loss amounted to $42 billion, or $135 billion minus $93 billion.[2]

As depression followed boom, the losses became greater. The loss to the American people of unproduced goods amounted to $51 billion in 1930, to $59 billion in 1931, to $70 billion in 1932, and to $65 billion in 1933. The total loss for the five-year period 1929–1933 reached the astronomical sum of $287 billion.[3] As a measure of what we might have had, it is sobering to compare this figure with the postwar public debt—of approximately $292 billion—contemplated in the President's annual budget message of January, 1945. To put it another way, the wealth we failed to avail ourselves of during the 1930's exceeded in value the total cost of this country's participation in World War I and World War II.[4]

Mr. Robert Nathan, former chairman of the Planning Committee of the War Production Board, once pointed out that

with the manpower, the management, and the materials which lay idle throughout the 'thirties, we could have much more than rebuilt every factory, every office building, every bridge, every railroad, every dam, every power plant, every piece of furniture and clothing, and all other reproducible assets which exist in the United States today.[5]

We possessed the tools, the resources, and the willing workers. The overwhelming majority of Americans were in dire need of food, clothing, shelter—everything they themselves were capable of producing. But a dead hand lay upon them. Some strange paralysis afflicted them. A kind of economic witchcraft had placed them under its spell. The superstition of those who starve rather than eat the "sacred" cow is surely no greater.[6]

The National Survey of Potential Product Capacity may be charged by some with having dramatized a depression phenomenon and ignored the long period of "normalcy" which preceded it. But a $42 billion loss in 1929 occurred in what was then the most productive year in our history.

It may be emphasized, too, that the basis for estimating our capacity to produce was not some hypothetical modern, highly rationalized productive system, but our existing plant, with all its obsolescence and other imperfections. Finally, it can be contended that in a market that has been sustained since 1914 by two world wars and their aftermaths, and by such devices as installment buying and the kind of indiscriminate lending to insolvent foreign customers as prevailed during the 'twenties, the depressed 'thirties were a normal rather than an exceptional period.

The National Survey simply tells us statistically and more accurately what anyone might have surmised from the presence of millions of jobless in our midst.[7] However, if there is still a remnant of doubt concerning the magnitude of our failure, our experience during and after World War II has provided fresh evidence in a new and startling way.

Few achievements are more spectacular than the growth of American production during the war. Where adjectives falter, cold statistics tell the story better. If a value of 100 is assigned to our average volume of production for the years 1935–39, the index of our industrial production, as compiled by the Federal Reserve Board,[8] stood at 106 in August, 1939, when Hitler invaded Poland. In May, 1940, when the Nazis swept over the Low Countries and France, the index stood at 116. By December, 1941, the first month of our participation in the war, the index stood at 169. In November, 1942, as we were finishing the first year of the war, it was 191. By November, 1943, the FRB index stood at 247 percent of the 1935–39 average! At the same time, the volume of agricultural production was more than a third greater in 1944 than the 1935–39 average, and, despite the enormous requirements of our allies and our armed forces, the amount available for civilian consumption on a per capita basis was 8 percent above the pre-war average.[9]

While this unprecedented record was aided by the employment of an unusual number of women and other workers not ordinarily engaged in heavy industry, and by the abnormal scale of overtime work,[10] it was accomplished despite the most unusual handicaps: the cream of our manpower was meanwhile being drained into the armed forces; our industries had to undergo a drastic conversion from peacetime manufactures to the mass production of armaments.[11]

The record is one of which the American people are properly proud. It was a thrilling and unprecedented achievement. But it was also a measure of the magnitude of their earlier failure. For this spectacular success was a startling and inescapable proof of what America could have done in time of peace but had not done. The proof no longer rested upon possibly controversial and widely varying surveys and estimates. The hard, ineluctable fact was that for four brief years under most adverse circumstances we had produced a volume of goods which shamed the vaunted productive achievements of any other equivalent period.

Once, "practical" men told us that "it couldn't be done." Once, men who professed a love of liberty told us that the planning, organization, and regulation which made our wartime production possible would enslave us. But no one was enslaved: men still chose their church, aired their grievances, listened to their favorite radio oracle. Congress debated, pamphleteers protested, columnists denounced, reformers pleaded, and businessmen harvested lush profits. To be sure, there were "ceilings" and priorities and rationing and some limitation on profits, wages, and the freedom of occupational choice; but where these were burdensome the difficulty stemmed mostly from the scarcity of consumer goods in time of war.[12] Surely, if we had been making consumer goods instead of armaments, many of the restrictions would have been unnecessary and the resulting comforts would have made the remaining restrictions, those associated with planning, appear utterly negligible.

The Postwar Record

Before reviewing the record of the postwar years, it will be useful to emphasize two important distinctions. First, we must be careful to differentiate between total production or Gross National Product (GNP), which is the value of all goods and services produced, and "industrial production," which does not include consumer goods and personal services. Also, it is important to bear in mind the difference between a per capita increase in production (either "total" or "industrial") and production measured in absolute terms. If the rate of growth in population should seriously outstrip the rate of growth in production, the level of living would fall, even though, in absolute terms, the value of the national product increased. Hence it is the per capita rate of increase, whether of total or industrial production, that is significant.

The wartime increases cited above were in industrial production. The annual rate of growth in total production— henceforth called GNP—was about 9.5 percent.

The period following the war falls into two parts, the years of the Truman Administration, extending from the last phase of the war until 1952, and the years of the Eisenhower Administration, from 1952 to 1960. Because of this, and because the Eisenhower years were in an important sense a test of the competence of the business community to define and guide public policy—"We're here in the saddle as an Administration representing business and industry," declared Eisenhower's Secretary of the Interior, McKay[13]—the interpretation of the record has been obscured in a fog of partisan controversy.

GNP grew at an annual rate of 4.6 percent from 1947 to 1953. In the span 1953–1959 it grew at an annual rate of 2.5 percent. The so-called "historic" growth rate (1922–1960 and measured in constant dollars) was 3.4 percent. The per capita GNP (using constant dollars) increased at an average annual rate of 3.7 percent during the postwar Truman years 1947–1952. During the six Eisenhower years, 1952–1958, the average per capita growth rate of GNP was one-third of one percent. The big spurt in the following year brought the 1952–1959 average up to just under one percent. The postwar period has been marked by four "recessions"[14] three of them during the Eisenhower Administration, and all of them featured as usual by widespread unemployment[15] and idle plant and equipment. But the slack has not been limited to recessions. As Walter W. Heller, Chairman of the Council of Economic Advisers to the President, warned: "Economic recovery in 1961 is far more than a cyclical problem. It is a problem of chronic slack in the economy—the growing gap between what we can produce and what we do produce."[16]

Slightly earlier, Professor Paul A. Samuelson had cautioned, in a special report to the President-elect on economic conditions in the United States, that the recession with which the new Administration found itself confronted should not be permitted to obscure an even more serious condition. "More fraught with significance for public policy than the recession itself is the vital fact that it has been superimposed upon an economy which, in the last few years, has been sluggish and tired."[17]

What should the rate of growth have been during these years? Clearly, during the years 1953–1960 we were far below the optimum as comparisons with the historic growth rate and the growth rate from 1947–1953 suggest. It does no good to contend, as conservatives often do, that the growth rate during the Truman period was "exceptional" because of the momentum imparted to the postwar economy by the pent-up needs and savings accumulated during World War II and the later impetus provided by the Korean War. To say this is to concede what conservatives are hardly in a position to admit, namely that, in the absence of such extra-economic forces as war, war preparation, and war recovery, the economy is incapable of generating the forces necessary to its maintenance at a reasonably high level of production. The important point is that, *in maintaining such levels, it was not necessary to exact strenuous, abnormal, or special use of our human and physical resources.*[18] In point of fact, during the *peacetime* period 1922–1929, the average annual growth rate was more than 4.5 percent, significantly higher than the rate achieved between 1953 and 1960. It even averaged 4 percent during the peacetime period 1947–1950, although this interval was marked by a high level of unemployment and a recession.[19]

The extent to which we have fallen below the optimum level of production can be demonstrated in another even more convincing way, namely, by noting the only partial use made of our human and physical resources during the period under review. Unemployment will be discussed later in a different context. Here it need simply be noted that approximately 18.5 million available man-years went unused between the years 1953 and 1960 (not to mention the loss of manpower during the Truman recession of 1949–1950).

Nor is this because machines replaced workers. During these years idle plant capacity increased more rapidly than unemployment. Between 1954 and 1960 about 19 percent of our iron and steel capacity was idle on the average, rising to 48 percent in September, 1960. The percentage was even higher in some other basic industries. By the end of 1960 estimates of idle industrial production capacity ranged from 12.5 percent to 23 percent. Leon Keyserling, former chairman of the Council of Economic Advisers, concluded that "the deficiency in total national production in the 'boom' year 1959 was about $50 billion . . . and in the 'recession' period, fourth quarter 1960, the deficiency in total national production was at a seasonally adjusted annual rate of more than $70 billion. . . ." *The total deficiency for the eight year period 1953–1960 inclusive is calculated by him as more than $260 billion* (in uniform 1959 prices).[20] Even if this figure is challenged, the sum by any reasonable calculation is astronomical.[21]

All this reinforces the contention of liberal economists that an average annual growth rate of 5 percent (or near that) is not an unreasonable expectation for the American economy.[22] This is an optimum rather than a potential level, which is to say, what our human and physical resources are able to yield without strain. "The Report on the American Economy," issued in 1958 by the Rockefeller Brothers Fund, considers 5 percent as good and 4 percent as more or less satisfactory. The economy has failed since the war to sustain a 5 percent and, for extended periods of time, even a 4 percent level.

Confronted by awkward comparisons like those just cited, conservatives and leaders of the business community have responded with understandable ambivalence. Dazzled when they contemplate the absolute volume of American output, they suddenly denounce, as did the Republican policy-forming Percy Committee, the "cult of growth." Those who have proudly boasted of our prolific economy when they have considered its output in the aggregate speak flippantly of the "5 percenters" and "growthers" as in the pages of *Fortune*, and also find that "growthism" is "a new mask for big government." Demands by liberal Democrats (and by a few high ranking independent Republicans like Nelson Rockefeller, Douglas Dillon and Allen Dulles) during the 1960 presidential campaign that we abandon policies leading to a lagging growth rate were tortuously construed in the pages of *Fortune* as evidence that Democrats "seem to have abandoned entirely [sic] the idea of limited government."[23] All this was echoed by Mr. Nixon who scoffed at what he called "growthsmanship."

What are the consequences of the failure to realize our productive potentialities? Are they negligible and may liberals therefore be fairly accused of making a fetish of production? Are they indeed fostering, as the Percy Committee charged, a "cult of growth"? Their answer is likely to be that the test of productivity is a test which conservatives themselves have invited. More important, to limit this test to a comforting recitation of figures concerning our aggregate production, however impressive these may be, without relating such figures to what we could and should produce is a piece of self-deception which obscures profoundly serious consequences any one of which is enough to justify a liberal's concern. Some of these will be dealt with in a later chapter.[24] The consequence of concern here is that we are unable to understand the phenomenon of mass unemployment and therefore precluded from coping with it intelligently.

Growth and Unemployment

We are dealing with a comparatively simple mathematical equation. The size of the labor force is increasing. It is increasing primarily because of the growth of our population. As will be seen shortly, other factors could and should affect its size, but, apart from these, the increase is about 1.5 percent per year.[25] In addition to this, the productivity of labor, or output per man-hour, increases at a fairly predictable annual rate. Growth in labor productivity is brought about by technological improvements, including—on an increasing scale—automation, by modernization of plant and equipment, and by the more efficient utilization of labor itself. Improvement in labor productivity has steadily accelerated in the last fifty years from an average of 0.5 percent for the decade 1910–1920 to one of 3.0 percent for the decade 1940–1950 to 3.8 percent between 1950 and 1955. It declined for the succeeding five years largely because productivity is directly affected by the business cycle as well as by progress in science and technology.[26] In any case, 3.5 percent is not an exaggerated estimate of the average annual rate of increase, based upon the projection of historical trends and assuming a moderately healthy economy.

The conclusion follows inescapably. If employment is to be maintained, the gross national product must expand at a rate equal to the rate of growth of the labor force plus the rate of growth in productivity or output per man-hour. To be sure, increments to the labor force and increased efficiency in production might be used, not to increase aggregate output, but to provide more desired leisure for the total labor force. In part, this is what has happened as evidenced by the reduction of the work week from as many as 70 hours to 40 hours. No doubt a still shorter work week may be anticipated in the future as the impact of automation makes itself felt. But, by general agreement, for the present and the near future the shortening of the work week will not significantly affect the result simply because workers would resist a shortening of hours which did not permit them to maintain or expand their income.[27] Unless total output expands at a rate sufficient to employ the increased number of workers resulting from population growth plus the workers who are released because fewer workers can produce more, there will be unemployment. And, since the war, the economy has not expanded at such a rate for any sustained period of time.[28]

The number of workers increased by 8 percent between 1953 and 1960, but the number of man-hours worked in the private sector of the economy remained virtually unchanged. During the same period production in manufacturing increased by 17 percent while the number of jobs decreased by 900,000.[29] In the absence of adequate utilization of displaced workers the experience of the next decade will be worse. Such is the perversity which transforms increases in labor productivity into a threat to our wellbeing, and regards the willing new workers who are part of our population increase as the "kennel dogs" of the late Secretary of Defense Charles Wilson's strange new *Animal Farm*.

Concealed Unemployment

Later chapters will review liberal proposals for dealing with unemployment in its several varieties.[30] It remains to be noted here that, while economists quibble over whether the full time unemployment of 4 or 3 percent of the civilian labor force is consistent with maximum employment,[31] vast numbers of unemployed never get included in the statistics. Since they present us with some of our most baffling problems, their omission from discussions of unemployment is a sad commentary on the unrealism of much of our approach. Perhaps the omission is less glaring because, among these, many may be classified as *misemployed* rather than unemployed.

There is, to begin with, a large number of redundant farmers in the United States—including two million who operate marginal farms—whom we support at fantastic cost. One important reason is that there is no place for them in an already glutted labor market. Of the farm products sold in this country 82 percent are raised on only 30 percent of the farms. Even if the requirements of all segments of our population for foods, fibers, and biological oils were being met, which is not at present the case, and even if more of our surpluses were sent abroad, we should still find ourselves with an unneeded army of farmers for whom we have no other employment.[32] When we remind ourselves that, during what might be called the Benson years, from 1952 to 1960, U. S. government investment in surplus farm commodities increased almost eightfold and that the over-all outlay of the government for agriculture rose from about $1 billion to over $5 billion, the economic cost—not to mention the human cost—of our inability to solve the farm problem becomes painfully apparent.[33]

We may cite the proverbial charms of rural life and stress the power of habit, both of which no doubt root people even to Tobacco Road, but experience has shown that, if remunerative employment in commerce and industry is available, surplus toilers of the soil will yield to the blandishments of the city. Meanwhile, much of the work in which they are engaged must be regarded as misemployment, which is to say, concealed unemployment.

Another vast and unacknowledged area of unemployment is to be found among the so-called aged. Since 1900, life expectancy in the United States has increased an average of twenty years, and gerontologists are generally agreed that the sixty-fifth year may no longer be regarded as marking the advent of old age.[34] It is notorious that for those past middle life remunerative employment is systematically discouraged by present-day retirement practices.[35] The overwhelming majority of workers aged sixty-five or over, unless they possess unusual skills, are barred from employment without reference to their individual capacities.[36]

As a result, hundreds of thousands of workers are not only deprived of an opportunity to make a contribution to society; they are thrust into a state of dependency, and society must make provision for their support. Certainly our arbitrary retirement practices account in part for the fact that at least half of the aged—about 8 million people—cannot afford adequate housing, nutrition, or medical care.

This is not all. Enforced idleness and the loss of opportunity to earn a living are contributing factors to ill health, both mental and physical. It is a striking fact that, during World War II and the Korean War, when older persons were able to find work with relative ease, their death rate dropped.

At least as significant as the unemployment prevalent among the aging is a waste of manpower which is one of the favorite themes of employers, but is rarely related by them to mass unemployment. This is that same "conscientious withdrawal of efficiency" discussed earlier as it pertains to business, but widespread among workers as well. Such deliberate effort by workers to reduce their productivity goes by the homely name of "featherbedding," which American railway operators say costs them some $500 million a year and which is said to cost American industry about $2 billion a year. Even if these figures are exaggerated, there is no hyperbole in the railway fireman without a fire to stoke on a diesel engine, who is nevertheless able, with the help of his union, to tag along even if there are two men on the cab; or in the union compositors some newspapers must employ in setting so-called "bogus" or "dead horse," that is, in resetting advertisements which have been received in mat or plate form;[37] or in the four standby musicians who receive about $70 a performance while two pianists actually play the accompaniment to Broadway's *Billy Barnes Revue*.

Such make-work is senseless, but the indignation of editorializers is not likely to prevail against it so long as workers live in a world where there is an endemic scarcity of jobs and are haunted by the fear of unemployment. America has made its featherbed, and it will have to sleep in it—until it solves the problem of mass unemployment.

Four other areas of un- or misemployment deserve at least brief attention. One of these is the handicapped, of whom 2 million reportedly could be rehabilitated and partly or wholly support themselves if they were not condemned to waste their lives in a society that has not yet learned to use its able-bodied citizens. A second area comprises the juveniles whose inability to find steady work is surely one of the major causes of delinquency. One need not propose the reintroduction of child labor to urge that large numbers of young people, many of them incapable of more than an elementary education, could be saved from delinquency if they were not the victims of enforced idleness—in school or out. But an already overstaffed labor corps will resist, except on an occasional, catch-as-catch-can basis, even their part-time employment, and the schools must perforce function in a custodial role to which they are entirely unsuited.

To discuss, in the context of mass unemployment, such matters as the waste of technical and professional talent among trained and educated women who might be better wives and mothers if society enabled them to make part-time use of their skills, may be regarded by some as whimsical. But the fact is that such women, to their own detriment and society's loss, are also partly unemployed and never get into the count.[38]

A final example of concealed unemployment concerns what may be called private boondoggling. The term "boondoggling" came into popularity during the Great Depression as an opprobrious designation for public works regarded by critics of government intervention as frivolous or useless. "Leaf-raking" was presumably worse, for it was intended to designate a pretense at working; nothing came of it, not even a boondoggle. The idea that such titles, whether apt or not to projects of the prewar Public Works and Works Progress Administrations, might be applied to the private sphere would have seemed strange, and will no doubt still seem strange in many quarters. It appears that, almost axiomatically, private works are useful because they would not be paid for if they failed to meet a need. It has always been a cardinal assumption of classical doctrine that the sale of a commodity forthwith establishes its economic usefulness, however the commodity may be reviewed by the arbiter of good taste or the censorious moralist.

Though it may flout the classical assumption cited above, many will agree that the army of salesmen engaged in cajoling and pressuring people into buying superfluous and often misrepresented articles for which no one has any real use, and the auxiliary army engaged in manufacturing such articles, are involved at best in private boondoggling, at worst in leaf-raking, no less so for being private. Surely the brush or magazine salesman knocking at America's door, the makers and vendors of elaborately packaged body deodorants, skin softeners, dandruff killers, and hair restorers, those who rescue us from "acid indigestion," "tired blood," and the like, and innumerable others engaged in satisfying the most bizarre and far-fetched "wants" are artificially employed. So too are the makers and sellers of "gimmicks," the devices used to allay or weaken buyer resistance and divert the buyer from a critical appraisal of his purchase.

Some of those who perpetrate such artifices may be confidence men by choice, but it is difficult to believe that, if the labor market afforded them an opportunity, they would not prefer more useful lives.[39] It is understood that a very wealthy society will be prone to certain frivolities and extravagances. Such human frailties are not under discussion here, although the way in which they affect our schedule of priorities will call for attention later. What is under discussion are the services which must be misrepresented or oversold before they can be merchandized. Surely these come under the class of "boondoggle" more appropriately than the depression art projects, recreational facilities, and post offices which initially earned the title. The man who, in Professor Galbraith's words, "devises a nostrum for a nonexistent need and then successfully promotes both"[40] is, of course, employed in one sense of the term, but the question is whether a wise (and sane) society should regard him as employed. Professor Alvin Hansen rightly calls all this "pyramid building" and the "modern version of the 'make-work'" philosophy.[41]

Economic Lag and Waste

A second consequence of economic stagnation is at least as serious as the first. By virtue of the failure of our economy to produce regularly at optimum capacity we waste vast wealth which could be made available to raise our level of living, improve our cities, expand our social services, and maintain our defenses. The $260 billion in wealth we failed to produce between 1953 and 1960 could have added $4,200 on the average to the income of every American family. As Mr. Keyserling and others have pointed out, had we produced this wealth, $90 billion in added tax revenues would have been available *without increasing existing tax rates*. That $90 billion could have provided enough help to wipe out every slum house and repair every blighted city block in America.

The unused potential for 1960 was estimated by the chairman of President Kennedy's Council of Economic Advisers as between 30 and 35 billion dollars. Testifying before the Joint Economic Committee of Congress, he declared: "This unused potential is equal to $500 per American household. It is two thirds the amount we spend on national defense. It is almost twice the amount spent on public education. It is about one and a half times the amount spent on new homes last year. Even the world's most prosperous nation cannot afford to waste resources on this scale."[42]

If, on the contrary, we have more wealth than we can use and sufficient tax revenue to meet our needs, the point made here is a slight one. For example, Professor Galbraith takes the view that we already produce enough to forget our concern about increasing production. *But the conservatives who contend that we are unable to afford the President's request for additional defense expenditures unless we cut back on his welfare program are hardly able to take this position.* The fact is that the combined cost of expanding our defense and social welfare programs (between $10 and $11 billion), as called for by the President, will be paid for *without increasing taxes* by revenues deriving from our expanded production.

It is a tragic paradox that those who cry that we are spending ourselves into insolvency have been oblivious to this waste. All too often the advent of a recession is dismissed, as by the president of United States Steel Corporation, with a comment that "We had to expect a leveling out sometime." The president of Owens-Corning Glass displays similar equanimity: "No one likes to be quoted that a recession is a good thing, but actually it's a damn good thing now and then. It's good for people, and I mean business as well as consumers, to get back to earth, cut off their debts, and correct their personal and business habits."[43]

Enough has been said to indicate that what is required to guarantee a comfortable life to every American family is not "equalization of income" or a "division of wealth"—goblins that have been used so many times to frighten the talented and the well-to-do.[44] We may wonder why the greatest rewards are often reserved for the least functional members of society. We may marvel at the moral callousness which tolerates ostentation and extravagance side by side with extreme poverty. But this is not the heart of the problem. Without addressing ourselves to existing inequities, we could end poverty and richly reward those who contribute most to society if we could realize our productive potentialities, if, that is, we only *could* do exactly what conservative apologists for the existing order erroneously argue we have done—produce. The basic flaw in the profit system as we have known that system is not that it creates a class of wealthy and sometimes functionless beneficiaries, which is bad enough, nor that the concentration of wealth in a few hands makes for an undemocratic use of power, which is worse. The flaw is that the rules by which such wealth is acquired, somehow, for whatever reason, impose restrictions upon the production of more wealth. The system breaks down at precisely that point where it was said to be most strong.

The Great Ambivalence

So much for the record of the prewar and postwar years and their aftermath. In the first quarter of 1962, our economy is said by business economists to be on the eve of a boom of impressive dimensions. For liberal economists the question is whether the conservative coalition in Congress and the key committees it controls will consent to measures which must be taken if we are to achieve high productive levels. The new Administration has been able to give some impetus to the economy because the Soviet threat to Berlin aroused Congress into voting a substantial increase in defense expenditures over the fiscal 1961 budget. Congress has also made minor concessions to the sluggish business conditions with which the Administration was confronted immediately upon taking office. However, it is doubtful that such partial measures will suffice to raise the economy to a high level of production.

If high levels are reached, panegyrists will hail them as a tribute to the American system and find in them a crowning vindication of a capitalist economy based upon a free market. Against a background of bursting granaries, endlessly moving assembly lines and mounting consumption, critics will be accused of carping if they resurrect the melancholy record of the last decade and much of the preceding period. The fact that this upsurge will have come about as a result of fiscal and monetary policies opposed by the business community and made possible in part by a fortuitous international crisis will go ignored—as will the fact that regenerative forces within the economy were not in evidence.

And yet spokesmen for the business community know, and in other contexts often say, that since about 1937, whenever the volume of production has been comparatively high, this has been achieved as the consequence of a *special* set of circumstances deriving from war: the reconversion, delayed repairs to plant and equipment, replenishment of exhausted inventories, spending of accumulated individual and corporate savings, and foreign aid which followed in the wake of World War II; the limited war in Korea; the cold war and all the defense commitments it has entailed both at home and abroad. The tacit implication has been that, in the absence of these circumstances, *which are political in origin and quite extraneous to the free enterprise system,* the production levels of the present and recent past would not have been achieved.

Here is evidence, among its most ardent apologists, of a deep pessimism concerning the normal operations of the free enterprise system. The striking fact is that American businessmen and industrialists do not themselves believe that high levels of production can be maintained, let alone raised. This is evident, above all, from the fatalism with which they recurrently resign themselves to recessions; one need not be surprised if these are one day christened Anna and Bertha and Carla, for imputed to them is an inevitability which suggests a strong resemblance to hurricanes.

Our fever chart has its peaks and valleys. In 1947 the financial journal, *Barron's Weekly,* could comment: "The 1947 depression recession, or shakeout, whichever one calls it, has advanced from a fear to a fad. Not to believe in its imminence stamps one as an ignoramus." In 1948, confidence was somewhat restored, but again only because *special* circumstances had intervened: Marshall Plan funds and a rearmament program occasioned by increasingly strained relations with the Soviet Union gave promise of large-scale help. Hope was inspired by an improvement of short-range business prospects, brought about by factors obviously extrinsic to the economic system—public works, in fact—and not by a conviction that the system was inherently capable of sustaining high levels of production. But this kind of hope betrays a pessimism as far as the "resiliency" of the economy is concerned, the kind of pessimism, however inadvertent, revealed by the words of Dr. Edwin G. Nourse, formerly chairman of the President's Council of Economic Advisers and generally regarded as a spokesman for the conservative point of view. "If the practitioners of communism had not thrust us back into the danger of war," he said, "we would soon have been thrust forward into the *difficulties of peace.*"[45]

Why have we failed, why must we fail now to produce in time of peace and for the uses of life what we have produced in time of war and all-out war preparation for the spread of death? What frame of mind, what habit of thought, what principle of right and equity, what primitive subservience to ritual and taboo prevents us from permanently realizing our productive potentialities? Until these questions are satisfactorily answered and the bonds of fear, bias, and inertia which keep us from fully employing our creative energies are sundered, we shall go on living in a strange and unstable world.

In that world some 70 million American workers will not provide an occasion for rejoicing because they are able to produce over $500 billion worth of goods and services; instead, these workers will be looked upon with gloom and foreboding. We shall focus with Dr. Nourse on the "difficulties" of peace, not on the blessings of peace. In that strange world we shall find ourselves talking, as we do now, of what we must produce, not to satisfy our wants, but to employ our manpower. Each new labor-saving device will add to our problems and contemplation of the hydrogen bomb will cause the Chamber of Commerce of the United States to issue a bulletin (as it did in relation to the atom bomb) reassuring its members that since "this energy cannot at once be used for purposes other than destruction, immediate jeopardy to our economy is not in sight." We may yet yearn for the comparative reasonableness of primitive life, where men starve because they have too little and not because they have too much.

Chapter 10

The Welfare of Nations

DESPITE ITS LIMITED success and frequent failure in making possible the use of our productive capacity, the free enterprise system, whether in its classical or modified form, may result in an equitable distribution of the goods which *are* produced, and it may provide an adequate standard of living. With this, it may achieve what may be regarded as a desideratum in any system, namely, the closest possible correspondence between what is needed, what is wanted, and what is produced.

"Equitable" is, of course, a value-laden word, but economists even in their most *wertfrei* moments have hardly been able to profess complete unconcern with the way in which the goods of society ought to be distributed. Certainly liberal economists are not unconcerned. And surely even the most resolute positivists among the others will not recoil from the proposition that wealth should be diffused at least as broadly as may be compatible with maximum productivity. The point at which the two objectives come into conflict, and the policies to be followed in the event they do, occasion prolonged debate, but it is well to have a general principle before us even though its application to particular cases will often be unclear.

The Distribution of Income

The two questions—an equitable distribution of goods and an adequate standard of living—are obviously closely related, but it makes for clarity if they are treated separately.

A discussion of distribution should begin by recalling that the profit system as it initially developed in the nineteenth century, first in England and then in the United States, did not function to achieve a broad diffusion of income, and that its dynamic character stemmed from this very circumstance. The point is worth elaboration.

In every society some allocation of resources must be made between the production of consumer goods and the production of capital goods. The production of capital goods will consist of replacement of existing tools—or, as we now say, plant and equipment—and the development of new tools. Nineteenth-century England and America may be called capitalist for *two* reasons: (a) because the means of production were privately owned and operated; (b) because a much larger proportion of their resources was allocated to the production of capital goods, or "capital formation," than had been the case before.

An economy may grow too rapidly as well as too slowly. A society which concentrates a disproportionate amount of its wealth on the production of capital goods to the neglect of consumer goods accomplishes this only by a high degree of regimentation. In particular, it must deprive workers— who are the bulk of consumers—of the power to reject such an allotment. Consequently, demands for higher pay, shorter hours, better conditions of work, social security, adequate public amenities, are made ineffectual by banning unions and restricting suffrage.

This is precisely what happened in nineteenth-century England and the United States. The profit system provided entrepreneurs and proprietors with lavish incomes. These, after appropriate deductions for "conspicuous consumption," were invested in expanding the means of production, which they owned. Merchants and manufacturers, lacking titles, fiefs, and sinecures (status, that is), could satisfy their desire for power only in this way. The result was an inordinate sacrifice of consumption by the unorganized and politically defenseless working masses, and by means of the factory system, a merciless emphasis on disciplined toil resulting in the fourteen- to sixteen-hour day and the use of women and children at hard labor. Lacking political and economic defenses, and inexperienced in the use of such weapons even after they obtained them, workers were incapable of effective resistance. The rapid rate of capital formation in nineteenth-century

England and America can therefore hardly be called a virtue or ascribed to the "genius" of the system. It was based upon reluctant and disproportionate sacrifices exacted from generations of totally unprotected workers. We today are the beneficiaries of this unwholesome diversion of the energies of society into the production of capital goods.[1]

It is worth noting parenthetically that the USSR has been passing through the same phase of economic development as did England and America in the last century. Indeed, in an important if disconcerting sense, the USSR is today more capitalist than western countries. By forcing the people of the Soviet Union to give up or defer consumption, the Kremlin is able to allocate a proportionately larger share of resources to the production of capital goods. The methods used by the Communists have been more direct and brutal—there were no slave camps or secret police in England and the United States—but fundamentally the result is being accomplished in the same way: by depriving workers of the power to protect themselves through use of the ballot and through genuine collective bargaining.[2] And, by the same law that accelerated our expansion when we sacrificed consumer wants to concentrate on investment in capital goods, the Soviet Union will also expand as it is now doing. It may do so more or less efficiently, with greater or less attention to the more exigent wants of consumers, certainly with more coercion and less attention to parliamentary forms, but it will expand at an ever increasing velocity.[3]

In the USSR a rapid rate of capital formation is achieved through the action of the state in withholding a large part of the national product, more of which would otherwise flow into income and be spent on consumer goods; in nineteenth-century Britain and America the same result was achieved by the free market operating in such a way as to dispense enormously disparate rewards. The results from an economic point of view have been approximately the same.

Meanwhile practices change. In mid-twentieth century America large incomes are no longer the chief source of private capital formation. Of funds amounting to $196 billion invested in the private sector of the economy between

1955 and 1959 inclusive, 70 percent derived from internal sources, in the form of retained profits, depreciation and depletion allowances, and so on. Previously such equity funds would have come from the savings of persons with high incomes, translated into stock subscriptions, bond issues, and bank loans. This shift has important implications not the least of which is that it removes one of the chief arguments for high incomes.[4] It is ironical that those primarily in control of private investment policy are the ones responsible for making this rationalization of wide disparities in income to a great extent irrelevant.

In 1869 a manifesto of the Noble Order of the Knights of Labor spoke of how "capital . . . crushes the manly hopes of labor and tramples poor humanity into the dust." Many changes have taken place between that year and August 26, 1961, when Walter P. Reuther reached an accord with American Motors Corporation on a profit-sharing plan and a continuation of annual improvement-factor wage increases and the cost-of-living formula. Also, much has happened since the "prosperous" year of 1929 when, according to a well-known Brookings Institution study, 21 percent of the total number of American families received annual incomes of less than $1,000, 42 percent received annual incomes of less than $1,500, and about 71 percent (20 million families) received incomes under $2,500. At that time, one-tenth of one percent of the families with incomes in excess of $75,000 received an aggregate income almost equal to the aggregate income of 42 percent of the families at the bottom of the scale.[5]

America has made progress in the direction of achieving a more equitable distribution of wealth, progress made possible in part by our great affluence, in part by government policies vigorously opposed, it so happened, by the upper echelons of the income hierarchy. Some have called it notable progress. This appears to be impressively documented by Professor Simon Kuznets' well-known study, *Share of the Upper Income Groups in Income and Savings.* We are told that the shares (before direct taxes) of the two lowest quintiles rose from 13.5 percent in 1929 to 18 percent in the years after the second world war. Meanwhile the share of the top quintile declined from 55 to 44 percent and that of the top 5 percent from 31 to 20 percent.[6] Here surely is evidence of a general tendency toward declining inequality in the distribution of income.

However, it is now established that, if Kuznets' calculations are modified to include gross undistributed profits, payments in kind, and other complicating factors, the optimistic conclusions drawn from them would not be warranted. Professor A. M. Cartter finds, for example, that a much-heralded 26 percent decline between 1937 and 1948 in the share of the top income group would amount to only 5.3 percent if undistributed profits were added to personal income.[7] In any case, in the boom year of 1947, the President's Council of Economic Advisers reported that the highest tenth of the population received a larger share of the national income (33 percent) than the lowest six-tenths (31 percent).[8]

In 1955, a study prepared for the Joint Economic Committee on the Economic Report declared, "While the Nation as a whole has displayed healthy indications of economic expansion during the past 10 years, it is still a fact that a significant portion of its population has not shared in the overall increase in economic well-being." It found that there were in 1954, according to the Bureau of the Census, 8.3 million families plus 6.2 million individuals with incomes under $2,000, and that after allowances were made for shrinkages in the purchasing power of the dollar, the number of families with incomes under $2,000 was about the same in 1954 as in 1948, and that they were worse off.[9]

A later 1959 study prepared for the Joint Economic Committee found that, while the condition of the lowest income group had been significantly improved, this had been accomplished "with little change in the share of total income going to the lowest income groups. Government policy aimed at moderating economic inequality seems merely to have prevented a fall in the share of income of the relatively poor."[10] The study notes that such shifts in income as have occurred have taken place within the top group, but even here the change is unimpressive. By means of corporate saving, the top group has been able to offset income losses *by increasing its share of capital.*

The author of this study, Professor R. J. Lampman of the University of Wisconsin, has released a new report published in 1961 for the National Bureau of Economic Research and described as "the most comprehensive report of very rich Americans ever compiled."[11] It finds that, while there has been an equalization of the distribution of incomes, concentration in the *ownership* of wealth has been increasing since 1949 and is almost as great as in 1933. The richest one percent of American adults owns 27–28 percent of the nation's personal wealth (including corporation stocks, government and corporate bonds, real estate, mortgages, cash, insurance) as compared with 28.3 percent in 1933.

Clearly, if the levelers have been at work, they have not labored with conspicuous success. America is still a place where there are great disparities in the distribution of wealth and income. If, often, the point is obscured by reference to the vast number of people among whom the ownership of American corporations is distributed,[12] the facts suggest that the "people's capitalism" is still not much more than a catchword: 1 percent of the population receives on the average approximately 65 percent of the dividends paid to individuals.[13]

There is a direct relationship, according to liberal economists, between prevailing disparities in the distribution of income and the failure of our economy to achieve optimum productivity. In their judgment, *the profit system as it has operated in the past has failed to provide a great group of potential consumers with the power to purchase goods the manufacture of which would keep idle workers and idle plants continuously employed.* Thus, by a curious historical paradox, that same disparity of income which once hastened the expansion of production now retards it. When, in the nineteenth and early twentieth centuries, Britain and America had not yet glutted their prosperous classes with material goods, and when they were, as England was often said to be, "the workshop of the world," they had no need to rely on the purchasing power of the masses of their population to buy the output of their industry. But, while they may still spend fortunes on paintings, rare books, *objets d'art*, and so on, not even the most richly rewarded middle class could have use for *all* the cars of Detroit, the tires of Akron, the garments of New York City, or for that matter the lemons grown in prolific groves on a narrow coastal shelf in Santa Barbara County, California. Today, unless their own teeming millions can afford to buy the cars, household appliances, and countless other material things which pour forth from their factories (including "factories in the field") the result will be chronic stagnation. In the final analysis, the moral criteria presupposed by "equitability" need not be invoked in discussing the distribution of income in America, important though they certainly are; the prevailing pattern of distribution impairs the *economic* viability of the system.

The Standard of Living

Even though we are not successful at realizing our productive potentialities and are still far from achieving an equitable distribution of wealth, we may nevertheless produce in such quantity that the overwhelming majority, including the lowest income group, enjoys an adequate scale of living. In that event, we might well hesitate to tamper with a system which, for all its shortcomings, is unique in thus having solved mankind's basic problem.

As observed at the outset, by nearly any standard, the volume of goods Americans consume is vast almost beyond our power to imagine. We are rich beyond the dreams of any other people. An enthusiastic spokesman for the business community, Mr. Eric Johnston, declares:

We [Americans] take for granted in the most offhand manner standards of living, our levels of health and longevity, the extent of our sanitation and facilities for amusement, and a thousand other indications of . . . progress. Only when we travel abroad, or when we see our abundance and leisure through the eyes of an amazed foreigner . . . do we become aware of the miracle.

Yet it is a simple, demonstrable fact that the United States of America is the wealthiest, healthiest, freest, best educated country in all history.[14]

The achievements to which Mr. Johnston refers are unprecedented and they are substantial. It may seem to an average beneficiary of the blessings Mr. Johnston is counting that only a malcontent could fail to appreciate them. Certainly, they must be taken into account in any fair appraisal of our economy. But certainly, too, whatever our appraisal, no easy inference can be drawn from the "miracle of abundance" Mr. Johnston celebrates to the merits of a free enterprise system. The system of free private enterprise took up its abode in France and the United Kingdom as well as in the United States. If, as Mr. Johnston points out, we greatly excel the French and British in the production of physical goods, is this the work of the profit system, or is it because we have been blessed, among other things, with great natural resources, a great land area unbroken by the trade barriers that have plagued Europe (and are only now being eroded by the Common Market), and relative isolation from Europe's conflicts? The answer is not as obvious as Mr. Johnston and others suppose.

In any event, enough has been said earlier to indicate that we may not indulge in unrestrained self-commendation. The Bureau of Labor Statistics estimated (1959) that an annual income of $4,000 is necessary for an urban family of four to maintain an adequate standard of living. In 1958, 19.7 million families (including unattached individuals) received incomes under $4,000 and, for the three years preceding, the number of families in this range had actually increased.[15] In the 1959 study prepared by Professor Lampman for the Joint Economic Committee, an annual income of $2,500 is taken by him as the minimum for a family of four, and on this his report determines "low-income" status. Using this austere standard, Professor Lampman finds that there were 32.2 million persons with low income status in 1957. Of these, at least 11 million were children under the age of 18.[16] According to Professor Alvin Hansen, about 20 percent of our population is still too poor to provide itself with the material goods it needs.[17] So, too, his colleague, the late Professor Sumner Slichter, testifying before the Joint Economic Committee (March 20, 1959), pointed out that, in 1958, one-fifth of the spending units in this country had incomes of less than $1,890 before taxes.

If this is true of the lowest one-fifth, one may conclude

that the brackets just above it hardly command goods, services, and leisure in amount sufficient to justify the ecstatic prose which flows in an uninterrupted stream from the U. S. Chamber of Commerce and many kindred societies. Sixty-one percent of the families (including unattached individuals) in the United States live on annual incomes of less than $6,000. Frequently felicitated on their good fortune by their prosperous fellow-Americans, they are not likely to be found engaging in self-congratulation. The lap of luxury—or of the "very mother of plenty," as Mr. Hoover once called it—may be capacious in our country, but no one seriously believes that it can accommodate even $8,000 a year families in the high priced American market of the 1960's.

The struggle to keep afloat on the sea of consumer goods is evidenced by a precipitate increase of consumer debt in this country which, despite exorbitant interest charges, rose (exclusive of real estate loans) from about $27.4 billion in 1952 to $41.7 billion by 1957. This remarkable increase in the size of consumer debt indicates that the wants of the American people are far outstripping their purses, and this in turn suggests an important and usually neglected distinction between *level* of living and *standard* of living.

Standard of living refers to the level of expectations. It represents not what the members of any given group would *like* to have (everyone might like to own a yacht) but what they believe they *can* have and *ought* to have as a matter of right and justice. When the requirements of a given group are crude and simple, we say that the standard of living is low; when the requirements are elaborate and complex, we say that the standard of living is high. A French peasant's conception of what is indispensable to a contented and justly rewarded life is more modest than that of a California farmer, and the requirements of a Chinese rice farmer or an African bushman are a great deal more modest.

Level of living represents the economic goods actually enjoyed by any given group. The physical quantity of economic goods represented by the level of living may be the subject of three comparisons.

First, it may be compared with the physical quantity of

goods available to other groups, past and present. On the basis of such a comparison, contemporary Americans, as a group, enjoy a far higher level of living than any other group. This is true despite a tendency to confuse the well-being of all with the comforts of the upper middle class. In America that class is numerically larger and more affluent than any other economically ascendant group in the world's history, and this has led some people to conclude that it constitutes or is on its way to becoming a majority of our people. In the judgment of liberals, this prospect remains remote in the absence of policies which the favored income groups in America have so far successfully blocked, at least in part.

Second, the physical quantity of goods represented by the level of living may be compared with a standard of consumption based upon the biological requirements of the group, as estimated by experts guided by the best technical information available to them. This standard is what qualified persons regard as necessary to the preservation of health. For example, the experts of the Bureau of Home Economics of the United States Department of Agriculture have estimated the requirements of adequate housing in terms of room space, lighting, land use, privacy, sanitary facilities, etc. Other estimates have been made for adequate diet, and so on. It has already been indicated that the level of living of approximately one-fifth of the American people does not meet this standard.

Finally, the physical quantity of goods represented by our level of living may be compared with the physical quantity of goods represented by what might be called our psychological standard of living. This standard is called "psychological" because it is determined in the end by a set of attitudes, a state of mind. It is what people have come to regard as obtainable and as necessary and proper to their welfare, where welfare is something far more inclusive than biological well-being. *A comparison of our psychological standard of living with our actual level of living is what is most often ignored by conservatives, and yet it is this comparison which can be fraught with explosive implications, just because there has been and still can be a large and unhealthy gap between what the American people have and what they think they should have.* This gap may well be larger—so that our level of living may be lower in relation to our standard of living—than is even suspected. There are a number of reasons why this is so and it will be useful to indicate some of them.

In the first place there is no country in the world where the art of the advertiser has been plied on such a scale and with such skill as in the United States. Nowhere else and never before has so great an effort been expended to make people want so much. The mounting volume of consumer debt is a tribute—in more senses than one—to the success of that effort.

Second, and by no means unimportant, motion pictures and television daily depict for millions of American viewers a scale of living which very few of them can enjoy. Movies and television serials are preoccupied mostly with the doings of the middle or upper middle class and, in any case, the scale of living presented is usually upper middle class, even if the characters are not. The result is that the average viewer takes for granted a standard of living which is actually quite remote from the realities of his everyday life.

Third, class stratification is much weaker in our country than in most. Our egalitarian tradition encourages us to think of ourselves as eligible to the "best circles." Universal education contributes to this tendency. In consequence it is possible for many Americans to view the comforts of the well-to-do, not as the privilege of a remote and inaccessible class, but as something which they might have for themselves.

Finally and most important, the average American knows that he is not living on an island incapable with its meager natural resources of adequately sustaining a large population —like England, for example, or Japan. He knows, too, that he is not an inhabitant of an industrially underdeveloped country, like China or India, or a not fully industrialized country such as Italy or even France. He finds himself the inhabitant of a rich continent, technologically advanced and highly developed industrially. If he should forget, *Life, Time, Business Week,* and periodicals like them are sure to remind him. It is no consolation to be told that he has more than the English or French or Chinese. He is aware, even if only implicitly, that he lives in a land of forested mountains and fertile valleys, of great cities and giant factories which can yield him more, much more, than he now has. This awareness becomes explicit in the presence of jobless millions and idle factories. The desire for more is not a vague yearning or passing whim; it is a steady conviction in the midst of potential abundance that more should be had—and, in many quarters, a determination to get it.

A final point deserves attention in any complete examination of the material well-being of our people. By a curious oversight, discussions of the American level or standard of living are almost invariably limited to a consideration of private incomes and what these incomes will buy. Hardly anything is said *in this context* about the contribution of social services and public amenities to the level of living.

The streams and rivers we live by, the air we breathe, the countryside we look at, the open areas we play in, the ease with which we move to and from work, surely these are at least as much a part of the level or standard of living as refrigerators, plumbing, television sets, and automobiles. It would be difficult to find a monetary equivalent for the loss of well-being suffered by the people of metropolitan Los Angeles after their once pure air became dangerously polluted; yet no one will deny that their level of living has been significantly impaired. If our coastline is almost entirely preempted by private owners, as the best part of it is, surely the level of living of those who once had access to it is thereby diminished.[18] If the drinking water of Omaha, Nebraska, is made unclean because Sioux City, Iowa, daily dumps ten tons of raw human sewage into the Missouri River, the way in which the people of Omaha live has deteriorated.

All this reminds us of what must be reckoned in any realistic appraisal of what is happening to the American level of living. It also prompts us to ask if the free enterprise system as it presently operates does, in fact, achieve that approximate correspondence, claimed for it by its advocates, between what is produced and what is wanted. An answer to this question takes one to the last of the four tests to which an economic system may be subjected before it can be described as viable.

The Problem of Priorities

If all the changes which nature has rung down the long corridor of time could be telescoped into ten years, they surely could not match the evolution of the tail fin, the rear light and the radiator grill. "Forced obsolescence," says iconoclast George Romney, president of American Motors, ". . . has become one of the most expensive factors in manufacturing cost and product quality. In the superficial change process, it is difficult to escape a sense of appalling waste. Refreshing change is one thing, but incessant change has a touch of idiocy."[19] But annual models have been decreed, motor car manufacturers and their spokesmen assure us, by the consumer.

On the other hand, where change could have been highly useful it has been neglected. Car fumes are no longer a mere nuisance; they are responsible for contaminating the air in most metropolitan areas and seriously threatening the health and comfort of great numbers of people. Experts report that there are a number of practical ways of reducing exhaust fumes. "Automobile engineers know now that for perhaps $10 per car they can eliminate 50 percent of the hydrocarbons; for something over $300 they can eliminate them totally."[20] Yet oversized cars carrying that much in unnecessary metal are not equipped with such devices. The automobile manufacturers have spent a minuscule $6 million on air pollution research, or less than one-half of 1 percent of the more than $1 billion cost of their annual model changeover.[21] This, too, we are asked to believe, has been determined by the consumer.

On the other hand, there are times when the myth of consumer sovereignty can be strained no further. When stereophonic sound burst upon the audiophile's world, a national periodical normally known for its friendliness to the business community point of view commented with remarkable candor: "Stereo seemed an answer to the wildest dreams of the hi-fi industry, which has always made the most of planned obsolescence. Whatever the hi-fi fan bought, it was declared outmoded by all the pseudo-scientific trade journals almost before he could get it wired up. . . . For the trade stereo had a classic simplicity; all the hi-fi fan had to do was exactly duplicate the equipment he already had. . . ."

It is tempting to leave the world of sound and turn to the world of odors where, women having been successfully deodorized, men have become the objects of solicitude. A reader of the magazine section of *The New York Times* of September 10, 1961 would have learned from a full-page advertisement, addressed to men, that "The stick and the roll-on are the great new advances in deodorants." They have different purposes. "If your aim is to find the most thorough protection against both perspiration and odor . . . if you want the very latest and safest formula to keep you dry and attractively fresh," choose the roll-on. "It's a masterwork of small improvements." On the other hand, if "you believe (as many men do) that a little light perspiring is a healthy thing . . . if what you want is absolute assurance of odor-free freshness," the stick is for you. If the prospective customer wants more he may turn several pages and learn about "Tweed Mist" for which, we must assume, males will also sweat, once they learn about it.

If it is difficult to believe that, without conditioning worthy of a Brave New World, the American consumer-voter could be quite so silly as his putative sovereignty requires us to assume, the difficulty is compounded when we return to more serious matters. Several examples will suffice.

This country faces a serious water shortage, yet consumption is expected to double within twenty years. The need for plentiful water to supply our rapidly growing population is urgent. Authorities agree that greatly expanded research is needed in the promising area of purifying salt water. Beyond filling our own need, a successful outcome would do boundless good for people living in parched areas of the world, where the need for water is desperate, and could yield us immeasurable good will. And yet the average annual budget of the Interior Department's Office of Saline Water is less than $1 million, and a modest 1960 bill to increase its development activities fivefold, although it passed the Senate, could not get committee action in the House. That this meager provision reflects the appraisal of a nation that spent $296 million on chewing gum in a recent year surely strains credulity, and yet this is what we are called upon to believe.

Sewage disposal has become one of this country's major problems. Experts tell us that our facilities are obsolete and inadequate and that in many areas the health of the nation is seriously threatened. The U. S. Public Health Service has stated that 10,000 new municipal and industrial treatment plants must be built and another 1,700 modernized. The cost would be about $2 billion. President Eisenhower's Secretary of Health, Education, and Welfare, Arthur S. Fleming declared: "The battle must be waged on a broad front. . . . If it is not, we may be confronted with a crisis of such gravity as to jeopardize the further growth and development of many areas of the country and even the health of millions of people." There is a note of real fantasy in this statement—as though Mr. Fleming were speaking of a mythical world. Why must a "battle" be waged? By what flight of folly would a people, if it could actually choose, court the epidemic hazards depicted by Mr. Fleming in preference to giving up $2 billion of the $322.7 billion it spent on personal consumption in 1960?

The richest nation in the world is short 195,000 teachers and 140,000 classrooms. One-third of the classrooms we have are potential firetraps. Despite this acute shortage, we spent in a recent year 3.7 percent of our national income on education, while tobacco and alcohol took 4.4 percent. Some may be interested in other comparisons, for example, that the sum spent on advertising in this country is approximately two-thirds of the total cost of education from kindergarten on through the university. These allocations, too, we must suppose, reflect the preferences of our people.

The point involved does not concern our ability to afford advertising ballyhoo, artificial obsolescence, capricious changes in fashions, the endless restyling of household appliances, the fabrication of those complicated devices for achieving simple effects that we call gadgets, and so on. Conservatives who speak for the business community say that we can afford all these and more, *while denying that we can afford to expand or in some cases maintain basic services; and they thereby seem to approve this strange order of priorities.* But this is not the point, significant and revealing though it may be. The question at issue concerns how these strange arrangements and dispositions have come about.

The conservative view, touched upon earlier in the discussion of consumer sovereignty,[22] is that this is the allocation of goods effected through the free market, and that, as such, it reflects the will of the consumer on the order of priority. Economically and politically he is the sovereign: this is what he decrees through his purchases; it is what he orders when he votes for taxes. "The free market is marvelously selective," declares a 1960 booklet of the National Association of Manufacturers. "It constantly establishes and changes priorities whereby resources are channeled into the most productive uses."

Liberals take a different view, expressed, typically, by Professor Alvin H. Hansen:

A not inconsiderable part of our productive energies is wasted on the business of manufacturing gadgets and trivialities, many of which in turn cause diversion away from an optimum allocation of our resources. Nowadays consumers no longer act on their own free will. The demand curve is no longer the product of spontaneous wants. It is manufactured. . . . Consumer wants are no longer a matter of individual choice. They are mass-produced.[23]

There could hardly be a more impressive confirmation of Professor Hansen's contention than the $11 billion spent on advertising in 1959. Or the $161.70 per car which, according to *Advertising Age,* General Motors spent on advertising the Pontiac Tempest in 1960.

Of the total outlay for advertising, $158 million was devoted to dilating on the joys of smoking. If Americans want to kill themselves by smoking, that is their affair; they spent $6.3 billion trying in 1958. But it verges on the weird to suggest, as the conservative thesis implies, that they *willed* the expenditure of $158 million to let themselves be persuaded that they should[24]—all the more bizarre, perhaps, in that this sum was 40 percent of the total outlay in the same year for medical and biological research.[25]

Clearly, more than the manufacture and capricious manipulation of wants in the realm of consumer goods is at issue. Much more serious is the complex web of arrangements and circumstances obstructing the allocation of adequate resources to basic public services. It is idle to contend that people get as much of these services as they are willing to pay for. If, in Kenneth Galbraith's telling phrase, we have a condition of private indulgence and public squalor, the answer is that public services are involved in a completely uneven competition. The scattered voices of a few civic-minded citizens, civil servants, and responsible politicians pleading for better schools, more adequate medical care, urban renewal, and the like are hardly a match for the shrill army of hucksters hawking their wares from every television and radio set and haranguing us from every newspaper and magazine page. It is like matching a piccolo against a trumpet. As Galbraith points out, "Every corner of the public psyche is canvassed by some of the nation's most talented citizens to see if the desire for some merchantable product can be cultivated. No similar process operates on behalf of the nonmerchantable services of the state." Accordingly,

Automobile demand which is expensively synthesized will inevitably have a much larger claim on income than parks or public health or even roads where no such influence operates. The engines of mass communication, in their highest state of development, assail the eyes and ears of the community on behalf of more beer but not more schools. Even in the conventional wisdom it will scarcely be contended that this leads to an equal choice between the two.[26]

In fact, we are dealing with more than the media of mass communication. Enticing shop-window displays, fashion shows, persuasive salesmen, glittering show rooms, neon signs, countless billboards, all combine to titillate the spirit of emulation, in effect, to exploit our weaknesses and break down resistance to otherwise manifest foolishness.

It is doubtful that the services of a glamorous movie star have ever been enlisted in behalf of ridding communities of slums. No brawny athlete has yet been asked to give a testimonial for sewage disposal plants or even—perhaps more appropriately—for public recreational areas. No neon sign on Times Square advises New Yorkers that their shabby public school system is a disgrace to a great and prosperous city.

Against such a background it takes stubborn conviction to maintain that the allocation of our resources is a product of meaningful choice. But the background is not yet complete. The cost of public services must necessarily be borne unevenly. Except for a lunatic fringe, the well-to-do are reconciled to a graduated income tax and understand that they are better able to afford the cost of defense, education, public health, foreign aid, etc., than their less prosperous neighbors. Indeed, on this score, prosperous Americans and Britishers far excel their continental European counterparts who, as in Italy and France, successfully evade much of the tax they should be paying (and thereby provide Communists with one of the weapons which give Communism its strength in these countries).

Even so, rich and poor pay the same price for a bottle of whisky, a refrigerator, a dishwasher, a motor car, and so on. But, given the graduated income tax, the rich may pay five or ten or a hundred times more for foreign aid, recreation facilities, urban renewal, education, etc. A $10 tax bill paid by a poor man may "hurt" infinitely more than $100 paid by his wealthier fellow-citizen; no "felicific calculus" can tell us. But that is beside the point. When the rich man buys consumer goods, the scales are equal or, if anything, balanced in his favor;[27] when he pays for social services the scales are weighted against him. Besides, he himself does not use many of the services and facilities he is expected to support, and, while the reasons are well known to him, the relationship between outlay and satisfaction is hardly as direct as the check he writes for the car he drives out of a showroom. Consequently, his response to requests that he support public services will range from grudging consent to apathy to bitter resistance. Accordingly, a large majority of our most influential citizens are arrayed against public services. Forces are at work that may change them;[28] but this is the way it has been.

This is not to say that wealthy Americans are without a social conscience. They are far more public-minded and generous than their rich European cousins. One does not find prosperous Europeans—including those who criticize Americans as materialistic—endowing universities, libraries, museums and foundations on a scale remotely like the gifts of Americans. Moreover, rich Americans historically have roused themselves in the interest of civic or municipal "improvement" —though one need only look beyond Pittsburgh's Golden Triangle or Chicago's impressive lakefront to realize that face-lifting turns out not to be face-saving. An all too small group of wealthy Americans is genuinely concerned with the problem of priorities and, with the liberals, seeking solutions. But the great majority of the well-to-do are impervious to talk about national needs, and content themselves with the kind of ersatz morality that confuses occasional personal services and gifts to the needy with building a balanced and healthy society.

To the hostility of the last group, and partly as a consequence of it, must now be added a bewildering variety of political contrivances which result in starving the public sector of our economy. The will of the majority cannot be expressed on appropriations bills either at the federal or state levels. To begin with, our bicameral system with its bias in favor of sparsely populated areas makes this inevitable. Also, large numbers of Americans, notably Negroes in the South and urban dwellers, who could be expected to support larger outlays for social services, are wholly or partly disfranchised.[29] More important, at strategic points so-called "strict economy" advocates, even though they reflect the views of a small minority, are able to obstruct the legislative process so that a revenue bill cannot even reach a vote. The blocking of proposals by a House Ways and Means Committee hostile to all social welfare legislation has been notorious and occasioned one of the fiercest battles on the New Frontier. In a state like California members of the upper house of the legislature from rural counties comprising about 5 percent of the population enjoy an absolute veto over revenue bills, if they choose to exercise it. This is not atypical.

Perhaps the most engaging device for obstructing the flow of funds to the public sector is the doctrine of states rights. When President Eisenhower, backed by the U. S. Chamber of Commerce and the National Association of Manufacturers, vetoed legislation authorizing $900 million over a period of 10 years for the construction of sewage treatment plants, he stated in his veto message that "because water pollution is uniquely a local blight, primary responsibility for solving the problem lies not with the federal government but rather with state and local governments." Similarly, federal aid to education was disposed of as "a problem of the states." Addressing the Ohio Municipal League, David Kendall, special counsel to President Eisenhower, summed up the Administration's position, and with this the position of most conservatives,[30] when he declared that urban renewal, housing, airports, and the like should be developed locally "without automatically assuming the federal government will do it." Such assumptions he described as undemocratic and as destructive of local initiative.

The projects are rarely disapproved. Who, after all, would declare against the importance of such basic needs as building classrooms, increasing teachers' salaries, constructing better houses, improving airports, building sewage treatment plants, and so on? We must meet these needs, but we must do so at the state or local level. Whether by design or accident the consequence is that, by and large, these projects are effectively and inevitably sabotaged. State and local governments have virtually exhausted their ability to cope with such needs. The hard facts and their harder implications were set forth in the cold, impersonal prose of President Kennedy's Council of Economic Advisers responding at the Hearings of the Joint Economic Committee to a question from Congressman Thomas B. Curtis, conservative Republican. "What," he asked, presumably with some umbrage, "is the basis for this statement [that the financial position of the state and local government is 'deteriorating'] which is certainly contrary to the fact of the rapid development of state and local expenditures in recent years?"

The Council's answer may be set forth in full, summarizing, as it does, some profoundly important truths affecting our national life:

The main evidence for the deteriorating position of the state and local governments is the growth of their deficits and their debts. These deficits . . . rose from an annual average of $0.4 billion in the period 1948–50 to an average of $2 billion in 1958–60. The Commerce Department projects a deficit of $3 billion for 1961. The total debt of states and localities rose from $18.5 billion in 1948 to $67 billion in 1960.

A state or local government is constrained in its ability to borrow by the market's evaluation of its debt-carrying capacity as based on its revenue-raising possibilities. Furthermore, many of these governmental units are subject to constitutional debt limitations. There is a serious danger that their increasingly difficult debt situation, together with their inability to increase their tax revenues sufficiently, will act to choke off some of the expenditures they urgently need to make.

The "rapid development of state and local expenditures," far from contradicting our assertion of growing financial weakness, is a prominent cause of that weakness. The States and localities have very properly responded to the need for better educational and hospital facilities, urban redevelopment, mass transportation, etc. They have not been able to afford to do enough in the past, and the needs will grow in the future.

At the same time, their revenues do not grow with GNP to the same degree as do Federal revenues. Moreover, a State or locality is inhibited from imposing a new or increased tax by the fear that economic activity will flee its borders, thus complicating its revenue problem.[31]

Since 1945, the total debt of the states has grown by 500 percent and the local debt by 300 percent. During the same period the Federal debt has risen less than 10 percent. In short, state and local governments are at or near the limit of their fiscal capacity. The Federal government with its greater freedom and power to raise revenue is alone able to meet the need. Against this background the posture of most conservatives with respect to fiscal support for the vital services on which our vigor as a nation depends is best expressed in an old English quatrain:

> Mother dear, may I take a swim,
> Yes, my darling daughter;
> Hang your clothes on a hickory limb,
> But don't go near the water.

On an inside page under a Washington dateline the UPI reported a minor event which could easily have escaped notice in our preoccupation with the more spectacular happenings of 1960: "The house rules committee today shelved a proposal to authorize $39,000,000 in federal grants for the construction of educational television stations. . . . Five Democrats voted to give the measure a go ahead. Four Republicans and one Democrat opposed it. Members said the vote killed the bill for this session of Congress."

In this quiet and nearly unheralded way, what the National Association of Manufacturers calls the "marvelously selective" market removed the possibility of a small island of refuge in an ocean of television bilge. For the market, as we know it, will not sustain education television stations, and, besides withholding its consent, generates actions—reflected in this case by five myopic congressmen—that frustrate the effort to find consent elsewhere. One wonders, however, if this is what the American people decreed, along with the other larger outcomes, laughable or lamentable, of which this action was a symptom and a symbol.

In the view of liberals, neither the self-regulating mechanism of the orthodox economists, nor the mechanism of the market as it has been tampered with in our time, meets the tests cited at the outset of this discussion. Only when government has intervened on a large scale, as during the war, has our economy realized its possibilities. The precise method and scope of similar intervention in time of peace and the economic problems involved are complex matters which must be left to professional economists, although their broad outlines will be sketched in the concluding chapters. First it is necessary to discuss the political implications of such intervention and the great controversy that it has aroused. The argument against classical liberalism and the classical liberal creed as interpreted among conservatives today has been traced, first in its psychological, then in its economic outlines. It must now be pursued in the realm of political theory and practice.

Chapter 11

The Positive State

IF THE FREE market as the sole and sovereign arbiter of our economic life is inadequate, both in pure theory and in corrupted practice, the alternative lies in collective planning, primarily governmental planning. Inadequacy is relative, however. If the only escape from the rigors of the "free" market is the "road to serfdom," one may well prefer the former. A final settlement of the economic problem takes one, therefore, to the arena of political controversy, where the lines are currently drawn—even if not always clearly—between the conservative who invokes the authority of the classical liberal for quietism in government and the present-day liberal who seeks a positive role for government. Inevitably, this controversy concerns the nature of government, of power, and of the historical and institutional contexts in which political power has been and is exercised.

In Historical Perspective

Twentieth-century liberals understand the fears which prompted men like Locke, Jefferson, Montesquieu, and Bentham to urge that government power be held to a minimum. The judgment of the political philosophers of that day was determined by the governments which they knew and these governments did not inspire confidence. Men who knew at close hand the tyranny of Bourbon and Stuart would hardly deserve a place in history if they had not insisted upon appropriate safeguards. Even the "mother of parliaments," in that day a harsh and aristocratic matriarch, was despotic enough to goad the Americans to revolution and, some decades later, to pass the repressive Six Acts. The representative, democratic government of present-day United States and Great

Britain was unknown to the seventeenth- and eighteenth-century liberals.

If the great classical liberals in denouncing tyranny often came dangerously close to identifying it with government as such, one can perceive the circumstances that drove them to this exaggeration, just as one can understand how in the struggle to assert their rights against despotic rulers they found the contract theory and the doctrine of natural rights congenial. Their indictment of *all* government was more inclusive than any necessarily limited experience might permit, and their contractualism and jusnaturalism were sheer fiction, but only a small mind would cavil over this. Their case was apt to their time, and in making this case out they were brilliant and often courageous. Lesser men, then and since, sought to deny others the freedom they won for themselves, but the greater ones left a legacy of freedom for all men.

Contemporary liberals proudly regard themselves as the trustees of this legacy. At the same time they denounce as a monstrous anachronism the attempt to apply to the democracies of the present arguments directed against the despotisms of the past. Those who insist upon employing these arguments against responsible, representative government are ignoring the principle of historical relativity and with it the proposition that what is wisdom in one century may be folly in another. Surely the Founding Fathers would have been the first to affirm this commonplace.

Institutional Changes and Interventionism

Although businessmen and industrialists, striving to avoid taxes and the regulation of their enterprises, would have been bureauphobes in any event, it can be contended that the great classical liberals would not have been fearful of the kind of responsible, representative government which now prevails in large areas of the Great Society. This, however, is inferential and by the way. More fundamental is the fact that great forces have been at work which have so transformed the commercial, handicraft society known to Adam Smith and the agrarian, sparsely populated country known to Jefferson as to make our world unrecognizable to them. And these forces have worked irresistibly to increase the power of government.

The first of these forces is represented by the transition from small-scale to large-scale enterprise. If it is not gratuitous to dwell upon a development which is familiar to every college freshman, this is because its implications are so often ignored. This epoch-making change is compounded of two parts: a change in the technology of production and a change in the organization of business.

The change from relatively simple tools to power-driven machinery, from the small shop or factory of the year 1830[1] to the vast industrial plants of today, from small-scale to mass production, made possible the enormous physical wealth which has been created in the last one hundred years. Only a few incorrigible romantics would wish to reverse this great revolution in technology. But the result of this revolution has been to repose enormous powers in private hands so that, at the turn of the century, a great steel baron could control the economic destiny of thousands of his workers, own the houses they lived in, the stores they spent their wages in, the legislators who made their laws, the police who arrested them, and the courts that tried them.

Even before the era of great corporations the industrialists, spawned by a machine technology, had become so powerful that they could control the press, dictate to the schools, silence the church, dominate the great political parties and, especially on the local and state level, make and break governments. Mr. Lippmann may argue that "the concentration of control does not come from the mechanization of industry,"[2] but quite clearly Andrew Carnegie was as much a product of such mechanization as the hearth furnaces which brighten the night sky over Pittsburgh. And just as clearly, there were only three ways in which to cope with the power of the Carnegies, the Fords, the Fricks, the Schwabs, the Huntingtons, the Guggenheims, and others like them: return to the day of the ironsmith, the stagecoach, and the spinning wheel; transfer the basic industries to public ownership; or provide government with enough power to curb and control the private owners of the means of production. The first was a romantic escape. At the turn of the century the second was a utopian dream. The only realistic alternative to an irresponsible and oppressive concentration of power in the hands of men whose code was "the public be damned"[3] was an increase in the power of government to control.

So far bigness has been viewed as an aspect of modern technology. But bigness is also an aspect of business as distinguished from industry. The brief discussion of monopoly in a previous chapter disclosed that the size of many of our corporations is determined not so much by technological as by financial considerations. As will be brought out in a fuller discussion of the corporate universe in the next chapter, liberals are not always in agreement about bigness in business. Nevertheless, whether good or bad, efficient or inefficient, necessary or unnecessary, big business has become a ubiquitous feature of our economic life. Corporativism antedated the government agencies which were set up to control or try to control it, and it was, moreover, the creation of businessmen. Cause and effect are well described by Dicey who writes in the tradition of classical liberals, and therefore as a critic of strong government:

. . . combination has gradually become the soul of modern commercial systems. One trade after another has passed from the management of private persons into the hands of corporate bodies created by the State . . . legislation [making combinations possible] was favored and promoted by [classical] Liberals, but the revolution of which it is the sign has nevertheless tended to diminish, in appearance at least, the importance of individual action . . . and supplied arguments for State intervention in matters of business with which in England the State used to have little or no concern.[4]

Dicey, writing before corporate trade had even approached its peak, concludes that "the modern development . . . of corporate trade has in more ways than one fostered the growth of collectivist ideas."[5]

There is an ironic quality in all this to intrigue the sensibilities of a Socrates. It appears that businessmen, of the very group that denounces collectivism and government intervention in economic affairs as collectivist, were themselves the first collectivists (as they use the term). Not content with the great power that came to them from the ownership of their own enterprises, they sought and secured the collective power of many owners, through combining and incorporating them. No wonder that, as long ago as 1899, Henry Adams, more perceptive than most of his contemporaries, could write to his brother Brooks, "They [the Capitalists] have abandoned their old teachers and principles, and have adopted socialist practices. There seems to be no reason why the capitalist should not become a socialist functionary. Solidarity is now the law. . . ." The parent may not be proud, but the fact is that in the United States private collectivists have sired public "collectivism."

Government has had to become stronger in order to cope with the power which has been reposed in private hands by a machine technology, a power vastly increased by incorporation and trustification. Besides this, there have been other forces, closely related to the great technological changes of our time, which have worked toward the same end. The railroad, the automobile, and television, to mention only three, have created problems and imposed responsibilities on government which simply did not exist when George Washington took the oath of office. The point is obvious enough: until the advent of the motor vehicle no government forbade pedestrians to cross in the middle of the block or against the signal at an intersection. Neither was a Federal Communications Commission needed to allocate wave lengths until the appearance of radio broadcasting. The forms of social intervention that atomic energy will require are still largely in the realm of conjecture.

Beyond this it is important to emphasize the general relationship of interdependence into which individuals and groups of individuals have been thrown in modern society. At the very moment when men were affirming their independence they might have affirmed, as Adam Smith in fact did, their interdependence as well. Acute in perceiving the implications of the former, nineteenth-century liberals rarely recognized the full implications of the latter. Men no longer live in scattered and relatively isolated communities in which they provide for almost all of their basic needs. The division of labor, the specialization of geographic areas, an enormous growth and concentration of population,[6] the development of rapid transit and communication[7] have vastly expanded the area in which Mill once said compulsion is justifiable because, to use his words, the "actions of each . . . concern the interests of other people."

Some men are only now learning that they live in one city, not to mention one world. The blighted areas of our great population centers, to take a pervasive example, concern more than those who own the slums and those who live in them; they concern the whole community. The senseless exploitation of land values and the general planlessness of our cities, which has prompted Lewis Mumford to call them "a crystallization of chaos," may represent an exercise of "freedom" for some; it restricts the freedom of most. A few have the profits and the rest have the problem. If we call upon government to intervene, that is because of a belated recognition that none of us can escape the consequences.

Nor could we escape the consequences of the series of events which rugged individualists set in motion when they heedlessly planted wheat where prairie grasses grew, thereby leaving the "Arkies" and the "Okies" free to harvest the "grapes of wrath" in California. Nor can one state remain oblivious to the backward social legislation of another to which its industries may move in search of lower taxes and cheaper labor. Nor can the flood victims of Louisiana avoid concern over what the citizens of Pennsylvania do about soil erosion. Nor can anyone who eats beef ignore the flooded cornfields of the Missouri Valley.

Today, as at no other time, we are affected in countless matters pertaining to our vital welfare by the decisions of individuals whose interests are remote from, if not in actual conflict with, our own. The central fact in this situation is that the individuals who make these decisions have no legal, they have not even a moral, responsibility—as our mores go—for taking our interests into account. The result is a growing demand that such decisions be made by parties whose responsibilities are clearly defined by law, and, if such responsibility cannot be fixed and enforced, that public agencies assume responsibility.

Quite apart from the influence of the forces described, the power and scope of government have been vastly increased in recent years for still other reasons. It is notorious that emergencies make for a concentration of power in the hands of authority, and emergency has been virtually endemic to our society since 1914. There were economic disturbances and wars in the period of capitalist expansion, to be sure, but these disturbances were of short duration, and the wars were confined to small areas. The nearly permanent state of emergency, punctuated by only short periods of specious security, in which we have lived has led inevitably to a reliance on government. Recourse to government is as surely a result of insecurity, of whatever kind, as plans in all other departments of life are the result of problems. Those who would reduce the power of government and avert planning would do better if they looked more to the cause than to the effect. So long as that cause, in the form of economic insecurity, is at work, along with the world insecurity which it produces, government will be with us, late and soon.

Finally, a psychological factor already touched upon deserves emphasis. Men once resigned themselves to drudgery and degradation. They saw no way out. But they have since caught a vision of something different. They made the exhilarating discovery in the nineteenth century that they were no longer the pawns of fate or providence; they could shape their own destiny.[8] Everyone knows that want, deprivation, poverty, are no longer a result of the niggardliness of nature. Mass poverty is artificial, man-made. It is institutional, not technological. To this the spectacle of idle factories and idle men in the midst of want has been eloquent testimony. Men endure what they cannot escape. But the glaring paradox of want in the midst of plenty is literally unendurable, in the end even to those who appear completely apathetic and resigned.

Inevitably, in such circumstances men turn to government.

They insist, that is, on collective deliberation and collective action to resolve the paradox. Whether in a highly productive society, where their expectations are correspondingly high, they will demand government intervention for more than their basic biological needs is a question which no one can answer with assurance. They probably will. That they will demand such intervention to meet their basic needs is certain. The history of modern reform is the history of this demand made more and more articulate through the institutions provided in a democracy. In the end that demand can be ignored only by destroying democracy itself.

These are the forces, relentless, implacable, which have combined to increase the power and scope of government. No one willed this change, although in an important sense it reflects the multitudinous wills of nameless men beyond mention. The change is a product of no fiat, no conspiracy, no sinister plot. It is the verdict of history. We can no more defy the forces which have brought the positive state into being than we can repeal the history of the last one hundred years.

The Commissional Revolution

Inevitably, the assumption by government of broad powers of intervention in affairs as various as unemployment, wages and hours, collective bargaining, the sale of securities, substandard housing, old-age security, radio broadcasting, television channels, the purity of food and drugs, etc., has required that it set up bureaus or commissions through which the declared will of the lawmaking body on these subjects is applied and executed. Inevitably, the proper exercise of their functions has required that these agencies assume considerable legislative and judicial or quasi-judicial powers.

The result has been a substantial change in the traditional conception of the separation of governmental powers. The change is most noticeable in this country, where we have always given special emphasis to a system of checks and balances and the principle of federalism. It is a wild exaggeration to charge, as many have, that we have abandoned the separation of powers.[9] But it is quite true that the power of the executive-administrative arm of the government has steadily increased at the expense of the legislative and judicial branches. At the same time, the power of the federal government has increased substantially at the expense of state and local government.

The "commissional revolution," as one may call it, is far from involving the drastic changes which the "managerial revolution" is effecting in business, but it has attracted much more attention and has become one of the most controversial issues of the day. In our country presidential elections are invariably fought over it, books have been written with terrifying titles, the bureaucrat has become the *bête noire* of every luncheon club and executive flight, and a famous economist has warned us that we are on the verge of becoming a nation of postal clerks![10]

It is not unnatural that the battle should be waged over the issue of bureaucracy. As government reaches out, it is through the bureau that it finally touches the individual, and he often feels no friendlier to it than to the traffic officer who gives him a ticket for speeding. Bureaus are favorite targets, too, because they are frequently vulnerable. Officials can become remote and preoccupied with routine. They can become little tyrants and big toadies. Everyone knows some civil servant who, in Churchill's words, is no longer servant and no longer civil. Bureaus often overlap and some of them linger on after the need has gone. They are constantly exposed to the danger of dry rot. Whoever minimizes these hazards does public administration no service.

In the judgment of the liberal, most of the attacks upon bureaucracy are, however, motivated by something deeper. They strike at the legislation which the bureaus have been set up to administer. Having failed in their attempt to defeat the legislation, the authors of these attacks now commend its objectives; they condemn only the *methods*. Apart from the usual charge that government administration is inherently inefficient, these methods are indicted because they involve a usurpation of power in the course of which administrative agencies are said to have arrogated judicial and legislative functions to themselves. What does this usurpation actually amount to?

Nothing is plainer than that the lawmaking body cannot legislate concerning the manifold details of a program as complex as the regulation of the sale of securities or the administration of veterans' affairs. The problems which will confront the administrator are at once too detailed and too varied. No legislation, however elaborate and prescient, could anticipate all the contingencies, and to attempt to do so would be to defeat the original legislation by strait-jacketing its administration. At best the lawmaking body can express its wishes, set up the agency for executing them, and indicate the broad policies by which the agency should be guided. Necessarily it must allow to such an agency a measure of discretion which represents, in effect, a delegation of legislative powers. Lawyers may debate and judges meditate concerning the extent to which the United States Congress may legally go in delegating such power. That a limited delegation must take place *if government is to act* is accepted among almost all competent students of government and recognized by our courts.

This does not mean that agencies and commissions have usurped the functions of the legislature. It is necessary, as Professor James Hart points out, "to draw a distinction between congressional abdication or transference of its legislative power and congressional delegation of rule-making discretion for the implementation of its policies." He goes on,

There is nothing in the nature of executive power which requires such content to be confined to clerical, ministerial functions. Neither is this required by the nature of the legislative power. The idea that it is, was merely an assumption of the transitory philosophy of the laissez-faire age. If in an era of interventionism the idea is utterly impracticable, then to hold that it is forever frozen into the Constitution is to deny . . . Congress part of its legislative discretion . . . to determine that executive agents shall have choices in the implementation of its objectives.[11]

This is a judgment to which every liberal will give hearty assent. The Congress which delegates powers for the realization of specific objectives,[12] powers securely tethered by purse strings, powers that it may freely retract, is not the Reichstag which issues a blank check and abdicates. The facile identification of the two is part of the attempt to reduce the government of which Congress is a part to impotence.

The logic behind the acquisition of judicial functions by administrative agencies is equally compelling. In the first place, the procedure of the courts is notoriously slow and cumbersome. Whatever its relevance to criminal proceedings and civil disputes, it would be impossible with this procedure to adjudicate the countless cases which arise in connection with the administration of any major regulative legislation.[13] Prior to the increased load brought about by the last war some one hundred thousand cases came before the Veterans Administration each year, and the Social Security Board handles more than a million cases annually.

In the second place, most of the cases that come before the average administrative agency are highly technical and do not fall within the competence of the regularly constituted courts. Administrators are experts in fields where the facts cannot otherwise be understood and appraised. The generality of jurists would become lost in the mysteries of rate-fixing, for example, as quickly as the average layman becomes lost in the jargon of jurists.

Equally weighty reasons for investing administrative agencies with quasi-judicial functions involve a more intimate knowledge of the role of the courts and the nature of the judicial process. The federal courts are confined to the *lis inter pares* mode of operation. This means that no one has standing in a court unless he is either a plaintiff or a defendant, that is to say, unless he has "a legal interest relative to person or property which has been violated by the opposing party to the suit or which may be jeopardized by the decision of the court."[14] Consequently a disinterested party, solicitous of the public interest, finds it extremely difficult to invoke court action to protect the public interest against abuses.

Moreover, the courts are notoriously reticent about seeking out violations of the law, nor do they maintain staffs for this purpose. Criminal cases excepted, they do not ordinarily on their own initiative hale a culprit before them until an aggrieved party seeks their aid. Meanwhile abuses go uncorrected.

Finally, the courts are not concerned with removing the causes of litigation. They do not act until someone is brought before them who has already violated a statute, though the violation might well have been averted had it been possible to take preventive action in the first place.

These are some of the reasons why administrative agencies have been given quasi-judicial functions. Does this mean that we are to be deprived of the precious right to seek relief in the courts, and that, as some charge, we are substituting a government of men for a government of laws? It is no easy matter to steer a course which will avoid the arbitrary denial of private rights, on the one hand, and the inadequate administration of socially necessary legislation, on the other. A proper attention to private rights must provide an aggrieved party with some kind of recourse to the courts. On the other hand, rigid adherence to traditional judicial procedures and unlimited recourse to judicial review would defeat the very purpose for which administrative agencies are instituted. Practice varies, and no one contends that the perfect pattern has been evolved. Private rights would seem to be properly protected when an individual can challenge decisions which are not supported by a fair hearing and "substantial evidence," and decisions which exceed the authority granted under the statute. To insist that hearings must conform to the pattern followed by the courts and that courts may review the administrative finding of facts is, however, virtually to nullify the administrative process. As Fainsod and Gordon point out, "fact finding . . . is the very heart of the administrative process. If judicial review is extended to this field, administrative hearings become simply preliminary trials and the vital administrative role is transferred to the courts."[15]

To summarize: Administrative agencies are the sinews of any state which assumes a substantial measure of responsibility for the welfare of its citizens. If such agencies are to function, they must have certain legislative and judicial powers. Without agencies possessed of such powers, positive intervention by government in the affairs of society is an empty gesture. Undoubtedly, much criticism of the exercise of judicial and legislative functions by administrative agencies is motivated by a sincere interest in protecting private rights. But much if not most of the criticism is prompted by a desire to escape effective regulation.

The strategy of avoiding effective regulation runs something like this: First an attempt is made to discredit the proposed regulatory legislation before the bar of public opinion; this failing, the lobbies take over the legislature; if the proposed legislation survives their pressure, the next step is to appeal to the courts, until recently cool and often cold to regulatory legislation; should the courts sustain the constitutionality of the statute, the next maneuver consists of placing insurmountable obstacles in the way of effectively administering it.[16] Much of the effort to divest administrative agencies of indispensable legislative and judicial powers and to enmesh them in procedural restrictions is a *ruse de guerre* belonging to this fourth stage.[17]

Chapter 12

The Road to Freedom

THE LIBERTY OF the individual is necessarily the first love of liberals. One need not pause here to formulate the protean meanings of "liberty" and "individual," to erect distinctions and add qualifications. The actions of liberals are eloquent enough. They were the first and often the only ones to denounce the abuses of liberty perpetrated by the tyrants of fascist Europe. For them the trains which ran "on time" did not muffle the anguished cry of Matteotti, felled by fascist assassins; "stability" in Germany did not blind them to the systematic enslavement of the German people and the inhuman extermination of the German Jews; they were not tricked into neutrality in the war of the Spanish people against a fascist puppet; the specious promise of "peace in our time" did not buy their consent to the Munich surrender. Nor was their consent forthcoming to the second surrender of Czechoslovakia—engineered by Communists and self-styled left-wing Socialists. They have been among the first to protest against the travesty on freedom which is the daily experience of dark-skinned Americans or, for that matter, of the dark-skinned colonials of all the great powers. They have been the first to oppose encroachments upon the basic freedoms won by the classical liberals in the revolutionary dawn of liberalism, encroachments which can grow more sinister when demagogues like McCarthy stampede a frightened Congress. Moreover, they have demanded the living substance as well as the legal form of freedom; and they have insisted that it shall be available to all men, humble and obscure as well as great and powerful.

But the discussion has not so far run on this theme. Instead, the topic under consideration has been the collective exercise of power. Is this not a strange preoccupation for libertarians? Is it not anomalous that they should be ranged on the side of strong government? An answer to these questions must delve more deeply into the anatomy of power than did the preceding discussion.

The Anatomy of Power

Power may be defined as the ability to produce an intended effect.[1] Power may be variously classified: by reference to its source, by the methods employed in wielding it, by its extent, or by its effects.

If power is classified in terms of its source, one may for present purposes distinguish political power and economic power. There are, of course, many other sources of power—parental, ecclesiastical, and so on, through all the social institutions in their role as agencies of social control—but these are irrelevant here.

If power is classified by reference to the methods employed in wielding it, one may distinguish power achieved through (a) physical force, (b) perquisites, (c) persuasion. Power effected by the first method is often called naked power. A common error consists of identifying all exercises of power, particularly when its source is political, with the use or threatened use of physical force or violence. Although the state may invoke force and is, indeed, accorded an exclusive monopoly in its use, the threat or use of force is far from representing the only way in which the state exercises power. Examples of perquisites may be found all about in the form of "pork," patronage, and *pourboires*. Persuasion may take the form of an appeal to the emotions or an appeal to consistency or evidence. It comprises everything from the propaganda of a group to the proselyting of an individual. It may be based upon fact or built upon fictions, myths, legends.

Power classified as to extent may be limited or unlimited. Obviously, such terms have meaning only in a specific context. Unlimited power is, of course, a theoretical limit rather than an actual state of affairs. Even *der Führer* was restricted in manifold ways, and so is the Presidium of the Russian Communist Party.

In classifying power according to its effect, one may distinguish between power over things and power over people. It is with a view to the latter that power has been defined as "the possession of sway or controlling influence over others," and it is power as so defined which has been held dangerous in the traditional view, on the score that the exercise of such power must correspondingly diminish the power, and with this the freedom, of those over whom it is wielded. This conclusion was not usually applied to the relationship of employer to employee. Neither was it or is it now applied to other power relationships, of parent to child, of pastor to flock, of teacher to student, and so on, where it might lead to ridiculous consequences. It has been reserved primarily for the exercise of political power.

Critics of the traditional position take the view that power does not exist in a fixed quantity, so that if the amount apportioned to government is increased, the amount enjoyed by the governed is decreased. "Sway or controlling influence" may be exercised over others in a way to diminish their power, but also in a way to increase their power by increasing their ability to achieve intended effects. To say this is to say that their freedom is increased since freedom is, after all, the power to do what one wishes. Locke himself said, "That which has the power, or not power, to operate is that alone which is or is not free."

Now the classicists partially recognized this by reposing the police power in government. But if the state by the exercise of the police power obviously increases the power and freedom of all of us, so too does the state promote freedom and power when children are compelled to attend school, when workers are compelled to contribute a portion of their earnings and employers a portion of their profits to a social security fund, when taxpayers are compelled to subsidize adequate housing for slum dwellers. In each case, of course, some are restrained more than others: the professional thieves, the children who might have worked in factories, the workers who prefer to live in the present, the employer or taxpayer who thinks he can isolate himself from the "other side of the tracks." The point is that intervention by government does not, as such, diminish freedom and power in general. The question simply cannot be settled in the abstract, but only by reference to each situation as it arises.

In other words, whether an exercise of power is excessive or not cannot be determined, as Max Lerner has pointed out, by universals about power or about human nature and its urge to power.[2] This can be determined only by reference to the concrete situation, which calls for an exercise of power. The comparatively great powers which the President of the United States wields in time of peace are inadequate to the requirements of war; that is why the Founding Fathers wisely made the President commander in chief with complete power to dispose of our armed forces in time of war. Few people would urge that the President should have sought Congressional approval before sending our armed forces to North Africa or Normandy. In the end, there is only one test by which to determine an excess or a defect of power: does it resolve the needs which called it into being in such a way as to promote human freedom? If power is greater than the situation calls for, it is tyrannical. But if it is less, and this is what is often forgotten, the final result will also be tyranny.

As said before, in terms of effects accomplished, one may distinguish between power over persons and power over things. In the classical view, political power tends to be identified with power over persons, economic power with power over things. In general, classical liberals tended to ignore the possibility that an exercise of political power may increase our power over things. Above all, they neglected the extent to which the economic power represents a power over persons. How the contemporary liberal makes amends for this latter neglect now remains to be seen.

Economic Power

Economic power has its origin first of all in the ownership of wealth. The ownership of wealth represents the power to command goods and services. In the final analysis, especially when concentrated in a few hands, it represents power over *people*: the power of exclusion, which is the essence of the property right, the power to buy personal services, and the power to determine within broad limits what people shall produce and consume. However, the power derived from the ownership of wealth is more than the power to govern the disposition of goods and services. In its further reaches it is the power to shape the policy of major social institutions, such as the school and church, in matters which the owners of wealth deem vital to themselves, the power to control the great opinion-making agencies, like the press and radio, and, finally, it is the power to command the state itself. These all-pervasive though more or less elusive powers often escaped notice in the thinking of nineteenth-century liberals and are naïvely underrated by their twentieth-century conservative legatees.

It need not be said with Marx and Engels that the state in a capitalist society is the executive committee of the *bourgeoisie*. However, the owners of wealth wield an influence over government which is not only vastly disproportionate to their numbers (thereby mocking the Benthamite dictum that "each is to count as one and no one as more than one"), but disproportionate also *to their functional importance in the community*.[3] Anyone familiar with the routine operation of the major political parties knows how the wealthy normally can, and usually do, exercise the decisive voice in matters of economic import. Campaign contributions, newspaper support, the atmosphere of the "big time" by which underpaid officeholders can be dazzled, the lure of private patronage in the form of jobs, retainers, assorted commissions, these are at the almost exclusive disposal of the well-to-do. Only where, as in Great Britain, labor unions have made possible the political organization of wageworkers has the case been different, and when this happened for the first time in the United States during the presidential campaign of 1944, it occasioned a Congressional investigation.

The case would not appear to admit of debate, and yet it is sometimes answered that the palpable presence of regulatory legislation on the statute books and the victories of Roosevelt, Truman, and Kennedy are proof of the very limited political power of a wealthy class which opposed all three vigorously. However, one must remember to begin with that this legislation, and the Democratic Administrations which sponsored it, never challenged the fundamentals of the economic order and, hence, did not evoke the unlimited opposition of the dominant group as a whole. Even on lesser matters, such as monopoly and the tariff, Democratic Administrations hardly scratched the surface—a sure tribute to the power of business. In the second place, it is important to distinguish between "crisis" politics and routine politics. In time of crisis the lower income groups can and do assert themselves; otherwise we should be a plutocracy. The regulatory legislation of the New Deal is the fruit of crisis. But after the peak of the crisis, and between crises, the party machines take over. The party wheel horses, like the mills of the gods, may grind slowly, but they grind exceeding sure. So long as wealth can be held in such large quantity that it confers great powers on those who own it, truly popular government must be regarded as an unrealized ideal.

In conservative quarters it will be argued that the great fortunes are disappearing and that privately owned wealth, as it is spread among more and more people, no longer wields the great power it once enjoyed. Income taxes prevent the birth of great estates and death taxes prevent their survival, we are told. Witness also the enormous increase in the number of people who are shareholders in our great corporations. For example, no single shareholder owns as much as one percent of the stock of a great corporation like the American Telephone and Telegraph Company.

To this it may be responded that the actions of the upper income group are far more audible than its words. However, if words must be had, one may note again that about 2 percent of the families in this country still own about 29 percent of the wealth. Neither income nor inheritance taxes, so it would seem, have as yet reduced the owners of this wealth to a measure of power fairly proportionate to their functional importance in our society.

But even if it is given fullest acceptance, the proposition that ownership of wealth is becoming significantly diffused still misses the point at issue. It takes no note of a species of economic power which has come to be known as managerial control. Managerial control is a phenomenon relatively new in economic history. Managerial power is not derived primarily, if at all, from the wealth one owns, but from the wealth other people own. Managerial power is associated with the growth of giant corporations, in which ownership is divided among a multitude of stockholders and has in fact come to be absentee ownership. As the ownership of corporate property has become dispersed, write Adolph A. Berle and Gardiner Means, authors of the classic work on this subject, "the power formerly joined to it becomes increasingly concentrated," and a resultant system has arisen which "bids fair to be as all-embracing as was the feudal system in its time."[4]

The way in which such concentration of power is effected is simple enough, although it often takes complex forms. As the ownership of a corporation becomes diffused among a widely scattered and heterogeneous group, it becomes possible through the use of the proxy machinery for a few stockholders with larger holdings, which, however, still equal only a small fraction of the total, to select the board of directors and the management. In the case of the very largest corporations, where no single holder owns as much as one percent of the stock, the management may in this way be almost entirely separated from ownership and still exercise virtual control. In an extreme case like the Pennsylvania Railroad Company in its heyday not a single director owned as much as 0.1 percent of the stock, and the combined holdings of all directors were reportedly less than 0.7 percent. "In such companies where does control lie?" asked Berle and Means. This is their reply:

> To answer this question, it is necessary to examine . . . the conditions surrounding the electing of the board of directors. In the election of the board the stockholder ordinarily has three alternatives. He can refrain from voting, he can attend the annual meeting and personally vote his stock, or he can sign a proxy transferring his voting power to certain individuals selected by the management corporation, the proxy committee. As his personal vote will count for little or nothing at the meeting unless he has

a very large block of stock, the stockholder is practically reduced to the alternative of not voting at all or else of *handing over his vote to individuals over whom he has no control and in whose selection he did not participate.* In neither case will he be able to exercise any measure of control. Rather, control will tend to be in the hands of those who select the proxy committee by whom, in turn, the election of directors for the ensuing period may be made. Since the proxy committee is appointed by the existing management, the latter can virtually dictate their own successors. Where ownership is sufficiently subdivided, the management can thus become a self-perpetuating body even though its share in the ownership is negligible.[5]

Everyone will recall that in the great strike which occurred in the automobile industry following the war General Motors Corporation refused to open its books to a government fact-finding commission on the ground that the amount of its profits was its own affair. The remark of Harry Anderson, vice-president of the company, has since become famous. "We don't even open our books to our own stockholders," he declared. This is managerial control. Such is the impotence of the stockholder that Mortimer J. Adler and Lewis A. Kelso have recently issued *The Capitalist Manifesto* in which they urge "restoring shareholders to their full powers and rights as the owners of capital and the employers of management."[6] One is almost disappointed not to encounter the appropriate concluding summons: "shareholders of the world unite, you have nothing to lose but your gains!" What does such managerial control amount to in terms of power?

The American Telephone and Telegraph Company employs 729,035 workers and has almost two million stockholders. It has raised more "new" money since 1945 than was borrowed by any European government during the same period. Its total capital is more than $18 billion. Its managers were reported some years ago to control more than the total wealth of twenty-one states. That, if unregulated, is power.

In 1930 the combined assets of the two hundred largest non-banking corporations equaled nearly half of all the corporate wealth in the United States. Berle and Means estimate that this represented 38 percent or more of all the business wealth and 22 percent of the total wealth of the country.[7]

The statistics of the Bureau of Internal Revenue for 1935 indicate that 0.1 percent of all the corporations reporting owned 52 percent of the assets of all of them and less than 5 percent owned 87 percent of the assets of all of them.[8] That is power, which, then and now, is a function of more than actually owned assets. The power of an automobile or steel manufacturer or oil producer includes control or tangible influence over a vast network of suppliers and outlets or "dealers."

In 1941 the Temporary National Economic Committee in its famous investigation of the concentration of economic power reported that six closely interrelated corporate groups received 45 percent of all war contracts, and that sixty-two companies or interrelated groups received 80 percent of the total. That is power. It prompted the committee to declare that "It is quite conceivable that the democracies might attain a military victory over the aggressors only to find themselves under the domination of economic authority far more concentrated and influential than that which existed prior to the war."[9] In 1948, after noting a sharp upward movement during the years following the war in mergers and consolidations, the Federal Trade Commission repeated the warning: "No great stretch of the imagination is required to foresee that if nothing is done to check the growth in concentration, either the giant corporations will ultimately take over the country, or the Government will be impelled to step in and impose some form of direct regulation in the public interest."[10]

According to one of the most recent and authoritative studies, that of Professor M. A. Adelman of Massachusetts Institute of Technology, 135 corporations own 45 percent of the industrial assets of the United States or the equivalent of one-fourth of the manufacturing volume of the world.[11] That is power.

Berle and Means found that in a population of 125 millions, two thousand individuals through the device of incorporation and the use of the proxy system were able to control and direct half the industry of the country. The pattern has not changed since their book appeared in 1933. That is power.[12]

Even this is not all. If owners can pool their capital, managers can pool their control. We have observed the concentration of economic power and share the guilt of those whom Professor Robert Brady charges with having neglected the role of the "trade association, the intercorporate 'institute,' and the chamber of commerce." What scholars have generally missed, according to Brady, "is that these forms of organization, regardless of the initial purposes of their sponsors, rarely confine themselves for long to strictly 'economic' matters." On the contrary, the larger they become, the more clearly their social and economic policies come to the fore.[13]

Besides the foregoing, one must reckon with a comparatively small number of life insurance companies, mutual funds, and pension trusts which own a sufficiently large segment of the stock of America's major corporations to control most of them, if they choose. At the present time, the management of such companies and trusts, while they no doubt share a community of interest and outlook, do not act in concert; nor do they endeavor on a significant scale to control the policies or select the staffs of the enterprises whose shares they hold. At present, they prefer to get out if the executives or policies of an enterprise are not to their liking. But the foundation for close control by a handful of men is there—if anyone should decide to build on it.

The concentration of economic power took place at precisely the same time that the spread of democracy was accomplishing a diffusion of political power. Moreover, as Brady points out, this economic power came to be used with growing political and social consciousness. The result was inevitable: political power came under the influence of economic power.

The pressure of the owners and managers of privately owned wealth upon government may have several purposes. It may have a negative purpose—a maximum of freedom from government control, which, in our country, culminated in the era of the Insulls and Van Sweringens. Indeed, in recent decades, the business world has found a new weapon which it uses with great effectiveness to ward off substantive government controls. Like the seemingly weak woman who, having fainted several times, consciously or unconsciously dominates her otherwise powerful husband by playing on his fear that she will faint again, the business community threatens that it will be "uncertain" or "insecure." This has been called with some aptness a "confidence" game. Business threatens the larger community that it will "lose confidence." It is seriously contended that the Kennedy Administration has been deterred from taking necessary measures to warn consumers of the menace to health of cigarettes for fear of "upsetting" the business community (presumably at a time when its stomach is in delicate balance) and there can be no doubt that other more general measures have been withheld for just these reasons.

The pressure of ownership and management may have a positive purpose, involving the actual extension of government control when such control serves the interests of ownership and management. The subject is far too important to be dismissed with a paragraph, but a few examples may suffice to make the point. They will indicate that the apparent hatred of government which one finds in many business quarters is the hatred displayed by an employer who depreciates a loyal servant lest someone else, possessed of greater charm, covet him.

Our tariff policy has been and still is a use of government power on the grand scale, invoked by owners and managers to provide themselves with a monopoly of the domestic market. We no longer send the Marines to Nicaragua, but when we did, no amount of "ceremonial legitimation" could conceal the fact that we were not protecting the investments of the coal miner or truck driver or dirt farmer. Our railroads were built with government subsidy,[14] and our merchant marine has been maintained in the same way. Periodicals and newspapers, including those most vigorous in denouncing government "paternalism," are the beneficiaries of postal subsidies which amounted to approximately 163 million dollars in 1948.[15] The variety of government aids obtained by ruggedly individualistic farmers is bewildering. The list could be extended indefinitely.

The pressure of owners and managers on government has a third purpose, whose omission would do them a grave in-

justice. To say that they are exclusively concerned with manipulating the power of the state in their own interest is to be
guilty of oversimplification. They have manipulated the power
of the state in behalf of the public—otherwise many would
be overwhelmed by a sense of guilt—*but always in terms of
their conception of the public interest, with rare exceptions
a conception colored by and preserving their preferred economic position in the social order.*

When Ralph J. Cordiner, chairman of General Electric,
testified against farm subsidies before a Senate committee,
he did not plead that farm subsidies placed an unfair tax
burden on corporations; his was the brave argument (especially in the light of what has since happened to General
Electric) that all peacetime subsidies of any kind interfere
with the free market and are "contrary to the ideal of a free
society."[16] When the light and power industry protests government ownership, the protestation is invariably in behalf of
"American taxpayers who foot the bill." When the late Mr.
Fairless, as president of U. S. Steel, defended the size of his
corporation before the Celler Sub-Committee, he explained
that "it has had to be, in order to do the jobs that a big nation
has demanded of it in peace and war . . ." When, in large
advertisements, McGraw-Hill Book Company hailed the passage of the Taft-Hartley Act, this was not because the
bargaining position of employers was thereby improved;
McGraw-Hill sounded the Lincolnesque theme that " 'Slave'
Labor" had been freed. This is in the end the ultimate power:
no cheap grab for "pork," no covert subsidy, but the identification of the wealth and power of the few with the wellbeing
of the many. When an ailing and impecunious septuagenarian
defends his congressman's vote against a medical aid bill with
patriotic ardor as having saved the country from creeping
socialism—that is power!

The problem of limiting the private corporation to its proper
economic sphere and containing its power becomes more and
more complex as the power of the corporation increasingly
spills over into other institutional areas. Inspired by an understandable desire to improve their tarnished public "image"

with something more eloquent than words, corporations have become increasingly interested in the ideal of "corporate citizenship." This has manifested itself in a variety of ways. One finds a keen interest in providing for the recreational side of their employees' lives. One also finds increasing evidence of a concern for the spiritual in the form of generous church subventions.[17] Most of all, many large corporations have lately dedicated themselves to rescuing higher education from the condition of penury into which it has steadily been sinking.[18] Inasmuch as a great deal of the criticism of corporations stems from institutions of higher learning, the gesture would appear to be a magnanimous one. It raises some interesting issues.

Initiated by a number of distinguished business men, including Frank W. Abrams, Chairman of Standard Oil of New Jersey, Alfred P. Sloan, Jr., Chairman of General Motors, and Irving Olds, Chairman of U. S. Steel, aid has been flowing in ever increasing volume to our parched campuses. Dr. Wilson Compton, president of the Council for Financial Aid to Education, has predicted that, by 1970, corporation aid to higher education will amount to one-half billion dollars annually. There are no strings. Disposition of the funds is entirely in the hands of the academic authorities.

However, in the important decision by which Judge Alfred Stein of the New Jersey Superior Court upheld the legality of corporation gifts, he declared: "I cannot conceive of any greater benefit to corporations in this country than to build . . . respect for and adherence to a system of free enterprise." And Richard Eells, author of an authoritative study, and an eloquent advocate of corporation giving (which must be distinguished from the benevolences of individuals),[19] declares that "The justification for corporation philanthropy . . . is not what it achieves for the community alone, but *rather what it does to protect the wider corporate environment that sustains the share owners' profitable investment.*"[20] And Dr. Compton, in his tribute to corporation giving, finds that business and education have much in common: "Both are interested in freedom. Both understand that freedom, private enterprise, and public education are segments of the same circle."

For anyone in academic life to question these propositions might seem like a display of churlish ingratitude—which may explain why the *Annals of the American Academy of Political and Social Sciences,* in an issue largely devoted to education finances, refrained. But it is surely questionable whether "Business" takes a positive interest in freedom, except as freedom from regulation. There is no significant record of activity on the part of the business community against abuses of civil rights and civil liberties, or—in this context, in defense of academic freedom. The bland (or naïve) equation of freedom and free private enterprise and the enterprise of large corporations should be undergoing continuous examination by our university faculties. But dare one question holy writ in a denominational college? *Caveat beneficii acceptor!*

The corporation was once called "soulless." Perhaps it should remain so. This is not to impugn the ideal of good corporate citizenship. It is to say that there is an area for the exercise of such citizenship which avoids a hazardous extension of the corporation's already formidable powers. There is ample and largely unused opportunity for corporations to reimburse the community for many of the social losses which enter into the cost of production, such as air and stream pollution, to take a major example. They might commit themselves to honest and clear labeling, whether of pharmaceuticals, canned goods, or interest rates. They might direct the U. S. Chamber of Commerce or the American Manufacturers Association to abandon their undeviating opposition to all proposals for helping those who are casualties of the marketplace. They might pioneer in fair employment practices, as these involve minority groups and the aged.

There are indications of a greater sense of social responsibility among big businessmen than among small. In many areas the Committee for Economic Development (CED), backed by a minority of management, has shown the way. But most corporation executives have not followed their lead. Until they do, the majority of liberals will not, like Mr. Berle, drop their guard and applaud the corporation as the "conscience-carrier of twentieth-century American society." Instead they will remember Mr. Berle's other words concerning "the small directing group" that presides over America's corporations: "As yet the community has not created any acknowledged referent of responsibility, no group from which they take their power mandate or get instructions in dealing with serious streams of events they can and do affect. There is no recognized body of doctrine by which they themselves must test their choice as they act from day to day."[21]

The liberal concludes that no society, least of all ours, is a void as far as the exercise of power is concerned. Power is wielded, must be wielded, everywhere and always. The question is whether its exercise will be controlled or uncontrolled, whether it will be used clandestinely for private purposes or openly for social purposes, whether it will be manipulated by special interests or exercised by responsible public agencies. The exercise of power is not inherently evil: it may release as well as restrain. In any case the exercise of power in a complex society is inevitable. Our choice is not between more power and less power. The question is one of transforming power,[22] of making it responsible, of legitimizing it. By whom shall it be wielded and in whose behalf? Shall it be wielded by two-thousand-odd managers who are not even accountable in many cases to their stockholders, let alone the public at large?[23] Or shall it be wielded by absentee owners, who, ignorant of the enterprises which belong to them, have not even management's functional justification for the power they possess?

The issue may be stated in another way. The large-scale enterprise and the device of incorporation which makes it possible emerged in response to the economic needs of a complex and highly mechanized society. Clearly such large enterprises are necessary to satisfy the requirement of efficiency and economy in production. Mass production would not be possible without them. The size necessary to the achievement of maximum efficiency in any given enterprise may be a matter of dispute and will vary, of course, in different industries. Nevertheless it must be evident that, beyond a given point, increase in size no longer serves the economic purpose[24] of efficiency in production, but an entirely different purpose, namely the desire of those who manage the enterprise for power. But at this point the private corporation ceases to be a merely economic entity; it becomes a political entity as well and, as such, must be viewed in terms of a wholly new set of criteria. For, by the verdict of corporation managers themselves when they are thinking in a different context, power is precisely what a society must regulate and control—and even diffuse—if society is to rest upon something more than a system of coercion. No one has said this more vehemently than they. Clearly, power must have some justification other than the desire of those who have it to acquire and wield it; otherwise it is illegitimate.

Some of our very large corporations are large beyond the requirements of efficiency. It would require a most resourceful apologist to establish that the size of General Motors, A. T. & T., U. S. Steel, Aluminum Company of America and scores of other corporations (not to mention the Du Pont Corporation which, to dirges sung by the corporate world, has been required by the Supreme Court to divest itself of its General Motors stock) is *functionally* justifiable, if only because much smaller enterprises, at least as efficient as their rivals, are awkwardly in evidence.[25] It is not unfair to suggest that we are, in fact, evolving a system of private government. Since our largest corporations are no longer merely economic entities and are as much agencies for acquiring and disposing of power, it is in such terms that they must be regarded.

Sometimes, to be sure, the power wielded by management may be quite unsolicited and have unwelcome consequences. At this very time the steel industry is considering an increase in the price of steel to compensate for an automatic wage increase which has just been granted under the terms of a contract with the steel workers' union. The decision to raise prices is likely to initiate an inflationary price spiral which will affect the entire economy. Consequently, the President of the United States has written to the heads of twelve steel companies urging them to hold the line on prices and promising to discourage inflationary demands by labor when contract talks open next year. But he is dealing with men of steel. They can be quite as unbending as their product. They dislike government even when its activities are at some remove from their own. When, in time of peace, the government endeavors to influence if not to dictate their pricing policies, their reaction is predictably negative. Mr. Roger Blough, head of U. S. Steel, has rejected the President's reasoning, although it is not yet clear that he and the others who have responded are categorically rejecting the request. And Mr. Conrad Cooper, executive vice-president of U. S. Steel, has described the President's request as a "first step toward . . . the demise . . . of a free market and, therefore, of a free society."[26]

Meanwhile, the issue of power and its responsible exercise could hardly be drawn more sharply. The decision reached by Mr. Blough and his fellow-executives concerns not merely themselves, but the whole country. However, it is bound to be made by reference to its bearing on the steel industry or, more precisely, *their notion* of what its bearing will be. It would seem reasonable to insist that the power to reach such a decision be limited by those who are responsible to the country as a whole. This is the price that management must pay when it accumulates power in such vast quantity. Not to agree is to invite confusion. This, at any rate, is the view of a liberal Administration in Washington armed only with the power of persuasion. Should that fail, it would be reasonable to urge that it be armed with more.

It must be recorded that there has been a tendency in recent years, even among some liberals, to neglect considerations of the kind raised above. The ease with which our economy effected the transition from war to peace generated a spirit of grateful relief which diluted the acrimony of much of the pre-war feeling against big business. Mingled with this, no doubt, was a sense of contriteness over what some came to call the "stereotyped" thinking and the "muckraking spirit" of the 'thirties, as far as large corporations were concerned. The stereotype may well have led to uncritical eulogy of small business and equally uncritical denunciation of bigness as such. Reinforcing such feelings has been a human tendency to find virtue in the inevitable, and, in our world, bigness in business surely exudes an aura of inevitability.

It is within some such framework that we must interpret

David Lilienthal's panegyric to bigness, called *Big Business: A New Era*,[27] and A. A. Berle's recent writings. Both are liberals. In his *20th Century Capitalist Revolution*, Mr. Berle points out that the traditional notions concerning how the power of corporations is checked are largely archaic. Major corporations, because they increasingly finance the replacement and expansion of their plants from internal sources, no longer seek capital and are therefore no longer checked by the judgment of the security market. Neither are they checked effectively by competition in the classical sense. But this is not a cause for serious concern, Berle contends. New checks have emerged. One of these resides in the system of oligopoly, as giants like General Motors and Ford struggle for leadership in a given industry; the other is the force of public opinion, which, to take an example, was strong enough to keep car manufacturers from inflating prices in the sellers' market following the war.[28]

Galbraith's *American Capitalism: the Concept of Countervailing Power* is similarly optimistic. In his view, as also in Mr. Berle's, even though competition in the old sense has been to a great extent destroyed, the power of many corporations is nevertheless checked by other firms offering a similar service as an acceptable alternative, as in the case of trucking versus railroading, coal versus gas, etc. In addition, there is another kind of restraint, or system of restraints, with which Galbraith's name has become associated, and which he calls "countervailing power." The concentrated power of producers evokes and is balanced by, he tells us, a corresponding concentration of power among those large-scale distributors who buy their products (chain and department stores, mail order and discount houses, etc.), as among those employee aggregates that form labor unions. These exercise countervailing power.[29]

Galbraith's hypothesis, to the extent that it assumes the *spontaneous* emergence of countervailing power, has been rather thoroughly discredited,[30] and Galbraith himself recognizes a role for government in the process. Buyers are protected, not by concentrations of power represented by chain stores, etc. (monopsonists and oligopsonists), but by the fact that merchandizing remains a predominantly competitive area. Labor unions, as a counter to the power of corporate industry, would not have emerged without government intervention. As for Mr. Berle's checks, the public opinion on which he relies is indeed effective within limits, else it would be pointless to speak of the possibility of government intervention, but a sophisticated observer like Mr. Berle ought not to need reminding that large corporations own the instrumentalities for conditioning public opinion and these enterprises are heavily biased in favor of their kind. Finally, if oligopolistic giants do contend with each other, their encounters are too suggestive of professional wrestling matches. Even when they do really contend, the upshot is all too likely to be a prettier package (including the metal packages in which our automobiles come) rather than a better commodity at a lower price.

Accordingly, the answer of the great majority of liberals is that the vast power now enjoyed by the managers and owners of large-scale enterprise should either be effectively controlled or, if this is impossible, actually wielded by responsible public officials subject to removal if their conduct is not in accord with the public interest. The same experts who now turn the wheels of industry must necessarily continue to turn them, but in response to policies either controlled or dictated by accountable public officials, policies determined by lawmaking bodies after open hearing and not by bankers behind a door marked "Private." Liberals vary from those who would impose strict controls on "big business" to those who would convert the private power based on ownership of large-scale enterprise into public power. On the other hand, most liberals are agreed that individual private enterprise *in the true sense of that term*—not the collective, quasi-public enterprise of the great privately controlled corporation—should be scrupulously preserved.

In a much-quoted statement Franklin Roosevelt said as much:

The power of a few to manage the economic life of the Nation must be diffused among the many or be transferred to the public and its democratically responsible government. If prices are to be managed and administered, if the Nation's business is to be allotted by plan and not by competition, that power should not be vested in any private group. . . .[31]

Power, it has been said, corrupts.[32] This the liberal denies. Unlimited and irresponsible power corrupts. Economic power when it becomes concentrated in a few private hands is irresponsible power. The alternative is positive intervention by government. But this, some contend, must eventuate in the use of unlimited power: interventionism must result in totalitarianism. Such a choice between irresponsible economic power and unlimited political power is a grim one indeed. Enough has been said to suggest that the dilemma is not real. But the case is not complete until the proposition that interventionism leads to totalitarianism has been re-examined in one of its most influential versions.

Totalitarianism: A Faulty Diagnosis

Political power has lately come under increased suspicion. The Nazi horror is still close enough to remind us of the terrible excess to which abuse of power can be carried. We had come to think that such things were no longer possible in the Western world, that we had left them behind in some dark period of the human past. It was by sheer luck—the arrogant confidence of the *Ubermensch* who sought to dispose of his victims simultaneously instead of one by one—that we averted destruction of the most precious values for which civilization has come to stand. We know, moreover, that although the most powerful citadels of fascism are now demolished, it can easily manifest itself in other forms. It held strong positions in pre-war France and it could conceivably reoccupy these positions, especially if the departure of De Gaulle should leave France without an effective third force to keep frustrated military men and dogmatic Communists from each other's throats. In the past there have been many places in America that have harbored fascist tendencies, some as holy as the Shrine of the Little Flower, as high as the Tribune Tower, and as vast as San Simeon. The new militancy of the lunatic right in this country is a reminder of ever-present danger. Fascism, along with communism—to which reference will be made later—represents the supreme abuse of political power and it is all-important that its causes be understood. Whoever confuses the issue does us no service. We do not want fascism to reappear in Europe and we do not want it here.

During the 'thirties there was a substantial measure of agreement concerning the causes of fascism. Subsequently, however, a small group of conservative economists and writers challenged the accepted interpretation. The most celebrated of them are two former Austrians, Friedrich A. Hayek and Ludwig von Mises, both of whom have had a great influence in America. Indeed, the reception of Hayek was strongly reminiscent of the triumph of Herbert Spencer in this country during the several decades following the Civil War. Even Walter Lippmann fell, if only temporarily, under their spell, as his *The Good Society* attests. Since the issue raised by them brings to a focus the many problems explored in connection with government interventionism and the use of power, and since clarity concerning the causes of totalitarianism is the most vital desideratum of our time, one may well examine their position.

What, asks Professor Hayek, prompted the majority of Germans to embrace Nazism? No inborn German vice, not their defeat in World War I, not even the suffering of the depression or the excessive German nationalism of which the *Junkers* and the general staff were the incarnation—these were minor factors—but socialism, particularly Marxian socialism. If Hayek means that the Socialists were an indirect and unwitting cause, in the sense that fear of them drove the capitalists and *Junkers* into the arms of the Nazis, and if he were to give this as one of the links in the chain of causes, he would find little disagreement. But Professor Hayek's thesis is much more original. The proletarian Socialists (Hayek and von Mises use the term "socialist" in several different senses) themselves deliberately promoted Nazism, declares Hayek. The capitalists, the middle classes, were innocent.

It was not merely the defeat, the suffering, and the wave of nationalism which led to their [the authors of Nazism] success. Still less was the cause, as so many people wish to believe, a capitalist reaction against the advance of socialism. On the contrary, the support which brought these ideas to power came precisely from the socialist camp. It was certainly not through the bourgeoisie, but rather through the absence of a strong bourgeoisie, that they were helped to power.[33]

If the critical reader wonders how many if not most of the German capitalists became members of the new "elite," Professor Hayek neglects to explain—an oversight which Herr Thyssen's repentant *I Paid Hitler* abundantly underscores.

We also have the authority of Professor von Mises that the "economic distress in Germany does not account for Nazism's success."[34] The great depression, he observes, was international; only in Germany did it result in Nazism. As for the German workers who voted against Nazism by voting for the Social Democrat, the Communist, or the Catholic ticket, they did so "out of fear and inertia";[35] they were really Nazis at heart!

For von Mises as for Hayek all interference with the free market, limited or total, interventionist or socialist, is evil.[36] The purpose of intervention, whether for private advantage or public good, whether secretly solicited or openly planned, whether secured through consent or imposed through coercion, is of no matter. The result is the same: brutal dictatorship on the Nazi model. Thus, whether inadvertently or deliberately (sometimes one is implied, sometimes the other), the German Left built and now the British Labourites and American progressives are building the foundations of totalitarianism. One would think that Hayek and von Mises might at the very least have saddled the private monopolists and cartelists with a major share of the blame for interfering with the free market. But it is the Left, the Social Democratic labor movement in Germany and "unorthodoxy" in England, which is almost exclusively anathematized. Although "the capitalist organizers of monopolies . . . are . . . one of the main sources of . . . danger," we are told that "it would . . . be a mistake to put the blame for the modern movement toward monopoly exclusively or mainly [sic] on that class." Rather, according to Hayek, we must look to the Left and its propaganda against competition which prepared public opinion to accept monopoly.[37] A similar spirit prompts von Mises to say that in Great Britain "Fabian and Keynesian 'unorthodoxy' resulted in a confused acceptance of the tenets of Nazism," leading to practical policies which "frustrated all endeavors to form a common front of all nations menaced by the aspirations of Nazism."[38] Runciman, Halifax, Lloyd, Lady Astor, Chamberlain, Hoare, and their kin—Fabians and Keynesians? Their harsher critics might say that all of them, both living and dead, would turn over in their graves.

The truth is that, like Procrustes, von Mises and Hayek have been committing mayhem on their victim in order to fit him to the size of their bed. Liberals hold no brief for the German Left. It had many faults. But the attempt to use the German case as proof of an unbreakable link between interventionism and dictatorship involves a gross distortion of recent history. History has been distorted before; the concern is that this distortion not leave us vulnerable to the real causes of totalitarianism.

German Nazism, the great majority of impartial students are agreed, was bred primarily of the widespread insecurity produced by mass unemployment and mass deprivation. The period between 1923 and 1928, the so-called Locarno era, was a relatively prosperous one for Germany. During this period the Nazi movement was without significance. Hitler's voice hardly reached beyond the rafters of a Munich beer hall until the depression gave him his opportunity. Fascism has threatened elsewhere with the advent of difficult times, and it is safe to predict that it will threaten in our country if we have a repetition of the mass unemployment of the 'thirties. Fascism rose primarily out of the *impotence* of German capitalist democracy, its powerlessness to solve the problem of mass insecurity.

The working-class movement in Germany had many faults, but Hayek and von Mises need only have consulted the election returns from the working-class districts of Berlin or recalled the gaping shell holes in the Karl Marx Hof of their own Vienna to determine where the opposition to Nazism mainly lay. This opposition joined to the opposition of the Center might well have prevailed over the middle-class fascination for Nazism, had not German financiers and industrialists, fearful of the use of government power in behalf of the masses, come to the rescue. Oblivious to the causes of social unrest, they preferred to banish unrest by the more convenient method of suppression. Alarmed by the power of labor unions and frightened by the threat of socialism to private enterprise, they gullibly adopted the fascist movement as a useful device for curbing both.

But even if the Nazis had been defeated, the result would not have been a forthright use of political power in the public interest. So deep was the conflict among the people that they were unable to find an area of agreement. The Nazis promised action; the great tragedy was that democracy had come to stand for stalemate, paralysis, inaction. This was so in Germany, and it was nearly so in prewar France. Here is the secret of life and death as far as democracy is concerned, and this is what the tragic fate of the German Republic can teach the democracies which by tradition as well as circumstance are sturdier than the fragile thing created at Weimar: When the forces at work in a democracy become so divisive that agreement on fundamental aims and purposes is impossible, either one interest tyrannizes over another or government is condemned to inaction. In either case democracy perishes. Forced unemployment, mass want and insecurity, the wanton waste of creative energy, the needless frustration of normal expectations and aspirations, these render such agreement impossible.

In the end, democracy cannot exist unless men have a sense of community. A sense of community prevails only when there is a full release of creative energies in behalf of the social group as a whole. *Only within the framework of such a community can the democratic organization of power be intelligently discussed.*[39]

A New Separation of Powers

Intervention may, of course, take many forms yet to be examined. It may manifest itself in the systematic and deliberate encouragement of Professor Galbraith's "countervailing powers."[40] It may take the form of the kind of regulation presently exercised by the government over public utilities. It may involve the extensive use of monetary and fiscal controls of the kind with which we have become increasingly familiar. In its broader reach it may take the form of extensive ownership of the means of production. It is safe to say that, unlike Marxists and unlike neo-classicists of the Hayekian school, liberals are unencumbered by dogmas as they approach this problem. They simply argue that there is nothing in the nature of political power *per se* and nothing connected with the rise of fascism in Europe which leads to the conclusion that totalitarian dictatorship is a necessary consequence of such interventionism or, for that matter, of socialism. Interventionism in Britain has led to none of the dire consequences Hayek and von Mises predicted for it; and the same may be said for New Zealand, Australia, and the Scandinavian countries, where intervention has been carried much farther. On the contrary, totalitarianism is much more likely to result from a policy of nonintervention and inaction, of stubborn reliance on a market which fails to perform the functions imputed to it in the dreams of the devout and orthodox. In the final analysis, modern totalitarian government is the desperate political recourse of a social order, which, by failing to fully exploit its productive potentialities, is not justifying itself economically.

But the liberal cannot afford to neglect the threat of dictatorship even in a society which is solving its economic problems. The danger in such a society is much less. But the danger still remains. Until recently many thinkers of the Left, preoccupied almost exclusively with the economic components of power, which they were the first to study systematically, assumed that if the means of production and distribution were owned collectively, democracy would automatically ensue. The enormous power of the capitalist class misled them into supposing that in modern society the concentration of power is exclusively a function of the concentration of privately owned and controlled wealth. This error led, for example, to an oversimplification of Nazism as a rule of capitalists, based upon naked force. The idea that capitalists could be reduced to the status of junior partners in the control of the coercive power of the state, as they in fact were in the Third Reich, was generally neglected. The same error led also to the early, now discredited assumption that socialism in Russia would automatically be followed by democracy. Unfortunately this has not been the case. To be sure those who cite the Russian experience as an object lesson for the democracies—and there are many who do—need to be reminded of Russia's lack of a democratic tradition, her technological backwardness, and the capitalist quarantine. These factors thwarting the growth of democracy had nothing to do with socialism.[41] In any case, it is clear that the Russian managerial elite, having achieved a virtual monopoly of power during a period of extended emergency, will refuse to relinquish power even when the emergency has passed. Such a managerial elite does not own the wealth of Russia but neither does the managerial class in America own the wealth from which it derives its power.

As liberals are now keenly aware, there are in fact two countertendencies at work, one discouraging, the other promoting, the abuse of power as governments intervene in the economic life of society. On the one hand, if the reorganization of economic power in a liberal society reduces the sources of friction and conflict, if it releases the creative energies of the whole people, if it mitigates the sense of insecurity from which all men, poor and prosperous, now suffer, it will to that extent remove much of the temptation to abuse power. For much of this temptation, it must be clear, springs from fear, resentment, frustration. On the other hand, the ambitions and aggressions, the love for display, and the desire for prestige, which are now discharged in private economic activity, will seek release in the political sphere as public enterprise expands at the expense of private enterprise,[42] and in this sphere will dispose of both political and economic power. Here is a substantial source of danger.

The nature of the danger was well described by Bertrand Russell some years ago. Mr. Russell believes with liberals that "the political State must either increasingly take over economic functions or partially abdicate in favor of vast private enterprises which are sufficiently powerful to defy or control it." He adds, "If the State does not acquire supremacy over such enterprises, it becomes their puppet, and they become the real State." But if, as Mr. Russell concludes, "economic and political power must become unified," the fact remains that,

Under any form of socialism which is not democratic, those who control economic power can, without "owning" anything, have palatial official residences, the use of the best cars, a princely entertainment allowance, holidays at the public expense in official holiday resorts, and so on and on. And why should they have any more concern for the ordinary worker than those in control have now? There can be no reason why they should have, unless the ordinary worker has power to deprive them of their positions.[43]

Mr. Russell concludes that "if concentration of power in a single organization—the State—is not to produce the evils of despotism in an extreme form, it is essential that power within that organization should be widely distributed, and that subordinate groups should have a large measure of autonomy."[44]

Mr. Russell may appear to have produced an antinomy: how can power be concentrated and divided at the same time? It will be answered that power must be distributed not with a view to blocking action by government but with a view to securing the widest possible participation in its action;[45] so, too, checks and restraints are to be employed not to curb action by government but to make the action of government responsive to the declared will and expressed needs of the people. How can this be done? It is possible to trace only in outline the answer to a question which has come to occupy a central place in contemporary liberal thinking.

What has been said implies, to begin with, a devotion to the constitutional ideal and with it the idea of government by laws rather than by men. So far classical and contemporary liberalism are agreed. But in the more recent view, the constitutional ideal must be spelled out not to prevent the *use* but to prevent the *misuse* and *abuse* of power. A constitution must provide for an efficient organization of the use of power and for founding such use upon popular consent. At the same time, there must be a proper consciousness of the limitations of constitutionalism. At its best, a constitution reflects the settled wisdom of a people concerning the proper aims and methods of government. But at its worst, it can be an accessory to the abuse of power by becoming a device for perpetuating established interests at the expense of new needs and aspirations. The subversion of the constitutional ideal to effect such abuse of power can be prevented only if the imperative need for flexibility in constitutional law is not obscured by pieties about the "wisdom of the past," which mean the dead hand of the past, or about the "rule of the law," which mean law as identified with the interests of the rich and powerful.

As he takes over the constitutional ideal which came into its own in the seventeenth and eighteenth centuries, so too, the liberal takes over the related doctrine of individual rights. The worth of human personality, of which rights are the legal recognition, is fundamental to the ethos of the new liberalism. With this goes the recognition that popular consent is a sham unless individuals and groups of individuals enjoy certain basic rights. Clearly, the will of the majority is spurious, save in a context of free speech, free press, and free assembly, where majorities and minorities can crystallize and be truly ascertained, where, in a word, minorities can *become* majorities. But as in the case of the constitutional ideal, so in the case of the doctrine of individual rights, the emphasis varies. The doctrine of "natural" rights is abandoned as a fiction whose usefulness ended when kings no longer claimed to rule by divine right. The foundation of rights becomes ethical and humanistic rather than metaphysical. Moreover, there is much less emphasis on the property right as traditionally defined. The property right, since it is no longer "natural," must be justified functionally—an idea shared by some of the fathers of the classical liberal tradition, like Locke, but forgotten by their followers. Such an insistence on a functional justification of the property right means that government can no longer be restrained from, say, the nationalization of subsurface resources by the plea that this violates the sanctity of human personality and flouts a natural right. Even so, the doctrine of individual rights, not excluding a modified conception of the property right, continues to function for the contemporary liberal as a limitation on the power of government. *In fact, from another side it undergoes a fundamental extension, for the liberal includes among the basic rights of the individual some which the eighteenth and nineteenth centuries generally ignored: the right to security from the economic hazards of illness, accident, old age; the right to employment of a kind commensurate with one's abilities and to a training which will prepare one for such employment.*[46]

The extent to which the new liberalism would avail itself of such devices as bicameralism, federalism, the differentiation of government into executive, judiciary, and legislative branches, and the related use of a system of checks and balances would, of course, be dictated in part by tradition and circumstances. In principle, the liberal is not bound to any of these, and he often points to the example of Great Britain as evidence of the possibility of getting on democratically without them. As an advocate of change, the liberal has found himself blocked more often than not by these devices. Too often they have been manipulated by an entrenched minority so as to perpetuate established interests. Too often, also, they have led to stalemate in time of crisis, as in the last months of the Hoover administration. In each case the attitude of liberals has been conditioned, not by a desire to curb government, but by a desire to make it more responsible. A brief enumeration will make this attitude clearer.

Liberals are generally agreed that the traditional bicameral systems are archaic. Some favor unicameral legislatures, especially for state governments. Others favor a revision of the bicameral principle to provide for the representation, on the one hand, of population groups, on the other hand, of functional economic groups.[47]

All liberals recommend the distribution of power between federal, regional, state, and local governments as a means of making government more responsive to local needs and differences, and as a way of encouraging and preserving local initiative.[48] Liberals find nothing wrong with what Lord Bryce described as the American dogma that "where any function can be equally well discharged by a central or by a local body, it ought by preference to be entrusted to the local body." But the function must be performed equally well. For many reasons, as has been seen, some of the old functions and most of the new ones undertaken by the central government cannot now be performed adequately by local government. No one disputes the general competence of states and municipalities in such matters as automobile traffic control, zoning, licensing, the control of crime, and so on. But as noted earlier, costly social legislation cannot be undertaken by the states, in the first place, because many of them cannot afford it, and, in the second place, because industry, seeking the lowest taxes and the least restriction, will often migrate to states where costly social obligations and restrictive regulations have been avoided. Since much of the national wealth is concentrated in a relatively small area, while the remainder of the country serves as a colonial hinterland, it is not unnatural that large parts of the country are unable to finance adequate education, for example. This will be accomplished only by federal intervention in an area heretofore free of it. When appeals to local responsibility obscure such facts, we are making a fetish of localism. It should be added that "Washington" is not the opposite of local responsibility. While federal aid is bound to involve regulation, patterns of federal-state-local co-operation have lately been evolved, for example, in the field of public housing, which effectively combine federal financial aid and federal definitions of standards with local initiative and local control.

If liberals are critical of the doctrine of "states' rights," so too are they cool to Montesquieu's classic division of government into three coequal branches checking and balancing each other. On the whole, they favor the British system, in which the prime minister and his cabinet are, in effect, the executive committee of the popularly elected chamber. Such an arrangement makes a stalemate impossible, since the cabinet is bound to resign if it fails to have parliamentary approval. On the other hand, the instability of ministries, as in the prewar French system, is avoided by the British, because a chamber which can be dissolved by the ministry and forced to stand the test of an election will use its power over the ministry with discretion. Neither can there be a stalemate between the courts and parliament in Great Britain of the kind which partly paralyzed action in this country in the first years of the Roosevelt administration. If in Great Britain, and, to a lesser extent, in our country, the legislative function has been increasingly delegated to the executive-administrative branch, both in the matter of legislative initiative and the working out of legislative detail, this augurs no disastrous consequence in the judgment of the liberal. So long as a popularly elected chamber retains the vital power of investigation, of criticism, and of approval and disapproval, its great service in guarding against tyranny, whether public or private, has been rendered.

In general, however, the contemporary liberal places less stress on the importance of political mechanisms in limiting power than the political determinists of the eighteenth and nineteenth centuries. By far the more important safeguards against tyranny are to be found, he believes, not in the organization of the machinery of government, but in institutions outside the government.[49]

The first of these is the party system. The right to protest is meaningless unless such protest can be informed and organized. In the absence of organization and leadership, public opinion is diffuse and impotent, and government can mold it to serve the interests of those in power. Such organization and leadership can be provided in part by organizations like the League of Women Voters, Americans for Democratic Action, the Committee for Economic Development, or the British Fabian Society—organizations which must be reckoned as part of the pattern of forces which tend to make government responsible to the people. But most of all, this function is performed by the multiparty system. A single-party system is, of course, a device for mobilizing opinion behind the government in power and perpetuating dictatorship. But an opposition party subjects government to a cross fire of criticism, forces it to justify itself at every important juncture, threatens it with removal if it falls short, and, above all, provides the electorate with an alternative which is a great deal more than a simple *nein.* "To rule without an unlimited opposition," writes Max Lerner, "is to rule with a stick." He adds,

To rule without it is a mark of political indolence and immaturity, and of a basic distrust of one's own social program. The party system and the party struggle must become the center of politics, as distinguished from the process of economic control and planning, the detailed work of which is best left to a corps of nonpartisan experts. It is the party system, with its principle of free scope to the opposition, that represents the most reliable safeguard against the disease and corruption of power.[50]

The party system is not only a check on the power of government. It also makes possible the continuous scrutiny of business as a system of power and, as they become stronger, of labor unions as well.

The people are not only voters and citizens; they are also workers. The second of the institutions by which government power is made responsive to the needs of the people is an independent and powerful organization of workers. Such an organization is indispensable to democratic government. Labor needs protection from public managers as well as private ones, and this can be had only through autonomous organization. Some change of function might well occur, notably in the direction of employee-management councils of the kind which here and there made an appearance during the war. But some form of independent organization there must be. It is not without significance that totalitarian governments have allowed no place for an independent labor movement. Neither is it without significance that labor unions had to wage a bitter fight for recognition in a society dominated by industrialists and businessmen and that the labor union is even now regarded, in some quarters, as a marginal institution, irregular, shady, suspect. Labor unions are universally despised by those who seek, either covertly or overtly, a monopoly of power.

The people are also consumers and the exercise of government power must be made responsive to the needs of the people through a strong consumers' organization. In our country the consumer, as noted earlier, has been woefully impotent, despite the carefully cultivated fiction that he is "sovereign." Even the New Deal, which lent such great impetus to the organization of workers, made only feeble gestures in behalf of the consumer. In Europe, on the other hand, the consumer movement has taken on enormous proportions. The problem of organizing consumers is concededly no simple one, and in America, particularly, the task of organizing consumers is one to which the liberal movement has yet to address itself successfully. Meanwhile, President Kennedy has sought aid for beleaguered consumers by proposing that a Consumers' Advisory Council be set up under the Council of Economic Advisers and that every appropriate federal department have a consumer adviser. Such action is long overdue.[51]

The functions of a consumer organization should be at least four. First, such an organization might exercise a monitor function, calling attention to waste, extravagance, poor service, and unimaginativeness in the production and distribution of goods. Second, it might do what advertisers—for the most part fraudulently—now claim to do, conduct extensive educational work among consumers. Third, it might poll consumers to determine consumer preferences, a practice made feasible by the new technique of scientific sampling which has been employed with fair success in polls of public opinion. Finally, and most importantly, it might encourage the entry of consumers into Rochdale co-operatives which, as a quasi-public form of enterprise *would serve to check the efficiency of both public and private enterprise.* The social significance of the Rochdale movement is too well known to require elaboration here. It can and has reached into the field of production with the consumers' organization acting as owner and employer. In any case, the Rochdale movement might well occupy an important place in a mixed or managed economy.

One more institution remains through which the responsiveness of government to the people may be assured. This is the institution of private enterprise, in a mixed or managed economy no longer the axis about which all other institutions revolve but important enough to be one of the several extra-governmental sources of power and to serve as a check on public enterprise. Liberal opinion differs concerning where the boundary between public and private enterprise should be drawn, but in any case private enterprise, both large scale and small, continues to occupy a significant place in a liberal and even in a liberal-socialist society. Once perhaps guilty of a doctrinaire opposition to corporate bigness as such, the liberal is presently willing to judge by reference to the political and economic consequences of bigness. Often despairing, during the 'thirties, of making a market economy work, and hence disposed to consider the possibility of jettisoning it, he is ready today to affirm the central place of the market in a "good society," provided the market is not rigged. Still discouraged over the inability of the business community to abandon its "folklore" and understand the imperatives of the twentieth century, the liberal nevertheless recognizes the important role, if not the sacred immunity, of private enterprise in a pluralistic society.

These are the devices, within government and without, by which the power of government though greatly increased, and the power of business though correspondingly decreased, can be made responsive to the needs of the people. This has been a mere outline, but it is enough to show why, in the judgment of the liberal, the assumption of large economic powers by the state need not lead along the "road to serfdom." If the assumption of such powers removes the frictions which are such a harassing feature of the life of our time, we may have found the road to freedom instead.

Chapter 13

The Welfare State: First Phase

HISTORICALLY, THE IMPETUS to reform has come from the demand for a just distribution of wealth. In the nineteenth century, glaring disparities between the wealth of the few and the poverty of the many, and an increasingly higher level of expectations, intensified the demand among those who were disadvantaged for suffrage and the power to bargain collectively. Where reforms proved slow or inadequate, the masses, or, more correctly, those who expressed the aspirations of the masses, turned to socialism, demanding an end to the profit system.

In the United States a variety of circumstances combined to blunt the attack. Greater social mobility, a safety valve provided by the frontier, abundant natural resources, a strong union thwarting the particularism from which Western Europe is very slowly extricating itself, isolation from Europe's conflicts, all conspired to contain the reform movement within the framework of a capitalist economy. However, the existing system of property rights yielded to major modification on two notable occasions: when, during the first quarter of the nineteenth century, nearly all of the states abandoned the property test for suffrage—despite Daniel Webster's dire warning that equal suffrage was incompatible with inequality in property; and when, abortively first in 1894, and then by amendment to the Constitution in 1913, Congress obtained the power "to lay and collect taxes on incomes."

The nineteenth and early twentieth centuries paid the first instalments on democracy. In the 1930's a new instalment fell due. In the eighteenth and nineteenth centuries the middle classes won their freedom. By the twentieth century, the *forms* of freedom were being extended to all men—at any rate in France, Great Britain, and the United States. But only a few enjoyed its substance. Liberals demanded that substance, seeking it in a society where all men may live fuller lives. In the now common terminology, and by consent of both protagonists and antagonists, that society came to be known as the Welfare State.

Liberals have been loath to present blueprints. Good architects do not plan the details of a structure until they know the site on which it will be built. Doctrinaires and dreamers may quarrel about the outlines of Utopia; wise men will consider the problems at hand.[1] Accordingly, the method of liberals has been tentative rather than final, experimental rather than authoritarian, pragmatic rather than dogmatic. However, the outlines of the Welfare State, in what might be called its first phase, are now clear, even though still incomplete. They were shaped overwhelmingly by the classic paradox of the 'thirties—dire want and insecurity in the midst of potential abundance, unmet needs in the presence of idle men and idle factories. Accordingly, the objectives of the Welfare State, as these took form in the 'thirties, were three: (a) a readjustment of incomes in order to provide adequately for the disabled and the disadvantaged, (b) economic recovery, (c) the diffusion of such concentrations of power as make for economic disadvantage.

Governing the quest for these objectives has been the basic conviction that intervention by government in economic affairs, that is, the collective use of intelligence in planning our economic relationships, is not only compatible with, but in our present world is an indispensable condition of, democracy. This does not mean that the Welfare State is regarded as the Omnicompetent State. Ample scope is given to private initiative. While liberals do not regard "welfare capitalism" as a realistic or practical *alternative* to the Welfare State, they will surely applaud such proposals as Russell Davenport's that the business community turn its attention to plans for stabilizing employment, for providing pensions and medical programs, for "humanizing" industry.[2] Likewise, they will welcome such support as that provided by the Committee for Economic Development, composed of some of our leading businessmen, in an important statement of principles:

To the extent that the free-enterprise system fails to meet the imperative need for high employment and productivity, the cause of the difficulty must be identified and removed as promptly as possible. While taking steps to expand private employment and needed public employment, the government must do its best to provide for those who are unable to find work, never losing sight of the fact that unemployment benefits are at best but a poor substitute for the opportunity to work and earn a living. . . . Through their federal government, they [the American people] have wisely provided in the past, and should continue to provide in the future, a program of social security—unemployment insurance and old-age pensions—for the benefit of those who are unable to work or, if able and willing to work, are for any reason whatever unable to find sufficiently remunerative employment to protect themselves against want. Such individual protection against hazards should be extended as rapidly as practicable.[3]

With the business community addressing itself to the problem of welfare and social reformers stressing the need for increasing the national product, the climate may yet be provided in which government action seems less a form of coercion than a way of administering a general consensus.

From the Cradle to the Grave

If optimum productivity has come increasingly into the foreground of liberal policy, the first concern of liberals in a society already enjoying high levels of production was in the 'thirties, and still is, the basic economic security of every individual. This is a concern which was on the whole alien to the dominant mood of the last century. In the nineteenth century poverty and dependence were regarded as evidence of personal failure. Individuals were unemployed because they were unenterprising or indolent, poorly paid because they were incompetent, impoverished during periods of ill-health or during old age because they had been improvident. A few were victims of circumstance and these might be helped by private charity, and in extreme cases by the state, but only meagerly and never as a matter of right. In all cases the recipients of aid must be made to feel disgraced and humiliated, and poorhouses, workhouses, doles, and the like were in fact tainted with a social stigma which was destructive of self-respect.

Twentieth-century liberalism, on the other hand, holds society responsible for the protection of its members from threats to their basic economic security. It holds that nineteenth-century liberalism—in any case, those who popularized that creed or spoke in its name—grossly exaggerated individual responsibility for indigence (as well as affluence). It holds that in a society as productive as our own, every worker can and should be assured of a wage at least sufficient to provide him and his family adequate food, shelter, clothing, recreation, and leisure, while all who are prevented from working can and should be assured of adequate support. Sumner Slichter has asserted that "the essential principle of the welfare state is that incomes should not be tied too closely to production."[4] With the exception of the permanently disabled, quite the contrary is the case, according to the liberal. The essential principle of the welfare state is that the market, as we have known it, is *too crude a measure* of contributions to production.

Twentieth-century liberalism holds that the number of shiftless and lazy has been enormously exaggerated, in part to exempt cherished institutions of responsibility for unemployment, in part because an aversion to overwork and excessively monotonous work has been confused with a dislike of work itself. Moreover, it views the relative few who are really shiftless and lazy as the victims, if not of an actual physical disability (no doubt the apathy of hypothyroids was once charged against "human nature"), then of personal and social maladjustments having to do with repeated frustration, lack of opportunity, and the like. Such people should no more be viewed as morally degraded than the victims of tuberculosis or pellagra; on the contrary, they should be considered ill and receive the special attention accorded any invalid. Finally, twentieth-century liberalism denies that the assurance of adequate means of support dulls man's initiative, just as it denies the converse of this proposition that insecurity is a necessary spur to effort. These propositions rest on the psychological fiction that man is born lazy, a fiction now dismissed by psychologists.

Economic insecurity in our society stems mainly from (a) inadequate compensation, (b) inherited and congenital disability and disabilities incurred through accident, ill-health, youth, old age, widowhood, and motherhood, (c) unemployment. The details of the liberal program for coping with these problems are familiar enough, but their import cannot be properly appreciated until they are viewed as parts of a now fairly well-elaborated whole.

To meet the problem of inadequate compensation, liberals have proposed that the government assist in three ways: through legislation facilitating the growth of a strong labor movement enabling workers to bargain on equal terms with their employers; through minimum-wage legislation; through a guarantee of full employment. Until recently in our country the advantages of collective bargaining had been limited for the most part to skilled workers. Legislation passed during the Roosevelt Administration, notably section 7A of the National Recovery Act and the National Labor Relations Act, made possible the organization of unskilled workers on a large scale. Employers in increasing numbers have come to accept labor organization as part of the "scheme of things," and great progress has been made in providing workers with a form of security which was conspicuously lacking in the 'twenties. The historic 1950 contract between General Motors Corporation and the United Automobile Workers Union, subsequently emulated elsewhere, reflects an enlightenment on the part of management which would have been unthinkable only two decades ago. However, large groups of workers, notably in agriculture, in small enterprises, in domestic service, and in white-collar occupations are still excluded from the advantages of collective bargaining. While their organization presents a problem of peculiar complexity, an adequate program of liberal reform will give the solving of this problem top priority.[5]

To be sure, the security provided workers by trade unions has not been realized without certain adverse consequences. We have yet to evolve methods for coping with jurisdictional disputes and disputes comparable to a general strike in their crippling effects on the economy, and liberals have not been too ready with constructive suggestions. So, too, with the restrictive practices of which certain unions are guilty. More-over, a type of leadership has appeared in the labor move-ment which is reminiscent in many ways of the more ruthless and unscrupulous business and industrial tycoons of the nine-teenth century. If its influence has been greatly exaggerated, such leadership nevertheless presents a serious problem with which liberals have failed to grapple—in part because the logic of events has thrust both groups into an uneasy political partnership whose breakup might jeopardize the whole social security program. But none of this detracts from the indis-pensable role which labor unions must play in an economy of wage earners if security is to be built on something more than a flimsy foundation of *richesse oblige*.

Besides encouraging labor organization, the New Deal broke new ground with the passage of federal minimum-wage legislation. Earlier state laws had established minimum wages for women and children, but in a 1923 decision, the Supreme Court found even this meager legislation unconstitutional for the characteristic reason (the liberal Justice Holmes dissent-ing) that the basis for determining minimum-wage rates in these state laws "is not the value of the service rendered, but the extraneous circumstance that the employee needs to get a prescribed sum of money to insure her subsistence, health and morals." It reaffirmed this judgment twice in 1936, only to turn an about-face in 1937 under the pressure of President Roosevelt's proposal to reform the court. The federal govern-ment made the first effort to establish minimum wages for male workers in the codes of the National Recovery Adminis-tration and later in the Fair Labor Standards Act of 1938. The minimum set by this act was far from adequate, and important groups of workers were excluded from its benefits. However, it marked a historic abandonment of the principle that the determination of wages must be left wholly to the vagaries of the "free" market. After the war, a vigorous movement to raise the minimum and include additional classi-fications of workers resulted in successive improvements. The latest, sponsored by the "New Frontier," adds 3.6 million more workers, for whom the minimum will be $1.00 an hour initially, to the 24 million workers previously covered, for whom the minimum rises from $1.00 to $1.15.[6] The latter group will receive $1.25 by 1963, the former group, by 1965.

Of the newly added workers 663,000 are estimated by the Labor Department as drawing less than $1.00. Of the workers already covered, about 1.9 million, including 1.2 million in manufacturing, have been getting less than the new minimum. Farm workers are still excluded from coverage and sponsors of the legislation had to omit laundry, restaurant, and hotel workers in order to save the bill. Small businesses (e.g., retail establishments with gross sales under $1 million) are also excepted.

However, adequate weekly and hourly wage rates are far from assuring sufficient means of support even when they are adjusted to fluctuations in the price level. The need for housing, clothing, and food is a steady requirement which pays no attention to the cycles and seasons of the economic world, and it often happens that the recipient of a generous hourly and weekly wage finds himself impoverished even in "prosperous" times by frequent lay-offs. Accordingly, liberals have supported and workers have pressed for a "guaranteed annual wage." The grievance of workers was simply stated by the CIO.

A company pays for land and buildings by the year.
It pays for the use of money by the year (bonds).
It plans its dividends to stockholders by the year
(preferred stock and often common stock).
It pays for much advertising space by the year . . .
It sets aside money each year to buy new machines to
replace the old.
Why should it not plan to pay its wage-earners by the year, too?[7]

President Roosevelt appointed a Subcommittee on Guaranteed Wage Plans, which subsequently found[8] that a guaranteed annual wage "can stabilize the economy and contribute to enduring prosperity." The idea had already been adopted on their own initiative in a number of enterprises. More recently, bargaining agreements which embody supplementary unemployment benefits are a step in the direction of a guaranteed annual wage and emphasis is at present limited to getting recognition of the principle. However, the question of a

guaranteed annual wage raises the whole issue of unemployment and with this of full employment. Full employment by
providing a seller's market for labor and improving the
worker's bargaining position is obviously related to the problem of adequate compensation. But this is a separate issue,
an examination of which must be deferred until the liberal
approach to the problem of insecurity, as related to the several
forms of disability, has been considered.

The first gains in the struggle for economic protection from
the consequences of disability were won in connection with
industrial accidents.[9] The English common law, like the
French Napoleonic Code, afforded the victim of industrial
accident virtually no protection, and whatever chance for aid
there might have been was removed by court decision. Until
the passage by the English of the Employers' Liability Act of
1880, industrial accidents (not to mention occupational dis-
eases) were regarded as part of the risk which a workman
assumed when he accepted employment; his wage compensated him for the chance he was taking, and, if it did not, he
was free to seek employment elsewhere. In America almost
all the states followed the precedent of the English and passed
similar legislation. However, the Employers' Liability Acts
were an almost complete failure, and it required the introduction of compulsory insurance, first in Germany in 1884,
later in Great Britain, between 1897 and 1906, and belatedly
in the United States, between 1905 and 1915, to lay the
foundations of real security. Workmen's compensation legislation was the first form of social insurance in the United
States, that is to say, it represented the first application of the
principle that society must set aside or require its members
to set aside small sums of money in advance, in order to
provide against a future need. In the case of industrial accidents, the cost of insurance is now reckoned a part of the
cost of production and therefore imposed on the employer.

While the principle of social insurance found wide application elsewhere, as other nations turned their attention to
the problem of social security, the United States was to remain apathetic for some decades. There is, however, one

exception to our general tardiness in facing the problem of social security. During the progressive revolt which marked the first decade of this century, liberals succeeded in obtaining government aid for widows and deserted or orphaned children. Mothers' Aid Laws were adopted by almost all the states. Substantial additional aid was provided by the federal Social Security Act of 1935, and this has been increased by subsequent amendment. Most European countries have provided similar aid through their social insurance systems. Meanwhile, liberals everywhere continue to work for more generous benefits.

In general, dependent mothers and orphans have evoked more sympathy than the dependent aged. Useful and honored in societies where agriculture and the crafts predominate, the aged became the outcasts of an industrial society. Meanwhile their number increased enormously. It was not until Germany introduced contributory old-age insurance in 1889, and the English-speaking and Scandinavian countries introduced noncontributory pension systems during the two decades which followed, that anything substantial was done. In America the voice of liberalism was not yet strong enough, so that the aged were left to the weak social conscience of the states, and with this, to the humiliations of the almshouse and to the nostrums of quacks and demagogues. After 1914 most of the states adopted assorted pension bills, but it was not until the adoption of the Social Security Act of 1935 that the federal government intervened.

The federal act, with its later amendments, helps in two ways. First, an "Old Age and Survivors' Insurance" plan provides retirement benefits from a fund accumulated by requiring contributions in equal amount from employer and employee during the working life of the insured. The program is administered by the Department of Health, Education and Welfare. Almost everyone earning $600 or more annually is covered by the program and this now includes salaried workers, farmers, domestics, and many categories of self-employed. The maximum against which payroll taxes may be levied is $4,800 in yearly earnings, a hardly alluring prospect to middle-income groups. Benefits begin at age 62 (recently reduced from 65 for men). The spouse is entitled to half of what the primary beneficiary receives and continues to receive benefits (currently 75 percent) after the death of the primary beneficiary. Maximum payment to a beneficiary is $119. As of 1960, the national average payment was about $72 monthly and $82 for those currently retiring—still far from munificent. The average benefit for retired couples is $120 monthly.[10]

Second, under a "Public Assistance" program, the Social Security Act provides for the needy aged who, because of retirement before or soon after passage of the law, or because of insufficient employment, have not had enough contributed in payments to yield adequate benefits in their old age. Such assistance funds are provided jointly by the state and federal governments. The program is administered by the states, which make the determination of need. The average monthly payment as of October 1959 was approximately $65 with a range among the states of from $30 to $115.[11]

Such aid to the aged fails to compensate, of course, for their cruel exclusion from productive work in an economy which has not yet learned to use its abler workers. Certainly, older workers, having been provided with adequate security, should have an opportunity to continue in productive work adjusted to their declining powers and thus to supplement their income through earnings. But such humane and intelligent provision must await a solution to the problem of unemployment, shortly to be considered.

In all this, the hand of the liberal has been strengthened by the fact that the compassion of those ordinarily unmoved by the merits of social security is more easily stirred by the plight of mothers, children, the physically handicapped and old people. In the case of the aged, the calloused were softened by the alarming political success of crackpot movements like California's "Ham and Eggs." So far, the attitude has been different toward those disabled by illness. Proposals for a federal system of compulsory health insurance have encountered a stone wall of opposition in the form of the powerful American Medical Association and its state branches.[12] Not even the acute needs of the aged have breached this wall.

Health insurance is an outstanding feature of the social security systems of all the major countries of the world except our own. President Roosevelt's Committee on Economic Security was deterred from including health insurance in the original social security legislation of 1935 by the fear that opposition from organized physicians might result in a defeat for the measure as a whole. Bills incorporating current liberal thinking on the subject of medical insurance have thus far encountered insurmountable obstacles in Congress. It is the liberal position, shared by a small group of *avant garde* conservatives, that the traditional fee-for-service method of payment has generally failed to make adequate medical care (including preventive medicine) available to the people who need it. Here as elsewhere, we have great unused resources and great unfilled needs. State intervention through a system of compulsory health insurance is the method proposed to meet the need. Such is the strength of the medical lobby, however, that a modest proposal to extend the insurance benefits of the Social Security Act merely to include hospital and nursing home care for the aged has yet to be passed by Congress. An earlier proposal (the Forand bill) that included some surgical expenses was rejected even by the late Speaker Rayburn as "going too far."[13]

Each year one out of five of the aged couples receiving Social Security benefits is hospitalized. In one half the cases their medical bills are in excess of $700 a year, or about a third of their income. Many are unable to afford the care they need. However, they may go to their graves happily; theirs is the consolation of knowing that they are heroically preserving American freedom—at any rate, as understood by the American Medical Association.

Illness and accident impose a twofold financial burden— the cost of medical care and the loss of earnings during the period of disability. Until recently security legislation made no provision for either, not even, in the case of the latter, through unemployment compensation.[14] Federal Disability Insurance now provides income for workers with permanent total disability. Aid for disabled and blind persons is provided through federally aided state assistance programs. In California, unemployment compensation disability insurance provides income for workers with short-term illness. In most instances, the emphasis has been on income maintenance on the assumption that recipients of aid would rehabilitate themselves. This appears to have been mistaken and, as a result, President Kennedy has stressed programs of rehabilitation in recently proposed amendments to the Social Security Act and in the newly passed Manpower Utilization and Retraining Act of 1962.[15]

Security has been discussed from the point of view of guaranties of adequate compensation for those who work, and from the point of view of adequate support for those who are unable to work. A third phase of the problem remains. What of those who are able but are prevented from working by forces over which they have no control? The unemployed, sometimes known as the "able-bodied poor," have been libeled for so long that the problem of meeting their needs might never have been approached with humanity and understanding had not the mass unemployment of the 'thirties forced us to face the problem. But unemployment, as we are painfully aware, was not a phenomenon merely of the 'thirties. Neither is it always of the kind we call mass unemployment. Unemployment may be distinguished into two major types: frictional unemployment and mass unemployment.

Frictional unemployment is defined by Sir William Beveridge as "unemployment caused by the individuals who make up the labour supply not being completely interchangeable and mobile units, so that, though there is an unsatisfied demand for labour, the unemployed workers are not of the right sort or in the right place to meet that demand."[16] Workers may be displaced by a labor-saving device or a device which they are not trained to use (technological unemployment), because of climatic conditions or seasonal fluctuations in the market (seasonal unemployment), because of the failure of the enterprise in which they are employed, because of a disagreement with the employer concerning the conditions of work. The fireman and brakeman who lose their jobs because passenger and freight traffic shifts from railways to highways and airways, the glass blower whose work is now done mechanically, the fruit picker or construction worker who is prevented from working by rains, the automobile worker who is "laid off" during the "slack" period, these are all victims of frictional unemployment. Such frictional unemployment, although it can be reduced, is unavoidable and is excepted in all proposals for "full" employment.

Heretofore the victims of frictional unemployment have been left to solve their own problem. Usually without financial reserves, they are reduced to complete penury and, in the more extreme cases, thrown upon public or private charity. Liberals have insisted that the problem be met in a different way. Two solutions have been urged. The first is the guaranteed annual wage, to which reference has already been made. The second is unemployment insurance.

Unemployment aid, based on employers' contributions, had been a part of social security systems abroad for some time before it became a reality in America through the Social Security Act of 1935. Bitterly condemned by the opposition to the New Deal, its inclusion in the social security system marked a great triumph for liberalism, and even conservatives have become reconciled to it in its present limited form. Much is still undone, but a precedent has at last been set.

At best, however, unemployment insurance is not a complete answer to the problem presented by frictional unemployment. It solves the problem of want, but the problem of idleness remains over. In the words of Sir William Beveridge,

Idleness is not the same as Want, but a separate evil, which men do not escape by having an income. They must also have the chance of rendering useful service and of feeling that they are doing so. This means that employment is not wanted for the sake of employment, irrespective of what is produced. . . . Employment which is merely time-wasting . . . will not serve that purpose. Nor will it be felt worth while. It must be productive and progressive.[17]

In other words, once the wants of the frictionally unemployed are met, measures must be taken to facilitate their re-entry into employment and, moreover, into employment commensurate with their abilities and skills. To help the worker find a job, the federal and state governments have shared the cost of a system of public employment offices. Federal grants for this purpose were authorized by the Wagner-Peyser Act of 1933. Such aid must be accompanied by adequate facilities for retraining workers to perform useful, creative tasks.

Unemployment insurance, public employment offices, the retraining of displaced workers—these cannot and are not intended to cope with the problem of mass unemployment. Mass unemployment threatens the whole framework of social security, not merely because contributions to the social security fund, which are based on pay rolls, are thereby drastically reduced, but because a society cannot enjoy the "abundant life" at which social security programs ultimately aim unless it first produces the means. Mass unemployment is the most explosive feature of modern life. Its manifest irrationality is destructive of any social order which long tolerates it. Racism, militarism, fascism, communism, the whole hideous brood, have battened on it and it may yet be our undoing. For, as noted earlier, we have not yet solved the problem of mass unemployment, although there is evidence of a much stronger determination to face it.

Heretofore mass unemployment had been thought of entirely as a cyclical phenomenon, varying with fluctuations in the business cycle. More recently, one hears much of a noncyclical component of mass unemployment called "structural" (also "hard-core" and "prosperity") unemployment. Structural unemployment, so-called, is described as frictional unemployment of long duration.[18] Such long-term frictional or structural unemployment refers to those who are made jobless, not as a result of recessions or depressions, but by large-scale changes in technology, shifts in consumer taste, the development of new products, etc. It may also refer to changes in the composition of the labor force including new increments of young workers resulting from continuing population growth, increments of older workers resulting from extension of the life span, a new influx of female workers, the advent of unwanted or heretofore segregated members of minority groups.

This structural or "hard-core" factor is increasingly stressed by those who oppose the use of large-scale government expenditures (i.e., fiscal policy) to raise the level of effective demand and thereby achieve full employment, optimum productivity, and—in the case of recessions—economic recovery. Those who take this position contend that postwar mass unemployment has had little to do with the level of demand; it consists largely of displaced workers who need to be retrained or relocated. As matters now stand, however, most of the so-called structurally unemployed would still not find work. If they did, they would displace those already working. If the observations, made earlier,[19] concerning the growth rate of the economy mean anything, they mean that the structurally unemployed are without work for the same reason that the cyclically unemployed are without work: there is not enough effective demand for their services, that is to say, the economy does not function at a sufficiently high level to utilize its available manpower.

Professor Walter W. Heller has testified: "Some have attributed the growth of unemployment in recent years to changing characteristics of the labor force rather than to deficiencies in total demand. According to this view, the new unemployment is concentrated among workers who are intrinsically unemployable by reason of sex, age, location, occupation, or skill. . . . The facts . . . clearly refute this explanation of the rise of unemployment over the last 8 years . . . there is no evidence that hard-core unemployment has been growing as a percent of the labor force."[20] This is the verdict of nearly all liberal economists, if not of professional economists as a whole.

Mass unemployment must end; this is a categorical imperative recognized by all parties. But how? Upon the answer to this question everything else hinges. In particular, all discussions of social security are academic until this issue has been met. For the answer of the liberal we may turn first to the words of Sir William Beveridge. Full employment, he declares in his now famous *Full Employment in a Free*

Society, "must be made a responsibility of the State." He continues,

No one else has the requisite powers; the condition will not get satisfied automatically. It must be a function of the State . . . to protect its citizens against mass unemployment, as definitely as it is now the function of the State to defend the citizens against attack from abroad and against robbery and violence at home. Acceptance of this new responsibility of the State . . . marks the line which we must cross, in order to pass from the old Britain of mass unemployment and jealousy and fear to the new Britain of opportunity and service for all.[21]

So, too, Professor Alvin H. Hansen has taken the lead among American economists in urging that under modern conditions the maintenance of adequate employment opportunities is a primary responsibility of society.

Just as the right to free land was the watchword of economic opportunity a hundred years ago, so the right to useful, remunerative, and regular employment is the symbol of economic opportunity today. . . . If the democratic countries were not now planning and developing new institutional arrangements designed to make the market economy function more effectively than it did in the past, the future would be black indeed.

Referring to the Murray Full Employment Bill as a counterpart of the Homestead Act, he adds,

The Homestead movement of the 1840's represented a great struggle for human rights and economic opportunity. It was fought by the forces of reaction. But the issue could not be evaded. So also with the full-employment program today. It involves elemental human rights—the right to life, liberty, and the pursuit of happiness. So long as 80 to 90 percent of the population cannot earn a livelihood except by getting a job, the issue of full employment will not down.[22]

More recently, Professor Heller has declared:

Measures to improve the mobility of labor to jobs and of jobs to labor, to better our educational facilities, to match future supplies of different skills and occupations to the probable pattern of future demand, and to improve the health of the population— these are and should be high on the agenda of national policy.

But they are no substitute for fiscal, monetary, and credit policies for economic recovery. Adjustments that now seem difficult, and unemployment pockets that now seem intractable, will turn out to be manageable after all in an environment of full prosperity.[23]

Clearly these statements chart a course that departs from the familiar path we once traveled, a path to which conservatives would have us return. Encourage private enterprise, keep government out of business, reduce taxes, increase profits, these are the time-honored devices. If, as in the 'twenties and 'fifties, these are not enough, and mass unemployment does set in, the orthodox practice has been to ignore it on the assumption that the situation will right itself (especially if wages and taxes are reduced). This clearly was still the belief of a majority of management, who, as late as 1944, in response to the query, "Do you think it is a function of government today to see to it that substantially full employment is maintained?" answered 66.2 percent in the negative and 4.4 percent "don't know."[24] However, it is not insignificant that almost 30 percent of management shared the view of liberals who believe with Hansen and Beveridge that the way to escape our prewar unemployment impasse is not by traveling the same path more rapidly but by advancing along a new course, where society acting through government assumes responsibility for full employment.

The implications of such a program are momentous. The labor market has almost always been in peacetime a buyer's market. Liberals propose to make it a seller's market. Instead of catering merely to their customers, producers would have to cater to their employees as well—as they often had to during the war. If courting customers is not an intolerable humiliation, the liberal argues, neither should it be unbearable to woo workers. To be sure, some of the consequences of full employment—a reduction of output per man-hour, some inflation, an increase of absenteeism, a more rapid turnover of labor, etc.—might be adverse, and liberals are often accused of ignoring them. Their answer is that none of these effects is irremediable and that, in any case, the total effect would be ovewhelmingly beneficial. The contribution to production of a full use of our manpower is obvious. Beyond this, liberals point out that we have talked much of occupational freedom of choice and of the merits of a society which exists for the sake of the individual. In circumstances featured by a surplus of labor, these are mere slogans for vast numbers of workers.

Government intervention, often denounced as incompatible with "individualism" and occupational freedom, if invoked in behalf of a seller's market for labor, will convert these slogans into reality, according to the liberal. This is the substance of William Beveridge's argument in one of his most significant passages:

> The proposition that there should always be more vacant jobs than unemployed men means that the labour market should always be a seller's market rather than a buyer's market. For this, on the view of society underlying this Report—that society exists for the individual—there is a decisive reason of principle. The reason is that difficulty in selling labour has consequences of a different order of harmfulness from those associated with difficulty in buying labour. A person who has difficulty in buying the labour that he wants suffers inconvenience or reduction of profits. A person who cannot sell his labour is in effect told that he is of no use. The first difficulty causes annoyance or loss. The other is a personal catastrophe.[25]

It was such reasoning that inspired the Employment Act of 1946, an historic triumph for the liberal thesis that full employment must be a goal of national policy. The Employment Act goes well beyond the British White Paper on Employment Policy produced by Britain's wartime coalition government. The Act declares it to be "the continuing policy and responsibility of the Federal Government to use all practicable means . . . to promote maximum employment, production, and purchasing power." The President is required to submit to Congress at the beginning of each of its regular sessions an "Economic Report" which shall set forth "the levels of employment, production, and purchasing power obtaining in the United States and such levels needed to carry out the policy," along with "current and foreseeable trends in the levels of employment, production, and purchasing power." He is provided with a Council of Economic Advisers and, upon submission of his Report, a 14-man joint congressional committee will thereupon study the President's recommendations and propose appropriate measures.

As it finally emerged from Congress the bill was a diluted version of the original and a product of much verbal juggling. It sets up no actual machinery for combating unemployment. A great deal of exegetic skill has been expended on the words "maximum employment, production, and purchasing power." In the end much depends on the way in which the President himself interprets its provisions and avails himself of them. Nevertheless, the Employment Act marks a great step forward in the effort of our people to control their economic destinies.

How is full employment to be achieved? One of the provisions of the Murray Bill, which was the original Senate draft of the Employment Act, was bitterly opposed by conservatives and was deleted in the final measure. It explicitly committed the government to deficit spending, declaring that Congress should, "to the extent that continuing full employment cannot otherwise be attained, provide . . . such volume of Federal investment and expenditure as may be needed . . . to achieve the objective of continuing full employment." This provision was rejected in the House draft and the conference committee finally compromised on the statement that it is the "continuing policy and responsibility of the Federal Government . . . to co-ordinate and utilize all its plans, functions, and resources for the purpose of maintaining conditions under which there will be afforded useful employment opportunities for those able, willing, and seeking to work." The changed language actually provides a far more sweeping grant of power to the government than the original and is thereby a tribute to the power of word magic[26] to overcome ideological opposition, including Senator Taft's, but that is by the way. The original language indicated the specific direction in which liberals wished to go. After all, from an economic point of view the war was a gigantic public works project made possible by deficit financing. It had solved the problem of mass unemployment. Could not similar methods employed on a lesser scale for constructive purposes be similarly efficacious in time of peace? To describe how full employment is to be achieved is, however, no longer to consider the problem of security in its own terms; it is to consider production and how to expand it.

Economic Recovery and Compensatory Spending

Granted that full employment is a social responsibility requiring government intervention, precisely what form should this intervention take? Much of the answer to this question rests upon technical economic analyses that lie outside the scope and competence of this study. Consequently, the answer will be limited to a summary of the conclusions reached by representative professional economists, conclusions which are now part of the mainstream of liberal thought.

Employment is a function of outlay or spending. As the total outlay or expenditure of society increases, employment increases; as the outlay or expenditure decreases, employment decreases. The objective—and to this everyone assents—is to assure sufficient expenditure to keep workers employed making the goods which these expenditures buy. Expenditures have three sources: the spending of consumers for consumer goods, the spending of producers for producer goods, the spending of government at all levels, federal, state, and local. The position of the liberal has been that, *if* the expenditures of private consumers and producers when combined with the normal expenditures of government (for highways, police, defense, etc.) are not sufficient to employ the available labor force, *the government should use its monetary and fiscal powers* to the extent necessary to achieve full employment. Its task will be eased by the therapeutic effect of "built-in" stabilizers which, whatever conservatives may think of them, operate quickly and automatically to restore a measure of purchasing power. These are so-called "transfer payments," especially in the form of immediately payable unemployment benefits, and tax relief automatically resulting from reduced incomes.[27]

In the 1930's a great deal remained to be learned about

monetary and fiscal policy. However, in all cases such government intervention was and is now envisaged *within a framework of private enterprise which,* properly controlled and subordinated to social needs, is *taken for granted* in the liberal program under consideration. Thus in the Employment Act, government was held responsible for giving every possible encouragement to *private* spending before increasing its own expenditures. And this, following Keynes, led to an emphasis on government spending as *residual, supplementary, compensatory.* In short, if and as private spending employs the available labor supply, it was thought that public spending must shrink to the amount required to finance the ordinary and regular activities of government.

Where is the money coming from and how will the government spend it? These are questions which at once obtrude themselves. The sum of money which the government spends to achieve economic recovery and secure maximum employment must come either from borrowing or from current taxes. The economic considerations which should determine the government's choice as between these sources cannot be examined here. However, it must be emphasized that the liberal's criterion of "sound finance" is neither the orthodox concept of a balanced budget nor the orthodox economist's goal of low taxes, but full employment and optimum use of our resources. "Optimum" is preferred to "maximum" use, since the latter might be achieved at the expense of desirable leisure or improvident use of natural resources.

How empty was the prewar fear of a growing national debt is evidenced, according to liberals, by our actual war experience. Our debt has gone to what orthodox economists once regarded as impossible heights. Readers of Keynes and Hansen discovered long before the war that an unbalanced national budget is not comparable to the unbalanced budget of an individual or of a private corporation and that the persistent use of this misleading analogy results only in confusion.[28] Even *Fortune,* which can engage in the most open flirtation with Keynes, when it is not chaperoned by Hayek, refers to the "old-fashioned taboo against public debt."[29] If by deficit spending we can create income-earning assets, like those which have transformed the Tennessee Valley,[30] and if we can raise the national income, thereby expanding our tax revenues, no questionable accounting convention should be allowed to stand in the way. In the 'thirties, owing to our refusal to plan and to the reluctance of conservative opinion to concede that the relief of unemployment must be an object of national policy, public funds were spent too tardily, the amount was not sufficient to remedy unemployment, and the money was sometimes spent on useless projects. Nevertheless, the rise in total output from a low of $39.5 billion in 1932 to $67 billion in 1937, amounting during the first six years of the New Deal to an addition of $100 billion to the national output, was not unrelated to the government's expenditure of about one-third that amount.

In the case of borrowing, the government takes the savings of citizens who wish to lend them and pays interest for their use. Since the economic effect of taxation is, in general, to reduce private spending, borrowing is the preferred recourse during a period of economic contraction. However, the state may prefer to obtain the funds with which to finance its increased expenditures by the more direct, if politically more difficult, method of taxation. To this, liberal theory does not object, *provided that taxes are obtained from the proper sources;* otherwise, the very purpose of maximum production and full employment, for which the taxes are to be spent, may be defeated.

To indicate what these sources are, it is necessary to return to some of the considerations raised earlier in the analysis of the causes of mass unemployment. These are as follows: Our gross national income represents the value of all goods and services produced over any given period. The size of this income is expressed in terms of money. If X number of workers were required to produce the goods and render the services whose value is measured by our national income, it is clear that we must spend our income if the same number of men are to continue in employment. If for some reason we should fail to spend a portion of our income, a proportionate number of workers would fail to find purchasers for their services and would be forced into idleness.

Now, we may spend our income either in the purchase of consumer goods or by investment in capital goods.[31] It had been generally assumed in orthodox economic theory that the amount of money we save is determined by the interest rate, which is in turn determined by the prospect of investment, and that savings pass automatically into investment and are spent in that way. Consequently, saving had not been regarded as a way of withholding purchasing power and, hence, as affecting the level of employment.

It was one of the major contributions of J. M. Keynes' *General Theory of Employment, Interest and Money* to show that the orthodox assumptions concerning the relationship between savings and investment are wrong. As a result of this and other studies, it has been argued that the failure to achieve maximum production stems, at any rate in part, from an accumulation of savings, which do not automatically pass into investment as the orthodox economists too easily assumed. Different people or groups of people make the decisions concerning the amounts which shall be saved and the amounts which shall be invested, and these decisions do not coincide. The amount of saving is not in fact determined primarily by the opportunity for investment, but by the *total income of a community and the way in which that income is distributed,* whereas the amount of investment is determined primarily by the opportunity to make a profit.[32] If savings were invested, that is to say, spent in replacing, renewing, or expanding capital equipment (and inventories), a major cause of unemployment would be removed. But this happens only in part. Planned private investment is too low in relationship to the "propensity" to save. Large savings tend to lie idle because profitable investments cannot be found.

Why are opportunities for profitable investment lacking? Certainly in part because of a lag in spending among the great mass of consumers stemming from an unequal distribution of income. The same inequality of distribution which leads the favored group to save makes it impossible for the low-income group to spend. Some way must be found for correcting the disproportion between the desire to save and the desire to invest savings and undistributed profits. Some way must be found, that is, for rescuing the profit system from itself. An uneven distribution of income leading to a failure in aggregate demand can be averted by strong organizations enabling workers, farmers, and consumers to bargain more effectively for a larger share of the national income. But where these have not sufficed, the result can be accomplished by government, which may either borrow or tax uninvested savings and spend in any one of a number of ways yet to be examined.

It is at this point that the requirements of an adequate tax policy become clear to the liberal. Taxes, except during a period of overemployment, must be directed primarily at that part of the national income which is saved and less at that part which is spent. The low-income group spend virtually all their income. This will become true of somewhat higher income groups with the advent of an adequate system of social security, which will obviate the need of saving for purposes of security. Sales taxes, excise taxes, and the like— "regressive" taxes, so-called—are unsound so long as the economy is operating at a low level of employment simply because they reduce effective demand, by being collected almost entirely from the low-income groups.[33] The depression of the 'thirties was aggravated, in the judgment of liberal economists, by new consumer taxes levied by federal, state and local government.[34] Accordingly, taxes must be levied on the group whose income is so great that it cannot or will not be spent upon consumer goods, with the consequence that, if it is not invested, it is saved. Once it was supposed that a tax policy designed to redistribute income—a "progressive" in contrast to a "regressive" tax—was morally commendable but economically unsound. The Keynesian analysis endeavors to show on the contrary that this is one instance in which moral and economic imperatives coincide.

How much of unused savings (and undistributed profits) must be taxed is a matter of debate. The prospect is not as alarming as it at first glance seems. If the "multiplier" principle made famous by Keynes is valid, only a portion of the savings of the well-to-do needs to be taken in this way. That portion, when invested or distributed by government, creates purchasing power, which in turn creates investment opportunities for private enterprise, thereby draining the savings that remain.[35]

The foregoing may compound a sin in that it is a simplified version of views which have already been criticized as simplistic—those, namely, of John Maynard Keynes, easily the most brilliant and influential economist of our time. Keynes has been unjustly described as a "depression economist" excessively concerned with deflation and unemployment and with short-run tendencies. He has perhaps been more justly criticized for a theoretical framework which neglects such important considerations as price-cost disturbances and relies too heavily on fiscal policy.[36] But the fundamentals of the Keynesian analysis—his bold rejection of the classical thesis that depressions are self-correcting if wages are allowed to sink and thus set in motion forces that will restore equilibrium; his perception of the relation of wage rates to effective demand; his identification of the tendency in an advanced capitalist economy for high-income groups to oversave; his recognition of the role of fiscal policy, in particular deficit spending in correcting economic contraction; above all, his emphasis on the tendency of a developed capitalist economy to find equilibrium at a level of underemployment (the theory of secular stagnation) in the absence of adequate fiscal policy; all this and much more endures and has permanently influenced public policy. The theory of underemployment in particular has been tragically confirmed by our experience of the last decade.

Because Keynes came close to saying, if he did not quite actually say, that unemployment is caused by the unequal distribution of income,[37] he relies heavily on progressive income and inheritance taxation as the basis for a long-range fiscal policy. Although the principle of progressive taxation is now generally accepted, even among conservatives, the prevailing rate structure is subject by them to constant and bitter attack, mainly on the score that it weakens incentive. The issue is a critical one, but if the verdict of objective experts may be believed, this charge is unfounded.

A typical expert view was expressed by the late P. J. Strayer: "Although there is a very vocal group which insists that the equalization aspects of the income tax have been carried too far and have led to the destruction of work incentives and investment incentives, no objective analysis of this question can produce evidence to support this contention." Meanwhile, repetition of the charge obscures the steady erosion of the tax base with the result that, in Strayer's words, "current practices are so bad as to seriously weaken the income tax as a means of income distribution." He concludes that "as now applied the individual income tax is not as effective an instrument of income redistribution as generally believed."[38] In fact, as pointed out by Professor Walter Heller, exclusions, deductions, exemptions, credits, and unreported income total more than $60 billion.

Some of these defy justification. For example, about $900 million represents flagrant evasions on unreported dividend and interest earnings easily recoverable by a simple withholding system which Congress has thus far refused to authorize; and the 27½ percent depletion allowance on which oil tycoons thrive is a clear case of confusing extraction with extortion. More than half the benefit of the tax exemption on state and municipal bonds goes to taxpayers in the higher brackets in tax savings, and not to municipalities and states in lower interest rates. It is estimated that, if a rigorous policy of restoring the tax base were pursued, tax rates could be lowered from the present 20 to 91 percent range to a 14 to 60 percent range. A similar program for corporations would permit a reduction in the tax from 52 to 42.5 percent.[39] Since offering this testimony Professor Heller has become Chairman of the Council of Economic Advisers. The high priority of income tax reform on President Kennedy's agenda is therefore understandable.

Meanwhile, the controversy over the effect of the tax structure on incentive rages unabated. When, some years ago, Emil Schram, president of the New York Stock Exchange, referred to the federal tax structure as "an attack on the sources of venture capital" and as having "dried up the traditional sources of venture capital," he was expressing the settled conviction of the business community. So, too, does Crawford H. Greenewalt, president of E. I. du Pont de Nemours, when, more recently, in the *Report of the President's Commission on National Goals,* he supplements the statement of the Commission with a special admonition that present high income tax rates "strike directly at incentives for personal accomplishment and cannot fail to weaken the drive at all management levels," and "also tend to remove an important source for new venture capital."[40] But in matters involving taxation the business community is all too prone to reach hasty conclusions—all of them the same. H. R. Bowen, former dean of the College of Commerce at the University of Illinois, reaches a different conclusion:

Within recent years, present income tax rates have been frequently and somewhat irresponsibly attacked on grounds that they stifle incentive, initiative, and productive effort. Although a few isolated instances are cited, the deterrent effect of these rates is by no means self-evident. During the very period in which the allegedly excessive rates have been in effect, the number of new businesses established has been beyond anything in our history; the competition among business executives for promotion . . . is fully as great as it has ever been; the appearance of new products and the adoption of new methods of production have been rapid . . . and there is little observable tendency for businessmen to retire in advance of the normal retirement age. . . . It is more common for leaders of industry to suffer coronary attacks—presumably from overwork produced by an excess of incentive—than it is for them to let down because taxes are too high.[41]

Vital myths die hard; one suspects that the business community will not be persuaded even if reminded as by Alvin Hansen that "for the twelve year period 1948 to 1959 inclusive, the average ratio of private investment to Gross National Product was equal to that of any previous boom year in our history," a fact which Professor Hansen not unreasonably interprets to mean that "high income taxes, as far as we can see, have not had any unfavorable effect on private investment."[42] If doubters are still unconvinced, perhaps the issue can be resolved by appealing to the experience of Germany. By general consent West Germany has a dynamic economy with an abundance of incentive. The total tax in West Germany is 32.5 percent of its GNP by comparison with about 27 percent of the American.

In turning finally to a consideration of how the funds obtained by government shall be spent, one leaves the area in which fiscal policy is primary, and deals with "public works." From the point of view of securing full employment it does not matter—if the foregoing analysis is sound—how government spends the money, provided that it is spent. In a famous passage Keynes writes,

If the Treasury were to fill old bottles with banknotes, bury them at suitable depths in disused coal mines, which are then filled up to the surface with town rubbish, and leave it to private enterprise on well-tried principles of laissez faire to dig the notes up again . . . there need be no more unemployment and, with the help of the repercussions, the real income of the community, and its capital wealth also, would probably become a good deal greater than it actually is. It would, indeed, be more sensible to build houses and the like; but if there are political and practical difficulties in the way of this, the above would be better than nothing.

He goes on,

The analogy between this expedient and the gold mines of the real world is complete. At periods when gold is available at suitable depths, experience shows that the real wealth of the world increases rapidly; and when but little of it is so available, our wealth suffers stagnation and decline. Thus gold mines are of the greatest value and importance to civilization. Just as wars have been the only form of large scale expenditure which statesmen have thought justifiable, so gold mining is the only pretext for digging holes in the ground which has recommended itself to bankers as sound finance; and each of these activities has played its part in progress—failing something better.[43]

Everyone objects to "leaf-raking" and "boondoggling." Men put to work at such tasks add nothing to the wealth of society, even if the purchasing power thereby created does put others to work at useful tasks. Moreover, "made" work is at least as humiliating and demoralizing as the dole. But much of the criticism of made work is subject to challenge. In the first place aversion to boondoggling is often no more than an opposition to new forms of public enterprise, whatever the merit of the project. Many who found boondoggling in WPA art, theater, and music projects, or in the program of the TVA, see nothing unreasonable, as Keynes reminds us, in the laborious excavation of gold and its elaborate burial at Fort Knox, Kentucky. Moreover, some of the most vigorous critics of leaf-raking forget that they found "socialism" in proposals to place the unemployed at work in idle factories to produce for their own use.[44] Finally, these same critics forget that such boondoggling as there was or will be is primarily the result of hasty improvisation made necessary by a failure to plan. But it is precisely the careful planning of large-scale public works which these critics have fought with all their might, as evidenced by the sorry fate of the National Resources Planning Board and the stubborn opposition which even the modified Full Employment Bill of 1945 had to overcome. Indeed, instead of encouraging careful planning for public works the conservative Eightieth Congress repealed the law providing repayable loans to state and local governments for preparing blueprints, although a more liberal congress has since re-enacted a similar law.

Made work—and this does not include many projects unjustly called made work—is irrational. That is why President Roosevelt in his famous budget message of 1945 called for a "national budget" in which federal expenditures would be related to the economy as a whole, and why the authors of the Full Employment bill sought to include provision for a National Production and Employment Budget. The opposite of wasteful improvisation is a carefully planned, long-range program of public works which will add to the nation's wealth and contribute to the well-being of its citizens. But America, in the decades preceding the 'sixties, was incapable of guiding itself by such a compass. When Congress required that the more ambiguous term "Economic Report" be substituted for "National Production and Employment Budget" in the language of the Employment Act, this was a symptom and a symbol.

Thus, in nearly all cases public works were undertaken primarily because they stimulated the economy and only secondarily because they were intrinsically desirable. If they enriched the public realm this was a byproduct; it was the impetus they gave to recovery that mattered. A public housing program would never have gotten beyond the Congressional Committees set up to thwart this kind of mischief, if the building industry had not been sick unto death. Such have been the priorities of a market economy even when it is ailing and in need of rehabilitation.

The Limitation of Power

The third objective of the Welfare State was to limit such concentrations of power as make for economic disadvantage. It was here, in probing the roots of power, that liberals exposed the raw nerve of those in control of the economy. The fierce hostility with which the entrenched economic group regarded the New Deal was in large measure the rancor of those who perceive a threat to their favored position in society. They greatly exaggerated the threat, but that is what it was.

The attempt to counter concentrated economic power involved much more than a vigorous application of the antitrust laws. It involved more than the passage of legislation like the Securities and Exchange Act of 1934 and the Holding Company Act of 1935. It involved more than a revision of the tax system for *distributive* as well as revenue purposes in accordance with President Roosevelt's proposals in 1935 for accelerating "progressive taxation of wealth and of income" and "encouraging a wider distribution of wealth." For the first time the colossi of the steel, automobile, electrical, and other major industries, after decades of determined and even bloody resistance, had to bargain collectively with their employees. The union leaders with whom they had to deal in the 'thirties were not the labor hacks and dreary time-servers of another era, but alert, aggressive, politically conscious men who understood the anatomy of power and the broader social issues at stake. Here, certainly, was countervailing power.

On the political side, the power of the elite group was

reduced by the partial disaffection of one of the two major parties. The Democratic party, dominated during the 'twenties by conservatives, came under the leadership of a new and rejuvenated liberal wing, and hence was no longer subservient to the ideology of the business community. Liberal forces wielded increasingly great influence with the national administration and achieved ascendancy in such key states as New York, California and Illinois. Liberals from the urban areas also increased their power in Congress where the principle of seniority has traditionally given control to the preponderantly conservative South. When the Democrats are in power most of the key chairmanships are still held by conservative and even reactionary southerners, but the party organization itself is no longer dominated by them—as its quadrennial platform statements attest—and the alignment of forces has changed even in Congress. As good a token as any of the decline of southern hegemony in the party was the abandonment at national conventions of the notorious two-thirds rule, which had previously given the South a virtual veto power over the nomination of a presidential candidate.

The result has been the emergence of a countervailing power in the form of a major party which in a new sense was "a party of the people"—even if sometimes waveringly so—a party in which minority groups enjoyed new prestige and prominence, a party in the councils of which organized labor was well represented. Anyone familiar with the Democratic party knows that business, large and small, has an influential voice, but it clearly does not as in the Republican party speak for or impose the "official" American Business Creed.[45] This was foretold in President Roosevelt's famous first inaugural address of March 4, 1933. Contemplating the gloomy realities of that dark period, he passed the following judgment:

Plenty is at our doorstep, but a generous use of it languishes in the very sight of supply. Primarily this is because rulers of the exchange of mankind's goods have failed, through their own stubbornness and their own incompetence, have admitted their failure, and have abdicated. Practices of the unscrupulous money changers stand indicted in the court of public opinion, rejected by the hearts and minds of men. . . . They know only the rules of a generation of self-seekers. They have no vision, and where there is no vision the people perish. Yes, the money changers have fled from their high seats in the temple of our civilization. We may now restore that temple to the ancient truths. The measure of the restoration lies in the extent to which we apply social values more noble than mere monetary profit.

Five years later the President reaffirmed his position in a different way, in a message to Congress on the subject of curbing monopoly, when he urged that free government is incompatible with the accumulation of property in a few hands.

The promise has hardly been climaxed by the event. If the argument of an earlier chapter is valid, power is still dangerously concentrated in a few hands. Even so, the emergence of a strong labor movement, of organized farm groups, and of a party skeptical of the official business creed and responsive to heretofore impotent ethnic minorities, means that a new kind of power balance has been established.[46]

Not the least factor in this new balance, it may be noted in conclusion, is the defection of intellectuals—the men who interpret events and, as Archibald MacLeish once reminded us, dispense the applause:

> Have Gentlemen perhaps forgotten this?—
> We write the histories.
>
> Do Gentlemen who snigger at the poets,
> Who speak the word professor with guffaws—
> Do Gentlemen expect their fame to flourish
> When we, not they, distribute the applause?

Those who reckon the calculus of power generally omit their own influence and the influence of their kind from the reckoning. This is an oversight. Men of the academic world and the world of arts and letters rarely pillory or lampoon the business community in the manner of the 'thirties, but neither are they its captives or captivated by it, as in an earlier era. Their aloofness is not the product of a collective decision. Artists and intellectuals belong to no union and have no party. By and large they prefer ateliers and library cubicles (and, in their relaxed moments, bars or coffee houses) to political rallies. They tend to be undisciplined and politically innocent. Nevertheless, both the New Deal and the New Frontier have evoked politically potent loyalties and commitments in the world of arts and letters and science which the opposition can hardly command. It is somehow difficult to imagine Pablo Casals playing at the White House before an assemblage of the greatest artists in the world at the invitation of Mamie and Dwight Eisenhower or Grace and Calvin Coolidge. This, too, is part of the new balance of power.

Such were the outlines of the Welfare State as defined by liberals responding to conditions prevalent in America during the 'thirties. The reforms of those years were concentrated upon the pressing and urgent. The energies of reformers were largely absorbed in finding remedies for mass deprivation and mass unemployment. Security against want and protection from contractions of the business cycle were and still are revolutionary objectives for America, but they are defensive and minimal—a sturdy stockade in the wilderness, not a conquest of the wilderness itself. The 'thirties could not go beyond them. Social unrest could be enlisted to produce a bold contribution to the wellbeing of the nation like the Tennessee Valley Authority, but the broader purposes for which TVA was a grand demonstration project—regional planning of great territorial units like our river valleys, the extension of the yardstick principle to areas other than the production and sale of power—these were lost. The impetus provided by the reform movement of the 'thirties might have carried us beyond a greenbelt community here and there, beyond a cramped approach to housing in terms of the needs of slum dwellers and a sick building industry, beyond an approach to public works as a device for stimulating business, beyond an approach to old-age security confined in its concept to paltry monthly allowances. One cannot say. The war came and ranks closed. The President declared a moratorium on reform.

The close of the war brought with it the terrible fear of

a recrudescence of mass unemployment and frightened Congress into passing the Employment Act of 1946. But postwar prosperity and the surprising ease with which America effected the transition from war to peace momentarily nourished a new confidence in automatic progress—a condition in which one has a sense of moving effortlessly towards goals without knowing what they are. It may be that, as Arthur Schlesinger, Jr., has said, the tensions of years of crusading in peace and war finally exhausted Americans. Russia did not yet loom as a menacing colossus. We enjoyed a monopoly in atomic weapons. Underdeveloped areas were not yet caught in the ideological cross-currents which tear at them today. All this produced a soporific effect which was not conducive to change. The Korean War was a rude reminder of troubled times to come, but America preferred tranquilizers. For eight years the nation slept.

"I believe that phase is passing. Our foolish languor has been shaken if not shattered. We are more ready to examine ourselves and our record."[47] Mr. Stevenson may or may not have been prophetic. Today new problems tax our strength, test our vigor as a people. They require new goals, call for new vision. Liberal spokesmen—Stevenson, Kennedy, Lippmann, Kennan, Humphrey, Douglas, Reuther, and many more—have sought to reawaken the national conscience.

But nations do not normally rededicate themselves except at moments of great crisis. It is one of the tragic paradoxes of life that men seldom achieve true nobility except when they suffer greatly. During the blitz the British achieved a moral stature that won them the admiration of all decent men. One refers to more than their great courage. During those dark hours class barriers were leveled. Men were imbued with a spirit of mutuality. There was a sense of common purpose, a consecration to something more important than mere survival. Something similar happened here, if in a less profound sense, during the Great Depression. The opening words of President Roosevelt's first inaugural address were, "This is a day of national consecration." Large numbers of Americans caught this spirit. They discovered a sense of community and developed the kind of social conscience that produced the New Deal. It took the spectacle of mass deprivation and mass unemployment to arouse Americans—including many who were not themselves deprived—to a high pitch of idealism. Out of this came a great forward thrust, a moral momentum that produced the Minimum Wage and Social Security laws. Today we need a new momentum. We need what William James once called a "moral equivalent to war." We also need a moral equivalent to depression.

There is good reason to believe that forces are combining to produce such a renewal. The promptings of conscience are aided by the prodding of events. Whether we shall first have to suffer greatly no one can tell. Meanwhile, we may examine these forces and the responses which, in the judgment of liberals, they ought to call forth.

Chapter 14

The New Challenge

THE GREAT RECONSTRUCTION initiated in the 'thirties is well on the way to completion. It marks, in America, the third historic occasion on which the system of property rights has accommodated itself to the demands of the disadvantaged. The need for a juster distribution of wealth and for a more effective strategy to counter contractions of the business cycle continues. To refer to "pockets" of poverty and unemployment is a calloused understatement. However, the needs of the impoverished and of the *cyclically* unemployed are not now the major impetus to comprehensive reform. Such needs do, indeed (as has been argued), have a serious bearing on the health of our economy, and they are, of course, an affront to the conscience of the community; but they no longer have decisive political force.[1] The disadvantaged, though still a massive 16 million households when reckoned as an income group, are not only less numerous; large numbers of them are dark-skinned people—Negroes, Puerto Ricans, Mexican-Americans—as well as old people and marginal members of the majority group, all incapable of posing a serious threat to the social order such as that presented by the now legendary "one-third" who were the "ill-housed, ill-fed, and ill-clothed" of the 'thirties. Similarly, those unemployed as a result of the postwar recessions, thanks to the reforms of the New Deal, have represented a much smaller proportion of the labor force, and many if not most of such cyclically unemployed workers belong to minority groups or are politically apathetic members of the majority group.

The reforms initiated in the 'thirties were primarily a response to the needs of the lower income groups. True, few prosperous people were able to escape the ravages of the depression, and all ultimately benefited from the measures taken to cope with it. But here, as with the social security program, people in distress, including the unemployed, were most immediately and directly helped. The general welfare was regarded as deriving primarily from action taken in *their* behalf, rather than action taken in behalf of entrepreneurs and property owners from whom, in the heretofore accepted view, benefits would trickle or seep down to the less fortunate. Such were the social priorities of the New Deal, and this was partly why it provoked the bitter hostility of a great majority of the well-to-do. If, in practice, the priorities as thus defined did not always work out, this was how they were estimated by all parties, and here, as elsewhere, what was thought to be the case was at least as important as what actually transpired.

Today, perhaps uniquely in history, the impetus to reform does not come from the militant spokesmen of economically deprived and desperate people, and it does not primarily express itself in a demand that wealth be distributed more equitably. *If not quite today, then surely within the next decade the impulse to reform will have undergone an historic change. It will have its roots in conditions which directly and manifestly affect everyone, rich as well as poor, employed as well as unemployed, people of light skin as well as dark, young as well as old, able-bodied as well as handicapped.* To ignore this change is to miss one of the most striking features of our time. Powerful forces conspire to make this so, and it is important that we clearly identify them.

The conditions referred to are four: (*a*) the emergence of the Soviet Union as a great and dynamic power, (*b*) the rising expectations of underdeveloped nations, (*c*) the impact of automation, (*d*) the urban crisis. Each will be considered in brief detail.

Challenge of the Soviet Union

Morally sensitive Americans rightly cringe when an intrinsically excellent proposal must be justified, as it often is these days, with the warning that the Russians are doing it, or doing it better. Adequate foreign aid, the conquest of space, increased support for education, improvement of the physical vigor of our people, integration of the races, economic growth, these should commend themselves, whether to our moral sense or common sense, without the threat of a hammer and sickle over us. Nevertheless, it took the launching of Sputnik to initiate the most searching look we have given our educational methods in a long time. The amount spent on education by the USSR has been one of the most potent arguments in favor of increasing what we spend. When the Russians circled and photographed the moon, a spokesman for the Eisenhower Administration disdained running up "a high score in an outer space basketball game," but most thoughtful Americans became concerned about the level and prestige of American science and technology. And, most recently, many Americans have become more troubled about our lagging growth rate than they might otherwise have been because the USSR is outpacing us.

If in this fashion we are forced to do what we might not have done but should do in any case, perhaps the cold war will not have been waged in vain. Meanwhile, we must be aware of the facts and the fact is that on the critical economic front, while America is still easily the front runner, we are in real danger of losing the race. The issue has occasioned curiously bitter controversy. Too many of us are disposed to scold the barometer when it points to bad weather. And yet the facts are not only clear, they will become overwhelmingly intrusive as the years go on.

Even by the most conservative reckoning, the Soviet economy has been expanding at twice the rate of our own. The economy of the Soviet Union is somewhat less than half the size of ours, but if it continues exceeding our own at this rate, the outcome is inevitable. This, in any event, has been the conclusion of an impressive list of American economists as recorded in the testimony of many of them before the Joint Economic Committee of Congress.[2] It was the verdict not only of partisan critics of the Eisenhower Administration, but of highly placed members of his Administration such as Allen Dulles, then Director of the Central Intelligence Agency, and Douglas Dillon, then Under Secretary of State for Economic Affairs—men who patriotically insisted on warning the nation against great peril, even at the risk of damaging the prestige of the Administration of which they were a part.

In the comparisons which follow it will be useful to bear in mind the distinction suggested in an earlier chapter between "total" and "industrial" production. Our annual rate of industrial production averaged 5.6 percent in the period 1947–1953. From 1953 to 1959 industrial production rose less than 1.7 percent annually. On a per capita basis growth in industrial production came to a halt, so that, in 1959, output per capita in mining and manufacturing was no greater than it had been six years earlier. Thus, while industrial production did in fact increase by a total of 10.4 percent between 1953 and 1959, population increased by 11 percent, so that there was actually a net loss in industrial production per capita. Meanwhile, Russian industrial production has been growing at a rate variously estimated by leading authorities as between 8 and 9 percent annually.

Confronted with such embarrassing comparisons, most conservatives—with the notable exceptions already cited—have denounced arithmetic. *Time* magazine, for example, referred to the "international numbers game." Former Vice-President Nixon glibly dismissed such disclosures about our production lag as "the most fashionable parlor game of our time." The editors of *Fortune* recently invoked the authority of a distinguished British economist to prove that the economy of the USSR is not really growing and that we have nothing to fear. Professor Colin Clark (who has been impressively wrong before) arrives at his conclusion that the Russian growth rate is a myth and illusion by averaging the years 1913 to 1956, a singularly unconvincing device (except, apparently, to the editors of *Fortune*) when applied to a country twice overrun and devastated during this period, and involved in a prolonged civil war besides.

Professor Clark also argues that USSR growth rates are based on the immediate postwar record when a high recovery rate was to be expected, given the low base from which it started. Neither the authorities nor the facts bear him out. Our Director of Central Intelligence referred specifically to *recent* experience in citing the rapid growth rate of the

Soviet economy: "During the past 7 years, through 1958, Soviet industry has grown at the annual rate of 9½ percent," he says. Mr. Dulles added: "This is not the officially announced rate, which is somewhat larger. *It is our reconstruction and deflation of Soviet data.*" He went on to cite a comparable American growth rate of 3.6 percent for the seven years through 1957, observing that the comparison would be even more unfavorable if one included the year 1958.

Douglas Dillon, referring to the new Russian seven-year plan, has also warned: "We should not make the mistake of giving the plan less than our most serious attention. . . . According to the Soviet leaders, the basic objective of the seven-year plan is 'the maximum gain in time in the peaceful competition between socialism and capitalism.' " He went on:

The Soviet Union has already made substantial strides in this competition. This is borne out by cold, hard facts. Our best estimates of Soviet domestic expansion place the average annual rate of growth of the Soviet economy as a whole at between 6 and 7 percent over the past 8 years. Their industrial growth has averaged between 8 and 9 percent during this time. Over the same period our own average annual increase, both in gross national product and in industrial production, has been about 3 percent.[3]

Likewise, Robert C. Sprague, Co-Chairman of the Gaither Committee, appointed by President Eisenhower in 1957 to survey national security problems, testifying before the Senate Subcommittee on National Policy Machinery, said: "There is no solid basis to argue that the Soviet economy will not continue to grow at its present rate." Words like those of Dulles, Dillon, and Sprague have been echoed by America's most distinguished economists and Russian experts.[4]

It is useful to turn from generalities like "gross national product" and "industrial production" to bricks, pig iron, coal, electric power, and the like. The late W. S. Woytinsky makes the following comparisons based upon the *Monthly Bulletin of Statistics* of the United Nations (March, 1960).

The real challenge of the USSR is suggested in the table below which deals, it should be noted, not with gross national product, but with industrial production.[5] The challenge lies not in the present size of the Soviet Union's gross national product, which is reckoned at about 45 percent of ours. It lies in the ability of a dictatorship to deny consumer goods to the population in order to concentrate on investment.

	United States			USSR		
	1953	1958-59	Change in %	1953	1958-59	Change in %
Coal, mil. in tons	36.7	32.2	−12	18.7	31.0	66
Crude petroleum, mil. in tons	26.5	27.6	4	4.4	10.8	146
Iron ore, mil. in tons	10.8	5.8	−42	5.0	7.4	48
Cement, mil. in tons	3.8	4.6	20	1.3	2.8	115
Building bricks, billions	0.5	0.5	0	1.4	2.4	71
Pig iron, mil. in tons	5.7	4.6	−19	2.3	3.6	56
Crude steel, mil. in tons	8.4	7.1	−15	3.2	5.0	56
Passenger cars, thousands	510.0	466.0	−9	6.0	10.0	67
Commercial vehicles, thousands	101.0	73.0	−28	25.0	41.0	64
Electricity, billions KWH	43.0	66.0	54	11.0	22.0	100
Industrial output (1953 = 100)	100.0	102.0	2	100.0	170.0	70

One commodity, not cited in the table, deserves special consideration in this context because it affords a striking and even more disturbing illustration. It is education. In an important sense, money spent on education is a capital investment. While schooling may be intrinsically enjoyable, its cost generally represents a sacrifice of present enjoyment to achieve future benefits. To the extent that our schools are the foundation of progress in modern science and technology, the resources we allocate to our schools may well afford a preview of the future.[6]

According to the U. S. Government's Education Mission, the USSR spends from 10 to 15 percent of its much smaller income on education, while we have been spending only 3.7 percent. A more recent report (1962), that of the National Science Foundation, declares that Russia spends as much on education as the United States, although its wealth is only half as great. U. S. Commissioner of Education, Lawrence Derthick, reported that the teacher-student ratio in the Soviet Union is 1:17 against 1:26 in America. The Soviet teacher is paid the equivalent of beginning doctors and engineers. The working hours for secondary teachers are 18 hours a week; for elementary teachers, 24 hours a week.

Without doubt the Commissioner would not think of having our public schools copy the Russians. Neither would all but a handful of Americans. But the fact nevertheless remains that the Russians spend a much higher share of their income on education. Also, they honor their teachers more. The payoff is already evident not only in the race for space, but in the fact that, during the last decade, Russians, for the first time in forty years, were winning an impressive number of Nobel prizes in science. It is evidenced also by the fact that, in the 1960's, according to the National Science Foundation, Russia will produce more than twice as many at least equally well-trained scientists and engineers as we produce.[7]

The foremost authority in America on the Soviet Union is our former ambassador to that country, George Kennan. The second volume of his great work, *Soviet-American Relations*, has recently appeared. Perhaps more than anyone else in America George Kennan (now Ambassador to Yugoslavia) is qualified to comment about the outcome of our contest with the USSR. This is what he says:

If you ask me—as a historian, let us say—whether a country in the state this country is in today, with no highly developed sense of national purpose, with the overwhelming accent of life on personal comfort and amusement, with a dearth of public services and a surfeit of privately sold gadgetry . . . with an educational system where quality has been extensively sacrificed to quantity, and with insufficient social discipline even to keep its major industries functioning without grievous interruptions—if you ask me whether such a country has, over the long run, good chances of competing with a purposeful, serious and disciplined society such as that of the Soviet Union, I must say that the answer is 'No.'[8]

Clearly a persisting disparity between the growth rate of the Soviet Union and the United States indicates an outcome for the future with which we must increasingly reckon, even though we may differ concerning its implications. It is an outcome which would involve all of us, perhaps most of all those who have the largest stake in retaining the fundamentals of our economic system.

The Emerging Nations

Meanwhile the Soviet growth rate poses an *immediate* and different kind of challenge which we dare not ignore. It is true, as the anaestheticians assure us, that we shall not be overtaken in the next ten or probably even twenty years. Our defenses and capacity to retaliate against attack will not be in jeopardy. We have enough and will continue to have enough wealth to wage a war of annihilation against any aggressor. No doubt it is because he understands this that Khrushchev has charted a new course. We might well achieve military invulnerability only to find that we had lost the real war. We may assume that, in the present conflict, neither side will deliberately invite open military conflict. The war will be waged, as Khrushchev has generously warned us, economically and ideologically, and the "spoils" will be the loyalties of the distressed millions of the world.

The submerged peoples of Africa, Asia, and Latin America know little of the benefits of modern science and technology. Two-thirds of the people of the world go hungry. They know only poverty and despair. We have not yet begun to grasp the new dimensions of their predicament, caught as they are between the promise of modern technology and some of its most evil consequences.[9] No doubt they will one day evolve their own methods and solutions appropriate to their peculiar problems. But it is quite clear—as the example of Red China attests—that they will be greatly influenced by, if not directly allied with, the nation which provides them with (a) direct aid in sufficient quantity to help lift them out of the ancient morass to which history has assigned them, and (b) an efficient economic model adaptable to their needs.

Congress has recently approved (September, 1961) direct aid in the amount of $7.2 billion in development loan[10] funds to be spread over a five-year period. This is a large increase over the level of the preceding years. However, not even the Berlin crisis sufficed to keep a penurious Senate from reducing President Kennedy's request for $4.8 billion in foreign aid for the next fiscal year to $4.2 billion, and an even more penurious (and provincial) House of Representatives from reducing the sum to $3.87 billion. $7.2 billion represents an average of $1.45 billion per year for the next five years, an almost trivial fraction of a Gross National Product which is expected to go far beyond $525 billion during that period. It may be compared with the $2 billion we spend annually on barber shops and beauty parlors, the $2⅓ billion we spend on toilet articles and preparations, and the $9¼ billion we spend annually on alcoholic beverages. However, this is a matter of priorities, to which attention is given elsewhere. The point needing stress here is a different one.

To have real impact on the emerging nations of the world, American assistance must be multiplied far beyond anything contemplated by nearly all of the parties to the debate over foreign aid. And the tragedy is that we waste that much by our simple refusal to produce it. If we had allocated a tenth (the traditional tithe) of the wealth we *failed* to produce in 1960 to foreign aid we would be thrashing the Soviet Union thoroughly at her own chosen game. Are the stakes worth it? Doubters should consider Red China and the difference it would have made to our world posture today if we had given aid to China on a sufficient scale and, it should be added, in an intelligent way.

Is India, a subcontinent in itself, worth it? Or shall we wait for communism to pre-empt that area, too? Thanks to our expanded aid, there are signs of progress in India. But in what direction, in fact, will the masses of India go if, ten or twenty years from now, Red China has moved into the twentieth century while India remains mired in the middle ages? In 1953, when the Eisenhower Administration took office, there was brave (if quixotic) talk of rolling back the USSR in Central Europe and liberating the European satellite countries. Instead, the Soviet Union today threatens the unity of the Western Hemisphere and has taken the initiative from us in Africa where at least fifteen new nations are looking to the

Kremlin rather than to us for leadership and assistance. That is why it is suicidal to scoff at "growthmanship" and the "cult of growth."

Meanwhile, cult or occult, the USSR has not, in fact, been idle. The use of trade and aid to win adherents and to convert the non-communist world has become an avowed objective of Soviet policy. According to our State Department, since the Soviet Union launched its aid and trade drive in 1954, it has extended some $2½ billion in military and economic development credits, $1 billion during the last year alone. The number of Soviet technicians has increased in the newly emerging areas to 4,000. Since the beginning of their offensive, Soviet trade has doubled. And one may be sure that the scope of aid and trade will expand as their economy expands.

Quite apart, however, from the vastly expanded foreign aid we could afford if our economy were functioning efficiently, what kind of model do we offer submerged peoples looking for a way to help themselves? Here, as earlier, it may be well to cite highly placed Eisenhower appointees who can hardly be accused of bias against his Administration. As conservatives and Republicans, their comments may help to commend a thesis which the overwhelming majority of Republicans and so-called conservatives unfortunately regard as suspect.

President Eisenhower's Committee to Study the U. S. Military Assistance Program, headed by William S. Draper, declared: "Entirely aside from the threat of communist aggression, the United States and other free nations face the challenge of the revolutionary insistence on progress by the hundreds of millions of people in less-developed areas . . ." However, as Douglas Dillon pointed out when he was still a member of the Eisenhower Administration, "In their search for material progress, the power of the Soviet example is not lost upon the peoples of the newly developing lands. If they are not given reasonable hope of progress under freedom— as they would much prefer—then they will surely be tempted to try shortcuts which purport to offer solutions for all their problems."[11]

Elsewhere, Dillon makes the point more vigorously:

Soviet economic success is of vital importance to international communism in projecting an image of the Soviet system as the magic blueprint for the achievement of rapid progress by the less developed countries of Asia, Africa, the Middle East, and Latin America. We should not underestimate the appeal which such an image may have on men of influence in the underdeveloped countries who are desperately seeking to lead their peoples into the 20th century.

He goes on, ". . . the less developed countries cannot help but be profoundly affected by the example of purposeful and dramatic increases in output achieved under communism. In some of these countries highly organized communist parties and their front organizations work unceasingly to prey upon this susceptibility."[12]

We are assured that our lead over the USSR is so great that concern about our being overtaken in the near future is alarmist, even though its rate of growth *is* more rapid than ours. However this may be, the underdeveloped areas *are* concerned with growth rates; they, or, in any event, their more enlightened leaders, want to move as quickly as possible, and it is *speed of growth* that will impress them as more relevant to their situation than recitations about America's 62 million motor cars, 37 million vacuum cleaners, 50 million refrigerators, etc., etc.

The *New York Times* under a July 23, 1960, dateline reported that steel mill capacity in the United States had fallen to less than half of capacity, the lowest rate in twenty-one years, except during strike shutdowns. Unemployment at that time was rising steadily. At this writing (March, 1962), it is still high. From the point of view of the attractiveness of our system to the leadership of economically backward areas, such news is catastrophic.

The manner in which aid must be provided and adjusted to the peculiar needs of different areas is a technical matter and belongs to the province of experts. The misdirection of aid so as to bolster corrupt and reactionary regimes and frustrate popular aspirations and progressive leadership presents a special problem related to whether we have backward look-ing or forward looking leadership in Washington. However, all this is not at issue here. What is at issue is the contention that the requirements of survival in the cold war compel us to take a hard look at economic arrangements in our country which might otherwise have been tolerated indefinitely with-out significant modification.

A former Soviet Foreign Minister has told us: "Peaceful coexistence does not mean a quiet life. As long as different social and political systems exist, contradictions between them are inevitable. Peaceful coexistence is a struggle—a political struggle, an economic struggle, an ideological struggle." It is this struggle from which the chief beneficiaries of our own system have for the most part retreated—retreated because, in order to win the struggle, we must re-examine our system and remedy its defects, and because, with this, we may have to shatter some of their most cherished illusions.

It is to be hoped that, as the conflict and the challenge grow more menacing, enough thoughtful Americans, includ-ing those who have heretofore resisted change, will recognize the imperatives of survival. Happily these imperatives do not involve destroying but creating: we are not required to hinder other nations but to help them, not to oppress them but to liberate them; and, therefore, they coincide with moral im-peratives as well.

However, when all this has been said, our competition with the Soviet Union merely helps us see what might otherwise have been obscure, namely that it is no longer possible for a great and prosperous democracy either to exploit underdevel-oped nations or to isolate itself from them. The predicament of France in Algiers affords a tragic illustration. Even if Communism were miraculously to disappear, we should no more be able to ignore the needs of necessitous and importu-nate nations in a shrinking world than we have been able to ignore the demands of needy people within our own bound-aries. The alternative would be to live in a world of surly, jealous, hostile, quarrelsome neighbors who would regard us as a nation of misers and sybarites, indifferent to the suffer-ing of others and huddling for safety behind a shield of atomic bombs. Puerto Rico should commend itself as a better model to reasonable Americans than the Congo or Cuba.

The Impact of Automation

If we must have a growing economy to meet the challenge of the USSR and guide emerging nations into the twentieth century, means are happily at hand. Automation—the use of machines to run machines—presages changes comparable in their impact on society to those produced by the advent of power-driven machinery. Examples have become familiar.

A single machine has been installed by the Bank of America which will perform all the work connected with the handling of checks for the 87 branches of the bank in the San Francisco area. It will tabulate the checks, clear them, keep track of depositors' checking accounts and print their monthly statements. What IRMA, as the machine is called, will do in the event an account is overdrawn is not indicated in the reports. No doubt it will write the neglectful depositor a polite but firm reminder.

We are told of a Cleveland automobile plant where machines perform 530 operations on an engine block which emerges as a finished product without having been touched by a human hand. In another plant 2,163 machines and tools and 27 miles of conveyors turn out two refrigerators a minute. The sheet metal for the refrigerators is checked at the beginning of the process; everything else is done by machine. We learn of a lathe which, after gauging each part as it is produced, automatically resets the cutting tools as they show wear. When the cutting tools are worn and must be discarded, the machine automatically replaces them with sharp tools. Parts are automatically loaded into the machine and unloaded when they are finished. Except for an occasional check, such a lathe requires no attention over periods of from five to eight hours.[13]

These examples are not yet the prevailing pattern for industry at large, but they are the shape of things shortly to come. We are also confronted with a chemical revolution which is transforming the raw-material base of modern industry, and soon available for commercial use will be boundless supplies of atomic energy.[14] However, it is automation that presents us with the most urgent issues. For, if automation serves us in spectacular ways, it also exacts a price from those who fail to grasp its implications.

Automation is not a name for routine improvements in technology to which we readily accommodate ourselves after minor dislocations in our accustomed way of doing things. It presents us with a novel set of circumstances. We have a new wedding of science and technology. As Norbert Wiener has reminded us, the coming of automation is a second industrial revolution.[15] Consequently, to deal with automation requires far more than the retraining and relocating of displaced workers. Automation promises untold abundance or threatens confusion, depending on how we use it. It can give us access to desirable leisure and produce fabulous wealth in which the rest of the world can share, or it can inflict enforced and demoralizing idleness on millions of Americans.

This much is certain: within the near future, as will be indicated in the concluding chapter, the impact of automation will require major modifications in our traditional approach to many basic problems, of economic growth, of foreign aid, of attending to the neglected public sector of the economy. Meanwhile, the consequences of neglecting essential public needs, complicated by the burgeoning of our population, will have reached such critical proportions as to inject a new dynamic factor into American life. This is indicated by what has been happening to our cities.

The Urban Crisis

In the Commerce Department Building at Washington a light above the "U. S. population clock" flashes every eleven seconds. Each flash heralds the birth of a baby. The population of the United States, about 180 million today, will be between 220 and 244 million by 1975. Shortly after the turn of the century it will be somewhere between 300 and 400 million. It could be 600 million by the year 2050, almost the population of China today. At least 85 percent of this number will be concentrated in urban areas. Dense populations will stretch for scores of miles in great supercities. And, if we continue to do business as usual, we shall choke in these gigantic metropolitan concentrations.

Today, long before this vast increment of population, our cities sprawl formlessly over the countryside. Except for islands of high commerce and atolls of living and recreational facilities largely reserved for the well-to-do, our cities are rotten at the core. The spread of blight has more than canceled out our still feeble effort at slum clearance and urban renewal, eroding the tax base of our cities and contributing to the ever mounting cost of crime, delinquency and disease. The result has been, as the 1960 census showed, a steady exodus to the suburbs. Refugees from the asphalt jungle settle at the periphery of the city, abandoning the center to ethnic minorities, the elderly, and all the other poor who must content themselves with overcrowding in substandard dwellings if they are to have any housing at all. Increasingly, therefore, our cities become racial ghettos and dense slums, some areas of which are unsafe to peaceful citizens even in daytime. Ironically, middle income families can no longer afford to live in the city itself,[16] and in their flight they take with them much of the leadership which might otherwise impart vigor and vitality to the civic life of the community. Many of those below the middle income but above the poverty level tag along to settle down in drab, sprawling tracts.

Thereupon a great pendulum-like movement takes place as, in each metropolitan area, hundreds of thousands of commuters converge on the city in the morning and evacuate it at night. Whether by public conveyance or car, it is reported that the Los Angeles commuter, taken collectively, travels almost 40 million miles daily, the equivalent of about 170 trips to the moon. The case of Los Angeles is, no doubt, extreme; it is the first city to have become a large metropolis after the advent of the automobile. But it is the prototype of every major city of the future, unless we mend our ways.

For those who prefer motor cars, freeways and expressways have been provided at fantastic cost, so that, bumper-to-bumper, the vast throng can inch its way in and out. During the rush hours, the freeways of Los Angeles, most elaborate in the world, are jeered at as the world's longest parking lots.

A mordant wit tells the story of a driver who ran out of gas on the Hollywood Freeway and was carried along for ten miles without learning that his tank was dry. Freeway jokes multiply, but the joke is on us.

It would be ironical if the scientists working on a projectile intended to go from here to Mars were to be late for the countdown because they were caught in a traffic jam but, as someone has noted, this might well be their weird predicament. We are solving the staggering problem of traversing interplanetary space without solving the problem of how to cross a city.

When scholars write the history of our time they will, no doubt, say that more than any other artifact, the automobile has shaped our culture. The automobile has given us undreamed-of mobility. It has brought us within easy reach of otherwise inaccessible recreational areas. It has freed us from dependence on the inflexible routes and rigid schedules of older systems of transportation. It has enabled us to move in splendid isolation from one place to another, enjoying privacy when we wish it. For many years it has been our favored status symbol. The total number of cars in the United States is 62 million, and it is growing at a faster rate than the population.

But the automobile has also led us to become prodigal with the land on which we spread our cities. Vast areas must be allocated to the movement and storage of the automobile. It is wasteful of fuel and, as traffic grows more and more congested, of time. The roadbeds it requires, including the freeways and expressways, are inordinately expensive. It pollutes our air. Until we come to terms with the automobile, all talk of solving our metropolitan area problems is wishful thinking.

Many commuters prefer public transit, but, due to competition from the automobile, public transit is becoming more inconvenient and generally inefficient. Even so, a simple calculation will disclose that great armies of commuters have spent as much as two years of their lives in a small, metal chamber moving back and forth between their homes and their places of work. This sounds suspiciously like a jail except that jails are not usually in motion.

Because of its rapid growth, California affords an excellent preview of what is in store for the rest of the nation. Uncontrolled metropolitan sprawl is taking over large areas of its most fertile land.[17] While much of this urban spread is inevitable, a great deal of it is wantonly wasteful of the state's best soil. Santa Clara County, one of the richest farming areas in the world, about thirty miles from San Francisco, is an excellent case in point. If all the land withdrawn for urban use in the Santa Clara Valley since 1947 were consolidated it would equal about 26 square miles. Instead, an area of about 200 square miles has been given over to urban development.

"Scatteration," as it is called, involves much more than a waste of precious soil; it entails unnecessarily extended utilities and streets, it adds to the time and cost of commuting, and it usually occurs without reference to the proximity of schools, churches, and recreational facilities. Wherever one goes one finds the subdivider playing a game of hop, skip, and jump—ever hopeful that the horde of humanity will catch up with him.

Lacking open spaces, pleasing landscapes, inviting woodlands nearby, inhabitants of "megalopolis" use every opportunity to drive beyond their urban wasteland; but, since the idea seizes them simultaneously, they usually find the accessible sanctuaries overcrowded. In other cases desirable recreational areas have been pre-empted by private owners. The area embracing Massachusetts and New York City, the most densely populated and one of the most highly industrialized in the country, has virtually no public beach and no more is available along the entire Atlantic shoreline. In California, the state is paying $100 a front-inch for beach frontage near Los Angeles which foresight might have acquired before it passed through the hands of a succession of speculators.

"Year after year our scenic treasures are being plundered by what we call an advancing civilization," recently declared a distinguished general who loves his native land enough to cherish its countryside as well as defend it from aggressors. General Omar Bradley added: "If we are not careful we shall leave our children a legacy of billion-dollar roads leading nowhere except to other congested places like those we left behind. We are building ourselves an asphalt treadmill and allowing the green areas of our nation to disappear."[18] He might have added that we shall also leave them a legacy of polluted air and streams, of billboard alleys, of garish neon-lit strips snaking endlessly out to characterless suburbs. This is the posture of urban life in America in 1962. If we continue on our present course, it requires no seer to predict what it will be in 1980.

The road we must travel is clear. Quite literally we must rebuild vast sections of our cities. We must provide open spaces and recreational areas, large and small, within and without the city, many of them so distributed as to be within easy access of where people live. We must build adequate housing within the reach of middle income as well as lower income families, and make special provision for housing the aged. We must provide rapid, efficient, comfortable public transit, and subsidize it—if necessary, give its services away. This may be one way of luring people out of their automobiles and reducing the fantastic waste and extravagance in which the overuse of the automobile has involved us. We must rethink the relationship between our homes and where we work and shop and play, so that these are brought into some kind of rational juxtaposition.

We cannot rebuild our cities without supporting our often neglected schools and libraries and other public amenities and facilities more adequately than we have in the past. We cannot make our cities more livable until we learn that our present outlays for training and paying teachers, police and probation officers, mental hygiene staffs, and social workers, not only suggest a distorted sense of values, but are economically much costlier in the end. We cannot revive our cities unless we recognize that the concentration of vast populations in relatively small areas requires a re-examination and revision of many traditional practices which presently obstruct intelligent preparation and planning for the future. To this the testimony offered by a large-scale builder of notably well designed houses in the "low-medium" range bears impressive witness:

Both in the central city and in the suburb there is much pioneering yet to be done and much for builders and for community authorities to learn. But there are sharp limits on what the individual builder or the individual political jurisdiction can do alone. At the most, if the builder is lucky and determined and employs the best architectural and planning talent . . . , he may produce an island of beauty and good design in the sea of urban sprawl and disorder. At the most, if the community brings all of its resources to the task, it might raise the character and quality of a small segment of a metropolitan area.

. . . We have gone about as far—and in many areas farther—as disorganized private initiative alone usefully can carry us in the development of our large metropolises. Government guidance is needed badly in these areas if private industry is to do its best.[19]

In short, the rapid increase in our population and its concentration in metropolitan areas forces us to do what we have heretofore been indisposed to do, namely, re-examine our priorities, make more intelligent use of our great wealth, give direction to our growth. *The demand for such direction or redirection, including the allocation of a greater proportion of our resources to public services, is not inspired by a desire to take from the rich and give to the poor. The impetus to such a program does not come from an effective demand to redistribute the wealth. The traditional socialist and liberal exhortations are not at work here. To fail to see this is completely to have missed the point.*

The wealthy have at least as much to gain as the impoverished from the reconstruction of our cities and the adequate support of basic public services. A few years ago it was easy for the well-to-do to escape the chaos and confusion of the city by creating islands of beauty and order in the country or in a suburb or country club. This is less and less possible. Soon it will be impossible.

A Jaguar is held up as inexorably on our congested freeways as a jalopy. In Los Angeles County the smog floats in and smothers affluent San Marino as it does blighted Brooklyn Heights. The sadism and violence that seep up from the slums can invade the sanctuaries of the rich as they have the sandlots of the poor. The daughters of unhyphenated as of hyphenated Americans are unsafe several steps from the campuses of two of our greatest institutions of higher learning. The demagogue who flourishes on human suffering can despoil the wealthy as well as delude the needy.

Here, as in the case of our epic competition with the Soviet Union, a new force is compelling us to consider our ways. If we do, cities may return to their historic function of civilizing people and enabling them to live richer lives. If we do not, our cities and the areas around them will become increasingly unlivable, dehumanizing us and twisting and warping the lives of all who inhabit them. "The culture of cities," Lewis Mumford has written, "is ultimately the culture of life in its higher social manifestations." The force of circumstance may yet compel us to achieve this higher social manifestation, although the fate of President Kennedy's proposal for a Department of Urban Affairs suggests that we still have some distance to travel.

Such are the major challenges to Americans in the second half of the twentieth century. They already enlist the attention of responsible conservatives. Nevertheless, it was liberals who first felt their force and, thus far, only liberals have come forward with creative proposals and solutions.

Chapter 15

Liberalism Today

IT FOLLOWS FROM what has been said that, in the liberal view, the concept of welfare must take on new meaning. The wish is also a prophecy. In the coming years welfare programs will no longer be limited in scope, or seem to be limited, to the area of social pathology, but will more nearly embrace everyone and more closely approximate the *general* welfare contemplated by the Constitution. Such an interpretation of welfare does not imply an abandonment of the private enterprise system as the mainstay of our economy. On the contrary, a broader interpretation of welfare will be a way of imparting enough guidance to the system to give it vigor and protect it from the debilitating policies of some of its most ardent friends. Accordingly, two principles distinguish the new version of welfare from the old. The first involves extending the sphere of government to include explicit responsibility for optimum growth. The second provides for the guidance of growth so as to give priority to basic unmet needs.

Optimum Growth

Clearly, success in our competition with the USSR, the needs of our less favored neighbors, and the healthy functioning of our domestic economy, all impose the same requirement—a growth rate which reflects our productive potentialities. If, therefore, liberals were once content to cast government in the limited role of countering contractions of the business cycle, they now understand that economic recovery and high levels of employment are impossible of achievement without a steady rate of growth, which is to say, a rate sufficient *through the years* to utilize the manpower made available by increased labor productivity and the growing number of available workers. This is the significance of Walter Heller's reminder that economic recovery from the recession of 1960-61 has been more than a cyclical problem; it is inseparably tied to the phenomenon of *chronic slack* (secular stagnation) in the economy.[1] It is the meaning, too, of Professor Samuelson's warning in his special report to President-elect Kennedy that "Prudent policy now requires that we combat the *basic sluggishness* which underlies the more dramatic recession."[2]

Earlier the discussion sought the measure of a healthy growth rate and of the wealth we waste by failing to achieve it. In the preceding chapter the intent has been to show that new conditions, only dimly discernible and hardly felt during the first half of this century, now urgently decree that government assume continuing responsibility for assuring adequate growth, should such growth fail to materialize otherwise. The question must now finally be raised, how such responsibility is to be exercised.

It has become clear that what is needed is neither a crash program which deals tardily with one phase of the economic cycle, nor a patchwork approach directed at segments of the economy or particular sources of weakness, but a continuing, comprehensive, coordinated policy embracing the economy as a whole. What is called for is no one stabilization device, but an integrated and flexible application of the monetary, fiscal, and other powers of government in such a way as to achieve the best use of our human and physical resources.

The Employment Act of 1946 provides ample mandate for such a program. *It shifts emphasis from curing an ailing economy to maintaining a healthy one.* As noted earlier, it categorically calls upon the Federal government "to use all practicable means" and "to co-ordinate and utilize all its plans, functions, and resources" to achieve the objectives of "maximum employment, production, and purchasing power." It declares this to be the "continuing policy and responsibility of the Federal Government." Significantly, it enlists the aid of professionally trained economists as technical advisers *at the policymaking level.*

Specifically, it requires the President, with the assistance of such advisers, to set forth "(1) the levels of employment, production, and purchasing power obtaining in the United States and such levels needed to carry out the policy . . . (2) current and foreseeable trends in the levels of employment, production, and purchasing power; (3) a review of the economic program of the Federal Government and a review of economic conditions affecting employment in the United States or any considerable portion thereof during the preceding year and of their effect upon employment, production, and purchasing power; and (4) a program for carrying out the policy . . . together with such recommendations for legislation as he may deem necessary or desirable." Surely this is a firm directive.

The following words, spoken in Harlem on October 25, 1952, augured well for the enforcement of the Employment Act:

. . . Let me say . . . what I have said time and again and with the full concurrence of all these associates of mine in this political crusade. Never again shall we allow a depression in the United States. The Soviet Communism [sic] is looking for one great victory. That victory is the economic collapse of our country. They want to see us go broke. Why then would a nation such as ours refuse to mobilize all its resources to defeat a depression as we would mobilize all our resources to defeat an invasion? One is just as serious as the other.

So I pledge you this. If the finest brains, the finest hearts, that we can mobilize in Washington can foresee the signs of any recession, and depression, that would put honest, hard working men and women out of work, the full power of private industry, of municipal government, of the Federal Government will be mobilized to see that that does not happen. I cannot pledge you more than that.

These brave words were General Eisenhower's. This was the Great Crusade. But when he became President they were followed by a timid policy of inaction and in retrospect the "crusade" was more suggestive of a cruise. The Economic Reports required of him by the Employment Act did not set forth the "levels needed to carry out the policy" in meaningful quantitative estimates of the potentialities of the economy.

Instead, from 1953 to 1960, the President's Reports dealt in generalizations and platitudes which, while soothing to a somnambulant Congress, failed to prevent or banish three economic contractions marked by successively higher levels of unemployment. The promised "full power" of the Federal government which was to be "mobilized" against depression or recession proved to be a vintage program of reducing Federal expenditures and tightening the credit available to private industry.

A new President has promised to "return to the spirit as well as to the letter of the Employment Act of 1946." President Kennedy has said that we should not "treat the economy in narrow terms but in terms appropriate to the optimum development of the human and natural resources of this country, of our productive capacity and that of the free world." He has surrounded himself with advisers who believe in the Employment Act. Unlike the architects of the New Deal, they understand the requirements of a consistent stabilization policy and are the masters of a far more sophisticated science than the economic science available to the New Dealers. The New Deal often moved at cross-purposes, the exigencies of the depression resulted in hasty improvisations, there was little earlier experience on which to build and a paucity of information about the actual operations of the economy. President Roosevelt himself did not understand the potentialities of fiscal policy. He thought of deficits as an unsalutary consequence of spending to relieve distress, and not as a device deliberately employed to affect demand.[3] The Democratic platforms of 1932 and 1936 both declared an orthodox intention to balance the budget.

Today the case is different. Economics is by no means an exact science and much remains to be learned about the complexities of our economic system. Economic forecasting is still hazardous. But economists are now aware, as they were not before, of the scope and variety of the devices available for guiding the economy. They have an increasingly clear understanding of the interplay of such devices and of their effect on the economy as a whole. Recent research makes a wealth of accurate data available. Moreover, there is a re-

markably large area of agreement concerning the broad outlines of sound policy among professional economists. The
exception is a small minority employed in the business community. Ironically, the business community—as some businessmen have come to see—would benefit greatly if it appropri-
ated the elementary wisdom embraced by the larger consensus.

The question is whether certain limitations on private
economic decision-making (imposed upon those who claim in
any case to be vassals of the sovereign consumer) would be
justified to secure a vigorous, expanding economy. It was the
contention of the preceding chapter that in the 'sixties the
force of circumstance would persuade a significant number
of conservative policymakers, in this instance business leaders
and the more responsible members of the conservative coalition in Congress who reflect their point of view, to agree. If
so, what may we expect? What broad principles comprise that
area of agreement among professional economists which has
yet to be fully translated into policy?

There is general agreement that the vigor of the economy
depends primarily on maintaining and raising the level of
effective demand sufficiently to absorb expanding capacity to
produce. This is the crux of the problem. The area of agreement includes a commitment to deficit financing and an unbalanced budget, if such recourse is necessary to maintain
demand during a period of business contraction and increasing unemployment.

In general, liberals have always favored expanding the
government's share of effective demand through increased
outlays for public works. Such a greatly expanded public
works program may be considered (1) from the point of view
of a rational schedule of priorities, and (2) as a device for
stabilizing the economy. The question of priorities, which
has become increasingly prominent, will be left for the conclusion of this discussion. Quite apart from the intrinsic
merit of the projects themselves, as Keynes pointed out, a
public works program can be a potent device for promoting
stability and growth. There are vast areas in which the invest-

ment of public funds would in no way compete with private enterprise, and many areas in which a specific private sector of the economy would be directly benefited quite apart from any stabilization effect, as when, for example, property values are enhanced by an adjacent urban redevelopment program. The effects of a public works program are in most cases too tardy to be of help in the early stages of an emergency, but, if properly planned in advance, projects of less urgency can be programmed to coincide with anticipated slack in the private sector of the economy. That is why President Kennedy has requested stand-by authority to spend up to $2 billion for the kind of capital improvement that can be started quickly. Less urgent projects can, of course, be held back if activity in the private sector of the economy is straining resources.

However, current thinking reposes somewhat less confidence than an earlier decade did in the *economic* role of public works programs. Even though, as will be seen, public works can and should be expanded far beyond their present scope, there are, in fact, limits to which they may be carried in an economy based primarily upon private enterprise. Keynes' "multiplier" principle notwithstanding, exclusive or nearly exclusive reliance on public works programs over a long period for stabilization purposes might well require a volume of capital formation which, given the basic framework of our economy, would be permitted only for a major war effort. In the absence of such a contingency, it might ultimately be necessary, despite the vast needs of the public sector, to pre-empt private enterprise in areas where it operates with reasonable efficiency. It could justly be argued that this was not a transfusion, but a transformation of the system.

Resistance to such a program would be unlimited (in a sense that resistance to the New Deal never was), and therefore disruptive of, if not fatal to, the basic community of interest which all peaceful, democratic reform must presuppose. Even with defense spending at its present peak ($46.7 billion out of an expected 1962 total for government at all levels of $150 billion) expenditures in the private sector will amount to approximately $418 billion in 1962 or 73 percent of an anticipated total national product of $568 billion. It would be unfortunate if preoccupation with the stabilizing power of government spending led to a neglect of the policies required for expanding effective demand in the far larger private sector of the economy. As Mr. Keyserling once pointed out,

> . . . it is clear . . . that the price-wage-profit policies pursued within the enterprise system in peacetime must continue to exert a far larger direct impact upon the nation's economic health than any programs the government may undertake, unless the government should undertake to run practically the whole economy.[4]

It is, then, on price-wage-profit decisions that public policy must concentrate. Prices, wages, and profits may continue to be the subject of negotiation among the interested parties, may continue to be responsive to conventional market pressures, and still be subject to selective government intervention, nearly all of it indirect in that it alters the conditions which influence the decisions of the interested parties but avoids pre-empting their decisions. It would be difficult to find a responsible American who seriously advocates that government actually fix wages, prices, and profits on any large scale, except in time of great emergency. Nevertheless, at one extreme are minimum wage laws, agricultural price supports, and transfer (social security) payments, all of which represent now accepted forms of direct intervention in the distributive system, not merely for humanitarian reasons, but as a stabilizing factor in the economy.[5] Their contribution to maintaining effective demand is direct and immediate. What is needed without delay is the inclusion of agricultural workers and other excluded groups under the provisions of the minimum wage law, and flexible powers which would enable the President to respond immediately to fluctuations in the business cycle by increasing or decreasing unemployment benefits.

Falling short of such direct intervention are the great indirect devices for maintaining effective demand: tax policy, the power to adjust interest rates and hence control credit, the management of the public debt. The complex technical considerations governing their use are outside the scope and competence of this discussion. Some of the guiding principles have been indicated earlier.[6] However, one basic principle may well be restated by way of underscoring a still crucial difference between conservatives and liberals.

The value of the national product is the sum of the amounts spent by consumers on consumer goods, by producers on capital goods, and by government at all levels. The amount invested by producers in capital goods is a function of the aggregate amount spent by private consumers and all government agencies. However, quite apart from its own outlays, the government's tax and credit policies may profoundly affect the volume and direction of investment. Understandably, the business world has called for tax incentives to encourage investment and, when conservatives turn to fiscal policy, this is the course they favor. In times of declining employment or continued high unemployment, with plant capacity idle or threatened with a shutdown, liberal economists prefer to emphasize a tax policy that directly increases purchasing power. Hence they are likely to favor tax reductions for the lower income groups. They argue that, if industrial capacity is lying idle (about 75 percent of capacity was the average for U. S. manufacturing industries in early 1961), the funds derived from tax concessions to industry would hardly induce producers to *expand* capacity or launch new enterprises.

To be sure, tax concessions can be used to encourage modernization which, by reducing costs, can be profitable to producers even in a contracting market. But it is notorious that such reduced costs are achieved largely by displacing human labor, so that the very policy intended to reduce unemployment could increase it. Such a contradiction would be avoided, according to liberal economists, by using tax policy directly to improve purchasing power. Given conditions of ample demand and full employment, programs of modernization of plant and equipment resulting in increased productivity would come about almost automatically.[7]

Failing such a response, the government might well reconsider its tax policy, depending on the reason for the lag.

Productivity might slacken as a result of inadequate incentive, but the cause might be beyond the power of a tax incentive to remedy. The hostility of monopolies to technological innovation could be one such cause. Another could be insufficient support of education and research, or badly oriented research. It is no secret, for example, that basic research is inadequately supported in this country; nuclear research would have been far behind had we not been able to draw upon European scientists. In general, neglect of our universities will adversely affect technological advance and industrial productivity. Here is occasion for indirect intervention in a variety of ways. In each instance the nature of the remedy is fairly obvious.

In general, the economy has generated forces making for an acceptable rate of increase in productivity (i.e., output per man hour), except during business recessions. The problem has been to provide sufficient effective demand for the increased output thereby made available. For this reason liberal spokesmen are likely to emphasize that the American worker's ability to buy the output of his industry is dependent on the *wage level* of the employed as well as on the *extent* of employment. Industry, even if stimulated by incentive taxes, cannot earn profits, and capital will not therefore be invested in industry, unless the wage level of the American worker generates sufficient effective demand to buy its output.

Provided always that the wage level is related to productivity, no government action can take the place of stability in real wages as a foundation for growth and a counter to recession and the unemployment attendant on recession. Recent resistance of wages to the ordinarily depressing effect of mass unemployment, for example in the automobile and steel industries, may well be regarded as having prevented a further decline. If, despite a greatly expanded federal outlay, the Kennedy Administration in October, 1961, found itself confronted for the eleventh successive month with close to 7 percent of the working force unemployed, the answer may hinge on the inability of one-fifth of the spending units in the United States to provide themselves with the material goods they need, and hence to buy what the unemployed would produce. Economists tell us that a 3.5 percent increase in consumer expenditures is equivalent in its impact on the economy to a 15 percent rise in business spending or a 21 percent increase in federal expenditures. It would be well if we kept this differential in mind.

Effective demand is, of course, automatically increased during a recession as a result of a decline in income tax payments and an increase in unemployment and social security benefits. These function as built-in stabilizers since they require no special legislation. They are estimated to have reduced postwar swings of the business cycle by as much as 35 to 40 percent.[8]

It is recognized, to be sure, that not all problems affecting growth and stability can be solved by raising the level of demand. Certain kinds of structural unemployment, for example, the idleness prevalent in distressed areas, obviously require other remedies, although, as noted earlier, even structural unemployment can be dealt with more efficiently under conditions of high effective demand. The gold flow problem has its own peculiar requirements, although here again it may be argued that a vigorous, expanding economy would retard the flow of gold.[9] It is also recognized that inflationary tendencies may be encouraged by a condition of high effective demand. A great deal has been made of the latter point by conservatives, especially during the Eisenhower Administration. Since it has become a crux of the difference between conservatives and liberals, it deserves elaboration.

Liberals are acutely aware of the distributive implications of price instability, in particular, of the impact upon individuals with relatively fixed income of an upward bias in prices. On the other hand, liberal economists believe that the dangers of a mild rise in prices have received disproportionate emphasis. Typical is the statement of Professor Robert A. Gordon before the Joint Economic Committee:

It is clear that we do not want runaway or galloping inflation, but how much of a creeping rise in price are we prepared to accept, if necessary, to achieve satisfactory employment and growth? I share the view expressed by the late Professor Slichter and others that the dangers of a mild upward trend in the price level have been exaggerated. While the recipients of fixed incomes may suffer somewhat, interest rates are likely to rise with rising prices—unless deliberately held down through monetary policy—debt contracts do not run in perpetuity and adjustments can be made in pensions and in social and private insurance provisions. Nor is there much evidence that an upward trend of 1 or 2 percent in the price level causes people to "flee from money into goods." On the other hand, mildly rising prices help to maintain optimistic business expectations and provide an additional incentive for a high level of real private investment.[10]

Similarly, Professor Paul A. Samuelson has testified:

It is quite possible that no conflict between growth and price stability will arise. But economic science cannot be sure at this time that they will always be compatible. My own tentative advice would be to put the major emphasis on growth of real income at our high-employment potential, not letting concern over price inflation dominate our decisions prior to such time as sustained upward thrusts in consumer and wholesale prices have established themselves. In other words, I would run some risk on the price inflation front.[11]

The late Professor Sumner Slichter, an authority generally esteemed by all parties, in addressing a meeting of bankers declared that "ill-informed talk about inflation in the United States has aroused unjustified fears and has given Americans an inferiority complex on the subject of prices." He added that "the problem of inflation is less important than many people would have us believe and is diminishing in importance. The dire consequences predicted for creeping inflation have not happened and are not likely to happen." He concluded:

As the public realizes that the bad results of inflation have been greatly exaggerated and that some of the results will not happen at all, it will give attention to other problems—particularly the problem of unemployment and of achieving an adequate rate of growth. The greatest harm and waste caused by inflation and the fear of inflation is that they have made both government and industry afraid of expansionist policies and have deprived the country of billions of dollars of production and millions of man-years of employment which the country could have had if it had not made a fetish of a stable price level.[12]

An overwhelming majority of professional economists (again with the probable exception of those employed by large industrial and banking corporations) would concur in this judgment. In short, liberals are prepared to risk or accept mild inflation if this is necessary to achieve full employment and optimum growth.

On the other hand, while shunning government wage- and price-fixing, liberals are not content to have the government abdicate and leave to autonomous groups the determination of price levels. As Professor Gordon points out, both organized labor and large-scale business "have to some extent taken control of the price level away from those in charge of monetary and fiscal policy."[13] With certain notable exceptions,[14] such autonomous groups are in the nature of the case committed to a short-range conception of their own narrow interest and are not directly guided by policies consistent with the national goals of high employment, rapid growth, and price stability. If inflation comes, not from excess demand pressing upon scarce goods, as during wartime ("demand-pull"), but from monopolistic and quasi-monopolistic practices or prices "administered" by labor and management ("cost-push"), government cannot remain aloof.

Counter action may take the form of direct intervention, as by the Antitrust Division of the Department of Justice. On the frontier lies the still unexplored possibility of extending the "yardstick" principle from the power industry to other industries which are incorrigibly monopolistic. If Theodore Roosevelt's "big stick" fails to do the job, Franklin Roosevelt's "yardstick" may have to be the answer. Meanwhile, what is needed as a minimum is permanent machinery, supplementing *ad hoc* Congressional inquiries (such as those conducted by the Kefauver Committee into the drug industry) and including the power of subpoena, for impartial investigation of the facts and public presentation of them. Are collusive practices artificially inflating prices? Do increased costs justify a price increase, or are profits already ample? Is a demand for higher wages related to increased productivity? The zeal with which management has resisted proposals for setting up machinery to get the answer to such questions suggests that there is much to hide. Often only the threat of such investigation would suffice.[15]

For all their reiterated fears of inflation, conservatives, when they were in power under the Eisenhower Administration, made curiously little effort to use such methods, natural as they are to a democracy in the efficient conduct of its economic affairs. Instead, price stability was sought partly by fiscal measures in the form of cutbacks in Federal expenditures, but largely by reliance on monetary policy.

Monetary policy is the time-honored recourse of conservatives. It refers to action taken by the Federal Reserve Board primarily to influence the cost and availability of money by directly controlling bank reserves. In this manner banks were restrained during the Eisenhower Administration from making new loans (i.e., creating new money) and interest rates were forced higher. Such a policy of "monetary restraint" is commonly called "tight money." Its effect is to reduce the demand for goods and services and thereby abate the inflationary pressure that occurs when there are too many dollars available for too few goods. Such a policy is appropriate when inflation is the result of a condition in which buying power exceeds the capacity of the economy to produce goods and services ("demand-pull"). But *where resources are unemployed* and inflation is largely brought about not by free market forces but by "administered" prices, i.e., by the decisions of big business, big labor and (with government help) of farmers ("cost-push"), it is difficult to see the relevance of a high interest rate policy that reduces effective demand.

It would be difficult to determine how, in a slack economy, with a 6.1 percent rate of unemployment and 17 basic materials industries operating at 76.5 percent of capacity, increased Federal expenditures could cause prices to rise. Yet such was the odd reasoning to which conservatives had become committed. It would be equally difficult to determine how, in a slack economy, a tight-money, high-interest policy that discouraged private spending could stabilize prices; and, in point of fact, the price level rose by a total of 10.6 percent during the years of the Eisenhower Administration. Indeed, where resources are only partly employed the effect of increased demand (government or private) may well be to *lower* prices because, given fixed costs for plant, equipment, management, etc., the cost per unit is likely to be higher when demand is low and a plant is partly idle, and correspondingly less as the slack is taken up.

It is worth remarking that the distributive implications of such a tight-money, high interest-rate policy were much more biased against middle and low income groups than the price instability which this policy was intended to cure. Moreover, such a policy did not hurt large, established corporations because they are relatively independent of the money market. On the other hand, it did penalize small businesses and growing businesses because they are not independent of the money market. Finally, in the true colonial tradition, the policy was regionally biased against the West and other areas where rapid growth has generated an enormous need for credit. In sum, tight-money policy imposes a private tax on all who borrow money.[16] However, in many quarters private taxes are acceptable if levied by bankers in the name of sound money, and monetary policy is, after all, under the aegis of Federal Reserve bankers. Such a private tax is even more acceptable if its effect is to discourage public spending to stimulate recovery. To be sure, immediate and pressing public projects are also discouraged, but at least the illusion of solvency has been preserved. If, under a conservatively oriented Federal Reserve, monetary policy, by discouraging private as well as public spending, curtailed production, this was embarrassing. But at least the shibboleths were not dishonored. The dollar was, or seemed, safe.

If the foregoing fairly reflects the thinking of most professional economists, what is the machinery by means of which this thinking may be translated into policy? The best hope probably lies in some version of the Employment Act's provision for a Council of Economic Advisers. Everything should be done to enhance the stature of this Council (or one like it), to emphasize its importance, to assure its technical competence, to preserve its independence, to give it access to the best professional opinion as well as to all avail-

able economic data. Its judgments should come to be surrounded by that same aura which envelops the verdicts of the Supreme Court (though not, to be sure, with similar finality).

This could and should be so, not because of any putative omniscience, but because the members of such a body occupy, or should come to occupy, a unique position: chosen for their professional competence, they view the economy *as a whole,* and the purpose governing their recommendations is not any segment's special advantage, nor anything other than "maximum employment, production, and purchasing power." This means that they must speak *qua* economists (so far as this is possible) and not as moralists, social reformers, politicians concerned with the art of the possible, or apologists for the policies of the President. The last point suggests that serious consideration be given to converting the Council into a National Economic Commission which would report to Congress and the people—an alternative seriously considered by Congress when it debated the Employment Act, and one which does not, of course, preclude the President from having his own economic staff.

An Economic Council which is an adjunct of the Executive could well be (and has been) in an awkward position, so far as Administration policies are concerned. In the nature of the case such policies are bound to be heavily influenced by political considerations and, if the Council is the *President's* Council and writing *his* Economic Report, there is no room for public expressions of disagreement. Nevertheless, in issuing its pronouncements, the Council should not only be independent in fact, it should have the *appearance* of independence. An arrangement worthy of serious consideration would be one which also provided an independent Commission of prestigious professional economists. Both would report to the Joint Economic Committee of Congress which already enlists professional testimony as well as the testimony of interested parties at its highly useful hearings on the President's Economic Report. It might be hoped that the Hearings would endeavor to reconcile differences between the Reports, or focus attention on agreement, as the case might be. Much more could be done than is at present to make verbatim and condensed versions of the hearings available as a kind of economics text for the American people—at any rate those among them who read, study, and influence, or will influence, policy.

An Economic Council and/or Commission would have available a complete inventory of America's productive resources: our working force, our natural resources, our plant and equipment. Specialized staffs would presumably be enlisted to provide the data (largely already gathered by various public and private agencies) concerning each of these categories: the changing size and composition of our work force, its skills and work habits; the shifting supplies of minerals, water, energy, soil, etc., available, and alternative sources of supply; the degree of obsolescence or maintenance characterizing our industrial plant and equipment. Also required would be the services of a specialized staff making available a tax profile of the country including all state and local taxing units. Obviously, there can be no intelligent Federal fiscal policy without detailed reckoning with the fiscal policy of state and local government, with the relationship of state and local tax programs to per capita wealth and income, and related information. The bland refusal of most conservatives to reckon with certain indisputable facts about state and local tax resources[17] might become awkward when spotlighted by the findings which such a staff would inevitably bring to light.

Finally, in order to advise the Congress and the President intelligently, an Economic Council or Commission (or both) must also have available the recommendations of a different kind of body, equally competent, equally august, and equally vital to the well-being of the country. Such a body might be called, as a pale prototype of it has been, a Commission on National Goals. To discuss the role of such a Commission is, however, to consider once again the crucial question of priorities, to which the discussion must now return.

The "Public Sector"

Earlier the question of priorities was raised with a view to determining the extent to which the prevailing pattern of resource allocation is really decreed by us in our role as consumers and voters. The discussion called attention to built-in forces which bias the allocation of resources, so that basic needs are imperfectly met and often grossly neglected. This is not to say that the average American, if freed of these influences, would display the sagacity of Aristotle's high-minded man. We have our share of human frailties. It is simply to urge that the average American may not be held responsible for the irrationality of many of our present allocations. The term "irrationality" is used advisedly, for to be irrational is to act contrary to what one really wants.

The problem before us is how to correct this bias. As suggested earlier, such an undertaking would have been hopeless several decades ago. Russia posed no serious problem. Most of the colonial world slumbered. Tensions which today threaten our cities had not yet become acute. Moreover, *any drastic increase of the resources allotted to public purposes could not have been accomplished without either reducing the private comforts of the dominant middle and upper income groups or eroding the economic base of their power.* The reallocation of resources to better serve public purposes had significant *distributive* implications: it was inextricably tied up with the explosive issue of inequality and economic privilege; it involved the very class structure of society.[18]

Such is no longer the case. Although, in recent years, our national goals and community needs should have taken precedence over the gratification of artificially induced consumer wants, the immediate future need not put our social conscience to the test—provided our economy is allowed to realize its productive potentialities. As noted earlier, our productive capacity, had it been fully employed between 1953 and 1960, could have yielded about $90 billion in additional revenue without increasing the tax rate.[19]

Writing with Great Britain's stagnant economy of the mid-thirties in mind, Keynes declared that he saw "no reason to suppose that the existing system seriously misemploys the factors of production that are in use . . ." Rather, he said, "It is in determining the volume, not the direction of actual employment that the existing system has broken down."[20] In the circumstances, Keynes' preoccupation with the volume of employment was understandable. It was shared by liberals, who accepted such a view for the United States as for Great Britain. Today liberals assert that this is a basic weakness in Keynesian doctrine and must be repaired precisely because, in the absence of selective interference with market processes as they now operate, the system *does* misemploy the factors of production.

We must go *beyond* Keynes and *beyond* the liberal position of the 'thirties, that government spending—apart from what is needed for its routine operations, or for defense—must be "residual" or "supplementary" or "compensatory." Many grossly neglected purposes for which public funds are desperately needed are too important to be regarded as "residual." Adequate school and hospital facilities, urban renewal, the "race for space," and numerous other inadequately supported projects are too essential to our welfare to be treated as incidental to a program of stabilizing the economy. They should be undertaken because they are needed on their own account, and not because or until they give a lift to the economy.

Surely, the $2.3 billion asked by President Kennedy for aid to elementary and secondary schools, the $3 billion asked for higher education, the annual $100 million needed for a Youth Conservation Corps to help unemployed young men who might otherwise be headed for delinquency, the funds required to provide the more than one million new hospital beds we need, these and other similar projects deserve priority over products requiring the most ingeniously contrived psychological pressures before the consumer can be persuaded that he wants or needs them.

Professor W. W. Rostow finds that our neglect of the public sector of the economy is not so much a function of the growth rate as of "certain American habits of mind, carried over from earlier phases of our history," and "the workings of the political process, as they affect the allocation of resources." He goes on:

This interplay of intellectual conception and conventional politics conspires to make it difficult for Americans to increase the scale of public outlays except at moments of acute crisis. Here lies an authentic danger to the national interest and a threat to the quality of American society.[21]

The question is, how can this "authentic danger" be avoided? It may be avoided (a) by making expansion of the public sector a function of the growth rate, and (b) by adopting measures that will counteract the enormous advantage enjoyed by consumer products in competition for dollars. Unfortunately, liberals have neglected both approaches and this may be a basic flaw in the strategy of contemporary liberalism. Indeed, the charge may fairly be made that liberals, in their preoccupation with tactics, have neglected basic strategy—at any rate, since the passage of the Employment Act. The tendency has been to rely on stabilization arguments for getting this or that project or program across, or on the skill with which some particular need, like the health of the aged, can be dramatized. The consequence is that liberals have had to stand by helplessly as worthwhile projects are nullified or whittled away by strategically situated congressional committees. The energy spent on one project could as well be invested in getting consent for a basic program.

Such a program would begin by recognizing that *any expansion of the public sector which requires a significant increase of existing tax rates or additional borrowing, is politically unrealistic so long as almost one-third of the total spent by government at all levels is required for the defense budget.* As matters now stand, every political candidate, no matter how strongly he believes that taxes can and should be raised must, with almost ritualistic regularity, declare his deathless opposition to tax increases. Two proposals may be suggested for avoiding this impasse. Neither would require from taxpayers an outlay greater than at present.

The first proposal is for legislation that would automatically transfer a significant percentage of reductions in defense expenditures, if such occur, to other public uses. Obviously, the public sector would not benefit from such a provision unless there were an easing of world tensions. However, despite the present gloomy outlook, a relaxation of tensions is by no means outside the realm of probability. Such legislation as that proposed might well win the adherence of those who would be more interested in its stabilization potential, in the event of a sudden drop in defense outlays. After all, it was the fear of what would happen to the economy in the absence of the stimulus provided by World War II that frightened conservatives into approving the Employment Act. Incidentally, such legislation might help to disabuse those under the spell of the Marxist-Leninist doctrine that a capitalist country must depend on the manufacture of armaments for economic survival. As matters now stand, many are persuaded by the argument that capitalism must have a large public works program to survive, and that the manufacture of armaments, because it does not compete with private enterprise, is the only kind of large-scale public works to which politicians dare lend support.

A second proposal would yield more immediate results and is not so dependent on an optimistic world outlook. It involves providing assurance in the form of legislation that, when the costs of government, including the special cost of the present emergency defense program, are being met from current revenue, and the budget is balanced, *the present ratio of federal revenue to gross national product be retained until certain stipulated goals are realized.* Such a legislative proposal might well be called the National Goals Bill. It would be a fitting complement to the Employment Act.

We are told (albeit, as time goes on, with somewhat less assurance) that the national budget will be balanced in 1963.[22] Thereafter the additional revenues produced by increments to the Gross National Product should be surplus. We know that every $10 billion increase of GNP will yield from $2 to $2.5 billion in added federal revenue. An increase of 5 percent of a GNP which will exceed $600 billion in 1963, could therefore yield a revenue increase of about $8 billion in that year. If we are to do justice to the public sector of the economy, it is essential that this revenue not be used to reduce the national debt (which, in the absence of additional borrowing, becomes smaller in any case, in relation to the increasing national product and an increasing population) and, above all, not be used to reduce taxes. The proposal would not involve freezing the prevailing tax pattern, which is obviously in need of major modification. Only the ratio of revenue to national product would be fixed—fixed, that is, until certain defined national goals were realized.

The needs of the public sector are not static. They expand and entail ever greater costs as population grows. Moreover, present needs are aggravated by prolonged neglect. If, in consequence, the surplus revenues to which we may look forward after, say, 1964, along with such revenue as may be saved in the event of a reduction in our defense requirements, do not suffice to meet the defined goals within a stipulated period of time, a federal sales tax would be justified. Such a tax at 3 percent, with food, medicine and clothing exempted, would yield about $3.5 billion.

For well-known reasons liberals are opposed to regressive taxes, that is, taxes which, like the sales tax, bear equally on all income groups. Such a tax would be justified only if the following conditions were already met: (1) full employment; (2) adequate and inclusive minimum wage protection; (3) adequate minimum allowances for individuals physically handicapped by virtue of age or any other cause, and unable to find work; (4) improved procedures for collecting taxes payable under existing income tax laws;[23] (5) a stricter interpretation of deductible "expense" allowances and (6) precautions in the law precluding use of sales tax revenues to lighten existing income tax payments.

Once all these conditions were satisfied, the temporary imposition of a regressive tax would be acceptable to an increasing number of liberals until the stipulated goals were met. As has been pointed out by Galbraith and others, our lower income groups in a $600-700 billion economy would be in a far better position to shoulder such a tax than would have been the case in the 'twenties and the public amenities provided by the tax would be primarily for them.

It is safe to say that tax legislation of the kind just suggested would not be feasible politically in the absence of an agency capable of alerting us to our problems and formulating our national goals in such a way as to awaken the national conscience and command the people's attention. We are thus brought back to the second part of the program referred to earlier for securing those unmet needs on which our welfare as a people depends.

It is imperative that the built-in bias of a consumer-oriented economy be corrected if we are to survive as a great nation. This means that we must have an authoritative body—such as a Commission on National Goals—which will define and dramatize the goals essential to our survival and, like the well-known Twentieth Century Fund studies of America's needs, give them a price tag. Such a commission would be charged with formally and systematically enlisting the advice of authorities in the major areas of need, and defining our goals with reference to our needs and, of course, our resources, and not by reference to existing government revenues. Since it would be concerned with social goals and policies it would consist of outstanding experts in the fields of education, health, conservation, urban planning, the arts and sciences, as well as distinguished business and community leaders. Necessarily, it would have the advice of professional economists—possibly the staff of the Economic Council or Commission—to advise on costs, the bearing of specific programs on economic growth in general as well as on related segments of the private sector of the economy, and much else.

A Commission on National Goals should be provided for by statute, and it should be charged with advising the President, the Congress, the Economic Council or Commission, and the *people*, concerning our basic unmet needs and the order in which they should be filled. In the course of preparing such advice it should have access to resources for ascertaining the preferences of people when they are not under the spell of pitchmen and have all the alternatives before them; and it should have resources for advising them through regional and local conferences (we already have White House and Governors' Conferences on various public programs, and private foundation studies such as those of the Ford Foundation, the Rockefeller Brothers Fund, the Brookings Institution, the National Planning Association, and the Twentieth Century Fund) and receiving advice from their ablest spokesmen.

There is every reason why a Commission on National Goals should be empowered to use the formidable resources of television (including prime time) on a grand scale to acquaint Americans *en masse* with the condition of their schools, housing, hospitals, parks, natural resources. Such a service from the television industry would be little enough compensation for the way in which the channels—a public property—have been used to warp our scale of values. *Life* magazine has brilliantly shown how a mass medium can use visual resources dramatically to confront the American people with the degradation of their cities. A recent example (January 26, 1962), a so-called "photographic essay," is captioned "These Children Are at Stake," and it begins with the simple warning, "They may not be yours but they're your problem." Even the citizen exclusively preoccupied with his tax bill can hardly avoid the obvious lesson that our slums incubate criminals on a large scale as efficiently as our farms produce chickens, and that an estimated annual $5 billion bill for juvenile delinquency is in great part a result of our failure to spend enough money for decent housing, schooling, and recreation, and guidance for the children of the slums.

The same economy-minded citizen might learn on another television program that a Missouri Valley Development would cost less than the loss from flood damage in that valley in the spring of 1947. On still another program Dr. Howard A. Rusk, an authority on the problems of the handicapped, might show him how $1 invested in rehabilitation saves $10 in income taxes—a rate of return that would cause Dr. Rusk to be hailed as a financial wizard if it were in manufacturing automobiles for sale instead of in rehabilitating the disabled.

No usurpation of the role of consumer preference in the determination of resource allocation is contemplated. It is not proposed that a few arrogate to themselves a monopoly on wisdom or the right to determine what others will consume. What is intended is some approach to the optimum conditions under which our people may themselves make an intelligent appraisal of priorities.

In the absence of a verdict from the market, how is it possible to allocate resources in such a way as to coincide most closely with the preferences of those who will be served? The question is a reasonable one. Clearly some kind of innovation must be substituted for the market, so that a determination may be made. Shall schools or hospitals be built first and, if it is possible to provide both, how much shall be allocated to each? How extensively shall resources be allocated to urban redevelopment and to what extent should it have priority over a highway program?

In *America's Needs and Resources,* which should be required reading for every American who loves his country, Dewhurst and Associates, after carefully marshaling the best available evidence, find that the total cost of bringing all urban and rural substandard housing up to minimum standard would be $67 billion at 1950 prices. They estimated the cost of an adequate educational program in 1950 at $17.6 billion or $7.1 billion above actual expenditures, and they predicted that expenditures would fall behind $6.6 billion (in 1950 prices) in 1960. Similar estimates are made for health, conservation, etc.[24] How should priorities be determined?

The question is not an easy one to answer. Much careful thinking has recently been given to methods of ascertaining preference that do not rely on the mechanism of the market.[25] However, if attention is limited to basic needs—as it must be—and not to marginal requirements, there is reason to believe that the American people would exhibit impressive agreement concerning what is important and what is trivial. Their personal budgets reveal remarkable similarity and there is no reason to doubt that they would reach a similar accord on the national budget. After all, accord is reached on a very substantial budget at the present time, even if often at the price of too much log-rolling. It would be the task of a Commission on National Goals to combat log-rolling and to assist us in arriving at a consensus.

In recent years serious concern over our national priorities has been expressed by a number of conservatives, who are not only alarmed by spreading urban confusion and increasing social disorganization, but no doubt understand that, in opposing allocation of more resources to public purposes, conservatism is fighting yesterday's battles. Among conservatives who have indicated such concern are Charles Taft,[26] the Rockefeller brothers, Paul Hoffman, Earl Warren,[27] Douglas Dillon, Senators Case of New Jersey and Aiken of Vermont, et al. In a 1959 Lincoln Day address, commenting on President Eisenhower's $4 billion cut in the budget at the expense of social programs like water resource development and housing, Senator Aiken declared: "Lincoln had to choose between conflicting values and he chose the greater ones. He could have balanced the budget and lost the Union. He could have held down the national debt and perpetuated slavery."[28]

Unfortunately, such thinking on the part of conservatives is still confined to a small minority. In the course of testimony before the Joint Economic Committee, Raymond J. Saulnier, Chairman of the Council of Economic Advisers under President Eisenhower, said: "As I understand an economy its ultimate purpose is to produce more consumer goods. This is the goal. This is the object of everything we are working at: to produce things for consumers." He added that this was what he regarded himself as having been "commissioned to maximize."[29] The statement has become celebrated. Professor Saulnier's words can hardly be misconstrued. He expressly indicated that he meant *personal* consumption. Besides, he proudly compared the record of the Eisenhower Administration with the record of the preceding Administration, pointing out that, while *total growth* (i.e., growth including private investment and public outlays) had lagged, the *rate of consumption* had increased.

Professor Saulnier did not distinguish among consumer goods and neither do those for whom he spoke. In effect, he was giving priority to oversized and overused cars, endlessly restyled household appliances, new fashions in male and female attire, cosmetics, gadgets, and luxury goods in general, *over* schools, hospitals, highways, parks, reclamation, flood control, research, libraries, urban redevelopment, mental health, recreational facilities, better police and probation staffs, public assistance programs, air and water purification, improved airports, the conquest of space, foreign aid, and even defense. For, given always a limit on means, the other side of *maximizing* personal consumption is minimizing the amounts spent for public purposes.

There can be no other conclusion, and this is precisely what the conservative Administration to which Professor Saulnier was chief economic adviser sought to do.[30] It is what the majority of American conservatives believe should be done and, as observed earlier, it is the bias which they have succeeded in imparting to our economy. It remains one of the major points at issue between liberals and conservatives. Walter Lippmann's comment on the Saulnier statement accurately reflects the liberal position: "There precisely is the root of our trouble," he wrote, adding:

Our goal is to maximize consumption. That is a very low national goal, and altogether unworthy of a great nation which has a great part to play in human affairs. The object of our economy is not to become fat with consumers goods. It is to use the wealth and the power which the economy can produce to support the national purposes which we so frequently proclaim. There is nothing very convincing or inspiring in loving our "liberty" to enjoy consumer goods so much that we cannot afford to educate our children. If we really believe in the ideals and the spiritual aims about which so much is said, we have something else to do besides maximizing the enjoyment of consumers goods.[31]

Liberals and American Conservatism

Against this background, it is one of the more baffling features of American public life that Senator Barry Goldwater, who would be in heartier accord with the Saulnier position than Professor Saulnier himself, can be taken seriously in some quarters when he writes that "The root difference between the Conservatives and the Liberals of today is that Conservatives take account of the *whole* man, while the Liberals tend to look only at the material side of man's nature. . . . Conservatism . . . looks upon the enhancement of man's spiritual nature as the primary concern of political philosophy. Liberals . . . —in the name of a concern for 'human beings'—regard the satisfaction of economic wants as the dominant mission of society."

Man's spirituality is furthered, one learns from Senator Goldwater, not by increasing social security "benefits," but by leaving people "free throughout their lives to spend their earnings when and as they see fit," especially the earnings of "uncommon men" who rise above the "undifferentiated mass."[32] The climax of this conservative testament which speaks often of man as a "spiritual creature," of the "dignity of the individual human being," and of his "immortal soul" is a cry of valiant protest against the income tax: "The graduated tax is a confiscatory tax. Its effect and to a large extent its aim, is to bring down all men to a common level."[33] Such are the shabby uses for which some who call themselves conservatives are today invoking man's spiritual nature. The "higher nature of man" and the "dignity of the individual" are somehow always inseparably linked with lower taxes.

There was a time when conservatism in America understood the meaning of welfare. This was when it spoke through the voice of Alexander Hamilton. In the debates over the general welfare clause in the Constitution, Hamilton argued that the clause was "as comprehensive as any that could have been used" and that it applied to "a vast variety of particulars, which are susceptible neither of specification nor definition"— including "whatever concerns the general interest of learning, of agriculture, of manufactures, and of commerce." The only limitation, he said, was that the purpose must be general and not local. And this, he added, "must be a matter of conscientious discretion involving considerations of expediency" and "not of Constitutional right."[34]

Senator Goldwater invokes the name of Theodore Roosevelt. But Roosevelt, like Hamilton, understood welfare in a different way:

We are face to face with new conceptions of the relations of property to human welfare, chiefly because certain advocates of the rights of property as against the rights of men have been pushing their claims too far. The man who wrongly holds that every human right is secondary to his profit must now give way to the advocate of human welfare, who rightly maintains that every man holds his property subject to the general right of the community to regulate its use to whatever degree the public welfare may require it.[35]

In justification of inheritance and income taxes, Theodore Roosevelt wrote: "No man should receive a dollar unless that dollar has been fairly earned. Every dollar received should represent a dollar's worth of services rendered—not gambling in stocks but services rendered." The really big fortune, he continued, "the swollen fortune, by the mere fact of its size acquires qualities which differentiate it in kind as well as in degree from what is possessed by men of relatively small means."[36]

The words of another conservative of the period are also interesting. Nicholas Murray Butler, sometime Republican candidate for the vice-presidency and longtime president of Columbia University, said:

Let me call your attention to the fact that the characteristic feature of the experiment in Russia . . . is not that it is Communist, but that it is being carried out with a plan in the face of a planless opposition. The man with a plan, however much we may dislike it, has a vast advantage over the group sauntering down the road of life complaining of the economic weather and wondering when the rain is going to stop.[37]

These are the voices of an authentic and responsible conservatism. Today such voices are drowned out by the strident radicalism of the far right.

The weakness of an authentic conservative tradition in this country is a great tragedy. Conservatism is a useful and important counterpart to liberalism. We need conservatives to alert us to the continuity of history and the role of tradition in human affairs. We need them to remind us of what the liberal and old-style radical often ignore: that man is not a completely rational animal and that we must address ourselves to his heart as well as his head, and reckon with his feelings as well as his cool, calm calculation of consequences. We need conservatives to warn us, also, that in human affairs the consequences are not easily calculated and often wholly unexpected, so that a known present should not be lightly discarded for a precarious future.

The conservative could be correct in finding that a stratified, hierarchical society, and the property rights that bulwark it, are at least one kind of foundation for stability in a world that verges always on the edge of chaos—provided (as is rarely the case) that the enjoyment of privilege is strictly conditional on the exercise of responsibility. The conservative's reverence of order, when it is not timid rejection of change *per se,* or a squeamish unwillingness to be bothered by the unfamiliar, may serve the same purpose. If, like Jonathan Edwards, we ponder man's wickedness and reflect that "mankind have been a thousand times as hurtful and destructive as . . . all the noxious beasts, birds, fishes and reptiles in the Earth, air and water put together," the conclusion may sometimes commend itself that we should not tamper with the gossamer institutional web which more or less successfully restrains each of us from leaping at his neighbor's throat.

But these formal attributes of conservatism are not enough. It must have a positive content, as men like Bismarck and Disraeli once saw. Otherwise it becomes a smug satisfaction with things as they are, a careless disregard of the needs of others, a form of snobbery and self-conceit, a preoccupation with large and small comforts, a set of empty pieties.

Other countries have been more fortunate than we with their present-day conservatives. In Great Britain and West Germany conservatives have avoided preaching anarchic individualism and an abdication of responsibility by government. In principle, the welfare state is taken for granted by all parties, and with interesting political consequences.

A Social Democratic Party congress recently convened in Bad Godesberg has adopted a new "program of principles" in which the party, after years of defeat, explicitly abandons the tenets of Marxism and with this the doctrine of the class struggle and the goal of liquidating capitalism. Transfer of the means of production to public ownership is completely subordinated to the idea of subjecting economic power to public control. The free market is accepted where there is real competition and the role of private enterprise and the profit motive in a balanced economy is freely acknowledged.[38]

Similarly, one of the major theoreticians of the British Labour Party, C. A. R. Crosland, reflects the judgment of an increasing number of erstwhile British socialists when he acknowledges that "many traditional Socialist attitudes are obsolete." He continues,

The Keynesian revolution has triumphed in terms both of the policies of governments and the expectations of the voters. Governments are prepared to intervene, through fiscal and monetary policy, to the extent necessary to preserve relatively full employment. Even right-wing governments will do so, because the electorate now believes that full employment can be maintained, and would administer a sharp reverse at the polls to any government which failed to maintain it.

This, plus the comprehensive welfare program which all parties in Britain endorse, explains why "the idea of further nationalization becomes increasingly unpopular,"[39] and why, in Britain, the "extreme positions have been obliterated" and "most people have moved towards the centre. . . ."[40]

For a different result America's ultraconservatives might look to Italy and France where the success of the economically privileged in avoiding income taxes and the inadequacy of welfare benefits and services accounts at least in part for the strength of the Communist (not to mention the Socialist) parties in those countries. British and West German conservatives have supported programs that have won them consistent success at the polls, and they have forced the socialist opposition drastically to revise its anticapitalist orientation. This is in part because they have not been exclusively obstructionist, have not opposed all reform, and, whether more or less adequately, have reckoned with the requirements of a complex, industrialized, urban society.

American conservatism has failed ingloriously to be influenced by the wiser of the two examples. It has no creed and no program—unless tax reduction and the "balanced budget" can be called a creed and a program. As a result, no significant dialogue has illuminated the deliberations of our people as we canvass the possibilities of action in a troubled world and grope for clarification of our national purpose. Liberals, both in office and out, often dare not demand the reasonable revisions of prevailing practices essential to our future, for fear of being branded as "reds" or "pinks" or "radicals." The opposition has kept them off-balance with charges that challenge their loyalty and divert attention from the particular problems at hand.

Thus, for too many years, the great debate has gone unargued. Even if liberals were not too often cowed into the espousal of weak compromises or sidetracked into the jejune manipulation of unreal opposites, there have been too few conservatives with whom to debate because conservatism in this country has so often succumbed to reaction. We very much need the revival or birth, as the case may be, of a responsible conservative tradition in this country. Otherwise reactionaries will continue to cramp our discourse and dictate its terms, and we shall be like a great giant flailing blindly in the dark.

America's economic problems are basically simple. It has been said a thousand times that, alone among the nations of the world, we possess the human and physical resources with which to satisfy our public and private wants in full abundance. No Grand Design is needed, only the forthright application of principles already accepted by the American people. All that is required is an exercise of the mind and an affirmation of the will and spirit. Perhaps this is difficult. But, as Spinoza long ago reminded us, "all excellent things are as difficult as they are rare."

Conclusion

IT WILL BE appropriate, in concluding an account of—and a program for—liberalism such as the foregoing, to restate briefly the similarity and difference between classical and contemporary liberalism, which it has been the main purpose of this discussion to define.

Liberalism in both its old and new manifestations has been a form of protest against established interests which balk the forces of progress. In the seventeenth and eighteenth centuries the protest was directed against a profligate and decadent feudal aristocracy; in our time it has been directed against the residual survivals of predatory capitalism. Functionless ownership and monopolistic controls over the economic life of society were decried as vigorously by the liberals of the eighteenth century as by liberals today. But the only effective force which the liberal spirit could invoke against social and economic ossification in the eighteenth century was the insurgent energy of modern capitalism, to which it became enthralled. Thus, classical liberalism fell into an ambivalence, on the one hand clinging to its initial inspiration, on the other, uncritically proclaiming the virtues of the profit system as such. In the creative youth of capitalism such contradictory tendencies might be ignored or reconciled. But as the profit system came more and more to serve monopolists and functionless owners, this ambivalence would have proved fatal had not contemporary liberals repudiated mere capitalist apologetics—yielding this to conservatives—and recalled liberalism to its original mission.

Second, and—because of its profound moral implications—more significantly, classical and contemporary liberalism share a common devotion to the dignity of the individual. In both cases, this emphasis upon the central importance of human individuality has expressed itself in *a categorical opposition to the exercise of unlimited power*.

In the case of classical liberalism, however, its proper emphasis on the dignity of the individual is vitiated by a failure to perceive the intimate dependence of the individual on the society of which he is a part. This is the failure explored earlier under the heading of "Atomism." Moreover, because of its historic association with the rise of capitalism the classical liberal emphasis on the importance of the individual is largely confined in practice to those individuals who compose the middle class, and it invariably tends to identify the furtherance of individuality with preserving the pattern of property relationships associated with middle-class ascendancy. In consequence, classical liberals regard social welfare primarily as the incident and byproduct of a process in which individuals are permitted and even encouraged to engage in a relatively uncontrolled pursuit of self-interest, that is to say, in acquisition or pecuniary accumulation. And their fear concerning the abuse of power takes the form of an emphasis on political to the neglect of economic abuses of power. This is also the emphasis of conservatives, as conservatism has been formulated in our time.

The contemporary liberal, on the other hand, understands that the individual is separable from the society in which he lives only by an act of violent abstraction. He understands, too, that for the same reason one may not speak of society apart from the individuals who compose it. The polarity which has been set up between the individual and society is a false polarity which, like so many of its kind—individualism *versus* collectivism, the one *versus* the many, freedom *versus* organization—diverts attention from the problems at hand and concentrates it upon the fruitless manipulation of abstract opposites. Consequently, advocates of the new liberalism refuse to build a philosophy upon the demonization either of private enterprise or of the state. They believe in the creative potentialities of modern capitalism, provided it is helped by collective intelligence intervening through effective public agencies. Only so will the vast wealth made possible by modern technology, soon to be fabulously expanded through the use of atomic energy, be transmuted into human betterment. They believe, too, that this can be, must be, accomplished in the crucible of democracy.

Democracy is a fraternity in which *all* men are free. In it there is no room for an economic any more than for a political monopoly of power. In this sense, contemporary liberalism is simply an extension and completion of the historical liberalism of the eighteenth and nineteenth centuries, providing for the first time for the majority of humanity the freedom heretofore reserved for the few.

The foregoing pages have presented the logic of the liberal case for a mixed economy in which the automatic harmonies of the nineteenth century are supplemented and at times supplanted by social planning. But liberalism is a philosophy of the heart as well as of the head. To forget this is to lose the key to an understanding of the liberal dynamic. It is to neglect the special meaning which social welfare has for the liberal, to whom "welfare" is no mere device for averting mass unrest but an end in itself and, as such, the foundation of all social morality. Thus the dispassionate syllogisms which decree the conditions of capitalist survival are suffused in the philosophy of the liberal by a compassionate regard for people—the "forgotten man" of Franklin Roosevelt, the average man of whom Harry Truman became the incarnation. This is the deeper wellspring of the liberal faith. This is the source of its enduring strength.

NOTES

Part One

Introduction

1. As Max Weber has pointed out, "the dominant doctrine rejected the spirit of capitalistic acquisition as *turpitudo*, or at least could not give it positive ethical sanction. An ethical attitude like that of Benjamin Franklin would have been simply unthinkable." *The Protestant Ethic and the Spirit of Capitalism*, translated by Talcott Parsons (London: George Allen & Unwin, Ltd., 1930), pp. 73-74.

On the other hand, the comments of some of Franklin's contemporaries would surely sound strange to a modern banker's ear. It was John Quincy Adams and not a disciple of Marx who said: "A bank that issues paper at interest is a pickpocket or a robber . . . an aristocracy is growing out of them that will be fatal as the feudal barons, if unchecked."

2. R. H. Tawney, *Religion and the Rise of Capitalism* (New York: Harcourt, Brace and Company, 1926), p. 61.

Chapter 1

1. *Introduction to the Principles of Morals and Legislation,* in *The Works of Jeremy Bentham,* edited by J. Bowring (Edinburgh: W. Tait, 1838-43), I, 1 ff.

2. It may be useful to have the words of America's foremost Protestant theologian as a contemporary verdict on this interesting issue. Commenting on the teachings of Jesus, Dr. Reinhold Niebuhr writes: "A special premium was placed upon actions which could not be rewarded. In other words, the prudential motive was treated with utmost severity. There are, of course, words in the teachings of Jesus which are not as rigorous as this. He promised rewards. . . . The judge will be judged severely. The proud man will be abased and the humble man exalted. Here the social rewards of social attitudes are recognized. Other offers of reward occur, but with one or two exceptions they can be placed in the category of ultimate rewards—'in the insurrection of the just,' 'treasures in heaven,' favor with God. On the whole, they do not seriously qualify his main position that moral action must be motivated purely by obedience to God, emulation of God's attributes and gratitude for the forgiving grace of God. An ulterior motive (desire for social approval, for instance) for a worthy action would destroy the virtue of the action . . ." ("The Ethic of Jesus and the

Social Problem" in *Love and Justice,* edited by D. B. Robertson (Philadelphia: Westminster Press, 1957), p. 31.

3. Of the elder Mill, John Stuart Mill writes, "So complete was my father's reliance on the influence of reason over the minds of mankind, whenever it is allowed to reach them, that he felt as if all would be gained if the whole population were taught to read, if all sorts of opinions were allowed to be addressed to them by word and in writing, and if by means of suffrage they could nominate a legislature to give effect to the opinions they adopted. He thought that when the legislature no longer represented a class interest, it would aim at the general interest, honestly and with adequate wisdom." *Autobiography,* Vol. XXV of The Harvard Classics (New York: P. F. Collier & Son, Inc., 1909), pp. 71-72.

Similarly, Henry B. Adams, the author of *The Education of Henry Adams* (Boston: Houghton Mifflin Company, 1935), commenting on the faith of the mid-nineteenth century, writes: "Education was divine, and man needed only a correct knowledge of facts to reach perfection . . ."

4. "If this [delight] were wholly separated from all our outward sensations and inward thoughts, we should have no reason to prefer one thought or action to another, negligence to attention, or motion to rest: and so we should neither stir our bodies, nor employ our minds; but let our thoughts . . . run adrift, without any direction or design; and suffer the ideas of our mind . . . to make their appearances there as it happened, without attending to them: in which state man, however furnished with the faculties of understanding and will, would be a very idle, unactive creature, and pass his time only in lazy, lethargic dream." John Locke, "An Essay Concerning Human Understanding," Book II, chap. vii, sec. 3 in *The English Philosophers from Bacon to Mill,* edited by Edwin A. Burtt (New York: The Modern Library, Random House, Inc., 1939).

5. I am indebted to John Dewey for this manner of formulating the contrast. Cf. his *Human Nature and Conduct* (New York: The Modern Library, Random House, Inc., 1930), pp. 117-24, 223 ff., 232, 249 ff., 265, 289; also his *Interest and Effort in Education* (Boston: Houghton Mifflin Company, 1913), chap. ii, and John Dewey and James H. Tufts, *Ethics,* rev. ed. (New York: Henry Holt and Company, Inc., 1932), pp. 319-24.

6. *Works of Jeremy Bentham,* I, 214. Although Bentham originally included the pleasure of skill on his list of simple pleasures, it is significant that he later dropped this from the list, for the reason that there can be no pleasure in labor as such.

7. Cited by E. F. Penrose, *Population Theories and Their Application* (Stanford: Stanford University Press, 1934), p. 25.

8. Melville J. Herskovits, *The Economic Life of Primitive People* (New York: Alfred A. Knopf, 1940), pp. 69-70.

9. Dr. J. Howard Beard, "The Contribution of Cholera to Public Health," *Scientific Monthly*, XL (November 1936), 515.

10. David Hartley, *Observations on Man* (London: printed for J. Johnson, 1791), prop. XIV.

11. Charles H. Cooley, *Human Nature and the Social Order* (New York: Charles Scribner's Sons, 1902), p. 7.

12. John Stuart Mill, *A System of Logic* (London: Longmans, Green & Co., Ltd., 1941), Book VI, chap. vii.

13. John Locke, *An Essay Concerning the True, Original, Extent and End of Civil Government* (Oxford: Basil Blackwell & Mott, Ltd., 1946), chap. ii, par. 15. Cf. also chap. viii. If Locke equivocates, as usual, and also suggests the opposite thesis, by regarding society as an ultimate principle, Hobbes is entirely consistent. Cf. George H. Sabine, *A History of Political Theory* (New York: Henry Holt and Company, Inc., 1937), pp. 524 ff. It is an interesting commentary on the ubiquity of the atomistic outlook that these two men, defending completely opposite political philosophies—the one, constitutional government, the other, absolute authority—should have started from the same atomistic conception of human nature.

14. In this respect Bentham might well have learned from Montesquieu, who in *The Spirit of Laws* (New York: Hefner Publishing Co., 1949) emphasized precisely these influences of time, place, and tradition on law and government.

15. John Stuart Mill's statement on this score is one of the most widely quoted. "It is better to be a human being dissatisfied than a pig satisfied; better to be Socrates dissatisfied than a fool satisfied." "Utilitarianism," chap. ii, in *The English Philosophers from Bacon to Mill*. The criterion of value on the basis of which these distinctions are made is obviously a nonhedonistic one.

Chapter 2

1. R. H. Tawney, *The Acquisitive Society* (New York: Harcourt, Brace and Company, 1920), p. 55.

2. John Stuart Mill, *The Principles of Political Economy*, edited by W. J. Ashley (London: Longmans, Green & Co., Ltd., 1920), chap. xv. The "remuneration of abstinence" and compensation for risk are, of course, additional items.

3. This concern is nowhere more evident than in John Stuart Mill's typical discussion of taxation as a way of reducing the inequalities of wealth. "I am as desirous as anyone," he writes, "that means should be taken to diminish those inequalities, but not so as to impair the motives on which society depends for keeping up . . . the produce of its labour and capital. To tax the larger incomes at a higher percentage than the smaller is to lay a tax on industry and economy; to impose a penalty on people for having worked harder and saved more than their neighbours." *The Prin-*

ciples of Political Economy, Book V, chap. ii, sec. 3. Slightly altered in the third edition.

4. *Ibid.,* Book II, chap. ii, sec. 3.

5. Mill went on to say, "and when the division of the produce of labour, instead of depending in so great degree as it now does, on the accident of birth, will be made by concert on an acknowledged principle of justice," *Autobiography,* Vol. XXV in The Harvard Classics (New York: P. F. Collier & Son, Inc., 1909), p. 149.

6. Children as young as six years of age were often classified as able-bodied and put to work.

7. Albert V. Dicey, *Law and Public Opinion in England,* 2d ed. (London: Macmillan & Company, Ltd., 1926), p. 203. (Italics mine.)

8. Herbert Spencer, *Social Statics* (New York: D. Appleton & Co., 1868), chap. xxv, sec. 6.

9. "Hard as it may appear in individual instances, dependent poverty ought to be held disgraceful. Such a stimulus seems to be absolutely necessary to promote the happiness of the great mass of mankind; and every attempt to weaken this stimulus, however ber volent its intention, will always defeat its own purpose." Th nas Robert Malthus, *An Essay on Population* (London: Eve yman, J. M. Dent & Sons, 1914, 2 vols.), Book III, chap. vi.

1J. Writing in 1748, before social negativism had come into its own, Montesquieu declared that every man has the right to work and to receive support from the state. "Whatever alms may be given to a man who is naked in the street, this will not fulfill the obligations of the State, which owes to all the citizens an assured subsistence, food, and proper clothing, and a mode of life which is not contrary to health." *The Spirit of Laws* (New York: Hefner Publishing Co., 1949), chap. xxix.

11. S. Maccoby argues, however, that historians have consistently underestimated mass pressures and overestimated personalities in describing the history of the reform movement. *English Radicalism 1832-1852* (London: George Allen & Unwin, Ltd., 1935), pp. 7 ff.

12. Herbert C. Hoover, *Challenge to Liberty* (New York: Charles Scribner's Sons, 1934), p. 45. More recently, Dr. Henry M. Wriston, college president and author of *Challenge to Freedom* (New York: Harper & Brothers, 1943), echoes Mr. Hoover with a fidelity already suggested by the title of his book. "Even at the bottom of the depression we did not lack bread or power or conveniences. Even among the underprivileged, while there was hardship, there was no famine . . ." (p. 8).

13. It may be added that the minority which voiced this criticism was led by one who can hardly be called a spokesman for the classical liberal tradition—Mrs. Sidney Webb.

14. Although this rests upon generalizations about human nature and would appear to apply to all men, "every man" imperceptibly

gives way to "average man," since there obviously are "exceptional" persons who are not satisfied with mere food, clothing, and shelter, and are willing to work for more.

In the absence of social legislation, company welfare plans might be cited as evidence of a feeling in high places that insecurity is not an indispensable spur to the lazy. In part this is true, but only in part, since it is demonstrable that in the case of most company welfare plans, security was only a secondary and even incidental consideration. For example, most of them have a service requirement of from twenty to twenty-five years. Cf. Abraham Epstein, *Insecurity* (New York: Random House Inc., 1938), pp. 141 ff.

15. Arthur Young, *Eastern Tour*, IV, 361, quoted by Harold Laski in *Rise of Liberalism* (New York: Harper & Brothers, 1936), pp. 237-38.

16. Patrick Colquhoun, *A Treatise on Indigence*, p. 7. Cited by Harold Laski, *op. cit.*

17. Abraham Epstein, *op. cit.*, p. 63.

18. Washington, D.C., January 27, 1931. Published and distributed by the National Association of Manufacturers. (Italics mine.)

19. The lines which follow suggest that the universality of human nature is sometimes forgotten by those for whom initiative is a frail flower that wilts with too much feeding.

"We face today a dreadful threat from fools who would destroy us,
  Of 'Socialized Security' they prate in accents joyous;
    Security? Its cost alone would drive us to perdition,
    Besides, it kills initiative and dries up all ambition;
  Security breaks down the will, the urge that keeps men free,
  It stifles effort, starves the soul—except in men like me."

From "Hymn to Free Private Enterprise," by J. D. K., *The Nation,* March 18, 1944, p. 329.

20. *Fortune*, October 1943, p. 12.

Chapter 3

1. To be sure, Adam Smith was interested in the commercial revolution rather than in the industrial revolution, but Arkwright and Adam Smith were both products of the same great historic forces.

2. Cf. Walter Lippmann, *The Good Society* (Boston: Atlantic Monthly Press, Little, Brown & Company, 1938), pp. 11-12, 29.

3. I.e., "the skill of that insidious and crafty animal, vulgarly called a statesman or politician." Adam Smith, *The Wealth of Nations*, 6th ed. (New York: Random House, 1937), Book IV, chap. ii.

4. *Ibid.*, Book V, chap. i.

5. *Ibid.*

6. *The Works of Jeremy Bentham,* edited by J. Bowring (Edinburgh: W. Tait, 1838-43), III, 3.

7. *Ibid.,* IV, 414. Addressing himself to his own countrymen on the subject of colonies, Bentham argues as follows: "Are you attacked at home? not a man can you ever get from them; not a sixpence. Are they attacked? they draw upon you for fleets and armies."

8. John Stuart Mill, *Dissertations and Discussions* (Boston: William V. Spencer, 1864), I, 453. Cited in W. J. Ashley's "Introduction" to Mill's *Principles of Political Economy* (London: Longmans, Green & Co., Ltd., 1920), p. x.

9. John Stuart Mill, *The Principles of Political Economy*, p. 796.

10. *Ibid.,* pp. 796-97.

11. *Ibid.,* pp. 956 and 968-69.

12. *Ibid.,* p. 964. In the fifth edition of 1862, Mill substituted "ten to nine hours" for "twelve to ten" hours. A lapse of fourteen years had already worked some change in the realm of the possible.

13. John Stuart Mill, "On Liberty," chap. i, in *The English Philosophers from Bacon to Mill,* edited by Edwin A. Burtt (New York: The Modern Library, Random House, Inc., 1939).

14. John Stuart Mill, *Principles of Political Economy*, p. 950.

15. Herbert Spencer, *Social Statics* (New York: D. Appleton & Co., 1868), chap. xx, sec. 6.

16. *Ibid.,* chap. xxii, sec. 8.

17. Not even Keats' "On First Looking into Chapman's Homer" could exceed Andrew Carnegie's eloquence on first looking into Spencer. "Light came as in a flood," declared the great industrialist, "and all was clear." Of the reception of Spencer in America, T. C. Cochran and W. M. Miller write, "Honored . . . as no philosopher ever was in Greece, no artist in Renaissance Italy, no scientist anywhere in his own day, Spencer left an impression on America that was much more profound than his work . . . From the Civil War to the New Deal, businessmen explained themselves to the 'public' in his terms; and during the decade of the 1930's his thought, or textbook variations upon it, formed the basis for conservative attacks upon the reforms of Franklin Roosevelt." *The Age of Enterprise* (New York: The Macmillan Company, 1942), pp. 119-20.

18. Albert Jay Nock, *Our Enemy, the State* (New York: William Morrow and Company, Inc., 1935), p. 52. Mr. Nock finally published these writings himself in 1940.

19. Cf. Charles Beard, *Public Policy and the General Welfare* (New York: Farrar & Rinehart, Inc., 1941), p. 124. This is one of the best short summaries of the American conception of the government's functions. I have borrowed suggestions from it freely.

20. *Ibid.*, pp. 75-76.

21. The Supreme Court has been reticent about providing a clear interpretation of the general welfare clause, at least until Justice Cardozo's famous decision in *Helvering* v. *Davis* in 1937. When it has appeared that the court would outlaw social legislation invoking the general welfare clause or invading an area of control traditionally allotted the states, Congress has found a way out by having recourse to its spending power in the form of federal grants-in-aid. Thus, the federal government has used its spending power to regulate indirectly what the court might forbid it to regulate directly. E. S. Corwin has written that "the success of the spending power in eluding all constitutional snares goes far to envelop the entire institution of judicial review as well as its product, constitutional law, in an atmosphere of unreality, even of futility." *The Twilight of the Supreme Court* (New Haven, Conn.: Yale University Press, 1934), pp. 178-79, cited by Merle Fainsod and Lincoln Gordon, *Government and the American Economy*, rev. ed. (New York: W. W. Norton & Company, Inc., 1948), p. 64. As early as 1802, Congress gave subsidies to the states to encourage education. Later Congress provided grants-in-aid for state militias, highways and canals, agricultural and vocational education, forest conservation, etc. However, as a potent device for social control grants-in-aid did not come into their own until the administration of Franklin Roosevelt. The Social Security Act and the United States Housing Act are outstanding examples of the recent use of grants-in-aid to achieve comprehensive social objectives.

22. Charles Beard, *op. cit.*, p. 105. Cf. also Charles Beard, *The Republic* (New York: The Viking Press, 1943), chap. viii.

23. The Louisiana Purchase is a striking example of Jefferson's departure from his conception of the role of government. Jefferson also advocated public education and a protective tariff. But all this falls far short of government action as we have come to know it. For an excellent discussion of Jefferson's point of view concerning laissez faire, see Carl Becker, "What is Still Living in the Political Philosophy of Thomas Jefferson," *American Historical Review*, XLVIII (July 1943), 691 ff.

24. These designated the practices of purchasing goods before they were offered on the market and offering more than the "value" of goods because of the prospect of immediate resale.

25. Albert V. Dicey, *Law and Public Opinion in England*, 2d ed. (London: Macmillan & Company, Ltd., 1926), pp. 237-38.

26. "When . . . in 1878, Fawcett protested with vigour against restrictions imposed by the Factory Acts on the liberty of women, he is clearly the brave defender of a lost cause." *Ibid.*, p. 256.

27. Considerations of this sort prompted the United States Supreme Court to characterize a minimum wage law for women as a "naked and arbitrary exercise of power." In finding the law un-

constitutional, Justice Sutherland declared that "women are as capable of contracting for themselves as men" and that the act "forbids two parties having lawful capacity . . . freely to contract with one another as to the price for which that one shall render services to the other in a purely private employment where both are willing, perhaps anxious, to agree."

28. Harold Laski, *Reflections on the Revolution of Our Time* (New York: The Viking Press, 1943), p. 142.

29. Merle Fainsod and Lincoln Gordon, *op. cit.*, p. 59.

30. Herbert C. Hoover, *The Challenge to Liberty* (New York: Charles Scribner's Sons, 1934), p. 51.

31. An acute English student of America, Mr. Laski writes, ". . . the state is everywhere compelled, by the drive of political democracy, to intervene for its [the standard of living of the masses] protection. But each phase of this intervention is fiercely resented and fiercely resisted by the privileged class; a positive state is denounced as 'un-American'; 'true' democracy is equated with laisser faire in every sphere where it seeks to aid the under-privileged." *Reflections on the Revolution of Our Time*, p. 242.

Another observer, this one with an opposite ideological approach and with his roots in Continental Europe, writes in 1942 that "the fundamental American idea of government and administration today is the same as it was almost a century ago." Gustav Stolper, *This Age of Fable* (New York: Reynal & Hitchcock, Inc., 1942), p. 38. For what it was a century ago, Stolper cites Mill's well-known comment—meant to be a tribute—that Americans prefer improvisation to government.

Chapter 4

1. Strictly speaking, the negative state merely calls attention to the medical quack by withholding certification; once his fraudulent claims have been made known, the individual must be left free to accept or reject his services.

2. This may explain why the aesthetic sense of the community has not been similarly protected. A billboard may be removed from the highway if it is a hazard to the safety or the morals of the motorist, but not because it mars a pleasant landscape or offends good taste.

3. The condemnation of unfit housing has never been one of the more energetic pursuits of the negative state, despite appropriate enabling legislation. This may be taken as symptomatic of the apathetic interest of the negative state in preventive action as such.

4. Henry Sidgwick, *The Elements of Politics* (London: Macmillan & Company, Ltd., 1891), p. 78.

5. *Ibid.*

6. Not all promises are, of course, involved. It is usually stipu-

lated that there must be reliance on the promise and that such reliance must have led to loss. Moreover, the general rule is that the promise must be deliberately made, without coercion (a term which occasions endless difficulties), that there must be no willful misrepresentation, and that there be no intention to violate the law or to injure the community.

Chapter 5

1. James Mill, "Government," chap. vi, in *The English Philosophers from Bacon to Mill,* edited by Edwin A. Burtt (New York: The Modern Library, Random House, Inc., 1939).

2. Strictly speaking, sovereignty implies absolute power and, as such, cannot be limited. In this strict sense it is quite true that "sovereignty as a conception is incompatible with constitutionalism." C. J. Friedrich, *Constitutional Government and Democracy* (Boston: Little, Brown & Company, 1941), p. 16. But in point of fact, as so defined sovereignty is a mere abstraction; it has never existed, cannot exist. As Harold Laski points out, "It is obvious . . . that no organization disposes in actual fact of unlimited force; and we shall fail completely to understand the character of society, unless we seek to grasp exactly how the sovereign is compelled to will things desired by bodies in law inferior to itself." *Grammar of Politics* (London: George Allen & Unwin, Ltd., 1938), p. 51. At best sovereignty is a difficult term, but one not easily dispensed with.

3. Opinion in this country is divided concerning the difficulty of amending our Constitution. As early as 1864 resolutions were introduced in Congress to reduce the size of the majority required to propose or ratify amendments. Such resolutions increased in number after 1900, but the adoption of four socially significant amendments between 1913 and 1920 and of two amendments in 1933 served to take the edge off the criticism that for all practical purposes it is not only difficult but almost impossible to amend the Constitution.

On the other hand, the child labor amendment is an example of how cumbersome the amending process can be. Statutory legislation outlawing child labor was approved in 1917, only to be declared unconstitutional by the Supreme Court. A proposal to amend the Constitution also won the approval of Congress but, even after this evidence of a mandate from the majority, the amendment, although it was submitted to the states in 1924, was not ratified by the required number.

4. Judicial review as it prevails in our country was not written into the Constitution by the Founding Fathers; it was read into the Constitution by Justice Marshall in the famous case of *Marbury* v. *Madison.*

5. The era of constitution-making is marked by a great em-

phasis on written constitutions, the general judgment coinciding with Tom Paine's that where a constitution cannot be produced in visible form, there is none.

6. Cf. *The Federalist*, edited by Henry Cabot Lodge (New York: G. P. Putnam's Sons, 1888), No. 84. Hamilton's point is an interesting one. Bills of rights, he says, "are, in their origin, stipulations between kings and their subjects . . . Such was MAGNA CHARTA . . . the *Petition of Rights* . . . The Declaration of Right . . . the [English] Bill of Rights. It is evident, therefore, that according to their primitive signification, they have no application to Constitutions professedly founded upon the power of the People, and executed by their immediate representatives and servants. Here, in strictness, the people surrender nothing; and as they retain everything they have no need of particular restrictions."

7. There is some variation, of course; for example, in the emphasis placed on the right of revolution.

8. Cf. Guido de Ruggiero, *The History of European Liberalism* (London: Oxford University Press, 1927), pp. 23-32, 50-73.

9. Article II of the French Declaration of the Rights of Man and of the Citizen, of 1789. Every American schoolboy knows that men are "endowed by their Creator with certain *unalienable* rights." The language of the Virginia and Massachusetts constitutions is equally strong. The former declares that the right of revolution is "indubitable, unalienable, and indefeasible," and the latter differs only in substituting "incontestable."

10. R. H. Tawney, *The Acquisitive Society* (New York: Harcourt, Brace and Company, 1920), p. 15.

11. John Locke, *An Essay Concerning the True, Original, Extent and End of Civil Government* (Oxford: Basil Blackwell & Mott, Ltd., 1946), chap. vii, par. 87. "Man being born . . . with a title to perfect freedom, and an uncontrolled enjoyment of all the rights and privileges of the law of nature equally with any other man or number of men in the world, hath by nature a power . . . to preserve his property—that is, his life, liberty, and estate, against the injuries and attempts of other men . . ."

12. Guido de Ruggiero, *op. cit.*, p. 27.

13. John Locke, . . . *of Civil Government*, chap. v, par. 31.

14. *The Works of Jeremy Bentham*, edited by J. Bowring (Edinburgh: W. Tait, 1838-43), X, 214, sec. 15. Particular target of Bentham's criticism in his "Fragment on Government" (*ibid.*, I, 221-95), was Sir William Blackstone who accepted the doctrine of natural rights. "The principal aim of society," Blackstone wrote, "is to protect individuals in the enjoyment of those absolute rights which were vested in them by the immutable laws of nature . . ." *Commentaries on the Law*, edited by B. C. Gavit from the 1892 abridged edition of W. H. Browne (Washington, D.C.: Washington Law Book Co., 1941), Book I, chap. i.

15. In some contexts jusnaturalism might coincide with the former instead of the latter, as when property owners would employ it to defend the immunity of private property from effective regulation.

16. In the constitution of 1793 the idea of a separation of powers was completely ignored, only to reappear in the constitution of 1795.

17. *The Federalist,* No. 47.

18. William E. H. Lecky, *Democracy and Liberty* (London: Longmans, Green & Co., Ltd., 1896), I, 361.

19. *The Federalist,* No. 62. Although the career of a measure through the two houses of our legislature is identical, a general differentiation of function is, nevertheless, imputed to them (apart from special differences like the Senate's treaty-ratifying power). The lower chamber is regarded as the seat of the passions and appetites; the upper, as the repository of "the cool and deliberate sense of the community." Madison (the authorship of this issue is in dispute as between Madison and Hamilton) wrote, "The necessity of a Senate is not less indicated by the propensity of all single and numerous assemblies to yield to the impulse of sudden and violent passions, and to be subdued by factious leaders into intemperate and pernicious resolutions." *Ibid.*

20. Thomas B. Macaulay, *Miscellaneous Works* (New York: G. P. Putnam's Sons), VIII, 8.

21. The measure was actually sponsored by the Conservative party under the leadership of Disraeli, who saw in it a chance "to dish the Whigs." "Shooting Niagara" was the phrase in which Lord Derby, nominal head of the ministry which Disraeli dominated, expressed his serious misgivings. The Conservative party had joined earlier with conservative Liberals to kill a less sweeping measure proposed by the Liberal Russell ministry of 1866.

22. The Declaration carefully avoids mentioning Parliament, which was even more responsible than the king.

23. *The Federalist,* No. 78.

24. *Records of the Federal Convention,* edited by Max Farrand (New Haven, Conn.: Yale University Press, 1923-37), I, 299. The sessions of the convention were secret. Our knowledge of what took place is based largely on Madison's careful and copious notes.

25. Thomas Hobbes, "Leviathan," chap. xiii, in *The English Philosophers from Bacon to Mill.*

26. For an excellent account of the relationship between the two, cf. Edwin Mims, *The Majority of the People* (New York: Modern Age Books, Inc., 1941), particularly chapters i and ii.

27. Although Hobbes preferred a monarch, the sovereign, he said, could be one or a few or many. At first a partisan of the Stuarts, he later transferred his loyalties to Cromwell.

28. John Locke, . . . *of Civil Government*, chap. xix, par. 229.

29. Guglielmo Ferrero, *The Principles of Power*, translated by T. R. Jaeckel (New York: G. P. Putnam's Sons, 1942), p. 168.

30. Cited by Mims, *op. cit.*, p. 38. A year before the signing of the Declaration even the president of Harvard might incite to revolution, as when he declared, "when one form of government is found by the majority not to answer the grand purpose in any tolerable degree, they may by common consent put an end to it and set up another."

31. Significantly, the Declaration of Rights in the French constitution of 1795 omits the references included in the abortive instrument of 1793 to tyrannicide and insurrection.

32. John Locke, . . . *of Civil Government*, chap. xviii, par. 203.

33. *Ibid.*, chap xix, par. 225.

34. *Ibid.*, chap. xix, par. 230.

35. David Hume, *A Treatise of Human Nature* (Oxford: The Clarendon Press, 1896), Book III, Part 2, sec. v.

Chapter 6

1. Adam Smith, *The Wealth of Nations*, 6th ed. (New York: Random House, 1937), Book I, chap. ii.

2. *Ibid.*, Book IV, chap. ii. "It is not from the benevolence of the butcher, the brewer, or the baker, that we expect our dinner, but from their regard to their own interest. We address ourselves, not to their humanity but to their self-love, and never talk to them of our own necessities but of their advantages." Book I, chap. ii.

3. *Ibid.*, Book I, chap. ii. The introduction in this passage of an "invisible hand" is a metaphysical departure from the otherwise strictly economic basis of Adam Smith's harmony of interests. The logic of his case does not depend, however, upon a *deus ex machina*. Some later economists have referred to the "invisible hand" as though Adam Smith employed it as an analogy. Thus T. N. Carver writes, "As Adam Smith said long ago, that we are sometimes led as [*sic*] by an invisible hand . . ." *Principles of Political Economy* (Boston: Ginn and Company, 1919), p. 61. The "as" is Carver's, not Adam Smith's, although the latter might have been better advised had he used it.

4. Bernard de Mandeville, *Fable of the Bees*, translated by F. B. Kaye (London: Oxford University Press, 1924), Part I.

5. The profit motive, it will be observed, is not confined to entrepreneurs. It permeates all the acts of exchange and becomes the central assumption of orthodox economics. Even the worker's wage presumably represents a profit to him of the goods which it will buy over the ills of "going without" and the irksomeness of labor. "For the final hours of all days in a year," writes John Bates Clark, "the (work) man will get a miscellaneous list of

pleasures and will decide whether the sum total of them offsets the sacrifice of almost three hundred final hours of labor. This is a difficult decision, but the man will make it; and in doing so, he will get a unit of final utility in terms of equivalent pain." *The Distribution of Wealth* (New York: The Macmillan Company, 1899), p. 384.

6. Economists traditionally divide their subject into two parts, one of which deals with production, the other with distribution. In *The Wealth of Nations* attention is largely focused upon the former, as might be expected in an era when production was the desideratum. With Ricardo attention shifts to the problem of distribution, to the problem, that is, of considering just how the wealth of society shall be apportioned among the various factors responsible for its production (i.e., distributed as wages, profits, interest, etc.). With this shift, the problem of value becomes central in economic theory, and shortly after, the labor theory of value, to which Adam Smith's preoccupation with production led him, is abandoned by orthodox economists for the hedonistic utilitarian theory of value expounded by Bentham.

7. Alfred Marshall, *Principles of Economics* (London: Macmillan & Company, Ltd., 1936), p. 15.

8. Walter Lippmann has been particularly vehement on this subject. In *The Good Society* (Boston: Atlantic Monthly Press, Little, Brown & Company, 1938), he writes concerning the usurpation by bureaus and commissions of the role of the market: "Those who formulate the laws and administer them are men, and, being men, there is an enormous disparity between the simplicity of their minds and the real complexity of any large society" (p. 28). Indeed, "the intricacy of one breakfast, if every process that brought it to the table had deliberately to be planned, would be beyond the understanding of any mind" (p. 30). However, it is a little difficult to know which Lippmann to believe, for Mr. Lippmann on another occasion has been just as vehement in disparaging the assumption, in the theory we are examining, that each individual knows his own interest. In his earlier *A Preface to Morals* (New York: The Macmillan Company, 1929) he writes: "The system of natural liberty assumes that if each man pursues his own interest his own way, each man will promote his own interest. There is an unanalyzed fallacy in this theory which makes it utterly meaningless. It is assumed that each man knows his own interest and can therefore pursue it. But this is precisely what no man is certain to know . . . There is nothing in the natural equipment of man which enables him to know intuitively whether it will be profitable to increase his output or reduce it . . . to buy or to sell . . . to pursue his interest his own way is a fairly certain way to disaster" (p. 245). No doubt Mr. Lippmann will return to this theme in a third volume, thereby assisting his perplexed readers who may well

wonder just what judgment should be followed if both collective and individual judgment are hopelessly inadequate.

9. The theory as initially expounded came to be challenged in all its ramifications, as by P. A. Kropotkin in his *Mutual Aid, A Factor of Evolution* (New York: Alfred A. Knopf, 1917), and by Lester F. Ward in his *Dynamic Sociology* (New York: D. Appleton & Co., 1920).

10. Herbert Spencer, *Social Statics* (New York: D. Appleton & Co., 1868), chap. xxv, sec. 6.

11. Echoing Spencer in America, John D. Rockefeller declared, "The growth of a large business is merely a survival of the fittest. . . . The American Beauty rose can be produced in the splendor and fragrance which bring cheer to its beholder only by sacrificing the early buds which grow up around it. This is not an evil tendency in business. It is merely the working out of a law of nature and a law of God." Cited by Richard Hofstadter in *Social Darwinism in American Thought* (New York: Oxford University Press, 1944), p. 31.

12. Sir Arthur Salter, *Recovery, the Second Effort* (New York: The Century Company, 1932), p. 17.

13. Perhaps one of the most brilliant of these is Professor Lionel Robbins' *The Nature and Significance of Economic Science* (2d ed.; London: Macmillan & Company, Ltd., 1937). By far the most popular with American readers until the appearance of Professor Friedrich A. Hayek's *The Road to Serfdom* (Chicago: University of Chicago Press, 1944) was Mr. Lippmann's *The Good Society*.

14. Mr. Arthur Bryant's description gives us a poignant picture of "the new England":

"The new England they built was housed not so much in towns as in barracks. These were grouped around the new factories, on the least expensive and therefore the most congested model attainable. Since the rate of profits was not affected if their inhabitants died prematurely, no consideration was paid to matters of sanitation and health. The dwellings which housed the factory population were run up by small jerry-builders and local carpenters, who like the mill owners were out for a maximum of profit with the minimum of responsibility. They were erected back to back on the cheapest available site, in many cases marshes. There was no ventilation and no drainage. The intervals between the houses, which passed for streets, were unpaved and often followed the line of streams which served as a conduit for excrement.

"The appearance of such towns was dark and forbidding . . . Overhead hung a perpetual pall of smoke, so that their inhabitants groped to their work as in a fog. There were no parks or trees; nothing to remind men of the green fields from which they came or to break the squalid monotony of the houses and factories. From the open drains and ditches that flowed beneath the shade of sulphurous chimneys and between pestilential hovels arose a fetid smell. The only symbols of normal human society were the gin shops." *The Pageant of England* (New York: Harper & Brothers, 1941), pp. 63-64.

15. Herbert C. Hoover, *Challenge to Liberty* (New York: Charles Scribner's Sons, 1934), pp. 42-43.

Part Two

Introduction

1. The Utopian writers of France and England (e.g., the Fourierists and Owenites), the Fabians and Keynesians, Marx and the Marxian revisionists, writers of the German historical school, the romanticists, American institutionalists, and pragmatists have all contributed in greater or less degree.

2. On the other hand, liberals once mistakenly withheld criticism of the Soviet Union lest they give encouragement to reactionaries.

Chapter 7

1. His later editions read "utility or benefit" instead of "utility or pleasure" and "surplus satisfaction" instead of "surplus pleasure."

2. This excellent distinction was made by Professor Wesley C. Mitchell. In contrast to postulates, preconceptions "shape the general trend of a man's thinking without being themselves submitted to critical scrutiny." *The Backward Art of Spending Money* (New York: McGraw-Hill Book Company, Inc., 1937), p. 203.

3. The egoist *seems* to exclude benevolent conduct when he says that all conduct is selfish, but clearly benevolence can have no meaning to him since, by definition, it is a variant of egoism (i.e., the generous man is doing what he likes to do and is in so far selfish). Consequently *no* kind of conduct is excluded by the egoist. Therefore when the egoist says that all conduct is selfish, he is saying no more than that all conduct is conduct.

4. "Every gallant life is an experiment in different ways of fulfilling it. It expands itself in predatory aggression, in forming friendships, in seeking fame, in literary creation, in scientific production. In the face of this elasticity, it requires an arrogant ignorance to take the existing complex system of stocks and bonds, of wills and inheritance, a system supported at every point by manifold legal and political arrangements, and treat it as the sole

legitimate and baptized child of an instinct of appropriation." John Dewey, *Human Nature and Conduct* (New York: The Modern Library, Random House, Inc., 1930), p. 117.

"Man is not a creature governed solely by his interests but also by his feelings, his convictions, his passions. Besides, it must be remarked that his so-called 'interests' include very various motives; for there is not only pecuniary interest, the desire for profit; there is also the desire for leisure . . . ; there is the desire for independence, which revolts the working class against the wage system; there is the desire for security . . . Personal interest expands progressively and becomes family interest . . . national interest, and even, reaching its last limit, the interest of humanity." Charles Gide, "Economic Man," *Encyclopaedia Britannica,* VII, 925.

5. Cf. John Dewey and James H. Tufts, *Ethics,* rev. ed. (New York: Henry Holt and Company, Inc., 1932), p. 331. In another place Dewey wrote: ". . . both self-love and altruism are acquired dispositions not original ingredients in our psychological make-up . . . Psychologically speaking, our native impulses and acts are neither egoistic nor altruistic; that is, they are not actuated by *conscious* regard for either one's own good or that of others. They are rather direct responses to situations." *Ibid.,* p. 324. Cf. also John Dewey, *Human Nature and Conduct,* pp. 116-17.

6. William James, *Principles of Psychology* (New York: Henry Holt and Company, Inc., 1890), I, 318-20. (The capitals and italics are James's.)

7. *Ibid.,* p. 323; also John Dewey and James H. Tufts, *Ethics,* p. 328. In 1890 when James's monumental contribution to psychology was published, he could say that only one author whom he knew, Herr Horwicz, had discussed the question whether the " 'pure ego,' *per se*, can be an object of regard." This may be an overstatement. Nevertheless, it indicates the extent to which self-interest was taken for granted as a description of human motivation.

8. Walter G. Everett, *Moral Values* (New York: Henry Holt and Company, Inc., 1918), pp. 109-10.

9. The sensualist who presumably abstracts the element of satisfaction from the experience producing it is a possible exception.

10. Edward Tolman, *Purposive Behavior in Animals and Men* (New York: The Century Company, 1932), p. 261.

11. The point is well made by John A. Hobson. "The formulas of early utilitarianists were wrecked on the hypothesis of pleasure or happiness being of a single kind, so as to admit of a 'greatest happiness' for a person or 'a greatest number.' J. S. Mill's recognition of the truth that pleasures and utilities are of different kinds and of incommensurable values destroyed the hedonist calculus that was the basis of the Benthamite utilitarianism. But unfortunately it survived almost intact in the economic science where it was sustained by an illusory interpretation of distinctively eco-

nomic conduct." *Economics and Ethics* (Boston: D. C. Heath and Company, 1929), p. 109. Cf. also John A. Hobson, *Work and Wealth: A Human Valuation* (London: Macmillan & Company, Ltd., 1914), pp. 331 ff.

12. Thorstein Veblen, *Essays in Our Changing Order* (New York: The Viking Press, 1934), p. 78.

13. John Dewey, *Human Nature and Conduct*, p. 118.

14. Melville J. Herskovits, *The Economic Life of Primitive People* (New York: Alfred A. Knopf, 1940), p. 70.

15. Cited by Herskovits, *ibid.*, p. 16. Another anthropologist, Richard Thurnwald, agrees that primitive people never limit work to an unavoidable minimum and that they engage in "assiduous" activity. However, he finds that their work lacks "concentration and discipline." "They are quite ready to make an effort when the work requires it, but they soon relax, and as they are not compelled to make any consecutive effort toward overcoming this tendency, they yield to the feeling of fatigue." To this Herskovits responds with some reason that "an ability to focus all effort on a task in hand when it is necessary to do so, to work hard when one must, and to relax when one is able, does not necessarily imply 'lack of concentration and discipline,' but rather a realistic sense of the physiological requirements of the human system." *Ibid.*, p. 71.

16. William McDougall, *An Introduction to Social Psychology* (Boston: John W. Luce & Company, 1926), p. 16.

17. Veblen in one of his most telling phrases comments that later psychology does not treat the organism as a "causal hiatus." "The Preconceptions of Economic Science," III, in *What Veblen Taught*, edited by Wesley C. Mitchell (New York: The Viking Press, 1936), p. 122.

18. John Dewey, *Reconstruction in Philosophy* (New York: Henry Holt and Company, Inc., 1920), pp. 86-87. In Dewey's *Quest for Certainty* (New York: Minton, Balch & Company, 1929), appears this significant comment: "The history of the theory of knowledge or epistemology would have been very different if instead of the word 'data' or 'givens,' it had happened to start with calling the qualities in question 'takens.' . . . as data they are selected from [the] total original subject-matter which gives the impetus to knowing; they are discriminated for a purpose; that, namely, of affording signs or evidence to define and locate a problem, and thus give a clue to its resolution" (p. 178).

19. *New York Times*, November 22, 1942.

20. Cf. Paul H. Douglas, "The Reality of Non-Commercial Incentives in Economic Life," in *Trends of Economics*, edited by R. G. Tugwell (New York: Alfred A. Knopf, 1924), pp. 151-88. Cf. also C. E. Ayres, *Divine Right of Capital* (Boston: Houghton Mifflin Co., 1946).

21. We are indebted to an essay of J. M. Keynes for this couplet.

22. Felix Frankfurter, *Law and Politics* (New York: Harcourt, Brace and Company, 1939), p. 203.

23. John Dewey, *Human Nature and Conduct*, pp. 123-24.

24. Cf. Arthur E. Murphy, *The Uses of Reason* (New York: The Macmillan Company, 1943), for an interesting indictment of a tendency on the part of some (e.g., Thurman Arnold, Burnham, Spykman) to pass from intellectual sophistication to cynicism.

25. William McDougall, *op. cit.*, p. 11; cf. also p. 351.

26. As Professor Karl Mannheim observes, "A new type of objectivity in the social sciences is attainable not through the exclusion of evaluations but through the critical awareness and control of them." *Ideology and Utopia* (New York: Harcourt, Brace and Company, 1949), p. 5.

27. This is far from denying that one can distinguish an ethical and an unethical use of such instruments.

28. P. T. Homan, *Contemporary Economic Thought* (New York: Harper & Brothers, 1928), p. 50.

29. Wesley C. Mitchell, "The Rationality of Economic Activity," *Journal of Political Economy*, XVIII (March 1910), 197.

Professor H. W. Stuart has devoted a brilliant essay to noting the unreality of this kind of description of economic conduct. Cf. his "Phases of the Economic Interest," in *Creative Intelligence* (New York: Henry Holt and Company, Inc., 1917), pp. 282-353.

30. Lionel Robbins, *The Nature and Significance of Economic Science* (London: Macmillan & Company, Ltd., 1937), p. 16. The object of choice is of no concern. Economic analysis is as applicable to a community of ascetics as to a community of sybarites, Robbins tells us. *Ibid.*, p. 26.

31. *Ibid.*, pp. 78-79.

32. I cannot forbear citing a 1945 *Fortune* magazine study of Wall Street in which the author asks whether the public will undervalue securities as it did in the depression. "One reason," the author finds, "it may undervalue them is that many investors still seem to allow their dislike of the [Roosevelt] Administration to distort their appraisal of their self-interest." *Fortune*, March 1945, p. 232.

33. Rexford G. Tugwell, "Human Nature in Economic Theory," *Journal of Political Economy*, XXX (June 1922), p. 340.

34. *Ibid.*, p. 332. What men have a right to expect from industry is a question which involves the vexing problem of the relationship of economics and ethics and ultimately of the place of value judgments in the social sciences. This problem is outside the scope of this study. However, the critic of classical economics takes the position that the "science of wealth" must reckon with welfare. He points out that the classicists constantly, albeit often covertly, import moral judgments.

35. Thorstein Veblen, *Essays in Our Changing Order*, p. 100.

36. "The motives of men as they go about their economic affairs are important for economists to understand whenever there arises a question of *why* it is human conduct follows a given line. It may be that all these *why* questions are irrelevant; but it would be less difficult to adhere to this belief if the whole school of classical economists and the present-day marginists, their successors, had not made such wholesale assumptions concerning those very motives. One great justification, for instance, for the distribution categories of rent, interest, profit, and wages lies in the fact that each furnishes an incentive to distinct individuals to do a distinct thing." Rexford G. Tugwell, *op. cit.*, p. 336.

37. K. W. Kapp in *The Social Costs of Private Enterprise* (Cambridge, Mass.: Harvard University Press, 1950), attempts to estimate quantitatively how much we pay in human health, in natural resources, and in social costs for the activities of private business and argues that the scope of economic theory be extended to take account of such costs.

38. The term is used to distinguish a growing group of economists who are critical of classical and neoclassical economics but who cannot be classified as belonging to the "historical" school (e.g., Schmoller), the romantic school (e.g., Ruskin), or to the Marxist school—although all these schools would concur in the criticism.

39. "In all stages of social development the economic motives that actuate men remain essentially the same," wrote J. B. Clark in *Essentials of Economic Theory* (New York: The Macmillan Company, 1907), p. 39, cited by P. T. Homan, *op. cit.*, p. 45. Clark, says Homan, "assumes uncritically the view of the utilitarian school of philosophers that utilities are quantities of pleasure, rationally measured."

40. It is, wrote Veblen, "the peculiarity of the hedonistic economics that by force of its postulates . . . it deals with . . . conduct only in so far as it may be construed in rationalistic, teleological terms of calculation and choice. But, it is . . . no less true that human conduct, economic or otherwise, is subject to the sequence of cause and effect by force of such elements as habituation and conventional requirements." Orthodox science was driven by its hedonistic preconceptions to ignore inquiry into the latter. *Essays in Our Changing Order*, p. 160. See also pp. 155-60, which are especially relevant.

41. Cf. Wesley C. Mitchell, "Quantitative Analysis in Economic Theory," *The Backward Art of Spending Money*, pp. 35-36. According to Professor Mitchell, "In the hedonistic calculus which Jevons followed, man is placed under the governance of two sovereign masters, pain and pleasure, which play the same role in controlling human behavior that Newton's laws of motion play in controlling the behavior of the heavenly bodies. Dr. Mar-

shall's conception of economic behavior as controlled by two opposing sets of motives is scarcely less mechanical in its logic. Indeed, any theorist who works by ascribing motives to men and arguing what they will do under guidance of these forces will produce a mechanical type of explanation." *Ibid.*, p. 34.

Even if, as Professor Homan notes, Marshall was sensitive of the importance of the evolutionary approach, "it must still be admitted that the concepts of physics and mechanics rather than those of biology are the ones that most affect his viewpoint and method as he approaches the scientific investigation of economic phenomena." *Op. cit.*, p. 214.

42. In his influential *Human Nature in Politics* (Boston: Houghton Mifflin Company, 1915), Graham Wallas wrote, "It [the classical political economy of the universities and the news-papers, the teaching of MacCulloch, Senior, and Archbishop Whately] . . . became identified with the shallow dogmatism by which well-to-do people in the first half of Queen Victoria's reign tried to convince workingmen that any change in the distribution of the good things of life was 'scientifically impossible' " (p. 13).

43. Albert V. Dicey, *Law and Public Opinion in England*, 2d ed. (London: Macmillan & Company, Ltd., 1926), p. 187. "By the people . . . I mean the middle classes," declared the utilitarian Henry Peter Brougham. Brougham in the same speech distinguishes between the "mob" and the "people": "If there is a mob, there is the people also. I speak now of the middle classes . . ." *Speeches* (Edinburgh: Adam and Charles Black, 1838), chap. ii, p. 600, cited by Dicey, *op. cit.*, pp. 185-86.

Chapter 8

1. Ludwig von Mises, *Omnipotent Government* (New Haven, Conn.: Yale University Press, 1944), pp. 49-50.

2. We are agreed, for example, that they may not buy nar-cotics. Do the same considerations which require that buying narcotics be an exception require other exceptions? Unfortunately freedom of consumer preference is simpler as a slogan than it is as a slide rule.

3. Cf. below, pp. 237-247.

4. G. D. H. Cole, *Economic Planning* (New York: Alfred A. Knopf, 1935), p. 61.

5. Barbara Wootton, *Freedom Under Planning* (Chapel Hill, N.C.: University of North Carolina Press, 1945), p. 57.

6. Adam Smith, *The Wealth of Nations*, 6th ed. (New York: Random House, 1937), Book I, chap. x, sec. 2.

7. "The Domestic Economy," insert to *Fortune*, December 1942.

8. Clair Wilcox, *Competition and Monopoly in American Industry*, TNEC Monograph No. 21 (Washington, D.C.: Govern-

ment Printing Office, 1940), p. 10. The term "monopoly" as I am using it refers to such control. Hereafter I shall refer to the Temporary National Economic Committee as TNEC. For a sympathetic study of the TNEC's hearings see David Lynch, *The Concentration of Economic Power* (New York: Columbia University Press, 1946); for a hostile criticism of the TNEC monographs, see J. Scoville and N. Sargent, *Fact and Fancy in the TNEC Monographs*, published in 1942 by the National Association of Manufacturers in New York.

9. Clair Wilcox, *op. cit.*, pp. 69, 98. Since the publication of the report changes have occurred. For example, the two companies providing domestic telegraph service have become one, molybdenum is commercially available now as a by-product of copper, a government action removed sleeping and parlor cars from the list, etc.

10. *Ibid.*, pp. 113-18.

11. A. A. Berle, Jr., *The 20th Century Capitalist Revolution* (New York: Harcourt, Brace and Co., 1954), p. 26. Among the pioneering studies of quasi-monopolistic and crypto-monopolistic practices were Mrs. Joan Robinson's *The Economics of Imperfect Competition* (London: Macmillan Co., 1933) and E. H. Chamberlin's *The Theory of Monopolistic Competition* (Cambridge: Harvard University Press, 1932). Cf. also *American Capitalism, The Concept of Countervailing Power*, J. K. Galbraith (Boston: Houghton Mifflin Co., 1952), especially Ch. iv; *Monopoly and Free Enterprise*, G. W. Stocking and M. W. Watkins (New York: Twentieth Century Fund, 1951); A. R. Burns, *The Decline of Competition* (New York: McGraw-Hill & Co., 1936); M. A. Adelman, "The Measurement of Industrial Concentration," *The Review of Economics and Statistics*, November, 1951 (Vol. XXXII, No. 4); "Administered Prices," *Hearings*, Sub-Committee on Antitrust and Monopoly, Pts. 1-10, 1957-1961. These are outstanding examples of an extensive literature.

12. Federal Trade Commission, *The Merger Movement: A Summary Report* (Washington, D.C.: Government Printing Office, 1948).

13. "Each of the two independently expresses its will; the schedules differ in form, style of type, printer's flourish. Yet by some higher telepathy the prices recited are identical." Walton Hamilton, *Patents and Free Enterprise*, TNEC Monograph No. 31 (Washington, D.C.: Government Printing Office, 1941), p. 99.

14. Having greatly advanced understanding of the phenomenon of imperfect competition in her influential earlier work, the distinguished British economist, Joan Robinson, tells us more recently that her *Economics of Imperfect Competition* "was a scholastic book" and not "a suitable basis for an analysis of the problem." ("Imperfect Competition Revisited," *Economic Journal*, Sept., 1953, p. 579.) So, too, Professor E. H. Chamberlin, whose theory

of monopolistic competition first drove home the importance of oligopoly, tells us more recently that "the subject needs to be re-written in terms of . . . cross-elasticity of demand, rather than in terms of the number of sellers in a market." (*Economica,* November, 1951, p. 355.) Cf. Sidney Weintraub's "Revised Doctrines of Competition," *American Economic Review,* 1955, Vol. 45, No. 2, pp. 463-479.

15. Cf. Joseph Schumpeter, *Capitalism, Socialism and Democracy* (New York: Harper & Brothers, 1942), Chs. vii, viii.

16. J. K. Galbraith, *American Capitalism: The Concept of Countervailing Power* (Boston: Houghton-Mifflin Co., 1952), p. 91.

17. *Ibid.,* p. 93. The kind of innovation involved is another matter. Cf. below, p. 237.

18. "Competition: Static Models and Dynamic Aspects," *American Economic Review,* Vol. 45, Pt. 2, p. 452. Professor Galbraith relies on what he calls "countervailing power" as a substitute for a no longer extant competition to protect the consumer. The power of oligopolists is countered in America by large-scale buyers who are able to protect the ultimate consumer from what would otherwise be the extortions of the producers. However, Professor Galbraith has himself been forced to concede that this happens only because retailing is still a competitive industry. Commenting on the critics who have pointed this out, he observes: "I suspect they are right. I am sure that I was more than a little reluctant, at this particular stage in my argument, to confess a reliance on competition. After all, it is a bit embarrassing after one has just murdered his mother-in-law to disinter the lady and ask her to help do the cooking." "Countervailing Power," *American Economic Review,* Vol. 44, Pt. 2 (May, 1954), p. 4.

19. "Technological Progress in Some American Industries," *American Economic Review,* Vol. 44, Pt. 2 (1954), pp. 178-189 (emphasis is added). Professor Maclaurin agrees with Professor P. T. Ellsworth, for example, that the "major innovations occurred under competitive conditions in the early years of the automobile industry as compared with the apparently minor changes since the industry has become monopoloid." This paper and the discussion following it would appear to indicate a heavy weight of professional opinion against the Schumpeter-Galbraith thesis.

20. *Ibid.,* pp. 190-200.

21. Wendel Berge, *Cartels* (Washington, D.C.: Public Affairs Press, 1944), p. 3.

22. *Ibid.,* pp. 19-20. The control of large areas of research either by company-owned research departments or, in some cases, by subsidies to the universities is a new and interesting chapter in the story of how monopolies perpetuate themselves. In an era when the research leading to technological advance is increasingly a collective undertaking requiring vast resources, the importance of such control is clearly evident.

23. *Ibid.*, pp. 28-30. When dentists began purchasing from industrial users at the lower price, the manufacturer sought ways of having the cheaper plastic barred under the Pure Food and Drug Act, even considering the inclusion of small amounts of arsenic as an ingredient!

24. E.g., the price of an important material like tungsten carbide, which rose from $50 a pound, its price in 1928 prior to the organization of a patent cartel, to $453 a pound after the cartel was formed. *Ibid.*, p. 43.

25. The TNEC comments as follows: "No one can read the testimony developed before this committee on patents without coming to a realization that in many important segments of our economy the privilege accorded by the patent monopoly has been shamefully abused. It is there revealed in striking fashion that the privilege given has not been used, as was intended by the framers of the Constitution and by the Congress, 'to promote the progress of science and the useful arts,' but rather for purposes completely at variance with that high ideal. It has been used as a device to control whole industries, to suppress competition, to restrict output, to enhance prices, to suppress inventions, and to discourage inventiveness." *Final Report and Recommendations of the Temporary National Economic Committee* (Washington, D.C.: Government Printing Office, 1941), p. 38.

26. Cf. Barbara Wootton, *Plan or No Plan* (New York: Farrar & Rinehart, Inc., 1935), pp. 130-33.

27. Cf. Barbara Wootton, *Freedom Under Planning,* chap. vi. In our country there have been, to be sure, times of excessive mobility, as during the depression and the war.

28. There are many areas, however, in which wages remain depressed. Moreover, the number of employable persons without work often exceeds the limits of "frictional" unemployment.

29. Restrictive practices of the kind already described often avert or delay a decline in prices in certain areas of production; so, too, with unit profits.

30. Cf. Wesley Mitchell, "Business Cycles," *Encyclopaedia of the Social Sciences* (New York: The Macmillan Company, 1935), III, 95.

31. The statement of Lionel Robbins is all the more valuable on this point because he writes in defense of the classical tradition: "Elementary equilibrium theory, as is well known, does not provide any explanation of the phenomena of booms and slumps. It explains the relationships in an economic system on a state of rest. . . . with a certain extension of its assumption it can describe differences between the relationships resulting from different configurations of the data. But it does not explain without further elaboration the existence within the economic system of tendencies conducive to disproportionate development. It does not explain discrepancies between total supply and total demand in the sense in

which these terms are used in the celebrated Law of Markets. Yet unquestionably such discrepancies exist, and any attempt to interpret reality solely in terms of such a theory must necessarily leave a residue of phenomena not capable of being subsumed under its generalizations." *The Nature and Significance of Economic Science,* 2d ed. (London: Macmillan & Company, Ltd., 1937), p. 119.

32. It is no wonder that orthodox economists gave scant attention—until forced as in recent times by the sheer impact of events —to the data under examination. Nor is it surprising that those who, like Sismondi, first called attention to the importance of business crises and depressions fall outside the classical liberal tradition. In our time also the great work on this subject, at any rate in America, was written by a vigorous critic of the classical tradition, Professor Wesley Mitchell. The author of *Business Cycles* writes, "One who turns from reading economic theory to reading business history is forcibly impressed by the artificiality of all assumptions of a 'static' or even a 'normal' condition in economic affairs. For, despite all efforts to give technical meanings to these ambiguous terms, they suggest the idea of an unchanging order, or of an order which economic principles are always tending to re-establish after every aberration. But a review of business annals never discloses a 'static' or a 'normal' state in either of these senses. On the contrary, in the real world of business, affairs are always undergoing a cumulative change, always passing through some phase of a business cycle into some other phase . . . In fact, if not in theory, a state of change in business conditions is the only 'normal' state." Wesley C. Mitchell, *Business Cycles,* 2d ed. (Berkeley, Calif.: University of California Press, 1941), p. 86.

Chapter 9

1. Edwin G. Nourse and associates, *America's Capacity to Produce* (Washington, D.C.: The Brookings Institution, 1934).

2. Harold Loeb and associates, *The Chart of Plenty* (New York: The Viking Press, 1935), p. 156.

3. *Ibid.,* p. 157. All figures are in terms of 1929 dollars.

4. The cost of our participation in the war for the years 1941-46, including appropriations subsequently canceled as a result of the ending of the war, was $450 billion.

5. Robert Nathan, *Mobilizing for Abundance* (New York: McGraw-Hill Book Company, Inc., 1944), p. 6. In economies which are not highly mechanized, the failure to utilize productive capacity is, of course, a failure in technology, not primarily a failure to utilize existing plants. In France the failure would be compounded of both. The failure of Great Britain and the Weimar Republic would be roughly comparable to our own.

6. In the light of the evidence cited above, the remarks of Professor Hayek on this subject verge on the fantastic. He writes of

the "irresponsible talk about 'potential plenty.' " This "snare," he says, "is still as palpably untrue as it was when it was first used over a hundred years ago." He adds, "The reader may take it that whoever talks about potential plenty is either dishonest or does not know what he is talking about." *The Road to Serfdom* (Chicago: Chicago University Press, 1944), p. 98.

7. The canard that most of the unemployed were so lazy as to be unemployable was decisively answered by our experience during the war. According to the *Federal Reserve Bulletin* of May 1944, p. 416, "By the spring of 1943, unemployment was down to a total of one million, a level heretofore thought impossible to achieve."

8. The index measures physical output, it should be emphasized, so that price variations theoretically have no effect.

9. *Federal Reserve Bulletin*, January 1944, pp. 2-3; *ibid.*, September 1944, pp. 841, 846.

10. The average hours worked per week in industry increased from thirty-seven hours in 1939 to forty-five hours by the end of 1944, or a rise of about 20 percent. Cf. *Federal Reserve Bulletin*, September 1944, p. 845. The most extreme estimate places the number of so-called "extra" wartime workers, i.e., people who either should not or would not work in normal times, at six million. There were approximately eleven million men in uniform at the peak of the war effort.

11. Other factors were of course at work. Patriotic motivation, especially as manifested in a decrease in the loss of man-hours from strikes, and a reduction in the variety of the goods produced contributed to the war effort. On the other hand, the hoarding of labor by producers with cost-plus contracts and the chaotic living conditions of workers in the mushroomed war industries were adverse factors. Granted the difficulty of casting up an exact account, it can be contended that the favorable and adverse factors roughly balanced each other and might, therefore, be discounted in an appraisal of the war effort.

12. Industrial output for civilian use in 1943 was approximately 80 percent of the 1935-1939 average, according to the *Federal Reserve Bulletin* of January 1944, pp. 2-3. The burden was also increased by factors which would be discountable from any long-range point of view, namely, our inexperience with wartime controls and the great haste with which we had to organize them. On the other hand, the requirements of war impose clear priorities, which render the problem of planning a great deal simpler in time of war than in time of peace.

13. Speech to the U. S. Chamber of Commerce, April 29, 1953.

14. 1949-1950, 1953-1954, 1957-1958, 1959-1960. One common recession feature has been absent, namely, a fall in prices.

15. Cf. below, pp. 213-219.

16. *Hearings,* Joint Economic Committee, March 6, 1961, p. 294.

17. *Hearings,* Joint Economic Committee, 1961, appendix. Pro-

fessor Samuelson continued ". . . our last recovery was an anemic one. 1959 and 1960 have been grievously disappointing years, as the period of expansion proved both to be shorter than earlier post-war recoveries and to have been abortive in the sense of never carrying us back anywhere near to high-employment and high-capacity levels of operation."

18. Hours of work actually declined during the Korean War.

19. The calculation of growth rates is a notorious snare for the unwary. Much depends on the base year taken as a point of departure. Thus the Committee for Economic Development (CED) finds that GNP expanded at an average annual rate of 5 percent over the 17-year period, 1938-1955, and 4 percent over the period, 1950-1955, a seemingly impressive record. Clearly, the increase from the depression year of 1938, taken by the CED as a base, and the war years which immediately followed is so great as to deprive the average as applied to the remaining years of significance. The second period, 1950-1955, is also deceptive since 1950 was a period of transition from recession to recovery and 1955 represented a new high mark. If the longer period 1947-1958 is taken a truer picture emerges: the average rate of growth then goes down to 3 percent.

20. "Jobs and Growth," pp. 20, 30. Conference on Economic Progress, Washington, D.C., May 1961. See also his testimony before the Joint Economic Committee (March 24, 1959).

21. The President's estimate in his economic message was more modest. He said, "Today most industries have the facilities to produce well above current levels. They lack only customers. As a Nation, we lose not only $30 to $40 billion of production per year. We also lose the vital incentives which capacity operation gives for expansion and modernization of plant and equipment."

22. The estimates of President Kennedy and the members of his Council of Economic Advisers start from a more modest 3.5 percent base. This is computed by adding the 1.5 percent annual increase in the size of the labor force to 2 percent annual increase in labor productivity. However, the President's message clearly indicates that the 3.5 percent growth rate is not high enough and the Chairman of his Council agrees that "it can and should be increased." (*Hearings,* Joint Economic Committee, March 6, 1961, p. 326.)

23. April 1960, p. 112 ff. The editors of *Fortune,* when they are not concerned with polemics and featuring articles about the sinister consequences of "growthism," accept a 4.2 percent growth rate as a fair expectation for the American economy. (April 1959, p. 105.)

24. Chapter 14.

25. During the 1950's the annual growth rate was about three-quarters of a million. The growth rate will be greater for the 1960's. An increase of from 1 to 1.2 millions was anticipated for 1961.

26. Since modernization of plant and equipment tends to lag during a business recession, labor productivity will be directly affected.

27. For many reasons the tendency of employers, as production expands, is to increase the hours of the work force already employed rather than add to the force. The length of the work week has not varied significantly since the war. It was 40.4 hours in 1946 and after rising and falling slightly was exactly the same 10 years later. Recently, Secretary of Labor Goldberg announced that a general shortening of the work week is not presently in sight. There is, of course, the hypothetically possible alternative of passing a law that would require the practice of both biological and technological contraception on a grand scale.

28. Between an $8 and $10 billion increase in the gross national product is needed to take care of the present annual growth of at least one million in the labor force. In 1961 it would take a $10 billion increase in the gross national product to take care of a 2 percent increase in productivity. These are Bureau of Labor Statistics estimates.

29. Federal Reserve Board and U. S. Department of Labor data.

30. Cf. below, Chapters 13, 15.

31. Four percent in 1961 would mean a true unemployment of about 4 million. "True" unemployment is counted by adding the full-time unemployed to the full-time equivalent of the partly employed.

32. Output per man-hour in agriculture since World War II expanded almost three times as rapidly as in nonfarming occupations. It is reliably estimated that productivity will rise another 85 percent in the next decade.

33. Our 2 million marginal farmers produce about 15 percent of the total agricultural output. They receive relatively little from the government in crop subsidies.

34. There are almost 16 million people over 65 years of age in the United States and, by 1970, increasing by about 400,000 a year, they will number 20 million, comprising almost 10 percent of the population.

35. The Federal income maintenance program for the aged now virtually forces retirement on beneficiaries because workers be-between 62 and 72 lose their benefits for any month in which they earn over $100.

36. The 1950 census indicated that, in California, for example, 17.1 percent of the aged worked after the age of 65, a comparatively large percentage. The figures do not indicate the amount of work done, nor the amount earned.

37. This was one of the chief issues in a costly labor dispute that shut down all of New York City's daily newspapers.

38. Surprisingly, the number of doctorates awarded women has declined from a peak of 17 percent to 10 percent, the proportion of women physicians is no greater today than it was in 1900, and

the pattern is similar for those receiving law degrees and appointments to university faculties. All this and more is reflected in *Who's Who* where the number of women listed has declined from 8.5 percent to 4 percent, a change which, except to the confirmed male chauvinist, must surely suggest a great waste of creative talent. (Cf. John B. Parrish, "Professional Women as a National Resource," *Quarterly Review of Economics and Business*, Feb., 1961, pp. 54-63.)

39. Western Europe is at least as overrun by supernumerary flunkeys, vendors, and the like. As for Communist Europe, it has its own problems, but it is doubtful that concealed unemployment of this type is one of them.

40. J. K. Galbraith, *The Affluent Society* (Boston: Houghton Mifflin Co., 1958), p. 269.

41. Alvin H. Hansen, *Economic Issues of the 1960's* (New York: McGraw-Hill, 1960), p. 78.

42. *Hearings,* March 6, 1961, p. 325.

43. Quoted by *Fortune* (April, 1958, p. 110 ff.) along with many other suggestive comments on the recession of 1957-1958. For the President of Emerson Electric the recession was an opportunity "to have Las Vegas shut down to a lower level and have the price of tickets to *My Fair Lady* cut from $50 to $25." And the executive vice-president of Shell Oil thought: "We have been on a fine long binge . . . We have to stop a bit and get a new surge of excitement." Comments such as these savor of *Alice in Wonderland.*

44. The authors of the *Chart of Plenty,* basing their statements on the National Survey of Potential Product Capacity, declare that even in 1929 "those goods and services which were *not* produced or rendered would have been sufficient to remove destitution . . . from every citizen, without taking away anything from the fortunate 8 percent possessing in 1929 an income of $5,000 or more per family.

"In fact these fortunate few could have enjoyed more comfort than they did enjoy, as well as a sense of security which at present is non-existent." (pp. 156-57.) A more recent study sponsored by the Twentieth Century Fund, *America's Needs and Resources,* by J. F. Dewhurst and associates (New York: Twentieth Century Fund, Inc., 1947), is somewhat less optimistic.

45. Speech to the Joint Orientation Conference (Pentagon Building, Washington, D.C.) (Italics added.)

Chapter 10

1. None of this stemmed from a conspiracy or sinister plot. As Bronterre O'Brien, a brilliant spokesman of the early Chartists, put it: "These spoliations they [the moneyed capitalists] commit not from sinister design, but from accidental position in society; or, rather the spoliations are committed *for* them by the silent opera-

tion of causes over which they have no control under the existing arrangements of society."

2. Even an assertion about the differences in degrees of brutality must be qualified when one recalls the company police of a 1920 Pennsylvania or Colorado mining town and notes that the Stalin terror is no longer (or rarely) invoked by his successors.

3. All this suggests that parallelism in the operation of profound economic forces may get obscured by the circumstance of timing and by great political and other differences. It is possible that, with the advent of an economy of plenty, the tight hold of the central government and its party guardians might relax even in the USSR. The relationship between a high level of consumption, i.e., abundance, and the degree of individual freedom permitted in all areas of action presents an interesting problem which has yet to receive the attention it deserves.

4. There are four classic defenses of high incomes: (a) the psychological argument that they provide necessary incentive; (b) the economic argument that they provide an indispensable source of capital formation; (c) the sociological argument that a leisure class is thereby made possible and, with this, the refinements associated with advanced societies, and (d) the meta-ethical argument that they are a reward for merit and, as such, part of the rational scheme of things.

5. Maurice Leven, Harold G. Moulton, and Clark Warburton, *America's Capacity to Consume* (Washington, D.C.: The Brookings Institution, 1934).

6. National Bureau of Economic Research, 1953. His results are confirmed by the Office of Business Economics' *Income Distribution in the United States*, a supplement to the *Survey of Current Business* (1954).

7. "Inequality in Income Distribution-Discussion," *American Economic Review*, Vol. 44, Pt. 2 (1954), p. 270. Professor Cartter agrees with George Garvey of the Federal Reserve Bank of New York that "an analysis of income changes which disregards corporate savings is somewhat unrealistic." Garvey's analysis (*loc. cit.,* pp. 236-253) also calls attention to special types of income currently charged as business expenses which are not reckoned as part of the income of the highest income group. Commenting on Garvey's reasons for the tendency to overstate decline in the inequality of income, Professor Margaret Reid observes in the same discussion: "My guess is that his list by no means exhausts the factors so far unaccounted for in the estimates, the net effect of which seems likely to support the hypothesis of relative constancy of pattern" (*loc. cit.,* p. 273). Clearly, the task of making an accurate estimate of trends in income distribution is beset by many hazards. Professor Kuznets, it should be said, qualified his own conclusions with many reservations.

8. *Midyear Economic Report of the President*, July 1948

(Washington, D.C.: Government Printing Office, 1948). Table I, Appendix B.

9. *Characteristics of the Low-Income Population and Related Federal Programs* (Washington, D.C.: Government Printing Office, 1955). Although this represented a decline between 1948 and 1954 from 25 to 20 percent in the proportion of families below the $2,000 a year level, the report points out that $2,000 purchased less in 1954 than in 1948 because of an average increase of 12 percent in consumer prices.

10. R. J. Lampman, *The Low Income Population and Economic Growth* (Washington, D.C.: U. S. Government Printing Office, 1959), p. 4.

11. By Sylvia Porter. Professor Lampman's report is entitled "The Share of Top-Wealth Holders in National Wealth, 1922-56" (Princeton University Press, 1961).

12. About 12½ million in 1959.

13. S. Kuznets, *Shares of Upper Income Groups in Income and Savings* (New York: National Bureau of Economic Research, Inc., 1950), p. 2.

14. Eric Johnston, *America Unlimited* (Garden City, New York: Doubleday, Doran & Company, Inc., 1944), pp. 40-41.

15. *Economic Report of the President*, January, 1960 (Washington, D.C.: Government Printing Office, 1960). Table C-8, p. 133. The decrease from the 1947 figure of 20.8 million, with which the table starts, is hardly spectacular. (A similar table is not contained in the 1961 Report.)

16. R. J. Lampman, *op. cit.*, p. 5. Professor Lampman explains: "If $2,500 is thought of as an appropriate minimum for a family of four, then some smaller income is appropriate to use for smaller consumer units, and a larger minimum is appropriate for families larger than four. A study of the variation of consumer needs by family size done by the Bureau of Labor Statistics provides a guide for such a range of cutoffs. They are $1,157 for a single person, $1,638 for two persons, $2,106 for three, $2,516 for four, $2,888 for five, $3,236 for six, and $3,750 for a family of seven or more.

"These several cutoffs for consumer units of different sizes were applied to the overall distribution of money income as estimated by the Bureau of Census. This leads to the finding that 32.2 million persons were in low-income status in 1957."

17. *Economic Issues of the 1960's* (New York: McGraw-Hill Co., 1960), p. 5.

18. Of the 3,700 miles of general shoreline from Maine to Mexico, only 240 miles or 6½ percent were in state or federal ownership for public recreational use, according to a 1955 survey of the National Park Service.

19. Quoted in *Time*, August 29, 1960, p. 58.

20. *Fortune*, January, 1960, p. 114. It is suspected by health experts that car fumes are one of the chief causes of the rapid rise in the number of cases of lung cancer.

21. Shortly after the foregoing was written, the automobile industry, under threat from the Secretary of Health, Education and Welfare of Congressional action, agreed to equip all 1963 model cars and trucks with anti-air pollution devices. (AP dispatch, December 12, 1961.)

22. Cf. above, p. 183.

23. Alvin H. Hansen, *Economic Issues of the 1960's*, pp. 75-76.

24. A 1960 report of the American Heart Association, based on years of study by qualified scientists, shows a statistical association between excessive cigarette smoking and death or illness from coronary heart disease. Death rates from heart attacks in middle-aged men were found to be from 50 to 150 percent higher among heavy cigarette smokers than among non-smokers. Also, a recent survey indicates that 25 percent of the doctors who smoked five years ago have stopped because they feared cancer. Reasonable men should be asking why that $158 million would not have been better spent persuading inveterate smokers and young potential smokers that smoking can be slow suicide.

25. Criticism such as the foregoing, it may be remarked in passing, is having its effect in advertising circles. We are presently witnessing the launching of a new campaign which advertises advertising; the resources of the industry are endless.

26. J. K. Galbraith, *The Affluent Society* (Boston: Houghton Mifflin Company, 1958), pp. 260-61.

27. The rich man actually buys more cheaply: his credit standing enables him to avoid the high interest rates on consumer credit; he buys his whiskey by the case, and the quality merchandise he can afford to buy may, in the long run, be cheaper than the highly perishable "bargains" on which the poor man must rely.

28. Cf. below, Chapter 14.

29. Cf. Gordon E. Baker, *Rural versus Urban Political Power* (New York: Random House, 1955).

30. Not all conservatives. The speech was bitterly criticized by Charles F. Taft, former mayor of Cincinnati, Ohio and brother of Robert Taft.

31. *Hearings*, Joint Economic Committee, April 10, 1961, p. 568. Conservatives may prefer the authority of a Rockefeller sponsored report, but they will not find it comforting. The Rockefeller Report on Education stresses the inability of state and local government adequately to meet the needs of education, finding that this is "due partly to the excessive dependence of state and local revenues—particularly the latter—upon the real property tax, which is notably laggard in its response to rising income,"

and "partly to the fact that state and local governments are reluctant to extend or expand their taxing systems for fear of placing their communities or states at a competitive disadvantage relative to other areas."

Chapter 11

1. It may be well to note that in 1830, some fifty years after the publication of *The Wealth of Nations,* large-scale enterprise was still distinguished by its absence and that Adam Smith, aware as he was of the dangerous power of the entrepreneurial class of his day, could hardly have foreseen the enormous increase which this power was to undergo.

2. Walter Lippmann, *The Good Society* (Boston: Atlantic Monthly Press, Little, Brown & Company, 1938), p. 13.

3. The remark is attributed to W. K. Vanderbilt.

4. Albert V. Dicey, *Law and Public Opinion in England,* 2d ed. (London: Macmillan & Company, Ltd., 1926), pp. 245-46.

5. *Ibid.,* p. 248.

6. It is estimated that the population of the world grew from 700 million in the year 1800 to 1,700 million in 1900. Thus, the population of the world increased a great deal more in a single century than during all the previous existence of the human species.

7. Josiah Quincy traveling in the year 1794 from Boston to New York marveled at the speed with which his journey was completed. The trip took seven days.

8. This is the essence of the idea of progress which swept the popular imagination in the nineteenth century.

9. Cf., for example, Eric Johnston, *America Unlimited* (Garden City, N.Y.: Doubleday, Doran & Company, Inc., 1944), pp. 82-83.

10. Ludwig von Mises, *Bureaucracy* (New Haven, Conn.: Yale University Press, 1944), p. 124.

11. James Hart, "Limits of Legislative Delegation," *The Annals of the American Academy of Political and Social Science,* CCXXI (May 1942), 87-100.

12. It was the failure on this score which led the United States Supreme Court unanimously to reject the NRA as "delegation running riot." Otherwise the court recognizes the need for delegation.

13. A typical short cut is the use by administrative agencies of trial examiners. Typical also of variation in procedure is the admission of hearsay evidence.

14. J. M. Pfiffner, "The Development of Administrative Regulation," *The Annals of the American Academy of Political and Social Science,* CCXXI (May 1942), p. 3. Provision is made for the appearance of a friend of the court (*amicus curiae*), but, as Professor Pfiffner points out, in most cases these are persons who

are litigants in a pending case that is similar. Persons anxious to protect the public interest must resort to a criminal complaint or a taxpayer's suit.

15. Merle Fainsod and Lincoln Gordon, *Government and the American Economy* (New York: W. W. Norton & Company, Inc., 1948), p. 73. The last word and unanimous opinion of the United States Supreme Court on this subject was spoken by Justice Frankfurter: "The history of Anglo-American courts and the more or less narrowly defined range of their staple business have determined the basic characteristics of trial procedure, the rule of evidence, and the general principles of appellate review. Modern administrative tribunals are the outgrowth of conditions far different from those. To a large degree they have been a response to the felt need of governmental supervision over economic enterprise which could effectively be exercised neither directly through self-executing legislation nor by the judicial process." *Federal Communications Commission* v. *Pottsville Broadcasting Co.*, 309 U.S. 134 (1940). Cited by Merle Fainsod and Lincoln Gordon, *op. cit.*, pp. 73-74.

16. There is a final step in the strategy of avoidance, and that is to staff an effectively functioning agency with officials subservient to the interests they are supposed to supervise.

17. It is significant, if this seems a harsh judgment, that most of the voices raised against the bureaucratic threat to individual rights have rarely been heard otherwise in defense of rights not associated with the property right.

Moreover, the career of the Walter-Logan Bill affords signal proof of the charge that what is involved is not an abstract devotion to the doctrine of the separation of powers in its traditional form but a desire to cripple certain agencies. This measure, sponsored by the American Bar Association, and passed by both houses of Congress in 1940, was vetoed by President Roosevelt because, in his words, it would "turn the clock backward and place the entire functioning of the Government at the mercy of never-ending lawsuits and subject all administrative acts and processes to the control of the judiciary." What primarily concerns one here, however, is not the logic of the presidential veto message but the fact that in passing the measure Congress exempted a long list of agencies (e.g., the Interstate Commerce Commission, the Federal Trade Commission, and the Federal Reserve Board) which happened at the time to enjoy Congressional favor. Congress knew that the Walter-Logan Bill would cripple them.

Chapter 12

1. Cf. Bertrand Russell, *Power* (New York: W. W. Norton & Company, Inc., 1938), p. 35.

2. Max Lerner, *It Is Later than You Think* (New York: The

Viking Press, 1938), pp. 223-24. Mr. Lerner's entire chapter called "Power Is What You Make It" is an excellent short discussion of this important subject.

3. The second disproportion is, from one point of view, more significant than the first. Even in the most egalitarian society the individual in a position of leadership, managerial or other, will count for more than one, although formally he casts only a single ballot. But there is no reason why any individual should wield power which is not proportioned to the function he performs.

4. Adolph A. Berle and Gardiner Means, *The Modern Corporation and Private Property* (New York: The Macmillan Company, 1933), p. 9. Cf. also A. A. Berle's *Power Without Property* (New York: Harcourt, Brace & Co., 1959).

5. *Ibid.*, pp. 84-85, 86-88.

6. Mortimer J. Adler and Lewis A. Kelso, *The Capitalist Manifesto* (New York: Random House, 1958), p. 127.

7. *Ibid.*, p. 32.

8. *Final Report and Recommendations of the Temporary National Economic Committee* (Washington, D.C.: Government Printing Office, 1941), p. 11.

9. *Ibid.*, pp. 3, 4. The Senate Small Business Committee has issued a report prepared by the onetime Smaller War Plants Corporation, "Concentration and World War II," which finds that "The relative importance of big business, particularly the giant corporations, increased sharply during the war, while the position of small business declined."

10. Federal Trade Commission, *The Merger Movement: A Summary Report* (Washington, D.C.: Government Printing Office, 1948), p. 68. The report finds that during the period 1940-47 "more than 2,450 formerly independent manufacturing and mining companies have disappeared as a result of mergers and acquisitions." The asset value of these firms is given as 5.2 billion dollars, or roughly 5.5 percent of the total of all manufacturing corporations in the country during the wartime year of 1943 (p. 17). Mr. Ickes has called attention to the fact that Mr. Garland Ferguson, Chairman of the Federal Trade Commission which issued the foregoing report, can hardly be accused of bias against business. He was a Coolidge appointee and has served as legal counsel to several large corporations.

11. M. A. Adelman, "The Measurement of Industrial Concentration," *The Review of Economics and Statistics*, November, 1951 (Vol. XXXII, No. 4). Cited by A. A. Berle, *The 20th Century Capitalist Revolution* (New York: Harcourt, Brace and Co., 1954).

12. A. A. Berle and G. Means, *op. cit.*, p. 33.

13. Cf. Robert Brady, *Business as a System of Power* (New York: Columbia University Press, 1943), pp. 8, 9.

14. Federal and state land grants to the railroads amounted to approximately 183 million acres. This is only a portion of the total aid provided.

15. Colonel Robert McCormick of the *Chicago Tribune* has estimated that the mail subsidies received by the *Time-Life-Fortune* publications are equal to their entire profit. Cf. "What Do You Mean, Free Enterprise?" by Nathan Robertson, *Harper's Magazine*, November 1948, pp. 70-75.

16. This was before General Electric's own interference with the free market led to the jailing of a number of its executives. Never was there a more striking contretemps.

17. "In Lone Star, Texas, this week, the Lone Star Steel Co. will open a new $40,000.00 building where the company will make no steel, transact no business. The building is a chapel. There, a full-time, specially trained Methodist chaplain will spend his time. . . . Similar pastor-counselor or devotional programs are fast spreading to dozens of other U. S. corporations. . . . Le Tourneau, Inc. maintains full-time chaplains at both its Vicksburg, Miss., and Longview, Texas, plants for on-the-job spiritual guidance . . ." (*Time*, October 31, 1955).

18. Even publicly supported education has suffered. In 1915, the states expended roughly 10 percent of their funds on higher education. By 1949 the proportion had dropped to 4 percent. The decrease has not been made up by the federal government. This is why the real income of college and university professors has declined since 1940 while the real income of other professional workers has increased. It is evident also in a shrinkage of space per student from the pre-war average of 155 sq. ft. The U. S. Office of Education recommends 180 sq. ft.

19. In both cases, the giving is decided upon by wealthy individuals, whether they sit as members of boards and dispense the funds of their stockholders, or dispense their own funds directly. The difference may strike some as negligible. The difference is worth pondering, however. Wealthy individuals are or may become many things from civil libertarians to uncivil libertines —roles to which their pecuniary interest may be completely subordinated. On the other hand, the individuals who manage corporations and sit on their boards are there primarily in their role as "economic men." They are bound to be thinking, and, indeed, required to think in economic terms. Moreover, individuals are mortal and their sins as well as their virtues die with them. Corporations—at least the large ones—enjoy a species of immortality. It may be contended that, in either case, boards of trustees, composed overwhelmingly of wealthy individuals, govern the colleges and universities. The answer is that, biased as such boards can be, their members, having been recruited specifically for their assignment, are likelier to be in rapport with academic ideals than the boards or management of business corporations.

20. Richard Eels, *Corporation Giving in a Free Society* (New York: Harpers, 1956), p. 29.

21. A. A. Berle, *The 20th Century Capitalist Revolution*, pp. 181-82.

22. "The quantum of power in political systems does not vary as widely as is often supposed. The lines of association and authority change from time to time, shifting the form, however, rather than the substance of control." C. E. Merriam, *The Role of Politics in Social Change* (New York: New York University Press, 1936), p. 103.

23. Even *Fortune*, in its difficult task of seeing the light and then diffusing it for the comfort of business-class eyes, has this to say: "The control of the typical big corporation is now in the hands of 'managers' who do not own it, and its ownership is in the hands of stockholders who do not influence its behavior. The corporation has become a disembodied, almost self-sufficient, socially 'illegitimate' force." "The Domestic Economy," p. 3, insert to *Fortune*, December 1942. If this is light, diffusion follows with familiar mechanical regularity. We are told among other things that managers are very unhappy about this state of affairs. Of the two managers quoted, one is Mr. Alfred Sloan of General Motors. Mr. Sloan's unhappiness did not prevent him from using his managerial powers to illegally appropriate some hundreds of thousands of dollars of the stockholders' money for a so-called retirement pension, as a result of which the courts found him guilty of violating his fiduciary responsibilities. Apparently only the editors' choice of an example was unhappy.

24. As noted earlier, Galbraith, following Schumpeter and others, strikes a different note (cf. above, p. 193), contending that large corporations and oligopolistic arrangements actually encourage technological innovations. Given Galbraith's caustic criticism in *The Affluent Society* of "preoccupation with production," the point—made six years earlier in his *American Capitalism*—may have come to carry less weight with him. Even so, the issue as it affects efficiency deserves pondering.

Some $13 billion is now spent annually on development and research in America. Of this, $1 billion is spent by institutions of higher learning and $7 billion by the federal government. That large corporations are not indispensable is evident in agriculture where, as everyone knows, technical development is almost completely socialized. Surprisingly, for one who was later to deplore the misallocation of resources, Galbraith does not deal with the way in which a large part of our total investment in research is heavily biased against pure science by its subordination to the profit motive (not to mention defense). Even in the area of technology (i.e., applied science) the emphasis is all too often on research to develop new gadgets.

Fortune quite forthrightly makes both points: "There is no doubt . . . that the division of the total expenditure between basic research and development has become inexcusably lopsided. Out of 1958's $10 billion, no more than $750 million went for basic research in all fields . . . and even this sum was heavily skewed in the direction of nuclear and sub-nuclear physics." (Jan., 1959, p. 76). Again: "By every criterion, the U. S. ought to be spending a great deal more on biological and medical research than last year's estimated $400 million." (p. 200). And yet again: "Experts may disagree on the seriousness of the Soviet 'economic threat,' but there can be no doubt that the U.S.S.R. has large cadres of well-trained scientists and engineers to assign to the productivity problem undistracted by the need to turn out annual engineering refinements in cars and a host of other consumer products." (*Ibid.*) (Cf. in this connection the Report of the President's Science Advisory Committee, November, 1960).

The words of Professor Walter Adams may well tell the story: "I do not believe," he says, "that any evidence has been presented to indicate that business sponsored research is more productive for equivalent expenditure than socially subsidized research. Subsidized research has the advantage of superior co-ordination and a lack of discrimination against promising research which does not promise immediate economic profit" (*loc. cit.*, p. 200).

25. Accustomed as we are to associate giantism with efficiency, we have too quickly taken for granted the relative inefficiency of small-scale enterprise. As Professor T. N. Beckman points out, "It is a matter of common knowledge among students of the subject that in essentially all branches of industry and trade some small firms have matched and even surpassed the efficiency record of the large companies." ("The Structure of Postwar American Business," *American Economic Review,* Vol. 34, No. 1, March, 1944, Pt. 2, supplement. Cf. also Monograph No. 21, pp. 309-15.) Professor Beckman cites a Federal Trade Commission study of company size in relation to production costs and rates of return, in which it was found that of fifty-nine tests the largest company had the lowest cost per unit in only one case; in thirty-seven cases companies classified as small had the lowest cost.

26. Conrad Cooper, speech, California Institute of Technology's Industrial Relations Center (November 12, 1961). See below, pp. 368-378.

27. David Lilienthal, *Big Business: A New Era* (New York: Harper and Brothers, 1952). "The argument about what is big enough and what is too big, I regard, generally, as not the central issue. My concern here is with the establishing to the fullest of a *climate of opportunity for growth and attainment of size,* as a means of greater productivity, better distribution of goods and income, and greater well-being for the country" (p. 36).

28. A. A. Berle, Jr., *The 20th Century Capitalist Revolution* (New York: Harcourt, Brace and Company) pp. 52-58.

29. J. K. Galbraith, *American Capitalism: The Concept of Countervailing Power,* pp. 117-23.

30. Cf., for example, George J. Stigler, "The Economist Plays with Blocs," *American Economic Review,* Vol. 44, Pt. 2 (1954),

pp. 7-14. Also, John Perry Miller, "Competition and Countervailing Power: Their Roles in the American Economy," *American Economic Review*, Vol. 44, Pt. 2 (1954), p. 24. "It is to be hoped," remarks Professor Miller, "that the stereotypes of the thirties of small business which can do no harm and large business which can be only evil, will not give way to the reverse stereotypes of small business which is inefficient and unprogressive and big business which can do no wrong."

31. Franklin D. Roosevelt, message of April 29, 1938.

32. Acton did not say "All power corrupts, etc., etc.," only that "All power tends to corrupt . . ."

33. Friedrich A. Hayek, *The Road to Serfdom* (Chicago: Chicago University Press, 1944), p. 168. Professors Hayek and von Mises do not appear to be in complete agreement on this point. According to the latter, "The inflation had pauperized the middle classes. The victims joined Hitler." *Omnipotent Government* (New Haven, Conn.: Yale University Press, 1944), p. 219. Elsewhere, when he is warning the English against a redistribution of income, Professor Hayek says, "It should never be forgotten that the one decisive factor in the rise of totalitarianism on the Continent . . . is the existence of a large recently dispossessed middle class." *Op. cit.*, p. 209.

34. Ludwig von Mises, *Omnipotent Government*, p. 219.

35. *Ibid.*, p. 221.

36. "Contrary to a popular fallacy there is no middle way [between the free market and totalitarianism], no third system possible as a pattern of a permanent social order." Ludwig von Mises, *Bureaucracy* (New Haven, Conn.: Yale University Press, 1944), p. 10.

37. Friedrich A. Hayek, *op. cit.*, pp. 194-96.

38. Ludwig von Mises, *op. cit.*, p. 228.

39. ". . . it is of the essence of democracy," Harold Laski notes, "that the central premises [*sic*] of action must be held in common by all classes which count." *Reflections on the Revolution of Our Times* (New York: The Viking Press, 1943), p. 143.

40. The paragraphs which follow are reproduced much as they appeared in my *From Wealth to Welfare*. They are clearly closely related to the theory of countervailing power which Galbraith elaborated with great skill about two years later in his *American Capitalism: The Concept of Countervailing Power*.

41. If I give more emphasis to the menace of fascism this is not because I underestimate the threat of Communism to other nations and the menace to us of the Soviet Union's expansionist ambitions. Neither would I minimize the danger of Communist espionage (and sabotage, in case of actual conflict). However, I write from the point of view of one who believes that Communism poses no internal threat to our established institutions and that fascism one day may.

As for the threat of Communism to other nations, it is not irrelevant to note that the Communist party is virtually without influence in the Scandinavian countries and among the members of the British Commonwealth (India included), where socialist or liberal-socialist parties have won comprehensive programs of social reform. Where this has not happened, as in France and Italy, the contrary is the case. Whether right or wrong about liberalism and liberal-socialism at home, conservative American critics of socialism abroad might ponder this fact. Those Americans who regard contemporary liberalism and liberal-socialism as "creeping Communism" and identify democratic socialism with totalitarian socialism (i.e., Communism) will, of course, derive nothing from pondering such evidence. Neither will they supply illumination for a foreign policy which must reckon with the distinction if we are not to drive the rest of the world into a position of aloof neutrality as between America and the Soviet Union.

42. The point is well made by Max Lerner: "When a society, as in a capitalist democracy, offers men these values of prestige, obedience, respect, enlargement of stature, sense of importance, in other walks of life than the governmental, the pressure to perpetuate governmental tenure is not so great." On the other hand, "What the process of socialization does is to effect a shift of the axis of the pursuit of power. The more that social activities are directed towards social ends, the more is the pursuit of prestige, importance, stature, withdrawn from nongovernmental (mainly economic) channels and drained into the governmental. This makes for a concentration of men's personal claims to stature, and therefore a concentration of danger." *It is Later Than You Think*, p. 227. That a militant progressive like Mr. Lerner can write in this vein is surely evidence that liberals are not unaware, as they are so often said to be, of the problem involved.

43. Bertrand Russell, *op. cit.*, pp. 285, 289.

44. *Ibid.*, p. 291.

45. The liberal charges, for example, that the current emphasis of conservatives on states' rights stems from a desire to curb the power of government to act, rather than from interest in local initiative and participation.

46. Cf., for example, Franklin Roosevelt's "Economic Bill of Rights," as presented in his annual (1944) message to Congress or the constitution of the Fourth French Republic.

47. Cf. Sidney and Beatrice Webb, *Constitution for the Socialist Commonwealth of Great Britain* (London: Longmans, Green & Co., Ltd., 1920), in which they propose a bicameral system, representing the consumer's or citizen's interest and the producer's or functional interest.

48. This point receives special emphasis in the Introduction to the 1920 edition of the *Fabian Essays* by Bernard Shaw, Sidney Webb, Graham Wallas, *et al.* (London: George Allen & Unwin,

Ltd.), p. xx, where Sidney Webb calls attention to the earlier Fabian neglect of local government. He notes that the Fabians had come "very vividly" to appreciate the significance of the manifold functions of municipal government "in ridding us from the hypothetical tyranny of a single national employer, inevitably 'bureaucratic' in character, no less than from the incubus of an all-pervading uniformity of social life." He goes on, "In the State of Tomorrow, as we realized, those who did not like the arrangements of Hampstead would always be able to move to Highgate and live under a different local government. We accordingly saw our way to a vast increase in the consciousness of personal freedom, a vista of endless diversity, the practical opportunity for an indefinitely varied development of human personality, under the most complete and all-embracing collectivism."

49. Professor Herman Finer has written, ". . . the instruments of restraint sought for in Montesquieu's time could be no other than those *within* the machinery of government. There is no trace in his writings of the moderating effects of party government . . . We know, today, however, that outside the machine, the parliamentary body, the bureaucracy, and the judiciary, there are great organized bodies of electors in a permanent state of tension, mutually restraining one another, and the problem of moderation is, in our day, formulable and soluble only in terms of them." *Theory and Practice of Modern Government,* rev. ed. (New York: Dial Press, Inc., 1934), p. 84.

50. Max Lerner, *op. cit.,* p. 237.

51. Prior to the war consumers' co-operatives, most of which are organized on the Rochdale plan, included over forty million members in some sixty thousand societies in thirty or more countries. For an excellent discussion of the movement, see the article "Consumer's Co-operation" by Charles Gide in the *Encyclopaedia of the Social Sciences* (New York: The Macmillan Company, 1935, IV, 285-91.

The states of California under Governor Brown and New York under Governor Rockefeller have pioneered in the consumer area by providing consumer counsels.

Chapter 13

1. Years ago Eduard Bernstein, father of German "revisionism," expressed unconcern with "the final arrangements of things." "I have at no time had an excessive interest in the future, beyond general principles; I have not been able to read to the end any picture of the future. My thoughts and efforts are concerned with the duties of the present and the near future, and I only busy myself with the perspectives beyond as far as they give me a line of conduct for suitable action now . . ." *Evolutionary Socialism* (New York: B. W. Huebsch, 1912), pp. xv-xvi.

2. Russell Davenport, "The Greatest Opportunity on Earth," *Fortune,* October 1949.

3. *Fortune,* October 1944, p. 162.

4. Sumner Slichter, "The Businessman in a Laboristic Economy," *Fortune,* September 1949.

5. 17,049,000 workers were members of trade unions in 1960. This was 68,000 fewer than in 1959, and 341,000 below the 1956 figure. Labor leaders attribute the decline in part to so-called "Right-to-work" laws and a growth in the size of the white collar group, which is notoriously difficult to organize. In all, about a fourth of the nation's total labor force and about a third of the employees in nonfarming occupations belong to labor unions. Only last year the AFL-CIO abandoned a costly attempt to organize farm workers. Liberals loudly deplored the surrender.

6. The original provision was for 25 cents an hour for the first year, then 30 cents an hour, and, by the end of seven years, 40 cents an hour, provided, however, that the higher wage did not throw people out of work, in the event of which the minimum might revert to 30 cents.

7. Pamphlet of the Department of Research and Education, Congress of Industrial Organizations. Cf. also J. Chernick and G. C. Hellickson, *Guaranteed Annual Wage* (Minneapolis: University of Minnesota Press, 1945).

8. November 1946.

9. The importance of the problem is underscored by the following paragraph from E. H. Downey, *Workmen's Compensation* (New York: The Macmillan Company, 1924). "Peace has its perils no less than war . . . Of deaths alone [from work accidents] the twelve months' total is four times the number killed and mortally wounded in the battle of Gettysburg; of permanent injuries the annual sum surpasses the yearly average of the Civil War. The total casualties of the American Expeditionary Force in the World War [I] did not equal the casualties to American workmen in peaceful employments between April 1917 and the signing of the Armistice. The toll of life and limb exacted by American industries during the second decade of the twentieth century exceeds the Nation's losses in battle from the Declaration of Independence to the present day [1924]" (p. 1). Cited by Abraham Epstein, *Insecurity* (New York: Random House, Inc., 1938), p. 578.

10. The major groups excepted from the operation of the plan are railroad workers, civil service employees and others already provided for under insurance plans administered by the federal or by state governments.

11. There are almost 16 million people over 65 years of age in the United States and about 80 percent of them have incomes from all sources of less than $2,000 yearly. Their rate of increase is about 400,000 a year and by 1970 they will number 20 million.

In 1950 they comprised 8.1 percent of the population and this will grow to 10 percent by 1975.

12. The activities of the American Medical Association in opposing public medicine will be seen in better perspective if it is noted that in the past it has opposed workmen's compensation, tuberculosis sanatoria, health centers, maternal and child health services, group practice, and voluntary health insurance. It now opposes federal aid to medical education, expansion of school health services, and disability insurance.

13. In 1960, an attempt was made by President Kennedy, then a Senator, to put through legislation providing limited medical care for the aged under the Social Security System. It failed and instead Congress passed the Kerr-Mills Law which increases Federal matching funds for medical benefits for aged persons already on relief and provides some funds for state use to help other older people who can prove they need money for heavy medical expenses. Conservatives introduced the bill to obstruct the extension of social insurance, even on this limited scale, to medical care.

14. The separation of programs of occupational and non-occupational disability insurance is an anachronism and has no justification. The need is the same in either case.

15. The liberal-sponsored Wagner-Murray-Dingell Bill of 1945 provided unemployment benefits for the victims of illness and injury, but the bill went down to defeat.

16. Sir William Beveridge, *Full Employment in a Free Society* (New York: W. W. Norton & Company, Inc., 1945), pp. 408-9.

17. Sir William Beveridge, *op. cit.,* p. 20.

18. "The Extent and Nature of Frictional Unemployment," Study Paper No. 6, Bureau of Labor Statistics, November 19, 1959.

19. Cf. above, pp. 213-19.

20. *Hearings,* Joint Economic Committee, January 1961, p. 295.

21. *Ibid.,* p. 29. The British White Paper on Employment Policy (May 1944) and a similar statement by the Canadian government (1945) represent the first official recognition of the principles affirmed by Beveridge.

22. Alvin H. Hansen, *Economic Policy and Full Employment* (New York: McGraw-Hill Book Company, Inc., 1947), pp. 16-17.

23. *Loc. cit.*

24. "Management Poll," *Fortune,* May 1944. Quite apart from the question of government intervention, the employer is necessarily a victim of conflicting tendencies, as far as full employment is concerned. This becomes evident when we consider the duality of his role as a seller of goods and a buyer of labor. As a seller of goods he favors full employment, which increases the number of his customers. But as a buyer of labor he fears full employment,

which increases labor absenteeism and turnover, enhances labor's bargaining power, and renders labor less docile in general. Hence a labor reserve of some five million unemployed—the figure we roughly approximated in the first part of 1950—may be regarded with equanimity as subclinical.

25. Sir William Beveridge, *op. cit.*, pp. 18-19.

26. The concern of Congress for semantic niceties decreed that the Federal government may not "assure" conditions of full employment, but it may "create and maintain" them; the government is not committed to spending what is needed, but it may "utilize its resources"; it may not seek the goal of "full employment"— the term is never mentioned in the final draft—but it may provide the "conditions under which there are employment opportunities, including self-employment, for all who are able, willing and seeking work"; and the President may not submit a "National Production and Employment Budget" but he must submit an "Economic Report."

Two informative books dealing with the Employment Act are *Economics in the Public Service* by Edwin E. Nourse (New York: Harcourt, Brace & Co., 1953), and Stephen K. Bailey's *Congress Makes a Law* (New York: Columbia University Press, 1950). Nourse was first chairman of the President's Council and came to differ vigorously with his more liberal colleague on the Council and the successor to the chairmanship, Leon Keyserling.

27. It is significant that President Kennedy's first action during the recession in which he found himself was to propose increases in transfer payments by temporary extension of unemployment compensation, aid to the children of needy unemployed under the aid-to-dependent children programs, improvement of old-age, survivors, and disability insurance.

28. A. P. Lerner's comments are typical. He writes, "The national debt is not a burden on posterity because if posterity pays the debt it will be paying it to the same posterity that will be alive at the time when the payment is made. The national debt is not a burden on the nation because every cent in interest or repayment that is collected from the citizens as taxpayers to meet the debt service is received by the citizens as government bondholders. It is not true that the national debt 'must be repaid sometime' any more than it is true that all the banks must call in their debts and repay their depositors on some catastrophic day or that all firms and corporations will have to be dissolved some day to repay the obligations to the individuals who invested in them." *The Economics of Control* (New York: The Macmillan Company, 1944), p. 303.

29. "The Domestic Economy," insert to *Fortune,* December 1942.

30. The term "deficit" as applied to the federal budget has misleading implications. United States government accounting is based

on cash receipts from taxes and total cash disbursements, not on "accrual" accounting as with business. No distinction is made between TVA (self-liquidating projects) and Congressional salaries (current expense); both are disbursements and may create a "deficit."

31. From the point of view of an individual, spending on capital goods would be regarded as savings, i.e., as income not spent on consumer goods. Savings may mean this, i.e., funds not expended on consumption, or it may mean funds held in a cash hoard. The context should make clear the sense in which "savings" is used. From the point of view of an individual, investment would include expenditures on bonds and shares; "investment" as used here is limited to capital expenditures, i.e., funds used to build factories, buy raw materials, and the like.

32. Beveridge summarizes the position as follows: "The amount which any community will try to save is governed, not primarily by the outlets for saving, i.e., the opportunities for investment, but by the total income of the community and its distribution; broadly speaking, if incomes are evenly distributed, less will be saved out of the total than if they are unevenly distributed. The amount which any community will seek to invest is governed, not primarily by the amount of savings available for investment, but by expectation of profits." *Op. cit.,* p. 94.

33. The violation of this principle was one of the basic inadequacies of the prewar spending program. According to the National Resources Planning Board, the tax burden for public aid fell most heavily on families with incomes of less than $1,000 a year. This was the result of state reliance on sales taxes for relief revenues and the use of pay-roll taxes to finance social security.

34. Cf. "Full Employment Through Tax Policy?" Gerhard Colin in *Essays in Public Finance and Fiscal Policy* (New York: Oxford University Press, 1955).

35. A comprehensive program of public works, and the fiscal policy associated with it, by no means exhausts the liberal program for coping with mass unemployment. A variety of monetary policies, such as a reduction in the discount rate, the purchase of government bonds on the open market, a reduction on reserve requirements, etc., is also included.

36. Liberal economists have repaired this gap in recent years. See below, pp. 362-64. For an example of more severe professional criticism, see Arthur F. Burns' "Economic Research and the Keynesian Thinking of Our Times," in *The Frontiers of Economic Knowledge* (Princeton: Princeton University Press, 1954), pp. 3-25.

37. See John Maynard Keynes, *The General Theory,* pp. 372-73. See also, "Keynes, the Economist," by Joseph A. Schumpeter in *The New Economics, Keynes' Influence on Theory and Public*

Policy (New York: Alfred A. Knopf, 1950), p. 99. This volume is a useful compendium of comment on Keynes' work.

38. P. J. Strayer, "The Individual Income Tax and Income Distribution," *American Economic Review,* Proceedings, XLV, No. 2 (May, 1954), pp. 430-31. Cf. also, J. Keith Butters, "Taxation, Incentives and Financial Capacity," *American Economic Review,* Proceedings, XLV, No. 2 (May, 1954), pp. 504-19.

39. *Hearings,* Joint Economic Committee (October 29, 1959), pp. 2996, 3008. Professor Heller's figures are based on studies by J. A. Pechman and W. F. Hellmuth, Jr., for the Ways and Means Committee.

40. *Goals for Americans* (New York: Prentice-Hall, Inc., 1960), p. 25.

41. H. R. Bowen, "The Personal Income Tax and the Economy," *The Annals of the American Academy of Political and Social Science,* November, 1949, p. 120.

42. Alvin H. Hansen, *Economic Issues of the 1960's,* p. 105.

43. J. M. Keynes, *General Theory of Employment, Interest and Money* (London: Macmillan & Company, Ltd., 1936), pp. 129-30.

44. One of the fiercest campaigns in American political history was waged over Upton Sinclair's 1934 EPIC (End Poverty in California) movement, which was based on such a proposal.

45. Conservatives simultaneously deny that there is such a creed and that the Republican Party reflects it. In truth, until the truculence and increasing power of the USSR produced an acute anxiety neurosis among those who have allied themselves with the Birch Society and like organizations, there was a virtual consensus concerning major policy issues among the overwhelming majority of businessmen, and there is no indication in the legislation it has opposed or supported that the Republican Party has gone contrary to this consensus even once.

46. Walter Lippmann has commented that "The great bitterness and violence of the 'thirties was due to the fact that the central issue then, unlike the central issue now, was a change in the internal balance of power among social groups. For many who felt that they were hurt by this change Roosevelt was regarded as a traitor to his class. The cutting edge of their bitterness was not that he provided welfare measures for the poor but that he pushed through changes in the relative status and power and privileges of banks, corporations, unions, farmers and Negroes." Lippmann believes that the issue is now largely settled and hence does not complicate the agenda of the Kennedy administration (*New York Herald Tribune,* October 27, 1960).

47. Adlai Stevenson, "America's Broken Mainspring," A. Powell Davies Memorial Lecture, Washington, D. C. Reprinted in *The Progressive* (March, 1959), pp. 9-13.

Chapter 14

1. This is, to a considerable extent, a result of partial disfranchisement brought about by alien status or southern chicanery or gerrymandering or hyper-mobility (as of migrant workers) or sheer ignorance. Minority groups or the elderly, if they vote as a bloc, may well hold the balance of power and may be able on occasion to swing an election, but this is far short of the power to initiate drastic social reconstruction.

2. November 13-20, 1959.

3. Department of State *Bulletin,* p. 760, May 25, 1959.

4. For example, W. W. Rostow (Massachusetts Institute of Technology's Center for International Studies), Oley Hoeffding (Economics Division of the Rand Corporation), author of "Soviet National Income and Product in 1928" and, in *Foreign Affairs,* April, 1959, of "The Soviet Seven Year Plan."

5. We must, of course, be on guard against exaggerations. Academician S. G. Strumilin, dean of contemporary Soviet economists, has just published data confirming Western charges that Soviet statistics on industrial growth are greatly inflated. As a result of his calculations, the Soviet statisticians will be forced to scale down the officially announced growth rate of 11 percent from 1955 to 1956 to 8 percent. American observers have already made allowances only now noted by Strumilin.

6. In its 1959 annual report on its studies of economic growth the National Bureau of Economic Research declares that "production in the United States has risen twice as fast as labor and tangible capital input combined, over the past two thirds of a century" and that, while a large part of the explanation is not yet determined, it is clear that the large and growing investments in education and in science and technology have been more important than the role of tangible capital goods. Cited by W. W. Heller in "Employment, Growth and Price Levels," *Hearings,* Joint Economic Committee, October 29, 1959.

7. Nicholas DeWitt, *Education and Professional Employment in the U.S.S.R.* (Superintendent of Documents, U.S. Government Printing Office, Washington, D. C.). Ours is still a commanding lead in the number of Nobel awards won. (See *Technological Review,* April, 1960.)

8. *Hearings,* Joint Economic Committee, "Comparisons of the United States and Soviet Economies", Part III, p. 587.

9. Clearly, one of these concerns the declining death rate and expanding birth rate of the so-called Malthusian areas.

10. Repayment (in dollars) can be spread over 50 years, and terms will be based "primarily on a judgment of the recipient country's overall capacity to repay." This is in contrast to the

restrictive, self-liquidating-project standard used by the Eisenhower Administration.

11. Address, Iowa Farm Bureau Federation, printed in the *Bulletin*, Department of State, Dec. 14, 1959, p. 855.

12. Address to the Overseas Press Club of America, "The Challenge of Soviet Economic Expansion," printed in *Bulletin*, Department of State, p. 761, May 25, 1959.

13. Cited by P. Einzig in *The Economic Consequences of Automation* (London: Secker and Warburg, 1957), pp. 5-7.

14. For an informative study, see R. A. Brady, *Organization, Automation, and Society* (Berkeley: University of California Press, 1961).

15. Norbert Wiener, *The Human Use of Human Beings* (2d. ed., rev.; Garden City: Doubleday & Company, 1954). The pioneer study of automation is John Diebold's *Automation: The Advent of the Automatic Factory* (New York: Van Nostrand, 1952).

16. "The median family income in urban areas is about $5,000 a year. If the family goes by the old rule of thumb and pays one quarter of income for housing, it will be able to afford roughly $100 a month. Since the family will have one or two children, it will need two bedrooms, at the very minimum, a total of four rooms—in other words, housing that rents for $25 a room.

"This is not being built. Except for public housing, for which the $5,000 family is disqualified, redevelopers cannot put up new housing in the city that rents for less than $35 a room per month, and in the great majority of new projects, the minimum lies somewhere between $40 and $50 a room.

". . . Barring any wholesale change of attitude . . . new housing will continue to be beyond the reach of the median family. And what of the people under the median? Twenty-five percent of American families who make between $3,500 and $5,000 [are] too rich for public housing, too poor for middle-income housing." "Are Cities Un-American?" William H. Whyte, Jr., *Fortune*, September, 1957, p. 126.

17. By the year 2000, when children now born will have reached maturity, the population of California will equal the present population of Great Britain. At a daily population increase of 1,500 people, California is consuming 375 acres of land every twenty-four hours. This amounts to 140,000 acres annually; and, at present densities, California can expect 3 million additional acres to be consumed by 1980—well over half the area of Massachusetts.

18. Quoted in *Sports Illustrated*, March 28, April 4, 1960.

19. Statement by Edward Eichler, Jr. of Eichler Homes before Assembly Interim Committee on Governmental Efficiency and Economy of the California Legislature, Los Angeles, California, September 28, 1961.

Besides changing the traditional practice of giving private enterprise an almost free hand by insisting on more government guidance, it must be evident that the existing pattern of local jurisdictions is wholly unsuited to the requirements of metropolitan areas and must be modified greatly.

Chapter 15

1. See above, pp. 215-221.
2. *Hearings,* Joint Economic Committee, 1961, Appendix, pp. 703-4.
3. Cf. Seymour E. Harris, ed., *Saving American Capitalism* (Alfred A. Knopf, New York, 1948), pp. 68-69.
4. *Ibid.,* p. 85.
5. Other examples are "fair trade" laws, tariff supports, rate controls on public utilities.
6. See above, Chapter 13.
7. A McGraw-Hill survey indicates that for the period 1958-1962 depreciation allowances already covered 94 percent of the proposed spending on plant and equipment by manufacturing companies. Although later surveys reduced this percentage in some measure for industry as a whole, there are impressive indications that it was conservative in many cases. In 1958-1959 the Ford Motor Co. spent only 45.5 percent of its depreciation allowance on plant and equipment. General Motors Corporation spent $589.3 million or 70.7 percent of its depreciation allowance of $883.9 million during the same period. The testimony of Walter Reuther before the Joint Economic Committee is extremely interesting on this subject. (*Hearings,* February 9, 1961, pp. 121-23.)
8. President Kennedy has asked for legislation giving him standby authority, subject to Congressional veto, to make temporary reductions in the income tax not to exceed 5 percentage points. This would amount to about $5 billion for a six-month period. He has also requested that the system of extended unemployment benefits provided by Congress as special temporary legislation on the occasion of the last two recessions be made permanent.
9. Foreign capital would be attracted by a high level of effective demand. Moreover, high levels of demand would encourage the plant modernization necessary to improving our competitive position abroad.
10. *Hearings,* Joint Economic Committee, October 29, 1959, p. 2959.
11. *Hearings,* Joint Economic Committee, January 30, 1959, p. 208. Cf. also, the testimony of Professor Walter H. Heller on the same day.
12. Sumner Slichter, "Inflation—A Problem of Shrinking Importance," in *Potentials of the American Economy,* pp. 134-49 (Cambridge: Harvard University Press, 1961).

13. *Hearings,* Joint Economic Committee, October 29, 1959, p. 2960.

14. The automobile workers' union sought to make pricing policy a subject of negotiation in the great strike of 1946, but was rebuffed. In 1958, the same union offered to adjust wage demands if manufacturers would cut car prices by one hundred dollars. In 1948, the textile workers' union offered to waive wage demands if employers would reduce prices.

15. In testimony before the Joint Economic Committee, Walter Reuther favored a plan similar to the one proposed in a bill of Senator O'Mahoney's. The plan proposes:

> the creation of a special government agency to hold hearings on proposed price increases by corporations which have substantial power to administer prices in their industries. Any corporation which controls more than a given percentage of sales in any industry—possibly 25 percent—would be required to notify the agency of any proposed price increase, and to testify and to produce all pertinent facts and records at a public hearing before such price increase could be made effective. If the corporation maintained that a wage or other economic demand by a trade union would necessitate a proposed price increase, the union as well as the corporation would be required to attend the hearing and to justify its demands. The agency, however, would have no power to control wages or prices. Its power would be limited to bringing out the facts . . . and making them available for public scrutiny . . . a public airing of the facts would in the majority of cases be sufficient to restrain unjustifiable increases. (*Hearings,* February 9, 1961, p. 121.)

The proposal would appear to be an eminently fair and reasonable one.

16. The average interest rate on the total outstanding Federal public debt was 28 percent higher in 1959 than in 1952, an advance about three times as rapid as the increase in consumer prices during the same period. For the seven year period 1953-59 interest charges on the Federal debt were more than $5 billion higher than if they had remained at the 1952 levels. During the same period interest rates on new general obligation bonds issued by state and local governments increased 68 percent, forcing them to incur excess costs of about $550 million. Excess interest rates paid by private borrowers for the same period amounted to about $17.5 billion. For all forms of debt, public and private, the total was $23 billion—better described as a hurricanefall than a windfall for lending institutions.

17. See above, p. 245.

18. The point is well made by Galbraith in his *The Affluent Society,* cf. p. 262.

19. This suggests the fatal flaw in Galbraith's otherwise plausible argument in *The Affluent Society* that our emphasis on production is "Highly irrational and founded on tradition and social myth" (p. 124). Quite apart from his overestimate of our affluence, Galbraith ignores the central issue. Which alternative is politically more feasible, that is, easier of attainment: government intervention which will assure a national product so large that expansion of the public sector and provision for necessitous groups would be relatively painless; or intervention to utilize our increasing supply of man-hours to reduce everyone's workload without reducing income, and to redistribute existing income in favor of helping low-income groups and expanding the public sector? From a political point of view the first alternative is plainly far more feasible.

20. John Maynard Keynes, *General Theory of Employment, Interest and Money* (London: Macmillan and Company, Ltd., 1936), p. 379.

21. W. W. Rostow, "The Problem of Achieving and Maintaining a High Rate of Economic Growth: A Historian's View," *American Economic Review*, Vol. L, No. 2, May, 1960, p. 111.

22. It becomes increasingly clear that, thanks to the slowness of the business recovery, the Kennedy Administration will fail to achieve its hoped-for budget balance by the end of fiscal 1962 and that a deficit is likely for fiscal 1963 as well. However, the size of the deficit depends on whether the calculation is based on what is called the "administrative budget," which is the traditional method, or by the so-called "national income" system of accounting, which provides a more accurate picture of Government expenditures and the effect of such expenditures on the economy. If the latter, more realistic method of accounting is used, the size of the deficit will be significantly less, if not negligible.

23. The reference here is to tax *evasion* and not tax avoidance which is referred to elsewhere (cf. above, pp. 322-323). One of the mysteries of our federal tax system is that taxes payable by those who work for a wage or salary are deducted at the source (and hence not evaded), while taxes payable on dividends and interest are not collected at the source, and hence evaded in the amount of about $900 million each year. Another mystery is the failure to expand the staff of the Bureau of Internal Revenue, although it is known that more thorough review of reports would yield many times the outlay for personnel.

24. F. J. Dewhurst and Associates, *America's Needs and Resources* (New York: The Twentieth Century Fund, 1955). Figures are from the "New Survey." See also, "Federal Expenditure Policy for Economic Growth and Stability," Joint Economic Committee, Nov. 5, 1957, especially Chapters VIII-XV.

25. Cf. R. A. Musgrave's *The Theory of Public Finance* (New

York: McGraw-Hill, 1959). A bibliography of recent literature on this important topic is provided (pp. 116-117).

26. Even Robert Taft, idol of right-wing conservatives, favored public housing and the Employment Act.

27. As Governor of California, Warren dared affront organized medicine by proposing that the State of California initiate a program of compulsory medical insurance.

28. *The New York Times,* February 15, 1959, p. 44.

29. *Hearings,* Joint Economic Committee, January 27, 1959, pp. 29-30.

30. "We shall reduce," President Eisenhower said in his first budget message, "the share of the national income which is spent by the government" (January 21, 1954). The President kept his word.

31. The *New York Herald Tribune,* January 21, 1960.

32. Barry A. Goldwater, *Conscience of a Conservative,* pp. 10-12 (Victor Publishing Co., Shepherdsville, Kentucky, 1960). The quotation marks around "benefits" are Senator Goldwater's.

33. *Ibid.,* p. 62.

34. Report on Manufacturers, Hamilton Papers, 2nd series. See *Alexander Hamilton and the Founding of the Nation,* R. B. Morris, ed. (New York: The Dial Press, 1957), pp. 269-70.

35. "The New Nationalism," p. 17, in *Social Justice and Popular Rule,* Vol. 17, *Works of Theodore Roosevelt* (National Edition).

36. *Ibid.,* p. 14.

37. Nicholas Murray Butler, speech, American Club, Paris, June 11, 1931. Cited by Charles Beard, *America in Midpassage* (New York: Macmillan Co., 1939), pp. 100-1.

38. On the other hand, large industrial combines are still subject to nationalization and the control of great economic power is still "the central task of a liberal economic policy." However, it is now affirmed that any concentration of power is dangerous, "even in the hands of the state."

39. C. A. R. Crosland, "Socialism in a Prosperous World," *New Leader,* February 29, 1960, pp. 12-14.

40. C. A. R. Crosland, *The Future of Socialism,* p. 498 (The Macmillan Company, New York, 1957).

Adler, Mortimer J., 270

America's Needs and Resources, by F. J. Dewhurst and Associates, 376, 416, 438

Atomism, psychological, as a creed of classical liberalism, 41-45; defined, 41; and theory of knowledge, 42; and view of society, 43-45

Automation, and productivity, 214; impact of, on industry, 345; promises and problems of, 346

Bagehot, Walter, 81, 144

Bain, Alexander, 33

Beard, Charles, 78, 79, 80-81, 107, 394

Bentham, Jeremy, 26, 32, 33, 39, 44, 45, 66, 70, 118, 124, 125, 177, 249, 391, 394; and hedonism, 28, 29, 31, 46, 161; "hedonistic calculus" of, 30-31, 36, 401, 404; "felicific calculus" of, 34, 36, 140, 242; and universal education, 35; on emotions produced by labor, 38, 390; and fruits of labor, 49-50; *Fragment on Government,* 67, 135, 398; on usury, 71; and national rights, 115; on universal suffrage, 121

Benthamism, 14, 26, 44, 72, 81, 83, 140, 161, 178, 267, 404

Berge, Wendel, 194-95, 196

Berle, Adolph A., Jr., 18, 190, 269-70, 271, 276-77, 280, 281

Beveridge, William, 84, 308, 309, 311-12, 313, 314, 430, 432

Big Business, and monopolistic practices, 187-97; role of technology and organization in, 251-53; power of, 251-53, 277-79; managerial control of, 269-72; pressure by, on government, 275-77; and "corporate citizenship," 275-77

Burke, Edmund, 26, 129; on government, 66; as liberal spokesman, 114, 115

Butler, Nicholas Murray, 380

Capital goods, production of, 226, 227

Carlyle, Thomas, 76, 86, 178

Casals, Pablo, 329

Cities, problems of, 254, 347-53

Clark, John Bates, 33, 171, 194, 400-01, 407

Cochran, Thomas C., 18

Commission on National Goals, proposed, 368, 374-76

Common Market, 232

Communism, 13, 242, 263, 264, 282, 284, 344, 380, 382, 426-27

Competition, 186-98; role of, in classical liberalism, 142-44; and theory of social Darwinism, 144-45; interfered with, by monopoly, 186-97; role of, in innovations, 193-96

Conservation, of natural resources, 254

Conservatism, 268, 365, 385, 386; origin of, in classical liberalism, 23; and law of human nature, 27; contrasted with contemporary liberalism, 154, 378; and level of living, 234; and problem of priorities, 240, 376-78; and government planning, 249; and problems of cities, 352; and tax questions, 379; and welfare, 379-80; role of, as political force, 382-83; effects of, on contemporary liberalism, 382-83

Consumer, 230; role of, in market economy, 182-86, 237; and freedom of choice, 183-85; and control of prices, 185-86, 193-97; and role of advertising, 237-38, 240-41

Consumer goods, production of, 226, 230, 233, 241

Cooley, Charles H., 42-43
Coolidge, Calvin, 61, 329, 422

Darwin, Charles, 144, 166
Davenport, Russell, 298
Dewey, John, 13, 18, 390, 405; on motivation, 37, 162-63; on theory of knowledge, 164; on labor *vs.* creativity, 167-68
Dicey, Albert V., 14, 15, 56, 81, 82, 83, 84, 178, 252
Diderot, Denis, 26, 32
Dillon, Douglas, 213, 335, 337, 343, 377
Dulles, Allen, 213, 335, 337

Economic power, 381; and ownership of wealth, 266-68; managerial control of, 269-72; pressure on government by, 272-73; and "corporate citizenship," 275-77; and size in business, 277-82
Economic recovery, and compensatory spending, 317-24
Education, financing of, 239, 370
Egoism, psychological, as a creed of classical liberalism, 28-34; as a "selfish system," 28-29, 157-59; and law of human nature, 33; fallacy of, 157-60
Eisenhower, Dwight D., 168, 244, 329, 335, 337, 341, 355, 362, 365, 377, 435, 439
Engels, Friedrich, 153, 267
England, 50, 66, 83-86, 107-09, 112-13, 114, 117-18, 130, 135, 232, 287, 398; liberalism in, 13, 15, 38, 42; poor laws in, 55-56; social insurance in, 59, 304; reform legislation in, 81-82; and universal suffrage, 121-22; beginnings of welfare state in, 297; conservatism in, 382
English Utilitarians, The, Leslie Stephen's, 15

Fascism, 149, 283, 285, 426
Founding Fathers, 77-78, 79, 132, 133, 250, 266, 397; and doctrine of laissez faire, 80; and Constitution, 107; and division of power in government, 117; and fear of the mob, 120; requirements for suffrage of, 121; and right of revolution, 133
France, 50, 67, 118, 130, 232, 400; liberalism in, 13, 15, 38, 42; Revolution in, 26, 112-13, 114, 135; social insurance in, 59; and Declaration of Rights, 115; and universal suffrage, 122; conservatism in, 382; and social reforms, 427
Frankfurter, Felix, 167, 421
Free market, role of competition in, 142-44, 240; social failures of, 146; triumph of, in present-day production, 146-48; role of supply and demand in, 181-82; economic failure of, 246-47, 249; and Welfare State, 300, 381
From Wealth to Welfare, Girvetz', 13, 426

Galbraith, J. Kenneth, 193-94, 219, 220, 241, 410, 426, 437-38; "countervailing powers," doctrine of, 18, 280-81, 286, 326, 327; and regressive taxes, 373; on technological innovations, 424
Germany, 428; social insurance in, 59, 304; causes of Nazism in, 283-86; Germany, West, taxation in, 323; conservatism in, 381, 382
Goldwater, Barry A., 378-79
Good Society, The, Lippmann's, 18, 146, 283, 401, 402
Government, 82-89; as instrument of the state, 66; functions of, 70-81; by constitution, 103-110; separation of powers in, 116-19; and suffrage, as check on, 120-23; positive role of, 249, 255-56; and big business, 252-53, 272-82; bureaucracy in, 257-58; doctrine of laissez faire in, *see* Laissez faire, doctrine of
Great Britain, *see* England
Growth of Philosophical Radicalism, The, Elie Halévy's, 15

Growth rate, 208, 210, 212-13, 370; and unemployment, 213-15; and productive potentialities, 353-57; and public works program, 357-62; and inflation, 362-66; and national goals, 366-68; and priorities for public purposes, 371

Hamilton, Alexander, 79, 110, 118, 125, 133, 379, 398, 399
Hansen, Alvin H., 219, 232, 240, 312, 313, 323
Hart, James, 258
Hartley, David, 31, 39, 42
Hayek, Friedrich A., 13, 18, 145, 402, 412-13; on causes of Nazism, 283-85; and interventionism, 287
Hedonism, psychological, 33, 34, 36-37, 157, 401, 404; a creed of classical liberalism, 28; and goal of greatest happiness to greatest number, 29-30; and "hedonistic calculus," 30-31, 140, 161, 171, 407; fallacy of, 160-61
Heller, Walter W., 210-11, 312, 354
History of European Liberalism, The, Ruggiero's, 15
Hobbes, Thomas, 38, 127-28; and human nature, 28, 391; "selfish system" of, 28-29; *Leviathan,* 28-29, 125-26; on revolution, 133
Holmes, Oliver Wendell (Justice), 75, 77, 80, 88, 302
Hoover, Herbert, 13, 58, 88-89, 147, 205, 233, 291
Hume, David, 124, 135; on mind, 42; as speculative philosopher, 114-15

Income, distribution of, 225-31
Inflation, 347-53, 362-66
Intellectualism, as a creed of classical liberalism, 34-36; and "felicific calculus," 34; role of reason in, 35-36, 169-70; and nonrationality in conduct, 35, 169-74; undermined by rejection of psychological quietism, 169-70

Interventionism, and Galbraith's "countervailing powers," 18, 280, 286, 326, 327; by government, 256-61; various devices of, 286-96; and Welfare State, 298; and unemployment, 314; and productive potentialities, 359-60
Investment, opportunities in, 319-20; and tax and credit policies, 360-61

James, William, 159-60, 164, 331, 404
Jefferson, Thomas, 79, 81, 112, 114, 121, 123, 250; and doctrine of laissez faire, 80, 395; and Declaration of Independence, 124, 130-31; on revolution, 131, 132; on government, 249
Jevons, William Stanley, 33, 140, 161, 407
Johnston, Eric, 231-32, 420

Kelso, Lewis A., 270
Kennan, George, 330, 339
Kennedy, John F., 244, 267, 273, 295, 308, 322, 330, 341, 352, 354, 356, 358, 361, 370, 414, 430, 431 433, 436, 438
Keynes, John Maynard, 13, 285, 319, 320, 321, 324, 325, 357, 358, 369-70, 382, 403, 406, 432-33
Keyserling, Leon, 212, 219, 359, 431
Krock, Arthur, 165
Kuznets, Simon, 228-29, 417

Labor, free choice of work for, 53, 197-98; improved conditions of, 167-68, 197; mobility of, 197; *see also* Trade unions
Laissez faire, doctrine of, 18, 81, 82, 84-85, 86, 87, 88-89, 144, 258, 324, 396; and classical liberalism, 18, 66; and John Stuart Mill, 72, 74, 75, 80; and Spencer, 77, 80; and Adam Smith, 80; and Founding Fathers, 80; and Thomas Jefferson, 80, 395; and Jean Baptiste Say, 80
Lampman, R. J., 230, 418

Laski, Harold, 14, 15, 85-86, 396, 397, 426

Law and Public Opinion in England During the 19th Century, Dicey's, 14, 15

Lecky, William E. H., 81, 119

Lerner, Max, 266, 294, 421-22, 427

Lewis, W. Arthur, 18

Liberalism, beginnings of, 13, 23; classical and contemporary, defined, 14, 17-18; and various spheres of interest, 15; as a battlefield, 17

Liberalism, classical, defined, 14, 17-18; as philosophy of life, 15; and doctrine of laissez faire, *see* Laissez faire, doctrine of; role of revolution in, 23; impact of physical sciences on, 23-24; and social responsibilities, 26; and law of human nature, 27

Liberalism, classical, various creeds: egoism, 28-34; intellectualism, 34-36; quietism, 36-41; atomism, 41-45

Liberalism, classical, present-day status of psychological creeds in, 45-46; and private property, 49-53; and free choice of work, 53-54; theory of rewards and labor in, 54-55; and relief for needy, 55-58; theory of deprivation as incentive in, 54-63; and distrust of state, 66-70

Liberalism, classical, on functions of government, various opinions: Bentham, 70-71; John Stuart Mill, 72-75; Spencer, 75-77; Founding Fathers, 77-80; Jefferson, 80-81

Liberalism, classical, and cultural laissez faire in America, 77-81; and beginnings of social legislation in England, 81-86; and political laissez faire in America, 86-89

Liberalism, classical, and protection of persons and property, 92-93; and state's enforcement of contract, 93-96; and open market, 96; and official standards, 96-97; and transportation facilities, 97-98; and freedom of competition, 98-99; and various meliorative functions of the state, 99-101

Liberalism, classical, and constitutional government, 103-10; and rights and liberties, 110-11; doctrine of natural rights in, 111-16; and governmental division of power, 116-19; suffrage as check on tyranny in, 120-23; as a child of revolution, 124-36

Liberalism, classical, and division of labor and exchange, 137-38; theory of "natural harmony of interests" in, 138-39, 146; role of price in, 139-41; and law of supply and demand, 141-42; role of competition in, 142-44; theory of social Darwinism in, 144-45; and free market's social failures, 146; and present-day production triumphs, 146-48

Liberalism, classical, judged on consequences, 178-79; and individual liberty, 263; and governmental interventionism, 282; and contemporary liberalism, review of, 385-87

Liberalism, contemporary, defined, 14, 17-18, 153-54; and the positive state, 17, 249, 250, 256; and law of human nature, 27; as critic of classical liberalism's foundations, 154-55; and fallacy of psychological egoism and hedonism, 157-61; and view of functional role of mind, 163-64

Liberalism, contemporary, as critic of psychological quietism, 164-65; and question of initiative and incentives, 165-66; and creative impulse *vs.* profit motive, 165-66; as critic of industrial system's failures, 166-67; plea for improved labor conditions by, 167-68; and undermining of influence of intellectualism, 169-74; and myth of "rational man," 169-74; and social welfare, 173-75, 178-79

Liberalism, contemporary, and question of productive potentialities, 223; and view of waste

Liberalism, contemporary (*Cont.*) of productive energies, 240; demand for Welfare State by, 298; and economic security, 299-316; and national goals, 330, 369-76; and priorities for public purposes, 371; contrasted with conservatism, 378; effects of conservatism on, 282-83; and classical liberalism, review of, 385-87

Lilienthal, David, 280

Lippmann, Walter, 13, 18, 66, 84, 146, 251, 283, 330, 378, 401-02, 433

Locke, John, 44, 47, 49, 53, 124, 125, 127, 130, 136, 153; as hedonist, 31; on knowledge, 38-39; on mind, 42, 163; on doctrine of natural rights, 113-14, 115, 290, 398; on government, 117, 249; on revolution, 128-29, 133-35; on power *vs.* freedom, 265; on human understanding, 390

Loeb, Harold, 206

McCormick, Robert, 423

McDougall, William, 163-64, 170

MacLeish, Archibald, 328

Madison, James, 114, 118, 119, 131, 132, 399

Malthus, Thomas Robert, 49, 56; *Essay on Population,* 32, 144, 392; and the "dismal science," 35; on birth control, 38; on overpopulation, 146, 173

Mandeville, Bernard de, 31, 139

Marshall, Alfred, 33, 40, 140, 157, 407-08, 181

Marx, Karl, 135, 153, 169-70, 267, 403, 407

Marxism, 149, 283, 287, 373, 381

Mead, Walter, 16, 164

Meade, J. E., 18

Means, Gardiner, 269-70, 271

Mill, James, 29, 32, 36, 81, 390; on role of pleasure, 46; on state power, 103; on universal suffrage, 121

Mill, John Stuart, 33, 43, 50, 51, 81, 123, 254, 390, 396; on role of pleasure, 46, 161, 404; and nonhedonistic views, 391, 404; on work, 54-55; and doctrine of laissez faire, 72, 74, 75, 80; on relief for poor, 73; *On Liberty,* 74; on universal suffrage, 121; on price-fixing, 188; on taxation, 391

Monopoly, and effect on competition, 186-97

Montesquieu, C. L., 117-18, 249, 292, 391, 392, 428

Mumford, Lewis, 254, 352

Nathan, Robert, 207

Nazism, 283-86

Newton, Isaac, 23, 24, 28, 111, 166, 176, 407

Niebuhr, Reinhold, 18, 389

Nock, Albert Jay, 77, 394

Paine, Thomas, 66-67, 135, 398; *Rights of Man,* 121

Paley, William, 32, 35, 135

Peattie, Donald Culross, 142

Population, 254, 346-47, 420

Power, anatomy of, 264-66; corruptibility of, 282; abuse of, in totalitarianism, 282-83; monopoly of, as in Soviet Union, 288; limitation of, in Welfare State, 326-29; economic, *see* Economic power.

Price, role of, in market economy, 139-41, 181-82; and law of supply and demand, 141-42, 181-82

Price-fixing, 186, 188, 192, 364

Priorities, for public purposes, problems of, 238-46, 334, 368-78

Producer, role of, in market economy, 141-42; effect on, of monopoly, 193-97

Production, and productivity, 146-48, 203-13; problem of waste in, 205-08; of consumer and capital goods, 226, 227; wartime and post-war record of, 208-13; and role of technology, 251

Profit motive, 381, 422; justification for, by psychological quietism, 166, 176; role of, in market economy, 176, 181, 186

Profit-sharing, 228
Property, private, 113-14, 121; protection of, 49-53
Public services, expansion of, 238-46, 357, 369-78

Quietism, psychological, 71, 81; as a creed of classical liberalism, 36-41; and theory of mind, 38-39, 163-64; and theory of indolence, 39-40, 165-66; discrediting of, by contemporary liberalism, 164-65; and justification of profit motive, 166, 176; as explanation for unemployment, 168

Rayburn, Sam, 307
Recessions, 198-201, 207, 212, 220, 222; causes of, 198; and equilibrium theory, 198-200; as exceptional and accidental data, 200-01; and contemporary liberalism's ideas, 201
Reuther, Walter P., 228, 330, 436, 437
Revolution, right of, 110; role of, in classical liberalism, 124; contractualism as doctrinal basis of, 125-35; and principle of utilitarianism, 135-36
Ricardo, David, 32, 33, 66, 84, 146, 181, 401
Rise of Liberalism, The, Laski's, 14, 15
Road to Serfdom, The, Hayek's, 18, 249, 426
Robbins, Lionel, 145, 171, 200, 402, 406, 411-12
Roosevelt, Franklin D., 13, 69, 88, 109, 267, 293, 301, 302, 303, 307, 325, 326, 327-28, 330, 356, 364, 394, 395, 406, 421, 433; on use of power by big business, 281-82; and the "forgotten man," 387; "Economic Bill of Rights" of, 427
Rousseau, Jean Jacques, 120, 125, 127, 136; and the "selfish system," 46; Social Contract, 124, 129; on sovereignty of the people, 129-30

Ruggiero, Guido de, 15, 113
Russell, Bertrand, 288-89

Samuelson, Paul A., 211, 354, 363, 413-14
Savings, and investments, 319-20; uninvested, taxation on, 320
Schlesinger, Arthur, Jr., 17-19, 330
Schools, 338-39, 434
Schumpeter, Joseph, 193, 410, 424
Senoir, Nassau W., 72, 181, 408
Sidgwick, Henry, 34, 94, 95-96
Sinclair, Upton, 92
Slichter, Sumner, 232, 300, 363
Smith, Adam, 26, 32, 33, 35, 47, 66, 67, 73, 81, 84, 135, 153, 187, 250, 253, 393-94, 420; on private property, 50; on government, 70; on payment of teachers, 71; and doctrine of laissez faire, 80; on division of labor and exchange, 137-38; on production, 401
Social legislation, in Welfare State, 298-316
Social security, beginnings in England and Germany, 59; role of psychological quietism in, 168-69; and Welfare State, 301-16
Sokolsky, George, 147-48
Soviet Union (U.S.S.R.), 353, 355, 425, 433; and "cold war," 155, 344; challenge of, 334-40, 344, 352; expansion of, 335-40, 426-27; role of, in underdeveloped nations, 341-42
Spencer, Herbert, 33, 87, 283, 394, 402; on relief for poor, 57, 76; on government, 66, 75-77; Social Statics, 75, 80; and doctrine of laissez faire, 77, 80; and social Darwinism theory, 144
Standard of living, 231-37; as distinguished from level of living, 233-35
State, the, negative role of, in classical liberalism, 91-101; positive role of, in contemporary liberalism, 250-60
Stevenson, Adlai, 330, 433

Suffrage, as check on tyranny, 120; and question of class *vs.* mass, 120-23

Supply and demand, law of, role of price in, 141-42, 181-82, 197

Tawney, R. H., 25, 50, 112-13

Taxes, 25, 219, 220, 247, 292, 360-61, 366, 369, 371-72, 380, 382, 438; and consumer, 240; graduated, on income, 242, 268, 297, 321, 322, 326; and deficit spending, 318-24; regressive, 320, 373; for public works, 324-26; and conservatism's position, 379

Tocqueville, Alexis de, 122, 123, 203

Trade unions, and restrictive methods, 53, 197, 301-02; role of, in Welfare State, 301, 302; and farm and white collar workers, 301, 429; and "right-to-work" laws, 429

Tugwell, Rexford, 173

Underdeveloped nations, needs of, 340; American assistance to, 340-41, 344; role of Soviet Union in, 341-42

Unemployment, 321, 333-34; as explained by psychological quietism, 168; and growth rate, 213-25; concealed, 215-19; frictional, 308-10; mass, 310-15; and Welfare State, 315-16

Unions, *see* Trade unions

Usury, 24, 25, 71, 81, 389

Veblen, Thorstein, 39, 40-41, 162, 174, 196, 405, 407

Voltaire, 26, 32, 120

Von Mises, Ludwig, 13, 145, 182-83, 184, 257n., 283, 420, 426; on causes of Nazism, 284-85; and interventionism, 287

Waste, problem of, in production, 205-08; and economic lag, 219-21; and planned obsolescence, 237

Wealth of Nations, The, Adam Smith's, 32, 47, 67, 70, 80, 81, 137, 138, 153, 393-94, 401

Webb, Beatrice, 427

Webb, Sidney, 427, 428

Webster, Daniel, 131, 132, 133, 297

Welfare State, objectives of, 298-99; and contemporary liberalism, 298; goals of, from "cradle to grave," 299-316

Whigs, as political party, 26, 114, 120, 121, 135, 399

Wiener, Norbert, 346